PLAINTIFF IN CHIEF

ALSO BY JAMES D. ZIRIN

The Mother Court
Supremely Partisan

PLAINTIFF IN CHIEF

A PORTRAIT OF DONALD TRUMP IN 3,500 LAWSUITS

JAMES D. ZIRIN

ALL
POINTS
BOOKS
New York

First published in the United States by All Points Books, an imprint
of St. Martin's Publishing Group.

PLAINTIFF IN CHIEF. Copyright © 2019 by James D. Zirin. All rights reserved.
Printed in the United States of America. For information, address
St. Martin's Publishing Group, 120 Broadway, New York, NY 10271.

www.allpointsbooks.com

Designed by Maura Fadden Rosenthal

Library of Congress Cataloging-in-Publication Data

Names: Zirin, James D., author.
Title: Plaintiff in chief : a portrait of Donald Trump in 3,500 lawsuits /
    James D. Zirin.
Description: New York : All Points Books, 2019. | Includes bibliographical
    references.
Identifiers: LCCN 2019012547| ISBN 9781250201621 (hardcover) | ISBN
    9781250201638 (ebook)
Subjects: LCSH: Trump, Donald, 1946—Trials, litigation, etc.
Classification: LCC KF228.T78 Z57 2019 | DDC 347.73/53—dc23
LC record available at https://lccn.loc.gov/2019012547

Our books may be purchased in bulk for promotional, educational,
or business use. Please contact your local bookseller or the
Macmillan Corporate and Premium Sales Department at
1-800-221-7945, extension 5442, or by email at
MacmillanSpecialMarkets@macmillan.com.

First Edition: September 2019

10   9   8   7   6   5   4   3   2   1

To Marlene

CONTENTS

CONTENTS

PROLOGUE

DONALD J. TRUMP, PLAINTIFF
(AND DEFENDANT) IN CHIEF

I have many (too many!) lawyers.
—Donald Trump, Tweet, April 15, 2018

When on January 20, 2017, Donald Trump took the oath of office to become the forty-fifth president of the United States, he assumed an obligation under the Constitution to "take care that the laws be faithfully executed."

Many saw Trump as the quick answer. He was the man who could fix things. He represented a garland of "isms"—populism, birtherism, nationalism, and protectionism. He understood the "art of the deal." He would lower taxes, deregulate our businesses, save American jobs stolen by China and other foreigners. He would crack down on the Muslim terrorists, build a wall on our southern border to exclude "murderers" and "rapists," tear up entangling treaties, and solve the 70-year-old dispute between Israelis and Palestinians.

But Donald Trump has proved to be, as Churchill said of Russia, "a riddle, wrapped in a mystery, inside an enigma." No political strategist or thinker can predict what he will say or do next, or what eccentric course he will take in violation of all norms of presidential behavior. The world seems to hang on his every tweet, no matter how false, no matter how misleading, no matter how half-baked, and no matter how cockeyed.

This book will attempt to decode and unpack Donald Trump, to explain his motivations and actions as president by examining his consistent antagonism toward legal standards—normative rules that he has regarded his entire professional life as made to be broken. It will show that he is the by-product of two primal influences: his father, Fred Trump, and his mentor, the unscrupulous lawyer Roy Cohn. It will unveil the core of his litigation history and show how this history defines his character. The ancient Greeks posited that character is destiny, a proposition with which most of us would agree.

American society today is just as polarized as plaintiff and defendant in a lawsuit. I would argue that Trump has made us more polarized. Our fragile democracy stands broken by gridlock and bitter partisanship. In 2016, looking for an "angry fix," the country was particularly vulnerable to Trump's "fake populism," sexism, and xenophobia, and his promises to eradicate political correctness, ban Muslim and Mexican criminals from the country, and drain the swamp of liberal bureaucrats and judges, the gnarled denizens of the "deep state."

There was a darker side to Donald Trump as well. Underneath the veneer of making America great again was a bullying style born of a lengthy litigation history and a pathological pattern of lying. It should have come as no surprise to those familiar with his background that he would seek to weaponize the justice system, use his power to bend the law, attack his enemies and critics, and claim victory when victory there was none. He had been doing this all his professional life.

Trump wakes up every morning with an irrepressible desire to win, to win big, and to win soon. Trump is a day trader. The finish line for him is always only hours away. Over the years of his professional history, he became more than litigious; he acquired a litigation mentality. He was possessed of an ugly combativeness coupled with the natural mendacity of a born salesman and promoter. His world is one in which reality is heavily spiced with make-believe, and fantasy is the new reality.

There is nothing wrong with wanting to win—most of us want to. What distinguishes Trump is that he lives in an alternate universe. He claims he has won even when he has lost. He insists he has persevered even when he has given up. He insists he has fought even when he has surrendered. And, he will tell any lie that suits his purpose. His word is meaningless; his claims are hyperbolic; his threats are hollow; his instinct for recrimination is out of control; and he will challenge the incontestable.

To a lawyer, facts matter, evidence matters, avoiding harsh and unfair results matters. Logic and reason matter too, just as they matter in a self-governing democracy longing for political stability.

Most people seek to avoid a lawsuit if they can. Litigation is costly, distracting, and time-consuming. The result can be imperfect. My law school ethics professor, the late Geoffrey C. Hazard Jr., was fond of telling his students, "Litigation is a disaster." Often, the court judgment leaves the parties—who once enjoyed friendly relations—bitter, filled with recrimination, and dissatisfied with the outcome. But litigation is supposed to be an orderly pursuit of truth and justice. The adversary system, the crown jewel of the English common law, was not designed to destroy the other side but to be the best method anyone ever devised to unearth the truth so the court could administer justice fairly.

As his life in court evolved, Trump saw litigation as being only about winning. He sued at the drop of a hat. He sued for sport; he sued to achieve a sense of control; and he sued to make a point. He sued as a means of destroying or silencing those who crossed him. He became a "plaintiff in chief." His pattern was more "float like a butterfly" than "sting like a bee." Often, he would sue and, shortly thereafter, drop the case. He sued to make headlines, for the entertainment value, and to reinforce his power over others. At the end of the day, he abused the process of the law.

According to *USA Today*, in the decades prior to becoming president, he became a perennial litigant, involved in more than 3,500 lawsuits, proceedings, and investigations (lest anyone think this is fake news, the American Bar Association counts 4,000). Bloomberg News reported in 2016 that Trump had racked up 1,300 suits since 2000, including 72 in federal court. A Google search for "Trump lawsuits" yields in a trice (0.42 seconds) roughly 21 million hits.

Trump saw law not as a system of rules to be obeyed and ethical ideals to be respected but as a potent weapon to be used against his adversaries or a hurdle to be sidestepped when it got in his way.

While real estate operators are a notoriously litigious bunch who commonly run into legal disputes with contractors, tenants, and architects, Trump has had cases or controversies, either as plaintiff or defendant, in virtually all of his business ventures. The sheer volume of his litigation is astounding. And, aside from filed lawsuits, he sent innumerable cease-and-desist letters threatening to punish competitors, journalists, publishers, or anyone else who might write or say unflattering things about him. He seemed obsessed with his reputation and the Trump name, which became his brand.

Lawsuits alleging serious wrongdoing, claims, counterclaims, false denials, inconsistent positions, investigations, subpoenas directed to close associates, carefully tailored testimony, scandalous allegations, and subversion of his adversaries were nothing new to him. The legal wagons protecting him had been drawn in a circle for many years.

It would not be feasible to list and treat each of Trump's many lawsuits. It would not be very interesting either. Many of the cases have been routine matters in which Trump refused to pay counterparties to a contract for goods or services. The records of most of the cases in which he has been involved are unavailable. Much has been sealed from public view by agreement of the parties because the controversies were settled after imposing large legal fees on his adversaries. Another group of records, more than 20 years old, has disappeared with the passage of time. But it is possible to discuss some groupings of cases. The nature of these cases tells a story and paints a picture of what has gone into the man who is now the president of the United States.

I discuss here certain telltale cases, culled from the lawsuits and legal proceedings to which Trump has been a party over the past 40 years, in which he abused the power of the lawsuit, mostly with little success in court but with remarkable success in attracting attention to himself, as well as the "Trump" brand—and chilling those whose interests he would frustrate. This pattern of behavior will present some insight into his conduct in office, in which he seeks public approval by attacking his critics and then portraying himself as the victim of a political witch-hunt, more sinned against than sinning.

My objective in presenting the cases is not to furnish a "witch's brew" of one Trump case after another. My purpose is to show representative cases that provide a window into his nature, temperament, and methods. If you connect the dots, there emerges a fully limned portrait of the man.

Trump's litigation history shows him more often suing than sued. It was how he engaged with people. He would sue almost anyone for anything. He never collected a big judgment, but he wasn't in it for the money. Trump enjoyed the possession of money and the things that money could buy. But more than money, his goal was the possession of supreme power, the joy of domination over those who crossed his path. He sued not necessarily to right a wrong but to satisfy some collateral objective to let others know he was Trump. And lawsuits against him have been considerable. He has been sued over almost everything he touches.

I deal later on with Trump's pit-bull litigation tactics—bluffs, obstruction, the undermining of his adversaries, temporizing, deflecting, false statements, denials, counterclaims, threats of meritless litigation, and the buying off of his mistresses—a kind of *WrestleMania* intended to strong-arm his opponents to the ground.

Some of the litigation may be categorized. If you partner with Donald Trump, chances are you will wind up litigating with him. If you question his professed net worth as overstated, he will sue you for defamation. If you enroll in his university or buy one of his condominium apartments, chances are that you will want your money back. If you are a pretty woman and you get too close to him, you may need to watch your ass, your breasts, or anything else he finds attractive. Then, if you try to sue him, he will defame you or deny it ever happened. If you purchase a membership in one of his golf clubs, you may find there were misrepresentations, or that you paid more to join than did some of your fellow members, and you will want a refund. If you make a deal with him, you better get it in writing. If you are a lawyer, an architect, a subcontractor, or even his dentist, you better get paid up front. If you render honest service to him, he will stiff you for your fee and threaten to charge you with malpractice if you dare sue. If you are a critic, you better write a rave review of a Trump project. If you venture an opinion that publicly criticizes him, you may be sued for libel. If you use the Trump name in a business he has never had anything to do with, he will sue you even if the Trump name is on your birth certificate. If you are a rapper, find someone else to dis or you will wind up in court.

If you sue him, a counterclaim for damages in excess of your net worth is almost inevitable. If he lives or does business in a locality, he is likely to sue the local government or the state for tax abatement, or even the nation-state, as he did with Scotland. If you are an Indian tribe entitled to operate a gambling casino under the law, you are in his crosshairs—he will question your lineage and claim that you don't look like an Indian. If you buy his bonds, the debt will be compromised when he files for bankruptcy. If you marry him, get an independent lawyer to draw up an airtight prenup giving you lots of money the moment he is dissatisfied with your companionship or is unfaithful and says, "You're fired." If you divorce him, he will not let go but will sue you years after the final decree.

If he takes you for a roll in the hay, he will attempt to buy your silence with six-figure hush money sums paid by wire transfer out of an offshore account owned by a shell LLC. A hush-money specialist lawyer-fixer with a nondisclosure agreement at the ready will structure the deal. The bizarre contract, together with a "side letter," its parties pseudonymous, will be called a "NON-DISPARAGEMENT AGREEMENT." He may then sue you for $20 million if he thinks you are about to spill the beans. Then, he will seek to enjoin you from telling your story.

Perennially, he has sued for breach of contract, fraud, breach of trust, government favoritism, RICO, misappropriation or adulteration of the brand name "Trump," and libel, apparently his favorite tort. He has sought the shelter of the bankruptcy court six times in 18 years, bragging that he has made millions by taking "advantage of the laws of this country, like other people." He has never had an independent board of directors to keep him in check. He was free to feed a seemingly insatiable appetite for litigation. His life in court took on an entertainment quality smacking of reality TV.

Nevertheless, surprisingly for someone who led a life of litigation, he has expressed contempt for the judiciary and the rule of law. Trump has rarely won in court. Mostly, after racking up large legal bills for everyone involved, he has settled, or—if he was the plaintiff—dropped the case. If England's "loser pays" rule, providing for shifting of attorneys' fees from winner to loser, existed generally in the United States, Trump may have had to sell his posh Palm Beach estate, Mar-a-Lago, to cover his adversaries' court costs.

At the time of the 2016 presidential campaign, Trump had been named as a defendant in more than 160 *federal* lawsuits, as well as other proceedings and investigations. He had been charged with race and sex discrimination, sexual harassment, fraud, breach of trust, money laundering, defamation, stiffing his creditors, defaulting on loans, and, as will appear, he had been investigated for deep ties to the Mob, which he has enjoyed over the years. For Trump—to paraphrase Clausewitz's *On War*—litigation was the continuation of his ego by other means. Trump's history has been one of legal conflict, with the law, as Justice Oliver

Wendell Holmes put it, a "brooding omnipresence in the sky" in his personal and professional life.

The cliché "you can't tell a book by its cover" may be debatable, but the nature of the lawsuits a man has been involved in tells much about him. They reflect his socialization, his commitment to compromise, his respect and feeling for other people, the nature of his relationships with his fellow human beings—in short, his very morality.

I tell the story of Trump's life in court not to show who was wrong or right in the myriad legal contests he waged. As noted, he settled most of the cases he was involved in. Occasionally, he even won. When you are in the ring so often, you may land a lucky punch. I have kept no scorecard. I tell the story using some of the cases as examples to show that Trump regarded the law as an arsenal of weapons to subvert his enemies with outlandish and exaggerated claims. When sued or investigated or threatened, he used the law defensively, employing scorched-earth tactics such as delay, counterattack, obstruction, deflection, confusion, threats of ruin, and blanket assertion of attorney/client privilege to avoid accountability. And, he did it largely with great success. Indeed, Trump confronted the law as though it were a defensive player in a football game and he were an offensive back—outmaneuvering with fancy footwork, or end runs, or bull-run charges up the middle.

Whether he was entitled to the benefit of the law, or whether he could support his positions with evidence, or whether his claims stated a cause of action, or whether he was really damaged was irrelevant to Donald Trump. What was important was to use the lawsuit to attract attention, to exert economic pressure, and to prove he was the kid on the block not to be messed with. And his adversaries largely gave way during his rise to celebrity and power.

A life of litigation was the building block for Trump's approach to public office. On May 25, 2018, the *New York Times* Editorial Board published a long list cataloging instances of Trump's abnormal breaches of "dignity and decency." These ranged widely, from meeting with

Justice Department officials about their investigation into his own conduct, to floating the prospect of presidential pardons for top aides charged with or convicted of serious crimes related to his election campaign, to calling our justice system, which he manipulated on his way up the ladder, a "joke" and a "laughingstock."

Trump had more experience in the labyrinthine corridors of our legal system than perhaps all of his presidential predecessors combined. "Trump tends to think of things in terms of real estate law—ways to get around legal requirements rather than enforcing and promoting them," says Corey Brettschneider, a professor of politics at Brown. He expressed contempt for the rule of law and, indeed, for any normative standard except winning.

And he brought this approach to the Oval Office.

Some will argue that Trump's litigation history is nothing more than the ordinary course of business for a young parvenu on his way up, particularly in the hard-nosed New York City real estate world. I would submit that Trump is very different. His instinctive litigiousness; his abuse of the legal process to obtain leverage, not justice; his mean-spirited statements and conduct; his overblown damage claims; his many lies, exaggerations, and prevarications; his willingness to sue, trash, or discard even those who did him a good turn along the way are abnormal by any standard.

Recent presidents have all had relevant experience in government and politics in one form or another. Trump's experience was in lawsuits. They were more than a necessary part of his doing business; they reflect his inmost ulterior motivation.

———————————

This, then, is the story of the lawsuit-freighted culture that surrounded Donald Trump's business career and his personal life. It is an account of the bullying techniques that catapulted him to the summit of the American political system. It helps us understand the man—why he thinks it gets him somewhere to launch mocking, vituperative attacks against the mainstream media or hector his political foes. Trump has been awash in lawsuits. He has experienced not only the expected business disputes over contractual interpretation or terms of sale. He has been mired up to his eyeballs deflecting investigations, avoiding his just debts, and defending himself against litigation alleging serious misconduct on his part.

I will treat in the course of this narrative Trump's scorched-earth tactics in which he abused the legal system to smear his apparent enemies, deflect accountability for his own wrongdoing, cheat his creditors, and silence his critics. I will describe the nature of the legal proceedings brought against him, which dot the landscape of his rise to the summit of American power; his pattern and practice of racial discrimination; his involvement with the Mob in the construction of Trump Tower and his three Atlantic City casinos; his depraved relations with women, including his spouses; the Trump University scam in which thousands of Americans were defrauded; and how his legal predicament as president might involve possible impeachment proceedings, should charges ever be brought.

Besides his consiglieres, originally Roy Cohn and later Michael Cohen, Trump surrounded himself with a squadron of lawyers—as he himself thought, too many. There was usually a new one for every lawsuit. In this respect, he was *sui generis*. Most of his lawyers were not paid at all or not paid in full. He told them they should be honored to represent him, and perhaps they felt that way. He fired many. Lawyers represent, among other things, the machinery and wheels of litigation. Businesspeople think of litigation as a pain in the ass. It is dangerous. Clients in the right can be wiped out financially, while their lawyers enrich themselves on a lush harvest of fees. Trump relished litigation. For him it was a cottage industry.

My background, training, and experience have been in the law, and it is a personal thing. I grew up in a legal household imbued with a deep respect for the legal process. Most of my parents' close friends were lawyers and judges, and they gathered at our home to discuss interesting cases in court. When I was admitted to the Bar on St. Patrick's Day 1965, my parents took me to lunch at an Irish bar and grill to celebrate. I thought it was the happiest day of my life.

My father, Morris G. Zirin, won success in the 1940s and '50s as a New York trial and appellate lawyer, particularly in the area of libel law, in which he found a deep interest. He was also something of a writer, publishing two novels that both featured a legal backdrop. The first was *The Don*, based on a true story about a Mafia vice-lord who "flips" and turns state's evidence against his don and then mysteriously dies while being held in police "protective custody" in a Coney Island hotel. In his second novel, *The Counsellor*, the hero, Saul Belinsky, whose parents own a candy store in Brooklyn, found that becoming a lawyer transformed all the wrongs, failures, and bad luck of his life into a personal triumph. My father taught me to rise when the judge enters the courtroom, not out of respect for the man or woman who wore the robes, but out of respect for what he or she represents.

My dear mother, Kate Zirin, was a public high school teacher who often spoke to me of "this wonderful Constitution we have" that all our public officials swore to uphold. It was the Constitution that protected the minority from the tyranny of the majority; that guaranteed basic human rights and freedoms; that was the "supreme law of the land." I have no doubt what she would have said about Trump's outspoken contempt for constitutional norms, as well as his repeated failure to honor our war dead. She would have been altogether disgusted.

My wife's grandfather, David T. Wilentz, prosecuted the Lindbergh baby kidnapping and murder case in 1935, otherwise known as the "trial of the century." Her uncles were lawyers: one, Robert N. Wilentz, became chief justice of the New Jersey Supreme Court; the other, Warren Wilentz, won his spurs as a prominent county prosecutor.

My experience has spanned over fifty years of professional service as a trial lawyer and federal prosecutor under the legendary Robert M. Morgenthau. I have crisscrossed the nation and the globe trying cases and deposing witnesses, including Margaret Thatcher on one memorable occasion. I have also written two books about the rule of law. The first, *The Mother Court* (2014), recounts some of the great cases that went down in the Southern District of New York in the mid-twentieth century. The second, *Supremely Partisan* (2016), is an analysis of the raw political tenor of certain constitutional decisions made by a deeply divided Supreme Court of the United States.

While my politics has been middle-of-the-road Republican (I voted for Ronald Reagan and both Bushes), it should come as no surprise that I found myself astounded by Donald Trump's war against the courts, the judiciary, and the Justice Department, as well as basic constitutional values. I was outraged when he called for a Muslim ban and an end to birthright citizenship; revolted when he wanted to strip flag burners of their citizenship; nauseated when he called the free press the "enemy of the people"; appalled when he cast aspersions on the Mexican ancestry of a federal judge who had ruled against him; and incensed, most recently, when he undercut the Constitution's separation of powers doctrine by declaring a "national emergency" over a border wall to subvert an appropriations decision of Congress. That matter is now in the courts.

I began to wonder where his antilegal approach came from. Was it sheer demagoguery that he used merely to get elected and stay in power? Or did it spring from something else in his background and education? I took a deep dive into Trump's litigation provenance, analyzed the record, and considered how his personal history has influenced his conduct in office.

In my years of prosecuting Mob bosses and representing Fortune 500 companies, international accounting firms, and malefactors of great wealth, I never encountered anyone quite like Donald Trump. Clients I have known respected the rule of law even when they ran afoul of it. All had some idea of what was the truth. Trump's position is an antinomian view, that he is either above the law or released from the obligation of observing it. While we may be alarmed by his racism, his callous comments over the tragedy in Charlottesville, his dog whistle calls to the lunatic fringe in our country, his sexist attitudes toward "bleeding" women, and his pathological lies and prevarications, his policies evoke a far more serious concern that his "bull in the china shop" approach to presidential norms has corroded our democracy and seriously threatened the world order.

I began to follow Trump in the late 1970s, when I happened to meet him at a New York nightclub called Le Club. Roy Cohn, whom I knew as a prominent fixer, lawyer, and man about town was also there, flitting from table to table. I appreciated Trump's brashness, his flair for publicity, and his skillful manipulation of the media to advance his personal interests and eponymous brand. When I dug deeper, however, I came to understand that Trump had a darker side. He often lived in an alternate reality in which he tried to cover up his responsibility for wrongful conduct, seeking to conceal it behind a veil of plausible deniability.

The law turns on the facts, and if the facts are concealed or misrepresented, the law cannot justly be applied. Facts matter in a democracy, as they do in court, as they do on the historical record, and as they do in life. Facts should never be sacrificed on the altar of some supposed larger good.

You cannot escape the truth, forever lying your way out of the facts. There is no alternate reality in which to take refuge.

All this aberrant behavior would be problematic in a businessman who professed to be a billionaire brander. Reporters who interviewed him in the 1990s questioned his mental stability. But the implications of such conduct in the man who is the president of the United States are nothing less than terrifying. In the words of civil libertarian Roger Nash Baldwin, "If America has a claim to glory among the nations, it is her service to human liberty. We cannot bear that America fail in justice." Frankly, we all should be very worried.

1

THE FIRST LAWSUIT

HOW TRUMP WAS
BAPTIZED IN LITIGATION

Well, this is my first affair, so please be kind.
—Sammy Cahn, "Please Be Kind"

In October 1973, the government accused Fred and Donald Trump of violations of the Fair Housing Act of 1968 (FHA) at 39 Trump-built-and-managed buildings in Brooklyn, Queens, and Staten Island.

President Lyndon Johnson had approved the FHA in the wake of the assassination of Martin Luther King. The measure was designed to eliminate all traces of racial discrimination from the housing field. Trump's father, a multimillionaire real estate operator, had repeated clashes with the Open Housing Center, a local fair-housing group that was working with the Justice Department, as well as the New York City Human Rights Commission, which asked the government to investigate racial discrimination in the Trumps' neighborhood housing.

The community groups handed their findings to the Nixon Justice Department on a silver platter. The Trumps were drowning in evidence of systematic racial discrimination. On at least seven occasions, prospective tenants had filed complaints against the Trumps with the human rights commission, alleging racially discriminatory patterns and practices.

It seemed that in a July 1972 test at the Trumps' Shore Haven properties in Brooklyn, when a black woman sought to rent an apartment, the superintendent turned her away, informing her that nothing was available. Shortly thereafter, when a white woman applied, the same superintendent told her she could "immediately rent either one of two available apartments."

The two women were "testers" from the Open Housing Center. One white tester said that a building superintendent admitted that "superiors" had directed him to follow "a racially discriminatory rental policy." As a result, there were only a few black occupants in the buildings.

There was also evidence that Trump employees had noted black and Latino applications with cryptic designations such as "C" or "No. 9." Also, the proof showed that Trump ghettoized his properties, packing minorities into Patio Gardens, his apartment buildings on Flatbush Avenue, Brooklyn, that were 40 percent black. He largely excluded African Americans from others, such as his Ocean Terrace Apartments, where blacks comprised only 1 percent of all residents.

Investigative journalist Wayne Barrett, writing in the *Village Voice*, reported that the evidence of racial discrimination against the Trumps was overwhelming. The government contended that no fewer than four rental agents had stated that applications sent to the Trump offices for acceptance or rejection were coded by race. Doormen stated they were instructed to discourage African Americans seeking apartments by saying the superintendent was out. A super stated that he was instructed to send black applicants to the central office, while he was authorized to accept white applicants on the spot. Another rental agent said that Fred Trump had instructed him not to rent to African Americans. The Trumps had quoted different rental terms and conditions to African Americans and made false "no vacancy" statements to African Americans for Trump-managed apartments.

The Trumps needed a lawyer to help them defend the case. It was the kind of case that any lawyer would advise the Trumps to settle. But Fred Trump was not inclined to settle. Donald, then 27, began searching for a lawyer to represent him and his father, and his life took a new turn.

Donald Trump grew up in the bedroom community of Jamaica Estates, Queens, a tiny chrysalis nestled in the heart of a great city. He represented the third generation of a family dedicated to making money. New Yorkers think of Queens as a low- to middle-income melting pot community, with African Americans, Latinos, and the foreign-born comprising its burgeoning populations. But the Jamaica Estates section where Fred and Mary Trump raised their family was monolithic. Donald grew up in a 23-room, 9-bathroom mansion. He was the fourth of five children, listed here in order of age: Maryanne Trump Barry, a retired federal judge; Fred Trump Jr., who died in 1981 at age 43; Elizabeth Trump Grau, a retired banker; and Robert Trump, now retired from the family business.

The Jamaica Estates neighborhood then was almost exclusively white, and other minorities would have had difficulty purchasing homes. When Annamaria Schifano's family moved to Jamaica Estates, Trump's older brother, Fred Trump Jr., who was dating Annamaria's best friend, confided that his parents were upset because the Schifanos were "the first ethnic family to move into the neighborhood."

Trump's grandfather, Friedrich Drumpf, was an immigrant, born in the southwest German town of Kallstadt. In 1885, at the age of 16 and having few prospects, Friedrich immigrated to the United States, landing in New York, where he lived with his older sister Katherine and her husband, who had immigrated earlier. Shortly thereafter, he decided to go west to seek his fortune, planting roots in Seattle, where he opened a dairy restaurant, which doubled as a house of ill repute. Things did not pan out well in Seattle for Friedrich, so he headed for Canada's Yukon Territory to participate in the gold rush, not by mining but by providing a restaurant, bar and grill, and "sporting ladies" for the miners. By the time the Klondike gold began to dissipate and the police moved in, Friedrich had made a small fortune and returned to Germany, where he married before returning to America in 1905 with his new bride. Back in New York, Friedrich worked as a barber and tobacconist—low-paying occupations for someone so obsessed with making money. Gwenda Blair, with whom the Trump family cooperated in writing their history, suggests that barbershops at the time were frequently fronts for the operations of organized criminals. In the 1910 census, Friedrich Drumpf became Fred Trump. In 1918, a worldwide influenza pandemic claimed the lives of 20 million people. One of them was Friedrich Trump.

Donald's father, Fred C. Trump, was only 12 years old when Friedrich died. Building on his patrimony, Fred started a residential garage-building business in partnership with his mother, Elizabeth. Fred's mother was a necessary partner as Fred was too young to enter into contracts or sign checks. In the 1920s, the garages morphed into single-family row houses, principally in Brooklyn and Queens. The houses went for just under $4,000 each, an affordable price at the time for middle-income families. At age 21, Fred was constructing single-family houses in Queens. In 1929, he shifted his business interest to a self-service grocery, which he sold for a substantial profit after a year. As World War II loomed, he procured government contracts for apartments and barracks for servicemen. Here he learned about government procurement, a skill he would employ in obtaining FHA loans enabling postwar housing for returning GIs. He constructed 27,000 subsidized apartments in the 1940s and 1950s, from which the Trumps still derive income to this day. Fred built Shore Haven in Bensonhurst, Brooklyn, in 1949, and Beach Haven, near Coney Island, the next year. The *New York Times* reported that he built "thousands of homes for the middle class in plain but sturdy rental towers, clustered together in immaculately groomed parks."

Fred was a tough customer. He prospered based on a borrow-and-build model, but he was not above fakery. Of German origins, he held himself out in the 1930s as Swedish because he thought it would be more palatable to his Jewish tenants. His row houses were not known for the best materials. Nor was Fred known for being the best of landlords—or the fairest.

He was anything but an equal-opportunity renter. In December 1950, troubadour Woody Guthrie became a tenant in Beach Haven, the second of Fred Trump's major Brooklyn buildings, where he lived for two years. Guthrie famously composed the song "This Land Is Your Land," a resounding appeal to an equal share for all in America. Guthrie wrote lyrics bitterly accusing Fred Trump of arousing racial hatred. Reworking his Dust Bowl ballad "I Ain't Got No Home" into a protest against "Old Man Trump," Guthrie wrote:

> Beach Haven is Trump's Tower
> Where no black folks come to roam,
>
> . . .
>
> Beach Haven ain't my home!

In 1927, the Ku Klux Klan marched with a thousand people in Queens to protest what they saw as the brutalization of native-born Protestant citizens at the hands of Irish Catholic police officers. According to newspaper accounts of the arrest, a Fred Trump of 175-24 Devonshire Road, Jamaica, Queens, was one of seven men arrested in connection with the demonstration, wearing the sheets and hoods of the KKK. Asked in 2015 by the *New York Times* whether his father had been arrested at a Klan event, Donald Trump said four times, "It never happened." When a reporter asked if his father ever lived at 175-24 Devonshire Road, Trump admitted that his father had lived there with his grandmother "early on," and then later denied that his father ever lived on Devonshire. But when Trump's parents were married in January 1936, nine years after the arrest, the wedding announcement appearing in the *Times* gave Devonshire Road as Fred Trump's address. Donald Trump dismissed the press reports as "totally false" because "there were zero charges against him." Lawyers know that you can't arrest someone unless there is a charge. There had to be a charge. The charges were dropped, as such charges often are.

Fred Trump was a shrewd operator, and Donald would later channel his father's unscrupulous behavior. Like Donald, he was a sensitized guardian of his name and reputation. "DENIES $4 MILLION FHA PROFIT," blared the banner headline on the front page of the *Brooklyn Daily Eagle* on July 13, 1954. Above the banner was the teaser: "BUT TRUMP HAS THAT MUCH SURPLUS IN BANK." And below, Fred's weepy answer: "BUILDER PROTESTS WINDFALL CHARGE BLASTS HIS NAME."

The story concerned Fred Trump's extraordinary testimony at an inquiry conducted by the Senate Banking Committee into the multimillion-dollar profiteering scandals surrounding the Federal Housing Authority housing program. Fred was a master at deflecting inquiry away from his affairs. Under oath, he admitted to engineering a transaction through which, based on the full faith and credit of the United States, he realized a windfall profit of $4 million with almost no investment. In 1944, Fred paid $180,000 for three contiguous tracts of vacant land in the Brighton Beach section of Brooklyn. He subdivided the tracts into six parcels for purposes of constructing 31 six-story elevator apartment buildings comprising 1,860 residential units, known as Beach Haven Apartments. He then turned around and gifted the land to his children, valuing the property at $180,000 for gift tax purposes. The IRS quarreled with the valuation and settled with Fred on $260,000.

Fred had his children lease the land to the corporations he formed to construct the apartment buildings. The ground lease was 99 years with an option to renew, and the annual rental was $60,000 for land valued at $260,000—a 23 percent return on investment. Trump obtained a nonrecourse FHA-insured construction mortgage on the property, the proceeds of which were $16 million. There is no way that a bank would have loaned him $16 million on the project without the FHA guaranty. The cost of construction, however, came to only $12 million, plus a general contractor's fee of $1.2 million, which Trump skimmed off the top. So at the end of the day, after paying off the construction contractors,

Fred had, with the assistance of the FHA, mortgaged out to the tune of $4 million ($55.5 million in today's dollars).

Only the buildings were mortgaged, not the land. The deal's documents provided that should the loan go into foreclosure, the FHA would have to pay a "recapture fee" to Fred's children of $1.5 million. So with an investment of $180,000 and no economic risk, Trump realized an income stream for his children, a guaranteed profit in the event of default, and, in round numbers, a cool $4 million bonanza.

Admitting to the essential terms of the deal before the Senate investigators, Fred Trump angrily denied any profiteering on the back of the FHA program with the spurious claim that *he had not withdrawn the $4 million from his corporate bank account*. He said the accusation of profiteering did "untold damage to my standing and reputation." Responding to a question from Senator Herbert Lehman of New York, Trump testified, "I have to take it out before I pocket it, Senator; isn't that right?" He told the Senate that the money in the bank not only did not constitute profiteering—*it was not even a profit*. Fred's prevarication was to deflect attention from the obvious fact that he had exploited the full faith and credit of the United States to make a tidy sum for himself. Although he was not charged, the FHA banned him from participating in future projects.

Donald Trump always wanted to be like his father; in fact, he was ashamed of not being like him. His need to be like his father accounts for his desire always to "look good," and its converse NOT to "look bad." It also accounts for his propensity to litigate—and to lie to justify himself.

For example, four decades later, Donald Trump channeled Fred's unscrupulous behavior in dealing with a housing agency of the federal government. In 1995, he applied for a HUD-insured loan of $356 million to fund the development of Riverside South, a sprawling Upper West Side of Manhattan development consisting of a public waterfront park and esplanade surrounding luxury apartments for well-to-do families earning more than $100,000 a year. The problem was that HUD-insured loans were intended for the development of low-income affordable

housing. Moreover, Trump inflated the value of the property by including the value of the city parkland, which accounted for 75 percent of
the funding. The loan application, later reduced to $180 million, was a
complete scam, and despite an endorsement by then mayor Rudy
Giuliani, HUD turned him down.

Trump tried to intercede by appealing to former governor Mario
Cuomo, whose son, now governor Andrew Cuomo, was the HUD secretary. Trump had been a heavy contributor to Cuomo's various political campaigns. When Cuomo declined to contact his son on the matter,
Donald exploded. As he later wrote in a chapter of his book *How to Get
Rich*, "I began screaming. 'You son of a bitch! For years I've helped you
and never asked for a thing, and when I finally need something . . . you
aren't there for me. You're no good. You're one of the most *disloyal* people
I've known and as far as I'm concerned, you can go to hell.'" After the
angry exchange, he said, "Whenever I see Mario at a dinner, I refuse to
acknowledge him, talk to him, or even look at him." Trump called
Cuomo a "loser"—another one of his favorite pejoratives. Trump told
the story in a chapter titled "Sometimes You Have to Hold a Grudge."
The "grudge" survived Mario's life just as Trump's grudge against John
McCain survived the former Arizona senator's. It continued into
Trump's presidency, with Trump attacking and taunting Mario's son Andrew over some anti-Trump remarks Andrew had made and claiming
that Andrew's "political career is over."

Fred also had ties to organized crime, just as Donald would later on.
Muscle and fear were ready recipes for making things happen. One of
his business partners was William Tomasello, who provided capital for
the Beach Haven Apartments as well as other projects and who owned
a 25 percent interest in ten Trump buildings. Tomasello, according to the
federal Organized Crime Task Force, was associated with elements of
both the Gambino and Genovese crime families.

Fred Trump was a towering figure, over six feet tall. Unlike Donald,
he was anything but ostentatious. An exception might be his use of
hair dye. Late in life, he wore his hair like Donald's, in a "comb-back," its

hue a striking shade of red. Fred's personal life flourished with his business success. In 1936, he married Mary Anne MacLeod, a brown-haired, blue-eyed immigrant from Scotland. She was what Fred wanted: a stay-at-home, behind-the-scenes housewife responsible for raising his children. Mary had been a maid in the household of Andrew Carnegie. It was perhaps here that she developed a taste for the trappings of wealth that she passed on to her son Donald.

Donald's older brother Fred Jr., called Freddy, was always an issue in the Trump family. He enjoyed life in the fast lane, driving a sporty Corvette, cruising in a Century speedboat, and flying his own plane. It was Fred Trump's dream that Freddy Trump would run the family business. Freddy had a brief flirtation with Fred's newest project, Trump Village, constructed in 1963–1964 in Coney Island, but his father sailed into him for installing expensive new windows instead of repairing the old ones. Freddy decided to stay clear of his father. He became an airline pilot for TWA and married a stewardess whom no one in the family liked. Donald Trump reflected on his brother's decision, which cleared the way for his succession: "For me, it worked out very well. For Fred, it wasn't something that was going to work."

Freddy Trump had two children named for his parents, Fred and Mary. In his twenties, he began drinking heavily. In the 1960s, things went south for him. He divorced, quit flying, and continued drinking. He returned to work for his father—this time on a maintenance crew. He died of drink in 1981 at age 43.

Freddy's bad luck was his legacy. His grandson William suffered seizures at birth leading to cerebral palsy. Donald Trump promised to help his nephew Fred III with William's massive medical bills, amounting to more than $300,000 a year. But then came Fred Sr.'s last will, drafted by Donald, which divided the estate among his children and their descendants, "other than [those of] my son, Fred Trump Jr." Freddy's children sued Donald, claiming fraud, lack of testamentary capacity, and undue influence. A prior will had entitled Freddy's line to an equal share of the estate. The last will was irrational. What kind of man disinherits one of his children's line of descendants, particularly when their father has predeceased them?

Donald Trump retaliated by withholding medical benefits from his nephew's child. "I was so angry because they sued," he told the *New York Times*. The case was later settled. Speaking in early 2016 about his deceased brother, Trump took a more conciliatory stance: "He would have been an amazing peacemaker if he didn't have the [liquor] problem. He's like the opposite of me." Trump does not touch the stuff.

Outside of his 23-room estate, Trump's father lived modestly without any pretense. Fred was a penny pincher. In his business, he curtailed expenses and raised rents. Many of his neighbors remembered seeing the Trump family grocery shopping on Union Turnpike, on the northern border of Jamaica Estates. Fred's only concession to flamboyance was his two navy blue Cadillac stretch limousines, each festooned with vanity FT1 or FT2 license plates, which he replaced every three years. A chauffeur collected him each morning in one of the cars and took him to work.

Donald was a problem child. He attended a private school on Union Turnpike, and later New York Military Academy. There were rumors he had slugged one of his teachers and had other behavioral problems, but no one remembers for sure. NYMA had the reputation as a school for educational underachievers. Many suffered from ADHD or were dyslexic, and today would be given Ritalin, Adderall, or some other drug therapy. NYMA would instill rigidity in Donald and, hopefully, a measure of academic discipline. Its graduates stood ramrod straight with outsized visions of worldwide fame. Some eventually overcame their learning handicaps. Donald said that his parents sent him to NYMA because "I was a wise guy, and they wanted to get me in line."

Fred Trump seemingly nurtured in his son a bunker mentality. A wall of separation surrounded the Trumps. One of his neighbors, Laura Manuelidis, recalled that Donald, then in his early teens, refused to throw back a ball that had bounced into his fenced-in yard, threatening to call the police. Trump's neighbors at the time did not give the Trumps a good report for kindness or willingness to share. There was a combativeness embedded in Donald's nature from the time he was a youngster. Trump, like his entrepreneurial father and grandfather before him, needed to win, and he needed to win without giving much quarter to the other guy. He craved his father's approval. But most of all, he must never acknowledge that he was wrong. Fred Trump disapproved of acknowledging wrongdoing. He thought it was disgraceful and even shameful.

From NYMA, Donald went to Fordham for college, later transferring to the Wharton School at Penn, from which he received his B.S. in 1968 at the height of the Vietnam War. A *New York Times* article, appearing on January 28, 1973, stated that Trump was "first in his class" at Wharton. The assertion has never been verified. Although he was a graduate of New York Military Academy, Trump was able to bypass the draft and military service at the height of the Vietnam War with a series of educational and medical deferments. Local draft boards were notoriously vulnerable to political influence, and many sons of wealthy men could readily find medical deferments if they wanted them. Trump avoided the draft, having been diagnosed with "bone spurs in his heels" by Dr. Larry Braunstein, a friendly foot doctor in Hillside Avenue, Jamaica, Queens, who happened to rent his office from Fred Trump. Another podiatrist, Dr. Manny Weinstein, a close friend of Dr. Braunstein with connections to the draft board, and who had offices in Shore Haven Apartments, another Trump building, may have assisted in the diagnosis. It was right out of the New York "favor bank." Both doctors had strong motivation to accommodate the landlord who controlled the rent. A self-styled playboy and womanizer, Donald famously joked to Howard Stern in a 1997 interview that serial sex instead of military service was his "personal Vietnam," adding, "I feel like a great and very brave soldier."

A 1968 graduate of Wharton, Trump had no greater business prospect than to join his father's business. In 1973, after some six years of idle pursuits, Trump, just 27 years old, formally took over management of his father's company, Trump Management, Inc. His role was to learn the business, become Fred Trump's first lieutenant, and assume responsibility for the company's legal affairs. He rose to become company president three years later, when he renamed the enterprise "the Trump Organization."

By the late 1970s, Fred Trump was one of the wealthiest men in America.

He died in June 1999 at age 93, after battling Alzheimer's for six years. He had accumulated a vast fortune, but no one knows with any accuracy exactly how much, as real estate valuations often present a moving target. He left a wife and four children, his son Fred Trump Jr. having predeceased him. When Mary Trump died in August 2000, the IRS valued the combined estates of husband and wife at only $51.8 million, some 23 percent more than the value declared on the estate tax returns. The most significant asset reported on the returns was a $10.3 million note receivable from Donald Trump. In fact, Fred Trump was most likely worth upward of a billion dollars.

When Fred died, only a small part of his real estate empire remained in his estate, as he had gifted over a billion dollars to his children during his lifetime to avoid estate taxes. The gift tax returns, according to a *New York Times* investigation, used "friendly" appraisals to grossly understate the value of the real estate holdings to the tune of hundreds of millions of dollars, and then discounted their ownership by as much as 45 percent by making dubious transfers designed to disperse control of the empire, thereby minimizing gift taxes. Using this scheme, the Trumps were able to transfer over a billion dollars in wealth to the next generation largely free of death duties, including at least $413 million at today's values to Donald. According to the *Times*, the Trumps paid $52.2 million in gift taxes, or about 5 percent on the billion dollars they passed to their children, which could have been taxed at $550 million using the 55 percent tax rate applicable at the time.

The Trumps relied on the fact that it is often difficult to value developed commercial real estate assets, as there are varying methods of depreciation, no broad and active market, and little clarity in rent rolls. It is axiomatic in real estate appraisal that the "value of a thing is the price it will bring." Besides, as every estates lawyer knows, the

IRS has notoriously lacked rigor in its enforcement of the gift tax laws.

Trump aspired to become an even more considerable real estate developer than his father. Despite the munificence of his inheritance, he liked to let on that he was a self-made man and had received little or no paternal financial assistance. But Fred lent more than moral support to his son's aspiration—he also loaned Donald money. Reports vary as to how much, with estimates of between $1 million and $60.7 million.

Presidential historians like to focus on relationships between presidents and their fathers as though they were characters in a novel by Turgenev or Philip Roth. They look at the contrasts between Joe and John F. Kennedy (isolationist, the father; internationalist, the son) or George H. W. and George W. Bush (restraint in Iraq, the father; rash invasion, the son). "I was never intimidated by my father, the way most people were," Trump said in *The Art of the Deal*, his first book, published in 1987; "I stood up to him, and he respected that." Relationships between fathers and sons can be as instructive as they are complicated. Trump described his father as his "hero, role model and best friend," saying that he "learned more from [him] than anyone else."

According to Gwenda Blair's book *The Trumps: Three Generations That Built an Empire*, Fred and Donald were always friendly but "talked right past each other." And Trump himself wrote about his father, "That's why I'm so screwed up, because I had a father that pushed me pretty hard," in his 2007 book *Think Big and Kick Ass in Business and in Life*. He always had lingering feelings of shame that he could not measure up to be the great business tycoon his father was.

———

Fred tasked Donald with funding legal representation in the discrimination case. Most of the lawyers Trump consulted told the Trumps to settle. "They all said, 'You have a good case, but it's a sticky thing,'" remembers Trump.

A "sticky thing," indeed! Trump's was one of the largest apartment management companies in New York City. It owned and managed 37 apartment complexes, comprising a total of at least 14,000 rental units. The government investigation revealed evidence of discrimination at seven of the buildings containing over 3,100 units, or about one-third of the total. Trump rental agents told the FBI that only 1 percent of the tenants at the Ocean Terrace Apartments were black, and there were no black tenants at the Lincoln Shore Apartments. Both housing centers were in Brooklyn.

In the 1970s, Donald often visited Le Club, located on 55th Street on the Upper East Side of Manhattan, an exclusive watering hole for demimondaine café society. There he met the lawyer Roy Cohn, who was seated at a nearby table. It was a fateful encounter. Trump explained to Cohn his legal predicament. He was thrilled when Cohn instantly declared, "Tell them to go to hell, and fight the thing in court." Most reputable lawyers take the time to examine the pleadings and to interview the client and witnesses before venturing an assessment of the merits of the case, and rarely guarantee the outcome. Trump was thrilled when Cohn instantly declared, without even examining the evidence, "Oh, you'll win hands down!" Trump instantly retained Cohn to represent him and his father, and there arose an extraordinarily close relationship, lasting until Cohn's death, almost two decades later. In Trump's eyes, Cohn was a sorcerer who could beat the system, and Trump eagerly cast himself as the sorcerer's apprentice.

They hit it off. "Roy had a whole crazy deal going," Trump said, "but Roy was a really smart guy who liked me and did a great job for me in different things." Trump's relationship with Cohn evolved into something transcending that of lawyer and client. The two became very close.

———————

In his heyday, Roy Cohn was one of the best known and most successful lawyers in the nation. He "lit up the town" during an extraordinary run.

Cohn lived high. He always managed to land a 50-yard-line seat at the Super Bowl, the owner's box at the World Series, and center aisle at the hottest Broadway openings. Cohn was thought of as "brilliant" and had been known as a "boy wonder." When Trump met him, Cohn had reached national notoriety as one of the prosecutors of Julius and Ethel Rosenberg, who were executed in 1953 for spying for the Russians, and a year later as chief counsel to Senator Joe McCarthy.

Cohn was a quintessential hypocrite, a classic Tartuffe. A closeted homosexual, he hypocritically attacked gay interests whenever the issue was presented. He was the prototypical Teflon man. He had beaten the system not once, but three times. Indicted by U.S. attorney Robert M. Morgenthau in the Southern District of New York on charges ranging from securities fraud to bribery to obstruction of justice, Cohn had been acquitted down the line, owing his success in court not only to some amazing luck but also to the fierce public counterattacks he waged against the government prosecutors, who he claimed were out to get him.

In 1969, in the most difficult to defend of the three cases against him—charges of bribery, conspiracy, extortion, and blackmail—Cohn's lawyer, Joseph Brill, who had cross-examined the government witnesses, professed to have chest pains just before summations and was hospitalized. Some thought Brill's removal from the case was staged. In any event, it was advantageous. Cohn, who had not taken the stand, summed up on his own behalf for seven hours without notes, ending with a declaration of love for America. He moved the jury to tears, and they acquitted him. After the verdict, Cohn held a courthouse press conference. The coda of his victory statement was, "God bless America."

Although many lawyers regarded Cohn as unscrupulous, he was without question a legal and political powerhouse. The more unscrupulous he became, the more his law practice grew. He was the man to see if you wanted to beat the system. Besides Donald Trump, his clients and circle of friends included, in addition to legitimate businessmen, fraudsters, mobsters, crooked politicians, Catholic prelates, club owners, and celebrities looking for an edge or to thwart the due administration of justice.

One of Cohn's clients was media mogul "Si" Newhouse, owner of Advance Publications, which owned Condé Nast magazines and many newspapers, who had been Cohn's friend since high school days. Newhouse, who met Trump through Cohn, was instrumental in transforming Trump from a minor local tycoon into a national figure. After he acquired Random House, it was Newhouse, at Cohn's behest, who signed off on the book that became the ghostwritten *Art of the Deal*. When Newhouse died in September 2017, however, all mention of Cohn and Trump was omitted from his *New York Times* obituary.

In his 1988 biography of Cohn, *Citizen Cohn*, Nicholas von Hoffman described what he called the "Roy Cohn Barter and Swap Exchange," specializing in "deals, favors, hand washings, and reciprocities of all kinds." Von Hoffman quotes a lawyer in Cohn's office describing how he practiced law:

> Lawyers are supposed to learn rules and then advise clients. Roy couldn't have given less of a shit about rules. He didn't read cases or care much about them. . . . He was a law-warrior. A lawyer should be dispassionate and detached. Roy didn't believe in that.

Cohn was an expert in making payoffs to politicians, buying off a woman scorned, exerting pressure, calling in a well-placed chit, or instilling fear of political reprisal. Cohn worked both sides of the room where it happens. A conservative backer of Richard Nixon, he had no problem working the floor and pressing the flesh at the 1968 Democratic convention, finally alighting in Senator Eugene McCarthy's box. Like Trump, Cohn's improvident business transactions led him to seek the shelter of the bankruptcy court. His power came not from money but from his uncanny ability to know the right people, give and get favors, and use intimidation to make people do what he wanted. He was never a "Master of the Deal" in the business world like Trump; yet he struck shrewd deals on the political rialto.

To some, he was a barefaced liar and con man, master of the art of the smear, an unscrupulous prosecutor, and lawyer to the Mob. Said prominent New York attorney Victor Kovner, who had known Cohn for many years, "You knew when you were in Cohn's presence you were in the presence of pure evil. He was a vicious, Red-baiting source of sweeping wrongdoing." To others, like gossip columnist Cindy Adams, news anchor Barbara Walters, and client Si Newhouse, Cohn was a lovable rogue. Harold R. Tyler Jr., former federal judge and deputy attorney general of the United States, said of Cohn, "He really amazed me, and I thought it was genuine." Tyler represented Cohn in his 1986 disbarment proceeding.

Cohn's unorthodox style even endeared him to some on the left, like columnist Sidney Zion and Harvard professor Alan Dershowitz, who said of Cohn, "I expected to hate him, but I did not. I found him charming." Zion helped Cohn write his "autobiography," which Zion organized and finished after Cohn died. Zion thus explained his affinity for Cohn:

> It was always hard for some folks to understand how a flaming civil libertarian like me could have truck with a guy whose name conjured up the trashing of the Bill of Rights; how a man so closely connected with the *New York Times* could stand, much less like, this rogue, this legal executioner, this notorious bastard who cared nothing for the conventions, who flouted the civil decencies.
>
> To all of this I invoked H. L. Mencken: "What a dull world it would be for honest men if it weren't for its sinners."

Cohn represented a number of Mob figures, many of whom would prove helpful to Trump. He advised them about their business affairs and many of the legitimate fronts they used in their illegal operations. Mob "business meetings" often took place in Cohn's townhouse office.

The participants reasoned correctly that the FBI would be hard pressed to seek a warrant to bug a lawyer's office, and, besides, Cohn had many friends in the FBI. Cohn's mobster clients included Carmine "Lilo" Galante, reputedly boss of the Bonanno crime family, who in 1979 was murdered in cold blood as he ate lunch in a Brooklyn Italian restaurant. Cohn paid his final respects to Galante at the Provenzano-Lanza Funeral Home in Manhattan's Little Italy. It was Cohn who introduced Trump to underworld clients like Anthony "Fat Tony" Salerno, who would be useful in the construction of Trump Tower, among other buildings in New York, and in greasing the skids at Trump's Atlantic City casinos.

Trump was fascinated by the Mob. His favorite movie was *The Godfather*, and he liberally quoted lines from it. In 2009, Kristopher Hansen, a high-profile bankruptcy lawyer at the distinguished law firm of Stroock & Stroock & Lavan, representing investors at risk of losing more than $1 billion in a Trump casino bankruptcy, received a phone call from a man "with a thick New York accent" who called himself Carmine. "If you keep fucking with Mr. Trump," the caller said, "we know where you live and we're going to your house for your wife and kids." The FBI found that the call was made from a telephone booth across from the Ed Sullivan. Theater, just before Trump was a guest there on the *Late Show with David Letterman*. The inference is that the caller was Trump himself.

Cohn opened a law office in the townhouse where he lived, at 39 East 68th Street. Atop a spiral staircase leading to his office was a wall featuring personally inscribed photographs of Cardinals Spellman and Cooke, J. Edgar Hoover, and even Richard Nixon. He wouldn't close the deal on the six-story house until his pal Barbara Walters looked over the space and gave her seal of approval. The townhouse was Cohn's in every way except on paper. It was held in the name of his law firm, Saxe, Bacon & Bolan. While Cohn was never officially listed as a partner in the firm, he held himself out as such and clearly acted as though he were a senior partner. Lawyers call this "partnership by estoppel." I therefore refer to his colleagues as his "partners." He wanted to live without income and, having no natural objects of his bounty, leave no taxable estate. Parked at the curb was Cohn's black Rolls-Royce, sporting the vanity license plate "Roy C." He acquired a 99-foot yacht called *Defiance*. No wonder Trump was impressed.

Fashionable in its exterior, the townhouse was central to Cohn's operations. According to journalist Marie Brenner in *Vanity Fair*, "It was a fetid place, a shambles of dusty bedrooms and office warrens where young male assistants made their way up and down the stairs."

Cindy Adams, a frequent visitor, told me that law books were strewn all over the second and third floors. Cohn would frequently greet people at any time of day wearing pajamas and a silk bathrobe. Visitors saw his collection of toy frogs, elephants, and puppets. He notoriously ate off companions' plates in restaurants.

The saga of McCarthyism reminded us that "guilt by association" is alien to our laws and our way of life. It is curious, however, that the lawyers closest to Cohn were all convicted of some form of criminal wrongdoing. Cohn's partner Thomas A. Bolan was convicted of a crime involving a plot to bilk more than $200 million from a fake charity of which Bolan was a trustee. Facing disbarment, Bolan resigned from the Bar, acknowledging "that he could not successfully defend himself against the charges." Another Cohn partner, Stanley M. Friedman, a Bronx political boss, worked for the city while he assisted Cohn and later went to jail for taking bribes in a parking-ticket-fixing mess.

In 1966, the government charged a third partner, Daniel J. Driscoll, with willfully failing for three years to file federal income tax returns. Driscoll's defense, rarely run in a white-collar criminal case, was temporary insanity, a "character neurosis" that "by reason of mental illness he was unable to conform his conduct to the requirements of law." A trial—in which Barbara Walters, FBI second in command Lou Nichols, and Cardinal Spellman's nephew Ned Spellman testified as character witnesses—ended in a jury disagreement. There was then a retrial, a conviction, and a successful appeal. Eventually, Driscoll pleaded guilty to one count of criminal failure to file, and the judge imposed no prison sentence.

After the plea, Cohn oddly called *the prosecutors* to offer his "congratulations," as though to rub it in that there was no greater penalty. Driscoll, who cheated the hangman, was fond of saying to new Cohn acquaintances: "Isn't Roy wonderful? He reminds me of Jesus Christ!"

The Trump-Cohn meeting proved to be an inflection point for both men: Trump found a lawyer to do battle with the government when he had no case and a mentor who left an indelible impression. Cohn landed a rich client, a comer, someone whom he could deeply influence in the ways of money and political power. Gossip columnist Liz Smith remarked, "Trump lost his moral compass when he made an alliance with Roy Cohn."

In 1981, Cohn published a Baedeker to beating the system, *How to Stand Up for Your Rights and Win!* In fact, he had total contempt for the law. In Cohn's dark world, his rights were more important than anyone else's. The law represented only an obstacle to maneuver around. The rule of law and judicial independence meant nothing to Cohn, and he impressed this attitude upon his apprentice. He was fond of saying to his colleagues, "Fuck the law, who's the judge?," which Trump would later seem to echo with his savage attacks on a "Mexican" judge, a "so-called judge," and an "Obama judge."

Understanding Cohn is central to understanding the rise of Donald Trump. Trump wanted to make inroads in New York society and politics. His father had made a fortune in real estate in the outer boroughs, but he never ventured into sophisticated Manhattan. Cohn, a prominent lawyer, could give Trump entrée to a brave new world of politicians, wheeler-dealers, mobsters, well-heeled men, and beautiful women. Cohn and Trump would cut an unholy and enduring bargain. Cohn was the priest and Trump the acolyte. Cohn taught Trump how to make common cause with the darkest angels in America.

Cohn unveiled for Trump an attack-dog approach to the law, in which you take no prisoners and inflict needless expense on the opposing party. Admit nothing, deny everything; lie, dissemble, and prevaricate. Make false and scurrilous accusations to demonize your adversary.

Drag it out as long as the courts will let you. Take depositions, propound interrogatories, demand documents, and then settle for the best deal you can. Seal the settlement papers so no one will know. Declare victory, bragging that you never settle—and go home.

In the McCarthy years, Cohn revitalized a "new" paranoid politics and leveraged the paranoia to achieve tremendous influence. Mid-twentieth-century America was the time of mass hysteria about the Communist threat, both external from the Soviets and internal from Communists and their "fellow travelers." There were deep divisions in the country about the tension between national security and civil liberties, just as there are today about how to deal with Islamic terrorism, border security, and wealth inequality. Cohn became a shadowy behind-the-scenes apparatchik, his signature pose whispering in the ears of the rich, the powerful, the beautiful young men he courted, and the Mob bosses, whom he guided in their nefarious pursuits.

Cohn knew how to work the press. He had his stable of favored reporters whom he served as a "reliable source." His information was largely accurate and found its way into the gossip columns of the *New York Post* and the tabloid press. The evidence shows that he leaked like a sieve. McCarthy and Cohn stole headlines as they called witnesses before McCarthy's Senate committee and smeared them for pleading the Fifth Amendment in response to questions about membership in the Communist Party or associations with others alleged to be Communists.

Cohn played fast and loose with his taxes. He devoted an entire chapter to tax avoidance in *How to Stand Up for Your Rights and Win!* "Only a fool pays more taxes than is legally required," he wrote. Not wanting to be a "fool," he erred on the side of nonpayment. "I decided to have no assets," he said. "I have no immediate family, and my law firm . . . pays the expenses I incur in developing and seeing through law business." After he died, the IRS had his estate in litigation, claiming he owed over $7 million in federal income taxes. Cohn's defense had been that he had no assets.

Trump learned at the feet of the master, reporting almost a billion dollars of questionable operating losses on his 1995 federal income tax return, which he could use to shelter substantial taxable income over a ten-year period. Giving the spurious excuse that his returns were under audit, he stubbornly refused to release them during his presidential candidacy lest the returns disclose some embarrassment. When challenged about his tax strategies, he explained in his first debate with Hillary Clinton, "That makes me smart."

Trump did not like to pay his lawyers. Sandy Lindenbaum, who knew Cohn, was a premier real estate zoning lawyer in New York. His father, Bunny Lindenbaum, a politically connected real estate lawyer, and Fred Trump shared a close political and personal friendship with Abraham Beame, a political hack who eventually became mayor. Sandy, like his father Bunny, was also politically connected in Democratic politics. Sandy Lindenbaum commanded high fees. He did some good work for Trump over the years, at one point stretching the zoning laws to squeeze some extra floors into a new building. Trump characteristically tried to chisel him on his fee. But Lindenbaum's long-standing political relationships gave him too much leverage for Trump to ignore, and it appears that he eventually got paid. At the end, friends said, they didn't speak.

When other, less well-established lawyers sought to be paid for their services, Trump threatened to counterclaim for malpractice, and that usually ended the matter. He said he paid little to lawyers, even to Cohn. "Roy charged less than any lawyer I've had," said Trump. Once, after Cohn turned a nice legal trick for him, Trump gave him what appeared to be a pair of diamond-encrusted cufflinks in a Bulgari box. After Cohn's death, Peter Fraser, his lover and beneficiary, had the cufflinks appraised. They were knockoffs.

Cohn may have charged *Trump* less, but he was known to gouge his clients. There is a story that when Cohn sent a bill for $10,000 to a client for advice given in a three-minute telephone conversation, the client called to protest. Cohn rejected the pushback and sent a bill for $20,000 based on the second telephone conversation.

Cohn taught Trump to focus on short-term victories and to use unscrupulous methods to achieve them. He rarely expressed a long-term objective. He never thought past the immediate situation. Cohn was not above trying to end-run the judicial process by either buying off or subverting judges, witnesses against him, or even prosecutors.

There are at least two time-honored tactics for impeaching an accuser: either show that what she says is unreasonable or improbable or contradicted by a prior statement or just not so, or attack her credibility by suggesting that she is unworthy of belief because she has a bad character, is "crooked," has been guilty of wrongful conduct, or is personally biased.

Cohn showed Trump that if he succeeded in blackening his opponent, nothing the opponent said would be believed. The best way to defend, Cohn knew, was to go on the attack, bashing your enemies. The best way to attack was to destroy the character of an accuser, even when the counterattack was untrue or exaggerated or irrelevant or prejudicial, and to repeat the bashing again and again. Cohn used this approach effectively with Morgenthau and Robert Kennedy, who he claimed carried personal grudges against him. The tactic resonates. Trump has called Special Counsel Robert Mueller a "conflicted prosecutor gone rogue"—a gutter attack without foundation that is vintage Roy Cohn.

For Trump, litigation became a way of life, a tool to get attention, to bring his enemies to book, and to achieve strategic advantage. The flaw in the American system is that, if you are willing to spend the money, scorched-earth tactics often work. In short, he abused the process of a lawsuit, making it into something it was never intended to be—a way to win out against whoever he considered to be his adversary.

A litigation mentality permeated Trump's character. In her book *Raising Trump*, his ex-wife Ivana recounts a revealing tale. When their first child was born in 1977, she suggested that he be named Donald Jr. Trump's immediate answer was negative. "What if he's a loser?" he lamented. Trump may have been right, but Ivana eventually won that one.

Trump and Cohn saw eye to eye as practitioners of an off-piste brand of politics. Politics was a business, a means of achieving power. Ideology was opium for the masses, while political power was the Holy Grail. Later, Trump tried to play down his relationship with Cohn, telling the *Washington Post* that Cohn was only one of many lawyers he used and he was only one of Cohn's many clients. He also dismissed Cohn's influence on his tactics: "I don't feel I insult people. I try and get to the facts and I don't feel I insult people," he told the *Post*. "Now, if I'm insulted I will counterattack, or if something is unfamiliar I will counterattack, but I don't feel I insult people. I don't want to do that. But if I'm attacked, I will counterattack."

Wayne Barrett, the journalist who spent years following Trump, disagreed. "I just look at him and see Roy," Barrett said. "Both of them are attack dogs." Others in a position to know also tell of a far more intimate relationship. Cohn once said that he was "not only Donald's lawyer but also one of his close friends." Roger Stone, the political dirty trickster who met Trump through Cohn, said, "Roy was more than his personal lawyer." Barrett said of Cohn, "He became Donald's mentor, his constant adviser."

In 1980, Cohn boasted of an extraordinarily close relationship. "Donald calls me 15 to 20 times a day," he told the journalist Marie Brenner in the presence of Trump over lunch at 21. "He is always asking, 'What is the status of this . . . and that?'" Peter Fraser, Cohn's principal lover for the closing years of his life, said of Cohn's influence on Trump, "That bravado, and if you say it aggressively and loudly enough . . . that's the way Roy used to operate . . . and Donald was certainly his apprentice." Cohn escorted Trump's mother to the opening of Trump Tower in 1983, where he posed for "cutting the ribbon" photo ops with Trump, Trump's mother, and Mayor Koch. There are even suggestions that Trump for a short time saw Cohn's doctor.

Cohn taught Trump the "art of the lie"—how to lie blatantly and without shame. To lie to the court in the litigation he brought or defended; to lie in his political positions; and to lie his way through life.

And Trump learned to do Cohn one better—*he would lie in denying he had uttered the lies he had previously told.*

Cohn preached political loyalty, a value that Trump also often professed. For Trump, you were either loyal or a "complete scumbag." "Roy was brutal, but he was a very loyal guy," Trump told the writer Tim O'Brien in 2005. "He brutalized for you." Cohn would always do a favor for his friends; he would never forget a favor either. "Loyalty," Cohn stressed many times during the Army-McCarthy hearings, "loyalty!" In the dark political world of shady deals and favor banks, loyalty is the gold standard. Trump asked James Comey for his "loyalty." Comparing Trump to various tyrannical characters in Shakespeare, Harvard professor Stephen Greenblatt, in his insightful book *Tyrant: Shakespeare on Politics,* reflects: "When an autocratic, paranoid, narcissistic ruler sits down with a civil servant and asks for his loyalty, the state is in danger."

According to journalist Sam Roberts, who wrote *The Brother,* the inside story of the trial of Julius and Ethel Rosenberg, Cohn's influence on Trump was profound. Roberts argues that Cohn taught Trump the golden rules of litigation: "1. Never settle, never surrender. 2. Counterattack, counter-sue immediately. 3. No matter what happens, no matter how deeply into the muck you get, claim victory."

In March 1986, when Cohn was dying of AIDS, Trump gave him a "farewell" dinner party in Florida. Donald and Ivana were there, together with Lee Iacocca, New York political operative Jerry Finkelstein, and his son Andrew Stein. One of Cohn's friends, Jay Taylor, recalled the evening: "The place settings were astronomical. The candelabra were more than I'm going to make in the next six months. Gold, everything. I was sitting at a $200,000-a-place setting at dinner. A great dessert; I had two of them. . . . It was fun, like we all gave him a tribute. 'I'd like to thank Roy.' They all knew. It was obvious at that time that he was going, and let's hurry up and give him a dinner and thank him."

The curtain fell in obloquy for Roy M. Cohn. His legal career ended in 1986 with his disbarment "for reprehensible conduct" before the very court his father had served as a respected judge. The court found that Cohn had, among other things, borrowed $100,000 from a matrimonial client in 1966 and refused to pay it back until 1979, when she sued him for debt; pressured the 84-year-old multimillionaire liquor baron Lewis Rosenstiel into signing a piece of paper making Cohn the executor of his estate as Rosenstiel lay dying in a Florida hospital room; and looted an escrow fund of some $200,000, which included an insurance payout on his yacht *Defiance*, which sank in 1973. A crew member died in the disaster at sea when a suspicious fire broke out aboard the ship. Not nice. But, as the Cohn character says in Tony Kushner's Pulitzer Prize–winning play *Angels in America*, "I'm not nice. Fuck nice."

Trump testified as a character witness at the disbarment hearing. He swore that Cohn was "loyal" and "possesses the highest degree of integrity." The courts disagreed. The *New York Daily News* of June 24, 1986, proclaimed Cohn's disbarment with a banner headline in 80-point type on its front page. A few weeks later, Cohn died. Trump attended his funeral. According to Wayne Barrett, he "stood in the back of the room silently, not asked to be one of several designated speakers, precisely because those closest to Cohn felt he had abandoned the man who had molded him." Cohn's 68th Street townhouse sold in 1987 for $3.7 million, with the proceeds impounded by the IRS.

Cohn's impression on Trump was indelible. In November 2017, with Special Counsel Robert Mueller closing in, Trump met with Jeanine Pirro, one of his favorite Fox News talk show hosts, to discuss the Russia investigation. A "visibly agitated" Trump told Pirro, "Roy Cohn was my lawyer," suggesting the bare-knuckled Cohn-type defense was just what he needed. When he wanted to get Attorney General Jeff Sessions to remain in charge of the Russia inquiry so he would have an attorney general to protect him, he told his White House counsel Donald F. McGahn to lobby Sessions to stay in the case. "Where's my Roy Cohn?" he fumed. It's no wonder that on election night 2016, once the result was known, Trump said to columnist Cindy Adams, who had known Cohn well, "If Roy were here, he never would have believed it."

––––––––––––

Back to the 1973 housing discrimination case. The lawsuit was one of the biggest and most sensational enforcement actions brought under the Fair Housing Act up to that time. It represented an existential threat to the Trump name and enterprise. Donald, although relatively new to Trump Management, Inc., his father's firm, where his duties were ill defined, took a personal interest in the litigation, interviewing witnesses and taking statements from them, attending key hearings, participating in the drafting of the final consent decree, and conferring with counsel. The government complaint, brought in Brooklyn's Eastern District of New York, charged that the Trumps had systematically denied people home rentals "because of race and color." The well-respected federal judge presiding was Edward R. Neaher.

Trump's defense against the federal case was deflection, denial, and counterattack. On December 12, 1973, Trump and Cohn held a press conference at the New York Hilton to brief the media on the case. Despite the damning evidence of racism, Trump rebuked his accusers, branding the allegations against him as "such outrageous lies." His defense was that he did not want to rent to *welfare recipients*, but he never discriminated based on race. If he was forced to rent to people on welfare, he said, "there would be a massive fleeing from the city of not only our tenants, but communities as a whole." Of course, none of the rejected black testers got far enough along in the rental process to be asked whether they were welfare recipients or not.

Nevertheless, Trump stuck to his story and continued to justify his conduct by saying he did not want to rent to welfare recipients. As quoted in the *New York Post* on December 12, 1973, Trump claimed that the "government is trying to force defendants to rent to welfare recipients who do not otherwise qualify for our apartments in our buildings." He again claimed that while he refused to rent to welfare recipients, he never discriminated based on race.

In those days the government routinely offered standard slap-on-the-wrist settlements where the defendant, without admitting or denying the charges, agreed to sin no more. But Trump and Cohn refused to settle. "The idea of settling drove me crazy," Trump wrote some fourteen years later in *The Art of the Deal*. Enlarging on his original "welfare cases" leitmotif, he said, "What we didn't do was rent to welfare cases, white or black," adding, "I'd rather fight than fold, because as soon as you fold once, you get the reputation for being a folder." He was even then living in a world of "alternative facts." In the real world, he settled many a case.

Fred Trump testified that he was "unfamiliar" with the Fair Housing Act, as though ignorance of the law was an excuse, but that he had changed his rental policies anyway after the 1968 law had gone into effect. Fred Trump knew all about the FHA. The Open Housing Center, as well as the New York City Human Rights Commission, had put him on notice, in and after 1968, that he was discriminating illegally, long before the government brought suit. This was a whopper that he could not have told with a straight face. The allegations all centered on discriminatory acts in 1972 and thereafter.

At the outset, Trump and Cohn announced with great fanfare a counterclaim against the government for $100 million, which Judge Neaher would call a "tidy sum." Trump contended that the government had sullied his reputation by bringing the suit and asserted that the charges were irresponsible and baseless. The court, although it recognized Cohn as a "big gun," was not impressed. The judge dismissed the counterclaim less than two months after it was filed.

The counterclaim was not the only line of attack Trump launched in his effort to undermine the government's case. Consistent with his "hit and run" strategy, he tried to smear one of the government lawyers, staging a sideshow to the litigation.

In 1974, Donna Goldstein was a relatively recent law school graduate employed by the Civil Rights Division of the Department of Justice. Her job was to obtain witness statements in possible support of the case against Trump. Goldstein's more experienced supervisor, Frank Schwelb, considered her to "have an excellent reputation, both with respect to her legal ethics and in relation to her professional competence."

Trump moved to cite Goldstein for contempt of court for improper conduct in the discharge of her official duties. The gist of the accusation was the myth that Goldstein told the witnesses, all former employees of Trump, that they would be charged with perjury unless they lied about the Trumps and that the government wiretapped the Trump offices and knew from wiretaps that they were lying. Of course there were no wiretaps, and no ethical lawyer would ever make such a misrepresentation to a witness. It was all sheer conspiracy theory paranoia.

The approach became ingrained in Trump's DNA. If the government attacks, charge prosecutorial misconduct or impugn its motives as political. That was the tactic that had worked so well for Cohn in his notorious legal duel with Morgenthau. In the discrimination case, Trump and Cohn would be hard pressed to suggest a plausible political motivation, since Trump was not then a political figure. Moreover, it was the Nixon White House that brought the discrimination case.

Trump supported his contempt motion with Cohn's affidavit describing a number of events at which Cohn was not even present. Cohn singled out Donna Goldstein for special savaging, alleging that before Goldstein arrived on the scene her predecessor, Elyse Goldweber, "observed legal and ethical strictures." And, to add some spice, he contended that once Goldstein was assigned to the case, the investigation turned into a "gestapo-like interrogation" during which Goldstein had made unspecified threats of an FBI investigation into the personal lives of the witnesses. His associate even complained to the Justice Department that its minions were "descending upon the Trump offices with five storm troopers."

Cohn attached to his own affidavit statements of four former Trump employees and two unsworn statements by a couple formerly employed as part-time rental agents at Trump's Beach Haven Apartments. All claimed that Goldstein had pressured them into stating their knowledge of discriminatory policies.

When the government, asserting that the allegations of misconduct on Ms. Goldstein's part were "false and scurrilous," asked for depositions and a hearing to resolve the issue, Cohn backed off. He desperately offered to mark the contempt motion off the calendar and to withdraw the motion "without prejudice," which is lawyer-speak for postponing the matter indefinitely and reserving the right to bring it on again any time he wanted to.

The government was not so easily going to let Trump and Cohn off the hook. The Department of Justice took a point of personal privilege, demanding a hearing to exonerate Goldstein from any suspicion of misconduct, which might be detrimental to her professional career. Besides, they recognized the contempt motion for the dishonest ploy that it was and wanted to expose the maneuver to Judge Neaher. Trump and Cohn were not about to hoodwink Judge Neaher, who stated at close of the hearing,

I find no evidence in the record that anything of the nature of Gestapo tactics was permitted by the FBI in doing the tasks assigned to them.

I consider that an extraordinary charge to make about an agency which, in my view, has always acted . . . with the utmost politeness and respect for the rules and laws of this country. . . .

I have found no evidence in the record to sustain such a charge and I think the charge is utterly without foundation. . . .

I feel that nothing here would amount to any reason why this Court should condemn them or punish them for what was done here. And that is my ruling in this matter, and therefore I grant the Government's motion to strike this application from the record.

Goldstein went on to become a respected superior court judge in Los Angeles until she retired in 2018.

Cohn's approach was to try to keep the government off balance and create a sideshow that would distract from the main event. A Justice Department memorandum of December 15, 1977, noted a "long series of delaying tactics,"

> among which were a $100 million counterclaim against the United States and a motion to hold a [Civil Rights] Division attorney in contempt of court for alleged "Gestapo-like" interviewing tactics. Defense counsel is Roy Cohn, who became well known in the fifties as an associate of Joseph McCarthy.

In Trump's eyes, the maneuvering to keep the government off balance worked. The case dragged on for years without resolution. After two years of fighting on collateral issues, the litigation ended where it should have ended in the first place: in a settlement. The consent decree between Trump and the government, filed June 10, 1975, was a slap on the wrist. Trump settled. The consent decree contained the boilerplate language, "without admitting or denying guilt." This was important to the Trumps. Never admit wrongdoing. This leads to shame and disgrace. Deny everything.

Donald said publicly that he was satisfied that the agreement with the government did not "compel the Trump Organization to accept persons on welfare as tenants unless as qualified as any other tenant," which was completely beside the point.

As part of the settlement, moreover, Trump agreed to a permanent prohibition on "discriminating against any person in the terms, conditions or privileges of sale or rental of a dwelling." The Trumps were further directed for a period of two years to implement an affirmative program of compliance with the Fair Housing Act, and they were required to "thoroughly acquaint themselves personally on a detailed basis" with the FHA. Trump was also required to send a weekly list of vacancies to the New York Urban League and to give the organization priority on certain locations.

Negotiations over the consent decree almost broke down on the issue of advertising. The parties attended a conference before Judge Neaher on a cool spring day in Brooklyn, on June 10, 1975, just before the consent decree was finalized.

The government had insisted that, as part of the decree, Trump must over the two-year period place three-inch ads in the *New York Times* one Sunday each month offering apartments in particular sections of New York City "on a rotating basis," with each ad at its foot containing the standard language "EQUAL OPPORTUNITY HOUSING." Government attorney Henry Brachtl advised the court that "when the purpose of this decree is to assure affirmative action . . . advertising is at the heart of the decree."

The Trumps pushed back and began to niggle, carping about the additional expense of adding language that had become standard under HUD regulations. "We have to pay for the extra line," Trump said. "It's a very expensive thing for us. It's really onerous. Each sentence we put in is going to cost us a lot of money over the period we are supposed to do it," he told the court repeatedly. Turning to Donna Goldstein, he asked the rhetorical question: "Will you pay for the expense, Donna?" Surely, the additional expense of one standard line in 24 ads over a two-year period would not be onerous for a billionaire.

Trump's father railed against the advertising sought by the government. The parties had the following colloquy with the court:

Mr. F. Trump: We were not convicted. We would win this case if we fought it.

The Court: Don't be too sure of that.

Courts rarely give neighborly advice. Trump lost the battle, and the Trumps were required to pay for the ads with the additional line directly soliciting minority tenants. The Justice Department claimed victory, calling the settlement "one of the most far-reaching ever negotiated." The black and Latino press, notably the *Amsterdam News* and *El Diario*, told their communities that "qualified blacks and Puerto Ricans now have the opportunity to rent apartments owned by Trump Management."

Trump, who had lost the case, also claimed victory, harping on the boilerplate language of the settlement agreement that he and his father had not admitted guilt. And he would write in *The Art of the Deal*, "In the end the government couldn't prove its case, and we ended up making a minor settlement without admitting any guilt." The Trumps didn't deny guilt either.

But it didn't end there. In January 1978, more than two years later, Drew S. Days, assistant attorney general in charge of the Civil Rights Division, advised Cohn that over the two-year period of the consent decree, the Department of Justice had received complaints of "discriminatory conduct by personnel at several different Trump Management buildings."

The government alleged that Trump had failed to comply with the consent order in the three years after it went into effect. It claimed that Trump had continued to make apartments unavailable to black persons on account of race, continued to discriminate against black persons in the terms and conditions of rental, made statements indicating racial preference and limitation, and falsely represented to African Americans that apartments were not available for inspection and rental when in fact they were.

Trump continued to be in court for discriminating against African Americans in violation of the terms of the 1975 settlement. The government charged that it was taking steps "to ensure realistic opportunity to nonwhite citizens to rent dwellings in predominantly white buildings." It again claimed that the Trump people had falsely told black applicants that apartments were not available. Government memoranda showed often-repeated instances of discrimination at seven Trump developments in Brooklyn and Queens and one in Staten Island. The racial statistics for the buildings where the incidents occurred showed relatively few black occupants (2.6–8.4 percent), and revealed that in one building with significant levels of black occupancy there had been an increase of only 7 percent, or 12 blacks, in a huge complex during the two-year period of the decree. The Department of Justice concluded that several of Trump's employees had engaged in violations and that Trump had not taken adequate steps to prevent a recurrence.

Cohn again tried the dispute in the press, fulminating against Trump's accusers and calling the new charges "nothing more than a re-hash of complaints by a couple of planted malcontents." He didn't dare repeat such statements before Judge Neaher, who had retained jurisdiction.

As late as 1983, the New York State Department of Housing and Community Renewal investigated two of Trump's apartment properties and found that they were 95 percent white. The case died a slow death as complaints subsided. The Justice Department closed the file in April 1982.

Trump should have listened to the other lawyers. After years of liti-gation, which was really a *sitzkrieg* in which nothing much happened—except for his frivolous counterclaim against the government for defa-mation, seeking $100 million in damages, and his attempted subversion of a government lawyer for doing her job—the Trumps had to settle the discrimination case anyway. As part of the settlement, they agreed not to discriminate anymore, and they continued to discriminate anyway. Cohn's presence in the case bought some time, but not the desired re-sult. Trump emerged from the case a big loser.

––––––––

Many see the discrimination case as evidence of Trump's racial bias. But there is the larger point—the early deployment of the attack-heavy, delay-and-deny, antilegal playbook, right down to some of the specific lan-guage we've heard over the course of this presidency. The Trump presidency—at war with his own Department of Justice, the FBI, and the intelligence community—his attacks on judges and lawyers who frustrate his objectives, and his demands that the investigators be in-vestigated and the prosecutors be prosecuted are all ripped right from the pages of the 1970s. Long before Rudy Giuliani used the term "storm troopers" to try to defend Trump, Roy Cohn did. From the discrimination case he developed an ophidian mentality—poised to attack his critics, to smear his adversaries, to position himself as ideologically antigovernment and anti–rule of law. Clad in this suit of armor, he was ready to go to war to preserve his buildings, his casinos, his projects, or his brand, whatever transaction he was engaged in. Sharply etched in the entrails of the discrimination case are elements of the personality in disarray that now occupies the White House.

2

TRUMP TAKES MANHATTAN

THE VOYAGE ACROSS THE EAST RIVER

Glittering crowds and shimmering clouds in canyons of steel
They're making me feel I'm home.
— Vernon Duke, "Autumn in New York"

In 1971, the time had come for Donald Trump to leave his father. He did not leave behind, however, Fred's wealth, connections, and sources of credit. Fred had staked him to tens of millions of dollars to get a foothold in the Manhattan real estate arena. Donald has always maintained that it was just a million. It was of enormous importance to him that he project the image of being a self-made man. Then 25, he moved across the East River from Queens to a small Upper East Side apartment. He had had it with Brooklyn and Queens. For young Donald, Manhattan was the Promised Land. In Manhattan, he would get in touch with the right people, he would make deals, he would build and buy luxury hotels, condominiums, and apartment houses and erect a tower to his self-anointed greatness. Speaking of his father, Donald said around the time of Fred's death, chuckling, "It was good for me. You know, being the son of somebody, it could have been competition to me. This way, I got Manhattan all to myself!" It was for Donald to attack

Manhattan and go for the brass ring. Fred Trump had become a major player in Queens and Brooklyn, yet for some unexplained reason, he never took his business model to Manhattan. Perhaps he felt uncomfortable in the real estate world of the Jewish Lefraks, Minskoffs, Milsteins, Tishmans, Resnicks, Roses, and Rudins. Whether for ethnic reasons or otherwise, he never became a member of the elite Real Estate Board of New York. He just did not fit in the club.

Donald became a major player in New York but never joined the club either. He was the parvenu, the new kid on the block from Queens. It is perhaps from this insecurity that net worth became such an obsession for Trump. He sued people who he claimed publicly underestimated it. He habitually misrepresented it. Trump had in 1982 made some strange phone calls to *Forbes* journalist Jonathan Greenberg in which he had posed as a fictitious Trump Organization executive called "John Barron," purporting to shed some light on Trump's net worth for the first "*Forbes* 400 Richest Americans" section. Although the caller "altered some cadences and affected a slightly stronger New York accent, it was clearly him," Greenberg wrote in 2018. "Barron" claimed that Trump really controlled in excess of 90 percent of his father's residential apartments. Although it became true a decade later, this representation was false. In 2018, Greenberg wrote of Trump's lies to *Forbes*: "Trump's fabrications provided the basis for a vastly inflated wealth assessment for the *Forbes* 400 that would give him cachet for decades as a triumphant businessman."

In late 2018, Trump's press secretary Sarah Huckabee Sanders put his net worth at "over $10 billion," when at roughly the same time Bloomberg estimated the correct figure to be $2.8 billion and *Forbes* estimated $3.1 billion.

He had no military record or passion for civic leadership, as the Rudins and Roses did, and no intellectual or cultural heft like the Minskoffs, Tishmans, and Milsteins. His philanthropy was minimal and almost always self-serving, just like his father's had been.

He was generally regarded as an *arriviste*, a playboy, an opportunist, a publicity seeker, a vulgarian—someone the elites didn't want to do business with. Mixed in him were many positive elements of entrepreneurial success: energy, showmanship, imagination, appetite for risk, a brash competitive nature, useful political connections, and the plausibility of significant capital. There was at least one absent quality, however: basic integrity. And let's not forget another tool missing from the box: old-fashioned charm. He wasn't nice. His bite was as bad as his bark. He left people feeling not very good about him. People didn't like Donald Trump. He made many enemies. His contacts were mainly his father's political cronies, like Mayor Abe Beame, and assorted Democratic politicians he met through Roy Cohn.

In 1977, Trump approached the bankruptcy trustees of the Penn Central Company to acquire an option on the 1,800-room Commodore Hotel, located next to Grand Central Terminal. This was Donald Trump's first major real estate deal. As will be seen, he eventually partnered with the Chicago Pritzkers, who were the source of the financing. The deal put him on the map. Amazingly, the Pritzkers put up *all* of the money, and Trump became the 50 percent owner of a multimillion-dollar property without contributing a dime. The partnership cratered, but Trump walked away with a cool profit after bringing major litigation against the Pritzkers.

The mayor at the time was Abe Beame, a product of the Brooklyn Democratic clubhouse. Beame was a close friend not only of Fred Trump but of Roy Cohn, whose birthday party he religiously attended each year. "Whatever my friends Fred and Donald want in this town, they get," Beame said. Trump produced Beame at a meeting with one of the Penn Central trustees, and that sufficed to seal the bargain. What Trump sought from the city was a 40-year tax abatement, worth $400 million at a time when New York City was on its financial keister, which turned on his acquiring the Penn Central option. He got both. The tax abatement was in the bag, a promised political favor from Beame. The man who engineered the tax abatement was Beame's deputy mayor, Stanley M. Friedman. Friedman became a Roy Cohn partner in 1978 the day Ed Koch succeeded Beame as mayor.

The option agreement with the bankrupt Penn Central was not yet signed because Trump was still trying to raise the $250,000 necessary to close the deal. So what did he do? He lied to the press and announced he had the option. Showing city officials an unsigned option agreement, Trump then nailed down the tax abatement. It was a shell game. Showing the banks the city's official commitment, he was able to get the option.

With the option and the tax abatement in hand, he enlisted his friend the well-connected real estate consultant Ben Lambert to find him a partner who would be a source of finance. At the time, Lambert was a Trump friend of long standing. They were both men about town. Lambert was close to the Pritzker family, who were stated by *Forbes* to be the seventh-wealthiest family in the nation, with assets exceeding $29 billion. The fortune dates back to A. N. Pritzker (died 1986), who created Hyatt Hotels with his sons Jay, Donald, and Robert and invested in holdings like industrial conglomerate Marmon Group, now owned by Berkshire Hathaway.

With Lambert's help, Trump was able to convince Jay Pritzker that he was a worthwhile partner on a new 1,400-room hotel to be called the "Grand Hyatt" on the site of the old Commodore. The Grand Hyatt would become the first Pritzker-owned hotel in New York City. Trump proposed to modernize the outside of the building and renovate the interior. It was a suitably ambitious Trumpian scheme, and the Pritzkers went for it. Fred Trump guaranteed the construction loan, and the Pritzkers did the rest. Trump went into the deal without putting up a dime of his own money.

The Trump-Pritzker relationship was contentious from the start. Over the years the parties became embroiled in at least three arbitrations. The records of the arbitrations are kept from the public view by court order, so we have none of the details. Suffice it to say that Trump charged the Pritzkers with negligently managing the property and failing to maximize the revenue. The soured relationship festered, eventually erupting into full-blown litigation. In 1993, Trump sued the Pritzkers in federal court under the Racketeer Influenced and Corrupt Organizations

(RICO) Act. He alleged that the Pritzkers had "systematically looted tens of millions of dollars from the Grand Hyatt through theft, fraud, waste and mismanagement." Specifically, he claimed they had used questionable accounting methods and made unauthorized payments to enrich themselves at his expense. The Pritzkers vehemently denied all this and quickly moved to dismiss. Their motion was never decided because Trump eventually dropped the case.

Trump was a great fan of RICO suits. RICO, both a criminal and civil statute, is, as the iconic Judge Learned Hand put it, the darling of a federal prosecutor's nursery. It furnishes a potent weapon against racketeers and mobsters engaged in a criminal conspiracy. It also provides a civil treble-damages remedy for certain types of business fraud. Prominent law firms, nationally known accounting firms, and even Fortune 500 companies have all been named in complaints alleging civil RICO violations. Most such allegations the courts dismiss as without foundation. RICO is a formidable legal weapon nonetheless because the exposure is terrifying. Win the case and you get your damages three times over plus your attorneys' fees; lose the case and you pay treble damages plus the winner's legal fees, which can be enormous. Trump told the *New York Post* that he brought the RICO case against the Pritzkers because "the rich have a very low threshold for pain," and "I don't like being pushed around, and now they're beginning to learn it." (As will be seen, Trump had brought another RICO suit in the 1970s, when he sued *a law firm* that had sued him on behalf of its tenant clients. The suit was dismissed; more on this later.)

Trump alleged that the Pritzkers' goal was to force him out of the partnership. Trump's goal was to extract a better deal out of the Pritzkers. "If you want to see what kind of partner Mr. Trump is, read his book," said Jay Pritzker with reference to *The Art of the Deal*, in which Trump brags he gets the best of any transaction.

The next year, 1994, the Pritzkers sued Trump in federal court for violating their partnership agreement in that he failed to remain solvent, he had collateralized his stake in the hotel for bank loans without obtaining the consent of the Pritzkers, and he refused to pay his stipulated share of necessary renovation expenses. Trump defended his dealings with the banks. He said, "Every 'i' was dotted, and every 't' was crossed." He claimed that the renovations proposed by the Pritzkers were "irrational and foolish." In an interview he gave to the *New York Times* on March 29, 1994, he said of the Pritzkers, "They're spending money like drunken sailors." Both sides agreed that when tales of the feud were bruited about in the press, the Grand Hyatt's ratings declined, and the hotel lost the coveted conference and convention business that was its mainstay.

Telling his story to the press, Trump said of the firestorm, "I see this thing ending when they give up the management of the hotel. This is a fractured relationship. I think Hyatt has done a horrible job in its management of the Grand Hyatt, and I want them out. That is the goal of my lawsuit." But the Pritzkers had had enough of Trump's lawsuits, and Trump wanted a divorce. The "fractured" 17-year relationship ended in 1996 when the Pritzkers bought out Trump for $140 million.

When David Rubenstein interviewed Trump at a meeting of the Economic Club in Washington in December 2014, he uttered not a word of criticism about the Pritzkers and said the Grand Hyatt was "very successful." Sure, it was "successful"—*for him*. He had contributed practically nothing to the cost of building the hotel or to the expense of maintaining it, and by intimidating his partners with a bogus racketeering charge, he walked away with a cool $140 million. The Pritzkers were seasoned hotel developers who today successfully manage 777 hotel properties in 54 countries. The claim that they had done a "horrible job" managing the Hyatt defied credulity.

Things did not work out as well for Donald Trump with the iconic General Motors Building at its prime block-through location on Fifth Avenue and 59th Street. Big litigation; small return on investment. In 2014, *Vanity Fair* writer Vicky Ward wrote a book about the entire GM

Building imbroglio titled *The Liar's Ball*. She expressed gratitude for Trump's help in the book and acknowledged he had met with her several times. The book told the whole story.

The GM Building was one of the most prestigious locations in Manhattan, across from the Plaza Hotel and bordering Central Park. Famed architect Edward Durell Stone was the designer. It was fully leased to such premier commercial tenants as the law firm Weil, Gotshal & Manges and international ad agency Wells Rich Greene. The presence as tenants of cosmetic giants Helena Rubinstein, Revlon, and Estée Lauder caused Leonard Lauder to quip that GM had become the "General Odors Building." Trump's plan for the building was to expand the usable rental area by leasing out retail space in the lobby and basement. A number of billionaire sharks in the real estate world, such as Sheldon Solow, Steve Roth of Vornado, Harry Macklowe, and Chicago's Sam Zell, had been swimming around the prime property. Trump was out to wrest the GM Building from their grasp without putting up very much money.

In 1998, the only problem for Trump was that he lacked the capital to acquire the building. So he found a partner in Conseco, a finance and insurance company based in Carmel, Indiana, to acquire the 50-story structure for $878 million. The guiding spirit of Conseco was a new Indiana millionaire called Steve Hilbert. The son of a maintenance man and a switchboard operator from Terre Haute, Hilbert had dropped out of college to sell encyclopedias door to door. A born entrepreneur, he eventually began to gobble up insurance companies until he made the run on Conseco, a multibillion-dollar insurance and financial powerhouse. As Conseco chieftain, he made $119 million in 1997 alone.

Hilbert was a conspicuous consumer. His bathrooms were gold plated. His antique collection was valued at $3 million. He was Trump's kind of guy. The only problem was that he was deeply in debt, and couldn't hold on to what he had. The bubble burst.

Conseco contributed all but $11 million of the $222 million equity in the deal. The lion's share of the purchase price, about $700 million, would be financed with money borrowed from Lehman Brothers. In recognition of his purported management skills, Trump obtained from Hilbert an extraordinary concession: he would get 50 percent of the equity in exchange for his 5 percent cash contribution. In the stew was the understanding that Trump would manage the property—of course, for a fee. Hilbert was fully under the Trump spell.

The acquisition was another exercise in Trump self-branding. With a comparably small equity position, he lost no time emblazoning the name TRUMP in gold letters on the building's façade. There were placards on the wall of the white-marble lobby that read, "The General Motors Building at Trump International Plaza." He ran a two-day ad in the *New York Times*, reading,

$700,000,000 . . . THE GM BUILDING . . .
A 50-story 2 million square foot office building . . .
Developer Donald J. Trump.

A drawback to the GM Building was an unattractive sunken plaza that had been slammed by *Times* architecture critic Ada Louise Huxtable. Trump raised the plaza, adorning its Doric simplicity with two 65-foot-long fountains, a marble sitting area, and steps. The new square eventually attracted CBS's *The Early Show*, which broadcast its program from the plaza. Passersby would stop to watch.

Trump had acquired a trophy—or part of a trophy. But could he hold on to it?

By mid-2000, Conseco was in deep financial trouble—which arose out of its other business operations—and sought the protection of the bankruptcy court. The board had ousted Trump's pal Hilbert from the company for his extravagant and highly leveraged acquisition program. The new management wanted out of the project, which was not throwing off much cash, and it decided to play hardball. It offered to sell its interest to Trump at a distress price of $295 million. The proposed deal was that Conseco would wind up not having to book a loss on the sale, and Trump would become 100 percent owner of the signature property, said to be worth at least $1 billion—a steal. The problem was that Trump did not have the money. Needing a source of finance to buy out Conseco, he promised a fee to his then friend Ben Lambert if Lambert found him a partner.

With Conseco on the ropes, Trump had lunch at Jean-Georges with Chicago billionaire developer Sam Zell. Located at the Trump International Hotel & Tower at One Central Park West, Jean-Georges is a high-end eatery, frequented by the movers and shakers of the city's commercial life. *Zagat* for 2017 says the restaurant features "'exquisite' New French cuisine that 'dazzles your palate' served 'with ballet-like precision' in a 'serene, luxurious' setting." *Zagat* adds that the tab is invariably a "king's ransom."

Zell had been interested in acquiring the GM Building in 1998. Needing a white knight to bail him out of his troubled venture, Trump pitched Zell on the GM Building over his favorite Jean-Georges hamburger. Zell turned him down. Zell told journalist Vicky Ward of the encounter: "I looked at him, and I said, 'Donald, you've sued every partner you ever had. Why would I want to be your partner in anything?'" Trump interpreted this correctly: "Zell was against me because of what happened with his friend Jay Pritzker." Explained Zell, "I was around listening to Jay when Donald was in big trouble on the Grand Hyatt Hotel. Jay saved his ass, and then after he saved his ass, Donald sued him." It is an axiom that what goes around comes around.

Lacking a new partner, Trump turned to his banker, Deutsche Bank, and made Conseco an unpalatable offer. Deutsche Bank would help Trump refinance the building with $995 million. Out of the loan proceeds, $700 million would pay off the existing loan to Lehman Brothers. Trump proposed to fund the $295 million Conseco wanted with $50 million in cash, *$200 million in notes*, and a $45 million residual interest in the property. Conseco knew its customer. The rub was the viability of the notes. In the fall of 2001, the parties were negotiating an "acceptable" guaranty of the notes when two planes took down the World Trade Center, and the financing collapsed. The attack took out

Deutsche Bank's downtown office headquarters, and it would not lend for months.

Conseco put the GM Building in play. So what was Trump to do? Out in the cold in February 2002, he sued his partner, just as Sam Zell had predicted he would. He commenced an action against Conseco for a $1 billion in the New York State courts, claiming that before the events of September 11, Conseco had torpedoed the refinancing by making "improper demands," insisting on a letter of credit from Deutsche Bank to secure the notes, and refusing the unsecured guaranty he had offered.

Conseco's reaction to the suit was a put-down worthy of Trump. Conseco said it assumed Trump now wanted to sell his interest, and that once he did, it would list on eBay the fake gold lettering of the building's TRUMP sign and donate the proceeds to charity.

In January 2003, Conseco sought to retain Ben Lambert to conduct an "auction" to sell the building, subject to the outcome of the litigation with Trump. Lambert paid a courtesy call on Trump to advise him of the request. Trump became livid. "I felt it was just disloyal of Ben, who'd been a friend for years, to go shop the building to the other side—and I haven't spoken to him since." In a transparent attempt to disqualify Lambert, Trump sent to Lambert's office a bundle of deal documents, but Lambert returned them unopened. Lambert readily perceived that the documents were a Trojan horse.

When in March 2003 Conseco applied to the bankruptcy court to approve Lambert's retention, Trump spitefully objected, asserting that Lambert was less than capable and also too expensive. Trump, ironically enough, would have been delighted to pay Lambert a fee three years earlier had he procured a deal with Zell or another white knight. "I couldn't believe it," said Lambert. "Donald had been prepared to pay my fees to find him a partner—but suddenly he told the court my fees were too expensive?" The court rejected Trump's application, ruling that there was no conflict and that Conseco could pay Lambert his fee.

In June 2003, there occurred a court-ordered arbitration between

Trump and Conseco, and Trump went down in flames by a 2–1 vote of the arbitrators. The court confirmed the award. Conseco won, Trump lost. The court directed Trump to sell his 50 percent stake to Conseco, formerly worth over $100 million, for a paltry $15.6 million. The golden TRUMP name came off the building the next day. Conseco had turned the tables on the dealmeister. It had bought him out for a song.

In September 2003, Ben Lambert conducted the auction to sell the GM Building. Conseco was seeking $1.4 billion for the property, and New York real estate nabob Harry Macklowe had the inside track. The underbidder, billionaire developer Sheldon Solow, hungered for the building, but Lambert regarded Solow, who was less litigious than Trump, as more litigious than Macklowe, and he worried that Solow might not close. The two bids were identical at $1.4 billion, except that Macklowe, unlike Solow, was willing to wire a nonrefundable deposit of $50 million, and Lambert wanted hard money up front.

Macklowe emerged as the successful bidder. He bought the GM Building out of the Conseco bankruptcy. At $735 per square foot, it was then the highest price ever paid for a North American office building. The sales proceeds went to pay off a $700 million mortgage, with the rest split $211 million to Conseco and $15.6 million to Trump. Conseco would get most of any remaining proceeds after transaction costs, with a reportedly small sum going to Trump. Nevertheless, Trump declared victory. "I made a lot of money, because we sold it for $1.4 billion," he bragged.

Solow felt that Macklowe and Conseco had screwed him. He did not believe that Lambert had conducted a fair auction. He had obtained security tapes from Lambert's offices showing that a Solow executive was denied admission beyond the lobby when he sought to deliver his bid, but Macklowe was immediately ushered upstairs carrying a folder presumably enclosing the sealed offer. When Macklowe emerged from Lambert's office, he was no longer carrying the folder.

Solow was outraged. One of his lawyers added the adjectives "hurt" and "offended." His high-profile attorney, David Boies, said that "the whole thing was a charade from start to finish. Even the opening of the sealed envelopes was pure theater. It was ridiculous. There was nothing fair about it." Solow sued in Delaware to try to block the sale, and later in New York federal court for damages. The first case was dismissed; Solow dropped the second. The Delaware court followed the deal documents, which provided that Conseco had the right to sell to whoever it wanted.

In real estate, staying power is the key to success; otherwise there is only lost opportunity. In May 2008, pressed by his creditors and confronted with the serious possibility of personal bankruptcy, Macklowe had to sell his prized possession. After holding the property for less than five years, he sold the GM Building at distress to a consortium led by Mortimer Zuckerman, Goldman Sachs, and two Arab governments for $2.9 billion, setting another new record for the highest price ever paid for a U.S. office building. Only six years later, the value of the building was said to be upward of $3.4 billion.

Even though Macklowe had bought the building in 2003 for $1.4 billion and had sold it in 2008 for $2.9 billion, a profit of $1.5 billion in just five years, the sale of the flagship property was considered a defeat. He was stripped of his trophy. Like Trump, who was forced to sell to Conseco, he might have reaped a bonanza had he had the financial wherewithal to hold on.

In 2008, Macklowe was at the nadir of his fortunes and reputation, but he had paid off his creditors and avoided going over the waterfall into bankruptcy. He would plan a comeback.

In the backwash of the record sale to Zuckerman and the Arabs, there was still more litigation. In September 2008, developer Leslie Dick, another unsuccessful underbidder to Macklowe, brought a RICO action in federal court against 17 parties, including George Soros, Macklowe, Deutsche Bank, and Trump, seeking $4.2 billion after trebling. Dick claimed that his 2003 bid was superior to Macklowe's "in every material respect." Dick had bid $1.5 billion, $100 million higher than Macklowe's offer, but he did not offer the $50 million cash down payment proposed by Macklowe. The bidding and award process, he claimed, was "permeated with fraud," part of a "racketeering enterprise."

Dick alleged that Macklowe had put no money into the deal and that Soros personally contributed $350 million to the purchase, including the $50 million down payment, making Soros the true owner of the building. He claimed that Trump was part of a money-laundering, bankruptcy, and bid-rigging scheme. Trump, it was claimed, conspired with Conseco to keep the negotiations going in 2001 so as to keep the GM Building in play for Soros and Macklowe to acquire it at a bogus price. Dick had brought a similar suit in 2006 in New York State Supreme Court, but that suit was dismissed. For the uninitiated, in the New York State court system, the Supreme Court is actually the court of original jurisdiction. In virtually all other states, the Supreme Court is the highest court in the state. In New York, the highest court is the Court of Appeals.

Macklowe's curt response, delivered by his publicist Howard Rubenstein, was, "This is an absurd lawsuit." Trump had at first tried to stonewall the case by ignoring it, and Dick tried to enter a default judgment. Then, Trump woke up and said that he wanted to actively defend the case. The court denied the request for a default, and the battle raged on. In October 2009, in a surprising turnabout, Dick dropped the lawsuit. The reasons were unstated.

Ten years after the event, Trump was still smarting over his defeat. He might have made billions on the deal, but he had only a pocketful of millions to show for his efforts.

Vicky Ward's portrait of Trump was unflattering, and Trump went ballistic. He smeared Ward and the horse she rode in on. In a scathing 2013 tweet, he said Ward's book was "poorly written & very boring." Trump had been tweeting harsh attacks on those who displeased him since 2009, three years after Twitter launched its platform. His tweeting salvos intensified when he became a presidential candidate, increasing from 275 tweets in the first two years to 375 a month in 2016. He told Page Six of the *New York Post*, "I made a tremendous amount of money in that deal. The book doesn't capture the essence, the glamour or excitement of what happened. It wasn't bad about me, but it should have been great about me. She did a lousy job." Trump's rant then turned personal. He claimed that Ward had begged him for help when she got divorced. "She came to my office in tears, she was a total mess. Her home was in foreclosure, and she said, 'Donald, you are the only one who can help me.' I called the bank and she got a one-year extension. Now she's laughing at my expense." Trump kept a thank-you note from Ward, who also stayed at Mar-a-Lago, Trump's Valhalla estate on the Atlantic, which reads, "If you do run for the presidency—I volunteer now to help!"

Trump had no love lost either for Ward's employer, *Vanity Fair* editor Graydon Carter:

She writes for failing *Vanity Fair* magazine and Graydon Carter is a sleaze bag and highly overrated. I figured that someday she would write a negative story about me for VF and I would show what a disloyal person she is.

There is never a shortage of recriminations in the arcane world of Donald Trump.

———————

Earlier, in 1994, Trump entered into a contract with a Japanese family to manage the 102-story Empire State Building. He let on to the media that he had an ownership interest in the building, which he did not. Under the terms of the deal, the Japanese would furnish $40 million in capital to acquire an ownership interest in the project from Prudential, and Trump would receive one-half of the increase in any profits resulting from his stewardship. In a press release announcing the venture, Trump chortled, "This is a great deal for me. I get 50 percent of all upside, and I don't have to put a dime in the deal. I intend to make my position worth a fortune." It didn't turn out quite as he had planned.

The building's 800 tenants generate $85 million a year in revenue, but under the terms of the master lease, a partnership controlled by Leona Helmsley and Peter Malkin would pay only $1.9 million a year to the building's owners. Trump's "mission: impossible" would be to break the master lease, which didn't run out until 2076.

The Japanese would also have issues. Three years after buying the skyscraper, the lead partner, Japanese billionaire Hideki Yokoi, was imprisoned in Japan for criminal negligence involving a fire in a hotel he owned. Yokoi sued his daughter and son-in-law, Kiiko Nakahara and Jean-Paul Renoir, who had partnered with him on the deal, alleging that they had stolen money and fraudulently transferred his ownership interest in the Empire State Building to themselves. The Renoirs took the position that the equity interest was a gift from Yokoi and that disgruntled half siblings had manufactured the claims. French authorities imprisoned Nakahara on suspicion of forging documents. Renoir was jailed in France for fraud. It is not known whether Trump knew he was partnering with such nice people, and, as every lawyer knows, guilt by association is alien to our laws and way of life.

Trump's interest would only have value if he could increase the rentals on the master lease with the Malkin-Helmsley group operating the building. To do this, as we have noted, would require breaking the lease—almost impossible as a legal matter. So, using the technique that had worked with the Pritzkers, he sued the Malkin-Helmsley group for $100 million in an attempt to wrest control, alleging mismanagement of the property. He claimed, among other things, that they had allowed the building to become infested with rodents and that its elevators were slow and its hallways and offices dark. The litigation went on for four years, going nowhere. One court called it "frivolous." It is not known what the litigation cost Trump in legal fees, but suffice it to say that he would not be eager to pay lawyers for losing a case.

Trump hated real estate powerhouse Leona Helmsley, also known as the "Queen of Mean." She had called him a "skunk" and a "sick, sick, sick, sick boy" in a 1990 *Playboy* interview. There she stole a famous knock on Trump by former New York City deputy mayor Alair Townsend: "I wouldn't trust Donald Trump if his tongue was notarized." Trump needed to jab at Helmsley whenever the opportunity presented itself. When a mentally deranged gunman on the 86th floor observation deck of the Empire State Building killed a sightseer and wounded six others before killing himself, Trump blamed Helmsley. He told the *New York Post*, "Leona Helmsley should be ashamed of herself." Trump and the Japanese sold their interest to Malkin in 2002, barely breaking even on the deal. Ray Hannigan of the prominent law firm Herrick Feinstein, Trump's attorney in connection with the sale of his stake in the Empire State Building, said, "Like many savvy New York real estate players, Donald Trump most certainly uses litigation as a tool to get what he wants." But suits like his RICO claims against the Pritzkers and his litigation over the Empire State Building were astounding attempts at legal blackmail. Other New York real estate operators may have regarded litigation as but another tool in the box, but no New York real estate player used the "tool" as promiscuously as did Donald Trump, who brought frivolous claims, like his claims against the Pritzkers and the Malkin-Helmsley group, to extract money from his adversaries and, most of all, from his partners.

Trump's lust for litigation extended to municipal governments. In 2002, Trump sued New York City for $500 million, concocting the claim that a tax assessor scandal had forced him to sell apartments in his 72-story Trump World Tower, near the United Nations, for below-market prices. He relied on testimony in a bribery case to contend that corrupt assessors had raised taxes for his property to cover up their conspiracy to lower taxes for other prominent landlords who were members of the elite Real Estate Board of New York. He argued that he would have gotten higher prices for his apartments had he also paid lower taxes. Nonetheless, Trump did manage to get $1.5 million for a two-bedroom apartment and sell 81 percent of the apartments at Trump World Tower. Trump also threatened to sue those competitors "whose taxes I was funding, because I was honest and used legal channels. The other people used illegal channels and got better results." The president of the Real Estate Board called Trump's charges "outrageous and unfounded," saying that the "individuals involved will be happy to respond to any frivolous lawsuit from Mr. Trump." Trump never sued. The suit against the city was dismissed. Trump, however, did receive some tax relief. In a settlement with the city, Trump wangled a 17 percent reduction in taxes, worth an estimated $119.5 million, on condition that, in return, he subsidize 200 affordable housing units in the Bronx that the city was partnering on. Why would the City of New York give Trump more tax relief than he was legally entitled to? Fred Trump and Roy Cohn had taught Donald Trump that there are more ways than a lawsuit to skin a cat if you have the right friends in City Hall.

The day Trump announced his candidacy for president, he spoke of his skill in dealing with the Chinese. He said, "I beat China all the time. . . . Am I supposed to dislike them? I own a big chunk of the Bank of America building at 1290 Avenue of the Americas that I got from China in a war. Very valuable."

In fact, court papers tell a different story of his dealings with China. Trump lost big-time to a group of Chinese partners—billionaires who broke off all ties with him after he unsuccessfully charged them with fraud. In 2005, Trump sued his two Hong Kong partners, Henry Cheng and Vincent Lo, in New York State Supreme Court for a staggering $1 billion over a land deal in Manhattan. He alleged fraud, tax evasion, and a litany of legal wrongs, including breach of fiduciary duty and conspiracy. Lo called the lawsuit "a shock."

Cheng and Lo were scions of two of China's most successful families. Cheng was one of Asia's wealthiest developers, with interests similar to Trump's in jewelry brands, real estate, hotels, and casinos. Lo's parallels to Trump were also striking. He was known as "the Donald Trump of China." His name branded high-end restaurants throughout the Chinese mainland. He had a reality television show. He split with his first wife in a highly publicized divorce to marry a beauty queen.

The four years of litigation with Cheng and Lo arose out of Trump's acquisition of the railroad yards later known as Riverside South, a 77-acre tract abutting the Hudson River and extending from West 59th to West 72nd Streets. In the mid-1970s, Trump, using the same formula that had worked with the Commodore Hotel, acquired an option to purchase the property from the Penn Central bankruptcy trustees. Lacking the requisite approvals from community groups and the city as to how the land should be developed, he let the option lapse in 1979, only to acquire it again in 1985 from another developer with $115 million in borrowed money. Trump's $4.5 billion development plan for the site included a skyscraper that would serve as broadcasting headquarters for NBC and would be the world's tallest building. Trump named the project "Television City," but we can only surmise that the building would be called "Trump Television City" if the plans matured. It would be the city's largest development since Rockefeller Center.

To accomplish his plans, Trump sought a $700 million property tax abatement from the City of New York. Unfortunately for Trump, his friend Abe Beame was no longer in office. The administration of Mayor Ed Koch denied the request.

A public feud broke out between the two flamboyant New Yorkers. Trump wrote a letter to Koch accusing the mayor of playing Russian roulette "with perhaps the most important corporation in New York." Koch wrote back accusing Trump of trying to "influence the process through intimidation." Trump said that the Koch administration was a "cesspool of corruption and incompetence." Koch said that Trump was "squealing like a stuck pig." Trump responded by holding a press conference calling on Koch to resign or be impeached. "Ed Koch would do everybody a huge favor if he would get out of office and they started all over again," he wrote, adding, "it's bedlam in the city." Koch subsequently announced that he would zone the railroad yards for a project about half the size of Television City. He then gave tax breaks to NBC to remain in Rockefeller Center. The situation smacked of the Kabuki.

In 1989, with Koch out of office, developer William Zeckendorf Jr. offered Trump $550 million for the property, but Trump turned him down—a strange decision, when the yards had cost him only $115 million in borrowed money. Then, the unexpected happened. In the 1990s, the New York City property market tanked. It is basic in real estate development that the art of the deal is holding on during a downturn. The developer must have enough capital to weather the storm until the opportune moment to cash in. Trump was being eaten up by $23.5 million in annual debt service, taxes, and other carrying costs. His bankers wanted him out of there. A cash-strapped Trump needed a white knight.

Here's where Cheng and Lo rode in to rescue Trump from the brink of bankruptcy. In 1994, he sold them the land comprising Riverside South. The terms of sale were that the Chinese would assume Trump's debts in return for promising him a 30 percent stake in any profits on the property, as well as fees for managing the site. The new investors constructed a series of high-end condominiums, using Trump's name on some of the buildings. The project proved to be highly profitable as the New York real estate market awakened from its doldrums. The problem for Trump was that the partnership agreement contained no requirement that profits be immediately distributed.

In 2005 the Cheng group announced a deal to sell the property for $1.76 billion to a consortium led by Extell Development Company and the Carlyle Group, a private equity firm. Trump claimed he could make a better deal. He told Cheng he had received unsolicited offers of up to $3 billion, and he took his Chinese partners to court in an uphill tilting-at-windmills legal battle.

Trump had Cheng and Lo in litigation for four years, until 2009, when Justice Richard Lowe of the New York State Supreme Court ruled against him and dismissed all of his claims. The judge found that Trump's $3 billion offers were not offers at all but simply indications of interest.

Trump was entitled to the agreed-upon 30 percent of the profits, which the Cheng group reinvested instead in two buildings: 1290 Avenue of the Americas in Manhattan and the Bank of America building in San Francisco. Trump attempted to throttle the deal with an injunction, but the court denied his application. Trump's payday will have to wait until the managing partner decides to make a distribution or the partnership is liquidated in 2044. Meanwhile, his interest in the two buildings is said to be worth $640 million, a far cry from the $1 billion that Zeckendorf's 1989 offer of $550 million would be worth in today's dollars. Trump had been sitting on a pot of gold, but he missed his shot to become the "wealthiest real estate developer in New York," as he and Roy Cohn falsely claimed he was to *Forbes* in 1981 and as he would later claim on *The Apprentice*.

Trump lost a golden opportunity, but he hailed the defeat as a victory. After the litigation, Cheng and Lo broke off with Trump entirely. They don't speak to him. Lo sold his partnership interest to Cheng, and Cheng sold out to Vornado.

But this was not the end. Trump would not let go of Riverside South. In October 2008, Trump sued the Carlyle Group and the other purchasers of the property from the Chinese, alleging that Extell and Carlyle had paid a $17.5 million bribe to his Chinese partners so they would sell the site for $1 billion less than it was worth. The suit was crazy. As Extell CEO Gary Barnett told *New York* magazine, "What, you think [the Chinese are] giving up a billion dollars in order to cheat Donald out of $17 million? The whole thing is a joke." The court dismissed the case.

In the Manhattan of the 1980s, it was not customary for a developer to name a building after himself. The only paradigm would have been Rockefeller Center, and even Trump, with his gigantic ego, would not have compared himself to Rockefeller. He did, however, seek to erect a flagship monument to himself, called "Trump Tower," which he would build in midtown Manhattan next to Tiffany's on Fifth Avenue between 56th and 57th Streets. Accomplishing this would involve cutting corners. And cutting corners would inevitably involve litigation.

Trump Tower is a mixed-use skyscraper that serves as the headquarters for Trump's business, known as the Trump Organization. It is also his New York residence, where he occupies a triplex apartment on the three top floors with a sweeping view of Central Park.

Construction of Trump Tower began in 1979. The architect was Der Scutt of Poor, Swanke, Hayden & Connell. Trump developed the property with a generous loan from AXA Equitable Life Insurance Company on the site of the old Bonwit Teller department store. The garish gold building is 58 stories in height. The plan was to have 6 floors occupied by the atrium space, 13 floors of office space, and 39 condominium floors. Trump of course exaggerated the size of the building. It had to be more "huge" than it really was. Trump labeled the top story as "68" because, he claimed, the five-story-tall public atrium occupies the height of ten ordinary stories. Journalists, however, concluded that Trump's calculations did not account for the fact that the ceiling heights were much greater than in comparable buildings, and the tower did not have any floors numbered 6–13. Thus, the 39 condominium floors start at floor 30 and ascend to 68 when they should begin at 20 and ascend to 58. The residential space was sold to wealthy tenants, including Arabs, foreign dignitaries, and Russian oligarchs.

Trump's fixer-lawyer Michael Cohen—later to plead guilty to an array of crimes involving payoffs to women in violation of campaign finance laws, bank fraud, and tax evasion—never lived in Trump Tower but had an office there. Cohen made a cool $3.3 million on a condo in Trump World Tower, near the United Nations.

Cohen was one of Trump's dwarves, his Nibelung, and he had a somewhat unsavory background. His ties to Russian oligarchs completed a galaxy of thuggery. He had worked for a lawyer convicted of bribing insurance adjusters. One of his former partners in the taxi business had a considerable rap sheet: assault in New York, a minor crime in New Jersey, and an arrest for battery in Miami. He organized businesses for several doctors, one of whom was charged with insurance fraud, another indicted for racketeering. Yet another doctor, Morton Levine, who happened to be his uncle, regularly rendered professional services to the Lucchese crime family. Levine ran the El Caribe social club in Brooklyn, which was said to be the headquarters of Russian organized crime in the United States in the 1970s and 1980s. Cohen owned a stake in El Caribe, which he divested in 2016 when Trump was elected president.

"Michael Cohen has a great insight into the real-estate market," Trump told a reporter in 2007. "He has invested in my buildings because he likes to make money—and he does." Trump added, "In short, he's a very smart person." Cohen also made a fortune with some suspicious non-Trump cash investments. According to a *New York Times* profile, "in 2014, he sold four buildings in Manhattan for $32 million, entirely in cash. That was nearly three times what he paid for them no more than three years earlier." Cohen's seller was a shell LLC; so was his buyer.

The construction of Trump Tower was riddled with controversy from the beginning. Community groups opposed the construction of a high-rise tower. As president, Trump said he opposed the destruction of Confederate statues that glorify slavery on the ground that they were "historic," but in 1980 he reneged on a promise to the Metropolitan Museum of Art to save a pair of iconic Art Deco bas-relief sculptures as well as the metallic grillwork appearing on the façade of the Bonwit Teller building. The museum wanted to include the objects in its twentieth-century sculpture collection. Although Trump personally gave the order to destroy the sculptures, he responded to the public outcry by blaming the undocumented Polish workers (discussed further below) whom he had hired to accomplish the demolition.

In the course of construction, Trump was involved in at least four lawsuits and investigations. He sued a contractor he decided he didn't want to pay for "total incompetence." He sued New York State over a 10 percent capital gains tax on real estate sales over $1 million, and took the case to the US Supreme Court. He lost. He sued New York City for a $50 million tax benefit, which Mayor Koch denied him. The suit bounced up and down in the courts for three years. Eventually, Trump won—perhaps because Roy Cohn stepped out of the picture and seasoned litigator Milton Gould assumed responsibility for the briefs in the New York Court of Appeals. Gould was a legal powerhouse in New York, a founding partner of the redoubtable firm of Shea & Gould. As will be seen, he tried the "Polish Brigade" case for Trump arising out of the illegal demolition work done at Trump Tower.

For the demolition work to take down the old Bonwit Teller building, Trump hired subcontractor William Kaszycki, an inexperienced vendor specializing in window and jobsite cleaning, for $775,000. Kaszycki had never before performed a demolition job where he was required to take down an entire building.

Kaszycki hired as many as 200 undocumented Polish immigrants to work side by side with 15 members of the House Wreckers Union, Local 95. Trump paid into the union welfare funds for the union workers on the job but not for the "Polish Brigade," which represented the majority of the workers. There was some urgency about the demolition, as there were tax savings to be derived once the land was vacant. The "Brigade" worked for far less than scale wages—as little as $4 an hour, with no benefits, when scale was at least five times that amount. Trump had them working 12 hours a day or more, and often seven days a week. Many were equipped with sledgehammers and wheelbarrows rather than power tools, as though they were working on a chain gang. Numerous workers were not even given hard hats. Those who worked with acetylene torches were not provided with masks.

In 1983, the workers sued Trump, Kaszycki, and others in federal court for unpaid union pension and medical obligations. Trump denied any knowledge that illegal workers were doing work at the site. To some of the lawyers preparing him for trial, he seemed distracted and inattentive, repeatedly making comments about the physical appearance of a female federal judge he fancied.

On deposition he tried to distance himself from the demolition, testifying that "the only thing I did was sign checks when they were sent to me." He swore that, *I really still don't know there were illegal aliens.*"

His testimony was false. He did know. According to attorney John Szabo, who represented the workers, a lawyer representing Trump called him and threatened to call the Immigration and Naturalization Service to have the men deported after Szabo got the Labor Department to open a wage and hours case in behalf of the workers.

The proof at the trial also showed otherwise. The job foreman testified that "he [Trump] liked the way the men were working on 57th Street. He said: 'Those guys are good, hard workers.'" When the Polish workers threatened a stoppage, Trump retained a labor "consultant," mobster Daniel Sullivan, who had bragged to Trump in 1981 about his ties to New York's underworld and his contacts at the FBI, for whom he was a sometime informant. Sullivan looked at the demolition problem and recommended that Trump fire the workers; the hiring of illegal workers jeopardized other Trump business interests. Sullivan pointed out that the New Jersey Department of Gaming Enforcement would take a dim view of a builder hiring undocumented immigrant workers, and that Trump risked losing his Atlantic City casino license. Sullivan testified that Trump knew he had hired illegal workers and that he had advised him in the strongest terms, "I think you are nuts."

In 1991, federal judge Charles E. Stewart, in what should have been a devastating blow to Trump's name and reputation, ruled that Trump had "knowingly participated" in the breach of duty to the workers. Stewart held that "there is strong evidence of tacit agreement by the parties ... [including the Trump defendants] to employ the Polish workers and to deprive them of the benefits ordinarily accorded to non-union workers on a union job, including contributions to the funds based on their wages."

Stewart found Trump's denials *"unworthy of belief"* and fixed damages of $325,415.84 in respect of unpaid contributions, interest, attorneys' fees, and court costs.

Trump's original lawyers in the case, Shea & Gould, who had tried the case so unsuccessfully, had to sue for their fees. The Gould firm's successor, premier lawyer Michael Armstrong, had won an important procedural round for Trump in the case. There now had to be a new trial, and a trial required an additional fee. Citing his own experience of being stiffed by Trump on fees in other matters, Armstrong sought a $500,000 advance retainer for his services going forward. When Trump refused to pay, Armstrong withdrew from the case.

In 1998, after 15 years of litigation, three rounds of discovery, a 16-day trial, and two appeals, Trump settled the case. The settlement was a complete capitulation. By agreement of the parties, the records of the deal were sealed and remained so until November 2017, almost twenty years after the settlement, when a federal court, over Trump's objection, ordered them opened to public view. After lawyering the plaintiffs to the ground, Trump paid a total of $1.375 million, with $500,000 going to a union benefits fund, and the rest for attorneys' fees. Normally, a settling defendant settles for less. This "settlement" was for 100 percent of the damages fixed by the court. Trump saved nothing by litigating. He had lost the case.

Using borrowed money, his father's wealth, and a trail of lawsuits, Trump eventually developed a real estate empire on Manhattan Island, with 15 buildings at the center of his enterprise. Startlingly, nine of the properties received huge tax breaks from the city totaling $885 million, including his flagship Trump Tower on Fifth Avenue, Trump World Tower at 845 UN Plaza, the AXA Building at 1290 Avenue of the Americas, 40 Wall Street, and the Grand Hyatt. There were also Trump Plaza, One Central Park West (site of the Trump International Hotel at Columbus

Circle), Trump Parc East, and Trump Place on the West Side. Trump surely must have called in a few chits in the municipal favor bank.

In 1988, he bought the iconic Plaza Hotel for $407.5 million in borrowed money, only to lose it to the banks when he couldn't handle the debt service out of the Plaza's operations.

Trump also proceeded to engage in a flurry of economic activity beyond New York. He bought a hotel in Washington in the shadow of the White House and built a 92-story waterfront skyscraper in Chicago on Wabash Avenue in 2008, featuring a hotel, condos, and retail spaces. He sought to construct a hotel in Moscow, built a skyscraper in Manila, and bought a skyscraper in Miami and another in California.

Eventually, in the 1990s, his business strategy evolved from borrowing to build and purchase assets to licensing his name to others who owned the venture. He franchised the Trump brand to a host of properties and products, including chocolates, home furnishings, fragrances, vodka, and steaks. Many of his ventures were unsuccessful, but he was out there, and the Trump name became a well-known and valuable marketing brand. He made speeches and wrote books. In addition, he owned, operated, or franchised seven Trump golf courses in the United States and three in Scotland and Ireland, with two others planned for Indonesia. He bought a winery in Virginia.

Many of his ventures tanked. In 1989, he bought the Trump Shuttle, an airline service between New York, Boston, and Washington, with $400 million in borrowed money, only to see it experience $85 million in operating losses in the year following its acquisition. The Trump Shuttle collapsed within two years owing to rising fuel prices and a declining market. The Shuttle simply ran out of cash and defaulted on its bank debt. In 1992, US Airways took over the Shuttle's debt, relieved Trump of his personal guaranty of $135 million made to Citibank in connection with the venture, and took over the franchise absent the Trump name.

He bought the Plaza Hotel for $400 million; it was repossessed by the bank. He bought a 282-foot superyacht from the Sultan of Brunei for $29 million; it was also repossessed by the bank. He developed, as will be seen, five Atlantic City casinos for $34 billion; he then filed for bankruptcy, and went out of business as he stiffed suppliers, contractors, and employees. His other ventures—Trump Mortgage, Trump Vodka, and Trump Steaks—all went out of business.

In 2004, Trump, licking his wounds, moved on to become the host of *The Apprentice*, an NBC reality TV show, broadcast from Trump Tower. He claimed he was paid an average of $15 million per year for the fourteen seasons he was on the program. Some have disputed this claim, and there is no way of verifying it since he has not released his tax returns. Along with others, he also owned and operated the Miss Universe beauty pageant, a fitting business for a Master of the Universe.

Trump had morphed from a real estate owner and manager to a big-time brander of the Trump name. He had used political influence to get an edge in his dealings with the City of New York. His political power, derived from campaign finance and access to the media, had won him significant tax abatements. He had used litigation to protect his brand, extract money from his partners, and attract publicity, which would enhance the Trump name for his purpose. He discovered Twitter as a tool to put down his critics and also to place his name before the public. He had enjoyed some business success, and much business failure. Through guile, instinct, and abuse of raw power, he had ascended the heights and patented a formula for future success. But the ethically questionable techniques he developed along the way would catapult him to the nation's highest office.

3

ATLANTIC CITY TAKES TRUMP

HOW TRUMP BANKRUPTED
HIS CASINO EMPIRE AND
EMERGED WITH MILLIONS

A lady never leaves her escort
It isn't fair, it isn't nice
A lady doesn't wander all over the room
And blow on some other guy's dice.
— Frank Loesser, "Luck Be a Lady"

Atlantic City, long an economically depressed area, legalized casino gambling in 1979. Instrumental in accomplishing the casino referendum was lawyer "Paddy" McGahn, an old-fashioned New Jersey political powerbroker whose older brother Joseph happened to be in the state senate the year the measure passed. In those days, the McGahns were Democrats. As an aside, Paddy McGahn's nephew Don McGahn, a Republican, served as Trump's White House counsel from the beginning of his administration until October 2018, when he resigned after spending some time talking to Robert Mueller. With Attorney General Jeff Sessions on the sidelines by reason of his recusal and Mueller tightening the noose, it was to Don McGahn that Trump erupted in anger in March 2017: "Where's my Roy Cohn?" History is indeed pro-logue.

For Trump, the advent of casino gambling in Atlantic City appeared to be a Mecca of opportunity. He obtained a casino license in 1982 and opened Harrah's at Trump Plaza two years later. Many wondered why a successful New York real estate operator would go into the casino busi-ness when he had no experience in it. Its waters were shark infested. Trump knew he would have to contend with well-funded competitors such as billionaires Steve Wynn, Sheldon Adelson, and Merv Griffin, as well as the parasitic mobsters of organized crime.

It was not uncommon for high-profile individuals to move from one venture to another. Merv Griffin had started his career in 1944 as a radio show singer. He had been a nightclub entertainer, a grade-B film actor, and a game and talk show host. In 1988 he went into the casino business, where he eventually lost a bundle in bankruptcy. Trump evidently be-lieved that if Merv Griffin could morph from game show host and creator of the popular TV game shows *Jeopardy!* and *Wheel of Fortune* to casino operator, then he could too. The business plan was all in his head.

Trump's ego led him to throw caution to the wind. He dreamed of building a casino empire under the banner of the Trump name. He craved the limelight, and the casino business, with its annexed hotels bringing with it popular entertainment, busty showgirls, sporting events, celebrities, media coverage, flash, and glitz, was perfect for him. His ex-perience in New York led him to believe he had a Midas touch, so why not roll the dice?

Trump came fast out of the gate in Atlantic City, but he faded in the stretch. There he embarked upon a greenmail scheme. (A greenmailer is a pejorative for someone who acquires large quantities of stock in a cor-poration in order to sell the holding back to the company at a premium. Trump's early Atlantic City activities fit the definition of greenmailer neatly, and he imagined that Atlantic City's streets were paved with gold.)

In November 1986, Trump began a four-month legal battle to gain control of Bally Manufacturing Corporation, which owned and operated a rival casino in Atlantic City. His objective was not to gain control—he couldn't afford the price—but instead to make a fast buck. In September, he had bought a 4.9 percent stake in the Holiday Corporation, an umbrella company, which owned the Holiday Inn chain, as well as casinos in Atlantic City and Nevada. Holiday's stock price spiked on rumors that he was going to make a run on the company. In November, he sold his Holiday shares at a $35 million profit. He then used the proceeds of the Holiday sale to make a run on Bally, which also owned two large Las Vegas casinos. He acquired a 9.9 percent interest in the company.

In December, Bally adopted a shareholder rights plan, or "poison pill." To avoid being the target of a hostile takeover by a larger firm, a corporate board might adopt this defensive strategy, which would allow existing Bally shareholders the right to purchase additional shares at a discount, effectively diluting Trump's ownership interest. The discount would not be available to Trump. Bally sued to declare its plan valid and sought to enjoin Trump from buying more Bally stock.

Trump counterclaimed for damages, alleging that the "poison pill" was illegal, and sought an injunction. Trump was ever vigilant to protect his name and reputation. It was a matter of importance to him to deny in papers filed in court that he was either a "greenmailer or corporate raider."

Two days later, Bally announced an agreement to buy the Golden Nugget casino in Atlantic City. This created an obstacle for Trump in the takeover fight, as New Jersey law provided for a maximum ownership of three casino licenses, and Trump already had two: the Trump Castle and the Trump Plaza. Bally would have owned two, the Park Place and the Golden Nugget. If Trump acquired Bally, he would have had to instantly unload one of the four casino properties. Trump moved in federal court to enjoin Bally from acquiring the Golden Nugget. The next day, the parties agreed to a settlement ending the litigation. Under the terms of the deal, Bally would not acquire the Golden Nugget, Trump would not buy any more Bally stock, Trump would sell 2.6 million Bally shares to Bally for $62.4 million, or $24 a share, and he would receive an additional $6.2 million for litigation and other expenses. Trump had paid an average of $17 per share of Bally stock. Trump would also retain 457,000 Bally shares, which Bally would buy in a year at $33 per share unless Trump decided to sell earlier on the open market. Bally shares at the time of the deal traded for roughly $20 on the New York Stock exchange. Four months after beginning his run on Bally, Trump walked away from the deal with at least $25.5 million.

A further wrinkle on the Bally litigation arose in April 1988. Trump became the target of a government suit seeking a civil penalty for his attempts to take over Holiday and Bally. The antitrust division of the Department of Justice alleged that Trump's 1986 stock purchases in the two companies "violated the notification procedures required by the Hart-Scott-Rodino Act." The law required buyers "to notify the government before purchasing more than $15 million worth of voting stock in a company and wait 30 days before completing the transaction." It was no trifling matter. As a result of the violations, Trump paid a $750,000 civil penalty. Even with the fine, Trump came out on top.

Seeking to live out his dream in Atlantic City, he entered the field with mobster partners, shaky financing, and a casino application that materially understated his litigation history. In the 1990s, Trump owned and operated three of Atlantic City's 12 casinos, making him the dominant player at the time. The casino ventures, however, were riddled with litigation, and Trump drowned himself in debt. In the end, he was willing to stake his reputation and his fortune on a dream that couldn't come true. He emerged a big loser.

The jewel in Trump's crown was the Taj Mahal, which he opened in April 1990. Featuring 135,000 square feet of casino floor, housing 160 gaming tables, including blackjack, baccarat, craps, and roulette, the Taj, according to Trump, was the "eighth wonder of the world."

The Taj was formerly known as the Resorts International. In 1978, Resorts had opened in Atlantic City as the nation's first legal casino outside Las Vegas. Resorts owner James M. Crosby had a vision of building the largest and most lavish casino in Atlantic City. Crosby had started life as an investment banker and had taken over the Mary Carter Paint Company in 1958. He diversified the company into real estate and then hotels and casinos in the Bahamas. He then changed the name of his enterprise to Resorts International. He once said that he found gambling to be boring because "the edge favors the house." He had made a fortune in the gambling business.

Crosby opened Resorts International in 1968 as the first casino hotel in Atlantic City. When Crosby unexpectedly died in 1986, Trump made his move. He bought a 72 percent control block of Resorts from the Crosby family for $79 million. Resorts was deeply in debt. With delusions of grandeur, Trump renamed the casino the Trump Taj Mahal. It was estimated that it would take another $805 million to renovate the property. Later, after a downturn in the stock market, Trump bought the remaining Resorts shares and took the company private. He was now the sole owner of the Taj, which became even more "huge" than anything Crosby had visualized: a 42-story hotel tower containing approximately 1,250 guest rooms; an adjacent low-rise building for meeting, ballroom, and convention space; and a 120,000-square-foot casino with restaurants, bars, and shops. Trump proposed to employ 6,500 people.

The Taj, like all the Trump casinos, was glitzy. Trump's Atlantic City signature was glitz. "I have glitzy casinos because people expect it," he said. "Glitz works in Atlantic City. . . . And in my residential buildings I sometimes use flash, which is a level below glitz." Part of the glitz at the Taj was the sign at the exit door of the breakfast buffet: "Have a Magical Day." Trump stole this banal expression from Walt Disney World, but Disney never complained about it. The sign was still there in 2013.

As Mark Singer observed in the *New Yorker*,

In Atlantic City, the idea was to slather on as much ornamentation as possible, the goal being (a) to titillate with the fantasy that a Trump-like life was a lifelike life and (b) to distract from the fact that he'd lured you inside to pick your pocket.

The day before Trump's Resorts deal was to be consummated, Trump hit a bump in the road. Merv Griffin made a competing bid, saying he would pay $245 million for Resorts if Trump would agree to the take-over and cancel the lucrative service agreement he had with the company. Trump sued Griffin for $250 million for fraud and interference with his contract negotiations with Resorts.

It was a bitter legal battle. The litigation ended in a settlement in which Griffin and Trump agreed that Griffin would pay $36 a share for 5.7 million shares of the publicly held Resorts Class A shares, and the same price for another 5.3 percent of the Class B shares not owned by Trump. Total package: $207 million. Griffin would also acquire all of Trump's Class B shares and sell the Taj Mahal stock back to Trump for an undisclosed price. Under the terms of settlement, Trump agreed to sell Griffin his controlling interest in Resorts, with Trump retaining ownership of Resorts' Taj Mahal Casino, then under construction.

The case was settled on terms that most analysts saw as a Mexican standoff. Some said Trump had backed down. Griffin got the existing Resorts assets. Trump got money from Griffin to cancel the services contract. He also got the Taj. Naturally, Trump claimed total victory. "I'm very happy with the deal and look forward to having Merv as a neighbor in Atlantic City for many years to come."

Trump took over the construction of the Taj from Resorts. Starting in 1990, he began to stiff his contractors while spending $1 million per week on personal expenses. One of the contractors, Atlantic City native Marty Rosenberg, had the contract for glass, mirrors, and doors. He was owed over $1 million, which Trump failed to pay. Rosenberg was not alone. Trump also failed to pay over 100 other contractors on the project. In all, he owed over $60 million for past-due goods delivered and services rendered. Rosenberg organized a committee of contractors, which negotiated with Trump and his lawyers. After several rounds of talks, they settled for pennies on the dollar. Some went bankrupt; others closed their doors.

The opening of the Trump Taj Mahal coincided with reports in the tabloid press of Trump's divorce from his wife Ivana, the mother of his three children. Trump had come out of the closet with his longtime squeeze, the nubile actress Marla Maples, whom he said he intended to marry. Trump said that the lurid publicity about his personal life was good for his bottom line, citing 1,500 media requests to cover the opening.

The Taj opened in a flood of publicity on April 2, 1990. Less than two weeks before, Marvin B. Roffman, a casino analyst at the Philadelphia investment banking firm Janney Montgomery Scott, told the *Wall Street Journal* that the casino would benefit from its opening publicity but was in for a tough time. "Once the cold winds blow from October to February, it won't make it. The market just isn't there," Roffman predicted. It would require $1.3 million a day just to pay debt service, a level of revenue that no casino could ever achieve.

Trump corresponded with Janney, threatening "a major lawsuit" unless it forced Roffman to recant and apologize or else fired him. Three days after publication of the *Journal* article on March 20, Janney fired Roffman for making unauthorized statements to news organizations. Roffman had initially signed a letter of apology to Trump to save his job but was fired after he signed a second letter repudiating the apology. This was not enough satisfaction for Trump. He needed to be vengeful. Smearing Roffman in the press, he asserted that Roffman was untalented and ungrateful, claiming without foundation that he had saved Roffman's job six months earlier. He also falsely accused Roffman of blackmail and fraud, telling *Vanity Fair* that the analyst had called "begging" him to become his stockbroker "with the implication that if I'd buy stock, he'd give me positive comments."

Roffman was a prophet in his own time. The Taj failed; it was underfunded. It filed for Chapter 11 in July 1991, the year after it opened. The other two Trump casinos filed for bankruptcy protection seven months later. As part of the restructuring, Trump gave the lenders a 50 percent stake in the business in return for lower interest rates.

Roffman eventually would have his day. He won a $750,000 arbitration award against Janney over his firing. He also sued Trump for intentional interference with contractual relations, and Trump settled the case by paying him an undisclosed amount. Roffman became known as "the man who beat Donald Trump."

The *Wall Street Journal* was skeptical of Trump's ability to make it in Atlantic City. When the newspaper was about to publish a piece on Trump's debt problems, Trump threatened to sue if they revealed the extent of his cash squeeze. The *Journal* published the piece anyway. There was no lawsuit.

In August 1990, New Jersey regulators focused on the "sheer volume of debt" on Trump's holdings: $3.4 billion, including $1.3 billion on the casinos and $832.5 million in personally guaranteed loans, which he later shifted to the casinos. The regulators warned of "the possibility of a complete financial collapse of the Trump Organization."

Litigation remained a storm cloud over Trump's Atlantic City venture. Steve Wynn, owner of MGM International in Las Vegas, sought to build a casino in Atlantic City's Marina District, the area of one of Trump's casinos. A vicious dispute erupted between the two titans, who vilified each other and hired away each other's executives. Trump called Wynn a "scumbag" and someone with "a lot of psychological problems . . . a very disturbed person."

In the midst of the controversy, the State of New Jersey announced it planned to build a 2.5-mile tunnel at a cost of $330 million, which would connect the Atlantic City Expressway and the Marina District. Although the Trump Marina Hotel Casino would benefit from the tunnel, Trump sued New Jersey in 1997 to throttle the project. He alleged that the tunnel would represent a "private driveway" to Wynn's resort, the Mirage. The *Newark Star-Ledger* reported Trump's exaggerated claims that if the state used casino funds to support the tunnel, it would be "taking money from widows and orphans," the elderly, and people with disabilities, an apt description of many of Trump's casino customers.

Trump spent over $500,000 on the antitunnel project, of which about $294,000 was for antitunnel litigation. Trump said, "Steve Wynn came in with a poorly conceived plan and he expects the public to pay for it." Trump paid $111,000 to the Neighborhood Preservation Legal Defense

Fund, established to mount a suit against New Jersey questioning the use of the eminent domain power to facilitate private enterprise.

Wynn countered with a federal antitrust suit against Trump, and Trump said he would counterclaim. He never did. Wynn and Trump settled all litigation between them on undisclosed terms.

Then, in 1999, the Mirage sued Trump for conspiracy to injure Wynn's casino by stealing proprietary information, notably lists of wealthy Korean gamblers. This time Trump counterclaimed, alleging that Trump's private investigator was a "double agent for Wynn who secretly taped conversations" with Trump. The three-year battle raged on and ended in 2000 with a confidential settlement agreement ending all litigation. At the end of the day, New Jersey built the tunnel, and Wynn got his casino. Wynn and Trump eventually buried the hatchet, and Wynn would wind up supporting Trump for president. He served as finance chair of the Republican National Committee until January 2018, when he resigned in the face of serious allegations of sexual misconduct.

Trump was never known for consistency. While he opposed eminent domain in his suit against New Jersey over the tunnel, he had earlier unhesitatingly championed eminent domain to take the Atlantic City home of Vera Coking, a widow whose house stood near the famed Atlantic City boardwalk. Coking's property was on the site of a proposed casino and hotel property owned by *Penthouse* magazine founder Bob Guccione. He tried unsuccessfully to buy her out. He began construction around the house but couldn't get a gaming license. He soon ran out of money. And after she turned down his offer of $1 million, he abandoned the project. Trump acquired the unfinished property from Guccione in 1995 and proceeded with demolition.

Coking sued Trump in 1996 for damage to her property. Evidently, the demolition company Trump hired had damaged her house in tearing down the remnants of Guccione's unfinished structure. Coking stood in the way of Trump's expansion plan. In a separate suit, Coking sought to prevent New Jersey from condemning her property.

Coking didn't want a New Jersey lawyer who might knuckle under to Trump. So through a lawyer's referral line she found a tough Philadelphia criminal defense lawyer named Glenn Zeitz. Zeitz, by reputation, played hardball. He was giving Trump a hard time in the case and was actually cleaning Trump's clock. He took Trump's deposition and asked if he could give a "ballpark figure" on how many times he had been deposed in his life. Trump testified he could not give even a ballpark figure, and instead answered, "No, but many."

Trump offered Zeitz $1 million for the properties, but Zeitz turned him down. Coking did not want to sell at all, but certainly not at that price; she had an appraisal of $2 million or more. It was a great example of a lawyer fighting hard for his client's rights.

Then Zeitz received a strange call from Donald Trump in which Trump offered to hire Zeitz to represent his interests in the fight against New Jersey and Steve Wynn to block the Atlantic City tunnel. Such a representation would have involved arguing the dead opposite of the position Zeitz was taking in the Coking case. Trump wanted to block eminent domain in the Wynn case but encourage it in the Coking case. Zeitz would have wound up arguing against himself.

Of course, had he accepted Trump's offer, Zeitz would have been enmeshed in an irreconcilable conflict of interest, and probably would have had to resign his representation of Coking at the very least. Trump was in effect saying to Zeitz, "If we can't beat you, we'll buy you." Zeitz of course refused. Coking prevailed in the demolition case and settled with Trump for $90,000 to compensate her for damage to her property. She prevailed in the condemnation case and was able to keep her home for an additional 18 years. Trump denied the conversation with Zeitz, who had shared the details with his associates at the time. No lawyer would ever make up a conversation like that, and no lawyer would ever forget it.

Controversy arose over construction financing, and here Trump flat-out lied to the regulators about his intentions. He had to convince them of the financial viability of the project, so he falsely claimed that banks were willing to lend him money at prime rates. "I mean, the banks call me all the time, can we loan you money; can we this; can we that." In sworn testimony, he went on to assure the regulators how important he thought it was to avoid junk bond financing—that is, the issuance of high-interest, high-risk paper. "I'm telling you that whether it's General Motors or Procter & Gamble, or any other company, if they have to go out and get junk bonds to do their borrowings, they are not a strong company," he said. "They make them junk, so it's like a self-fulfilling prophecy, almost." The regulators were healthily skeptical. But Trump reassured them. "It's easier to finance if Donald Trump owns it," he explained. "With me they know that there is a certainty that they would get their interest." It was not as certain as he said.

The principal financing for the Taj came not from bank loans at all but from a $675 million 14 percent first-mortgage junk bond offering underwritten by Merrill Lynch. The bond terms required Trump to pay $95 million a year to service the debt. Trump was only obligated to put in $75 million of his own funds, and the rest was to come from invest-ment income, lines of credit, and miscellaneous loans. The proceeds of the offering were also supposed to finance the purchase of the Taj from Resorts International.

Merrill Lynch was not the first underwriter to which Trump shopped the bond offering. Merrill's predecessor was the firm of Bear Stearns, which later went out of business. Trump and his younger brother Robert, who was a board member of the Taj, met with the Bear Stearns bankers to discuss the memorandum of terms. The bankers noted that there was another Trump corporation involved that owned a parking garage and transportation center that was to be connected to the casino-hotel by an elevated pedestrian bridge. When Bear Stearns bankers, doing their due diligence, commented that Trump could freely move the pro-ceeds of the offering to the garage, where Trump could use the money for personal purposes, thereby bankrupting the Taj, Robert jumped in and said, "He's got a point."

Then the Bear Stearns lead banker recalled a moment reminiscent of the scene in *The Godfather* in which Sonny Corleone speaks out of turn at a business meeting with a rival mobster and is rebuked by his father, Don Vito: "Never tell anyone outside the family what you are thinking again!" In real life, according to a Bear Stearns banker, Trump stood up and pointed his finger near Robert's face, angrily saying, "*You talk when I tell you to talk!*" The astonished Bear Stearns people were so horrified that they walked out of the meeting shaking their heads. Eventually Bear withdrew from the deal, and Trump turned to Merrill.

In the end, Trump could not meet his obligations to pay debt service on the bonds. Bondholders brought class actions under securities laws against Trump in various federal courts alleging prospectus fraud in connection with the junk bond public offering. The courts dismissed the actions on motion. The Trump lawyers, who had drafted the prospectus, made sure that it "bespoke caution," warning the reader of a parade of possible bad outcomes, which the investors failed to heed.

The principal Trump representation challenged by the bondholders was that "the Partnership believes that funds generated from the operation of the Taj Mahal will be sufficient to cover all debt service (interest and principal)." The bondholders claimed that Trump possessed neither a genuine nor a reasonable belief in its truth. Trump, however, pointed to an abundance of disclaimers, warnings, and cautionary language in the prospectus warning of the intense competition in the Atlantic City casino industry, the absence of an operating history for the Taj, the unprecedented size of the proposed casino, and the potential inability to pay interest on the bonds in the event of default and liquidation. The federal court concluded, "No reasonable investor could believe anything but that the Taj Mahal bonds represented a rather risky, speculative investment which might yield a high rate of return, but which alternatively might result in no return or even a loss."

Trump borrowed at high interest after assuring casino regulators he would not. He saddled the casinos with so much debt that they had no chance to succeed. He had to default on a $43 million interest payment on Trump's Castle, which he had opened in 1985 as one of his three Atlantic City casino properties. Later, when Trump's Castle needed to make an $18.4 million interest payment, Fred Trump came riding to the rescue, buying $3.35 million in chips. Then Fred wired in another $150,000, for a total of $3.5 million. This was later deemed an illegal loan. The casino control commission fined Trump $65,000 over the highly questionable transaction.

In financial distress, Trump sought to refinance. He went back to the public well. The equity refinancing was a sweetheart deal for Trump. Trump's public shareholders sued in 1996 for stock fraud because the stock price had slid in a single year from $37.50 a share to $12, and the proceeds of the public offering had been used to buy Trump's Castle at an inflated price, which included $175 million in cash to Trump's private holding company. Trump settled the suit. The bondholders sold Trump's Castle, later called Trump Marina, out of bankruptcy to Landry's in 2011 at the bargain-basement price of $38 million. Renamed the Golden Nugget, Landry's modernized the property and launched an online gambling platform offering 500 unique games. It leads the market in New Jersey online sites.

And when in 1990 Trump needed an emergency line of credit of $65 million to salvage his foundering Atlantic City enterprise, he once again dipped into his father's pocket, using his inheritance and a high-rise Fred Trump home for the elderly in East Orange, New Jersey, to collateralize the bank loan. Ninety percent of the construction cost of the East Orange property had been financed by a low-cost $7.8 million construction loan made by the government.

Trump had paid off his banks in part with the proceeds of public offerings of stock. The IPO at $14 a share in June 1995 raised $140 million for the casino operation. A secondary offering about a year later at $31 a share raised $380 million. Meanwhile, the casinos continued to rack up large annual operating losses, while Trump himself received $1 million in salary for a part-time job. In 1996, records show, he inexplicably received a $5 million bonus when by any standard he had badly mismanaged the assets.

The Taj continued to hemorrhage cash. In 2002, the SEC slapped

Trump with a cease and desist order for publishing misleading financial statements the year before.

In 2014, billionaire activist investor Carl Icahn—a friend and eventual political supporter of Trump's—committed $20 million in additional financing, eventually buying the casino out of bankruptcy for $350 million. In October 2016, Icahn shuttered the casino. Nearly 3,000 workers lost their jobs. He sold the property to the Seminole tribe of Florida in 2017. The Seminoles, through their Hard Rock International brand, paid Icahn four cents on the dollar.

Trump's casino businesses went six times to the Camden, New Jersey, bankruptcy court, where he told his creditors that they had to accept pennies on the dollar or be wiped out entirely. While he bragged that he left Atlantic City at the right time, he left because his investors threw him out, no longer wanting him in a management role. The last time, in 2004, the bondholders took a $500 million loss.

Trump got away with murder in Atlantic City because of his ability to convince his backers that the Trump name had real value on which they would one day cash in. However, his publicly owned casino company never logged a profitable year.

Analyst Marvin Roffman said, "There's something not right when every single one of your projects doesn't work out." David Hanlon, a veteran casino executive in charge of Merv Griffin's Atlantic City operations, said that the investors "were so in love with him that they came back a second, third, and fourth time. They let him strip out assets. It was awful to watch. It was astonishing. I have to give Trump credit for using his celebrity time and time again." And each time Trump claimed the benefit of the bankruptcy law.

Trump approached his Atlantic City venture as though he were a casino high roller, not a sophisticated businessman. The casino ventures were a complete disaster. They were too heavily leveraged. "Leverage is an amazing phenomenon," he said in 1997. "I love leverage. Plus I've never been a huge sleeper." Financial wise man Warren Buffett took a different view. Warning Notre Dame students in 1991 about the perils of overborrowing, Buffett said, "I've seen more people fail because of liquor and leverage—leverage being borrowed money. Donald Trump failed because of leverage. He simply got infatuated with how much money he could borrow, and he did not give enough thought to how much money he could pay back." Trump's Taj Mahal filed for Chapter 11 bankruptcy later that year.

The casinos staggered under a debt load of $3.4 billion, of which Trump had personally guaranteed some $833 million. Trump exited Atlantic City leaving bondholders with billions in unpaid debt. He also left behind a spate of unpaid local suppliers and contractors who had helped in the construction, many of whom were forced to go out of business. Although he pointed to the downturn of Atlantic City's economy as the cause of his failure there, the *New York Times* reported that "he was failing in Atlantic City long before Atlantic City itself was failing." Revenues at other Atlantic City casinos rose 18 percent in the period 1997–2002, while Trump's revenues declined 1 percent.

Trump continued to live the lie of alternative facts, telling *Playboy* in 2004 that "the casinos have done very well from a business standpoint. People agree that they're well run, they look good and customers love them." Who were these people? The bondholders? The stockholders? The suppliers? Certainly not his creditors. By 2004, all of Trump's Atlantic City casinos had filed for bankruptcy. Trump dismissed his financial failure as "really a technical thing."

In 1998, Donaldson, Lufkin & Jenrette, Trump's longtime investment bankers, pressed Trump for $13.5 million he owed them. The bankers pointed to the fact that the stock price of Trump Hotels and Casino Resorts had tanked. DLJ had a pressure point. Under its loan agreement with Trump, it was entitled to strip him of control of the company in the event that he defaulted on his obligation. Trump put his hand in the cookie jar in a self-dealing transaction. His publicly owned casino company loaned him the money to pay down the personal loan he had with DLJ. When a stockholder sued the board for breach of trust in authorizing the loan, Trump paid back the company, and the stockholder dropped the suit.

Later, DLJ sued him for $26 million in fees on the eve of his 2004 bankruptcy petition. DLJ alleged in court papers that the casinos would be back in bankruptcy court in four years because Trump's revenue predictions were unrealistic and the company was overloaded with debt. "The Trump name does not connote high-quality amenities and first-class service in the casino industry," the DLJ complaint alleged. "Rather . . . [the Trump name is associated with] the failure to pay one's debts, a company that has lost money every year, and properties lagging behind their competitors."

Trump settled the suit. Not a good idea to go against your bankers. They know where the bodies are buried.

———————

When it came to partnering over casinos, Trump's word was anything but his bond. In the early 1990s, Indiana passed a measure allowing gambling in the state for the first time. Some area businessmen, William Mays and Louis Buddy Yosha, sought to partner with Trump Indiana, Incorporated, to open one of the first casinos allowed under the new law. The businessmen hoped to lend their support to Trump and cash in on his well-known name. Eventually, they would claim that Trump failed them by not making them minority partners in his Indiana gambling enterprise and by refusing to create a charitable foundation—with the two of them on its board of directors—to benefit various worthy causes in Indiana. Initially the pair was awarded $1.4 million in damages, but the Seventh Circuit reversed the award, noting, "Mays and Yosha were essentially seeking millions for almost nothing because for a time they thought they were going to get exactly that, millions for almost nothing." But this complicated deal, the court held, "was never reduced to the kind of solid contract that could be comfortably enforced in a court of law." Trump reneged on an oral agreement by pointing out that it was never reduced to writing. As Samuel Goldwyn, legendary Mr. Malaprop and Hollywood mogul, once quipped, "A verbal contract isn't worth the paper it's written on."

Trump made a great show out of protecting his casino ventures in Atlantic City. In 1995, he unsuccessfully sued New York State when a video game called *Quick Draw*, based on the casino game keno, was introduced in New York restaurants and bars. Trump realized that *Quick Draw* competed with keno, a game featured in his Atlantic City casinos. Feigning concern for the public interest, he stated that he was really just worried that the game's presence in New York would bring "tremendous amounts of crime" and "destroy businesses in New York." Trump argued that gambling addiction would render New York residents unable to pay their rent, a strange argument coming from a casino owner. New York State continues to offer *Quick Draw* as part of its lottery program. Perhaps any casino operator would have sued New York for infringing on his keno license. That would make sense. But it was Trump's instinct for publicity that led him to plead all the nonsense about crime and impoverishment of New Yorkers who wanted to wager. In Trump's head there was rarely a fact without a fantasy.

In 1993, he sued the federal government over Indian gaming, claiming that the government had discriminated against him by allowing Indian casinos. He argued that the Indian Gaming Regulatory Act violated the Tenth Amendment to the Constitution in giving an advantage to "a very limited class of citizens," namely Native Americans, at the expense of other citizens. The suit was preposterous. He dropped it the next year.

From his casino days, Trump was on the warpath against Native Americans. His animus came from the fact that the tribes enjoyed state exemptions from the gambling laws and that they could legally operate casinos on their reservations, drawing away possible customers

from Atlantic City. Increased competition from Indian casinos infuri-
ated Trump. He even questioned whether Indiana casino operators were
legitimate Native Americans.

In 1993, Trump appeared on the Don Imus radio show and was
asked what he thought about an Indian tribe's plans to open a casino
in New Jersey. "A lot of these reservations are being, in some people's
opinion, at least to a certain extent, run by organized crime," he responded. "There's no protection. There's no anything. And it's become
a joke." Imus mentioned the Mashantucket Pequot Tribal Nation,
which had opened the successful Foxwoods Resorts Casino in Mashantucket, Connecticut, in 1991. "I think if you've ever been up there,"
said Trump, "you would truly say that these are not Indians. One of
them was telling me his name is Chief Running Water Sitting Bull,
and I said, 'That's a long name.' He said, 'Well, just call me Ricky
Sanders.'" The tribe termed Trump's comments disrespectful and
racist.

Trump loves to work both sides of the street. He did not tell Imus
that he was in negotiations to partner with the Agua Caliente Band of
Cahuilla Indians, which was seeking to develop a casino in Palm Springs,
California. The Agua Caliente chose another developer. In 1995 they
opened their first casino in a tent next to the Spa Resort Hotel in Palm
Springs. Today the tribe has two hotels, two casinos, a golf resort, and
the premier concert theater in Southern California.

The National Indian Gaming Association filed a complaint against
Trump with the Federal Communications Commission over the Imus
remarks, demanding an investigation into "obscene, indecent and profane racial slurs against Native Americans and African Americans." The
FCC turned them down, stating that their authority to regulate hate
speech was limited by constitutional boundaries "as deplorable or offensive as certain remarks may be."

Later, in 1993, Trump would testify before Congress that organized
crime "is rampant—I don't mean a little bit—is rampant on Indian reservations." Then he delivered the offensive lines he would repeat on

television again and again: "They don't look like Indians to me," he testified. "They don't look like Indians to Indians."

Trump's remarks about organized crime had no foundation. A top official in the Department of Justice testified, "To date there has not been widespread or successful effort by organized crime to infiltrate Indian gaming operations." Trump had simply made it up.

Congressman George Miller (D) of California said that Trump's was the most "irresponsible" testimony he had heard in 40 years in the House. Roger Stone, who had accompanied Trump to Capitol Hill, tried to sugarcoat Trump's outrageous remarks. "Because first of all, he's bold," said Stone. "He's brazen. He fears nothing. And it's how he really felt."

In 2000, with New York considering the possibility of more Native American casinos in the Catskills, Trump anonymously paid over $1 million for an ad campaign, designed by Stone, accusing the Mohawk tribe of having criminal records and ties to the Mob. The ads showed lines of cocaine and syringes with the caption: "ARE THESE THE NEIGHBORS WE WANT?" Another ad warned of the social ills that casino gambling would bring to the Catskills: "increased crime, broken families, bankruptcies, and in the case of the Mohawks violence." New York State laws required Trump and Stone to disclose the ad spend as a lobbying effort, which they had not done. State regulators, accordingly, fined Trump $250,000, its largest civil fine ever.

Again, Trump was working both sides of the street. At the same time he was lobbying against the Mohawks, touting the dangers of casino gambling in the Catskills, he was trying to help the Eastern Paucatuck tribe obtain federal approval for a Connecticut casino. The tribe had promised to pay Trump a percentage of the future casino's revenues as a management fee. The Eastern Paucatucks won approval, but the Bureau of Indian Affairs imposed a nasty condition. The agency found that the Eastern Paucatucks were part of another Connecticut tribe, the Eastern Pequots, a Native American tribe numbering fewer than 1,000 from southeastern Connecticut. The Eastern Pequots had their own plans for a casino that did not include Trump. A member of the tribal council, a dark-skinned Native American named Joseph Perry, had a long memory. Explaining his vote against Trump, he recalled for the *Washington Post* Trump's testimony before Congress. It was "a factor in my mind," he said. "What do Native Americans look like? . . . Some are dark-skinned like myself. We don't look all alike."

In 2003, Trump sued the Eastern Pequots. He claimed he had spent close to $10 million helping to promote the tribe's brand in exchange for the right to negotiate the tribe's casino agreements. Trump settled the suit in a deal that reportedly involved no payments to Trump. Nevertheless, he told Congress, "Nobody is more for the Indians than Donald Trump." How he could have so testified with a straight face boggles the mind.

Trump claimed he took out millions from Atlantic City even though he left bondholders and creditors holding the bag. This was because of his successful "greenmail" run on Bally, plus the fact that he put up little of his own money, transferred personal debt to the casinos, and collected millions in salaries and licensing fees in connection with the Trump brand name. Four of Trump's five casinos are now closed. Only the Castle is still in business, under different management and a different name.

In sum, Trump exited Atlantic City in total defeat. Nevertheless, he declared victory, claiming that "the Taj Mahal was a very successful job for me." He crowed, "Atlantic City was a very good cash cow for me for a long time." If truth be told, the blow to his business reputation was devastating. He had betrayed the trust of his investors, stiffed his contractors, and laid off his employees. He was drowning in litigation. As will be seen, he had dirtied his hands with the Mob. His claim of a business success in Atlantic City is belied by the facts. He left Atlantic City unable to get banks to lend him money. His luck appeared to have run out, but he would live to fight another day.

LITIGATION FOR LUNCH

HOW TRUMP USED THE
LAWSUIT TO PRESERVE
AND PROTECT HIS BRAND

*[For Trump] to file a lawsuit is nothing.
It's just like having lunch.*

—Vincent Lo, former Trump partner,
after Trump sued him for $1 billion and lost

As his business expanded, Trump became a serial litigant. At the time of his election, the reported 3,500 lawsuits in which he had been involved would average roughly three per business day spanning the 48 years from 1968 when he graduated from college until 2016 when he was elected president.

"I love to have enemies," Trump said in 1989. "I fight my enemies. I like beating them to the ground." Trump, in his various books, provided extensive advice on his combative approach to doing business. In *How to Get Rich*, Trump advises readers to use the courts to "be strategically dramatic." In *Think Big and Kick Ass in Business and Life*, he boasts of how he "love[s] to crush the other side and take the benefits." As president, in his meetings in London with Theresa May, he advised her to sue the European Union as the way to handle her negotiations over Brexit.

Trump's favorite lawsuit has been the tort of defamation. He has often used the threat of such a lawsuit to silence his critics. It is anomalous to say the least that Trump, whose ethics have been questioned since he began in business, is so obsessed with a cause of action intended to redress injury to reputation. In instance after instance during his 2016 campaign, Trump threatened to sue people for defamation, whether they were women, media, or political opponents. He rarely sued in fact, but a draft complaint for defamation seemed to reside in his top drawer. As will be seen, he almost invariably lost in those instances when he did sue anyone for allegedly defaming him.

As noted at the outset, Trump seemed obsessed with his name and reputation. His name was his brand, and it had to be out there. He featured it, promoted it, and ultimately licensed it for commercial purposes. The name "Trump" had to be protected even if it was not really threatened. The name Trump had to be promoted and bruited about even if the news was scandalous or salacious, as long as they spelled his name right. When he divorced his first wife, Ivana, just as the Trump Taj Mahal was opening in Atlantic City, the splashy publicity served his commercial purpose. As Jeb Bush noted, he played the media "like a fine Stradivarius violin." He knew he was good copy. The media was responsible for the building of Donald Trump, and later responsible for the massive effort to take him down.

If he appeared to have a thin skin by overreacting to fair criticism and bringing or threatening frivolous lawsuits, if he sought to avoid harmful scandal with nondisclosure agreements and threats of litigation, if he fought silly cases with a remarkable ferocity and fervor, it was all part of a deep-seated and feral need, perhaps stemming from childhood, to protect his brand and keep the lid on any conceivable public shaming or embarrassment.

The remedy for false statements demeaning the reputation of an individual is the tort of defamation. To make out a case of defamation, a person must show that the defendant communicated to a third person a false statement that tended to harm the person's reputation in the eyes of the community or cause others to shun him. Libel is a written defamation (but also includes television), as opposed to slander, an oral defamation. The distinction is made because a written defamation, being more enduring, is inherently more injurious. Libel is considered an injury to someone's personality.

Truth is always a complete defense in a libel action. To prevail, a plaintiff must show that he or she is not "libel proof," which means that they have a reputation unblemished enough in the first place to be damaged by the alleged defamation. A plaintiff in a libel action can win big even if there is no financial injury and there are only nominal damages. Punitive damages may be awarded where there is malevolence, spite, or ill will.

A defamation suit was the road Trump took in January 2018 with former campaign chairman and presidential adviser Steve Bannon, who reportedly made unflattering comments about him and members of Trump's family to author Michael Wolff for his book *Fire and Fury*. Wolff, among other things, had quoted Bannon as saying that it was "treasonous" and "unpatriotic" for Donald Trump Jr. to have met at Trump Tower with a Russian lawyer who professed to have political dirt on Hillary Clinton. Wolff also had Bannon's take on Trump's daughter Ivanka, who was not at the meeting, although her husband, Jared Kushner, was. Ivanka, Bannon said, is as "dumb as a brick." Trump's lawyers immediately dispatched a letter to Wolff's publishers demanding that they cease and desist publication, threatening "imminent legal action" based in part on "defamation by libel and slander." The publishers refused and Wolff's book became a number-one national bestseller. Trump never sued, perhaps because it is a principle embedded in our law that "equity will not enjoin a libel," which means that a court will not issue an order restraining publication of a book because it is alleged to be false and defamatory. The publication proceeds, and the publishers take their chances.

Moreover, governmental "prior restraints" on speech are not permissible. In America, we have not permitted censorship since the founding of the republic.

Fire and Fury immediately flew off the shelves, as though it had in another era been "banned in Boston." To threaten a lawsuit totally defeated Trump's purpose. Adding fuel to the fire, Trump retorted that Bannon "spent his time at the White House leaking false information to the media," and that since leaving the White House he had "lost his mind." Special Counsel Robert Mueller, probing Russian tampering in the 2016 election, didn't think so. Following publication of the book, he subpoenaed Bannon to testify before a federal grand jury. If Trump sues Bannon for libel, undoubtedly Bannon will counterclaim. Lawyers do not see much merit in either case.

Trump early in his career apparently brought libel actions against journalists, but the records cannot be found. Wayne Barrett, who for years covered both Cohn and Trump for the *Village Voice*, reported that Cohn in 1979 represented Trump in two defamation cases against journalists. Trump told Barrett that his legal fees came to $100,000 and said it was worth it because "I've broken one writer." Trump later told the *Washington Post* that he didn't recall saying that to Barrett, calling his work "total fiction." As Roy Cohn instructed his underworld clients, "It's no crime not to remember." (Barrett died on January 19, 2017, the day before Trump's inauguration.)

We do know that Trump's libel actions were somewhat quixotic. In 1985, Trump sued the *Chicago Tribune* and its architecture critic, Paul Gapp, for libel. Trump planned to build a 150-story tower on a landfill site at the southeast end of Manhattan, which would be taller than the Sears building in Chicago. Gapp didn't like the plan. He said that Trump's notion of the world's tallest tower would be "one of the silliest things anyone could inflict on New York or any other city." He went on to describe Trump Tower as "a skyscraper offering condos, office space, and a kitschy shopping atrium of blinding flamboyance." Trump admitted he had not chosen his architect and had no plan for the building. He lamented that the *Tribune* story "virtually torpedoed" his dreams by depicting his would-be tower as "an atrocious, ugly monstrosity."

The case came before Judge Edward Weinfeld in the Southern District of New York. Weinfeld was widely considered to be the greatest trial judge in the nation. He dismissed Trump's case because Gapp's published statements were matters of opinion absolutely immune under the First Amendment. The case is fascinating because Trump ignored the difference between statements of fact and expressions of opinion, a distinction he often blurs today when he speaks of "fake news." In the alternate reality of Donald Trump, opinions are facts to be disproved, and facts return the compliment because they are really opinions.

Weinfeld was also prescient in reminding Trump of the settled law that

> men in public life, whether they be judges, legislators, [or] executives . . . must accept as an incident of their service harsh criticism, oft times unfair and unjustified, at times false and defamatory—and this is particularly so when their activities or performance may be the subject of differing attitudes and stir deep controversy.

It is highly unusual for someone to threaten a libel suit before publication. But Trump was not a usual personality. In 2005, Trump threatened a libel suit against ABC. The network was doing a two-hour biopic about the Trump family. Trump told the *Washington Post* that he would certainly sue if the film were "inaccurate." But if it wasn't inaccurate, he said he would not sue them. The biopic wound up on the cutting room floor. It is not known whether it was Trump's threat that killed the project or whether there were other reasons. If the former, Trump's reputation for litigiousness, studiously burnished for many years, perhaps proved its value.

There was a certain kind of publicity that really seemed to get under his skin. No journalist could get away with challenging his exaggerated statements of net worth. Trump was burned, though not fatally, in 2006 when he unsuccessfully brought a libel suit for $5 billion against former

New York Times journalist Timothy O'Brien, author of a 2005 book titled *TrumpNation: The Art of Being The Donald*, which Trump acknowledged he hadn't even read.

O'Brien's book, a fairly balanced account of Trump's behavior, made a claim that stung Trump to the quick. The author revealed that Trump's net worth was between $150 million and $250 million rather than the $6 billion he told O'Brien he had amassed or the $2.5 billion reported on the *Forbes* 400 Richest Americans in 1996. In *TrumpNation*, O'Brien essentially repeated statements he had made in *New York Times* articles about Trump in September 2004 that focused on Trump's efforts to recapitalize his casinos. At that time he reported, in language very similar to that found in *TrumpNation*, that

> the largest portion of Mr. Trump's fortune, according to three people who had had direct knowledge of his holdings, apparently comes from his lucrative inheritance. These people estimated that Mr. Trump's wealth, presuming that it is not encumbered by heavy debt, may amount to about $200 million to $300 million. That is an enviably large sum of money by most people's standards but far short of the billionaires club.

O'Brien's comments triggered a defamation suit. Trump said the assertion was "egregiously false." He sued, he said, because he wanted to hurt O'Brien. He told the *Washington Post* that O'Brien was a "low-life sleazebag." Trump told his people, "Go sue him. It will cost him a lot of money."

In a defamation action, as we have seen, the truth is always a complete defense. Armed with internal documents obtained in discovery from Trump Organization files, O'Brien's attorneys—Mary Jo White, former U.S. attorney for the Southern District of New York and later SEC chair, and Andrew Ceresney—proceeded to quiz Trump on deposition about what was false about the book.

The two-day deposition was in December 2007. Ceresney laid a lawyer's trap from which Trump could not conceivably have escaped. He placed before Trump a handwritten note. The note, which Trump had sent to a journalist, stated Trump's objection to the journalist's characterization that he owned "a small minority stake" in a Manhattan property. On it, Trump had scrawled a rhetorical, misleading question: "Is 50 percent 'small'?"

Evidence in the case suggested that Trump owned a 30 percent interest. When confronted with the facts, Trump gave this amazing explanation for the discrepancy: "The 30 percent equates to much more than 30 percent." Why? Because he had not been required to put any money into the project so the 30 percent computed to "much more than 30 percent."

Ceresney sprang:

Q: Mr. Trump, do you own 30 percent or 50 percent of the limited partnership?

A: I own 30 percent.

Q: Are you saying that the real estate community would interpret your interest to be 50 percent, even though in [the] limited partnership agreements it's 30 percent.

A: . . . Smart people would say it's much more than 30 percent.

Ceresney continued:

Q: Have you ever lied in public statements about your properties?

A: I try to be truthful. I'm no different from a politician running for office. You always want to put the best foot forward.

This was the first of at least 30 times that Trump was on record exaggerating or misstating his assets, liabilities, sales, net worth, or other material facts about his business during a deposition. He egregiously misstated, among other things, that

- He had sold some California real estate for about $4 million. In fact, the sales price was $1.4 million.

- He had borrowed "zero" dollars from his father's estate. In fact, he had borrowed $9 million.

- He had 22,000 employees. In fact, the number was far less. He had included suppliers and subcontractors not on his payroll in this figure.

- The initiation fee for his Westchester gold club was $300,000. In fact, the figure was $200,000.

- He had been paid $1 million for a single speech in 2005. In fact, he was paid $400,000. Trump's astonishing testimony was as follows:

A: I get more than a million dollars, because they have tremendous promotion expenses, to my advantage. In other words, they promote, which has great value, through billboards, through newspapers, through radio, I think through television—yeah, through television. And they spend—again, I'd have to ask them, but I bet they spend at least a million or two million or maybe even more than that on promoting Donald Trump.

Q: But how much of the payments were in cash?

A: Approximately $400,000.

Q: So when you say publicly that you got paid more than a million dollars, you're including in the sum the promotional expenses that they pay?

A: Oh, absolutely, yes. That has a great value. It has a great value to me.

Q: Do you actually say that when you say you got paid more than a million dollars publicly?

A: I don't break it down.

Trump as a witness was like a cornered rat. A lawsuit in which he had accused a writer of defaming him by falsely questioning his net worth wound up completely destroying his credibility.

After the deposition, O'Brien had this to say about Trump: "A very clear and visible side effect of my lawyers' questioning . . . is that he [was unmasked as] a routine and habitual fabulist."

In 2009, Trump lost the case on summary judgment, and the appellate court affirmed. He later bragged to the *Washington Post* that he didn't mind losing after years of litigation: "I spent a couple of bucks on legal fees, and they spent a whole lot more. I did it to make [O'Brien's] life miserable, which I am happy about." Was it his purpose in bringing the suit to make O'Brien's life miserable even though he knew he would lose? It all seems quite weird.

Diminishing Trump's net worth has always been a sore point with him. In 2011, Trump trained his guns on MSNBC's Lawrence O'Donnell. O'Donnell had committed the unpardonable sin of implying that Trump's net worth was less than $1 billion. Trump erupted and sent a tweet protesting that he was in fact worth "substantially more than $7 billion." "Very low debt," he said. "Great assets."

In 2012, Sheena Monnin, a former Miss Pennsylvania and Miss USA contestant in the Miss Universe pageant, claimed that the entire contest was rigged and alleged that the top five finalists of the 2012 Miss USA contest were chosen prior to the show's live broadcast. Trump blasted Monnin as "a beautiful young woman who had sour grapes because she was not a top-15 finalist." He had the Miss Universe pageant bring a claim against her in arbitration, seeking, among other things, defamation damages. Needing to show that Monnin's statements damaged him, he claimed that British Petroleum pulled out of a $5 million sponsorship because of Monnin's charges that there was a fix—a claim that Monnin had no opportunity to refute. After Monnin failed to appear at the arbitration, the arbitrators awarded Trump $5 million for his claim against Monnin, which the court confirmed. After the decision, Monnin posted on Facebook, "When I stated my opinion that the Miss USA pageant was rigged, I was not aware of the clause in the Miss USA contract which says that the Miss Universe Organization, Donald Trump, and others have the legal right to choose the top five and the winner. This is irrespective of any publicized selection process." Trump's lawyer argued that Trump had never exercised this right and that the contest's judges had independently selected the finalists. Monnin's father later said that she did not pay one cent of the award. You would almost wonder what the flap was all about.

In 2015, Trump sued Univision for defamation and breach of contract, seeking damages of $2.5 billion after the Spanish-language network said it would not be airing Trump's Miss USA and Miss Universe beauty pageants because of his provocative public statements that some illegal immigrants from Mexico are "rapists." Trump claimed that an Instagram post created by Univision programming chief Alberto Ciurana was false and defamatory. The post depicted Trump side by side with a mass-murderer white supremacist. Univision rejected the complaint as "factually false and legally ridiculous." Trump dropped the defamation case. The rest of the case disappeared in a confidential settlement. You can be sure that Univision never paid anything remotely approaching $2.5 billion.

Despite his notorious record for insulting people, I can find only one case in which Trump was himself sued for libel, and there he prevailed. In 2016, political strategist and commentator Cheri Jacobus brought a libel suit against Trump. In mid-2015, Jacobus had interviewed with the Trump campaign for the salaried post of communications director. After two interviews, she decided not to go forward. On January 26, 2016, she appeared on CNN to discuss Trump's threat to boycott one of the Republican primary debates unless Fox removed Megyn Kelly as a moderator. Jacobus called Trump a "bad debater" and said he "comes off like a third grader faking his way through an oral report on current affairs." She claimed he was using the flap with Kelly as an excuse to avoid the debate.

On February 2, Jacobus again appeared on CNN, this time to discuss whether Trump's campaign was self-funded. She stated: "Look, Donald Trump also had a super PAC that he started out with, and he lied about it, and they had to quickly shut it down." She also said that the campaign had approached several Republican "fat cats," all of whom had refused to give Trump money.

Trump went ballistic. In the days following Jacobus's second CNN appearance, he tweeted "@CheriJacobus begged us for a job. We said no and she went hostile." After Jacobus's lawyer sent him a cease and desist letter, Trump launched another tweet, in his characteristically dumbed-down cadence: "Really dumb @CheriJacobus . . . Major loser, zero credibility!" He said she was "virtually incompetent" with a "failed career."

Justice Barbara Jaffe, sitting in Supreme Court, New York County, dismissed the case, citing Judge Weinfeld's 1985 dismissal of Trump's suit against the *Chicago Tribune* years earlier. Trump's knocks on Jacobus were the statement of an opinion, not statements of fact, which are capable of being proven true or false. She held that the "privilege protecting the expression of an opinion is rooted in the preference that ideas be fully aired." Justice Jaffe was affirmed on appeal.

Justice Jaffe noted that some of Trump's Twitter followers channeled his tweets by posting what she found to be "demeaning, sometimes sexually charged, comments and graphics, including insults [about Jacobus] aimed at her professional conduct, experience, qualifications, and her purported rejection by Trump." One such graphic was an image of Jacobus in a gas chamber, eerily reminiscent of Auschwitz, with Trump portrayed in a Nazi-style uniform about to push a button marked "Gas."

So when it comes to expressions of opinion he doesn't like, such as the architecture critic's views on his tower, Trump sues the media for defamation, claiming "fake news." But when someone sues *him* for demeaning them in their profession, he switches positions: "I was just expressing my opinion, Judge. So no defamation." Ralph Waldo Emerson said, "A foolish consistency is the hobgoblin of little minds." But, of course, he never met Donald Trump.

Trump sued to attract attention. I have earlier discussed the RICO case Trump brought against the Pritzkers. In the 1970s, he invoked RICO to sue the *law firm* that represented tenants opposing his efforts to evict them from their homes at a building he owned on Central Park South.

Trump wanted to demolish the building and build condos. The tenants hired a small law firm and resisted, complaining to the Department of Housing and Community Renewal, the relevant New York State regulatory agency. They also sued Trump in the New York State courts. Trump brought a separate action in the federal court seeking treble damages and attorneys' fees under RICO, claiming that the tenants' lawyers formed a "racketeering enterprise" and had conspired with the courts and agencies to commit acts of racketeering. The court dismissed Trump's allegations out of hand, and the Court of Appeals affirmed. When the defendants sought sanctions against Trump for bringing frivolous litigation, the district court judge ordered Trump to testify at a hearing. Trump promptly settled the matter, writing a low-six-figure check to the plaintiffs for their legal fees. The plaintiffs' lawyer framed a copy of Trump's check and hung it on the wall of his office. The building stands to this day.

Another example of suing to make a splash is the litigation he brought, long before he announced he was running for president, over the American flag waving on Mar-a-Lago's front lawn. An ordinary American flag on his property wouldn't do for Donald Trump. Whatever he did had to be huge. Patriotism was to be worn upon his sleeve. In 2006, the town of Palm Beach cited him for violating zoning codes by flying an oversized American flag atop an 80-foot flagpole. The town sought to fine him $250 a day for every day the flag continued to wave.

Trump claimed that "a smaller flag and pole on Mar-a-Lago's property would be lost given its massive size, look silly instead of make a statement, and most importantly would fail to appropriately express the magnitude of Donald J. Trump's and the Club's members' patriotism," He, in turn, sued the town for $24 million, claiming that the town's position violated his First Amendment free speech rights, and pledged to donate any recovery in the lawsuit to Iraq War veterans. "The flag is not going anywhere," he told the *New York Daily News* in November 2006 shortly before filing the lawsuit in January 2007, when town fines had reached $120,000. "And that's final." Not so final. Trump settled the case, agreeing to replace the flagpole with a shorter one.

The *Tampa Bay Times* said the town waived the fines when Trump dropped his $10 million lawsuit and donated $100,000 to Iraqi War veterans. The rub was that the settlement funds came not from Trump's personal accounts, but from the Trump Foundation. As will be seen in chapter 9, When she discovered that Trump had discharged a personal obligation with foundation money, New York attorney general Barbara Underwood suspected charity fraud and condemned the sleight of hand in a suit filed in June 2018 against Trump, the Trump Foundation, and the Trump family. In December 2018, the Trump parties settled the case.

The riddle is, why did Trump feel the need to chisel for a $100,000 tax deduction? Small potatoes in the scheme of things. We know Trump was not in want of tax deductions. He didn't pay taxes anyway.

Allegations of fraud dogged Trump's footsteps. As we have seen, stockholders, bondholders, and the SEC charged Trump with securities fraud in connection with his Atlantic City casino fiasco. But there were other frauds and rip-offs as well. I largely devote chapter 8 to the Trump University fraud, which merits its own discussion.

In 2013, Trump settled with more than 250 hopeful condo buyers over the failed Trump Ocean Resort to be located in Baja, Mexico, south of Tijuana. The plaintiffs, mostly based in Southern California, paid over $32.5 million in deposits to reserve units in the Trump development, a unit costing anywhere from $275,000 to $3 million. The individual deposits were for $50,000 and up. Trump had touted the project, a 525-unit oceanfront site featuring swimming pools, tennis courts, and sweeping views of the Pacific. The sales literature pictured a resort where purchasers "relax by the infinity-edge pool, margarita in hand, as the cabana boy brings fresh towels." Featured was a photograph of Trump smiling in a gold-leaf chair, under which he proclaimed that neither words nor pictures "can possibly describe what is about to take shape here, but it is certainly going to be the most spectacular place in all of Mexico."

What was "about to take shape" was nothing. The development was never built. Banks foreclosed on the property before construction even began. Trump tried to distance himself from the scam, taking the position that he was never the developer but merely lent his name to brand the marketing—the sort of claim he would make in the Trump University case. Nevertheless, the buyers sued, charging Trump with fraud and claiming they were gulled into believing he was one of the developers, which gave them a false sense of security. They had good reason to believe that Trump was one of the developers. "*We are developing a world-class resort* befitting of the Trump brand," Ivanka Trump said in a video on the Trump Baja website, in which she claimed she had reserved a unit in the first tower. Trump appeared in the same video, proclaiming, "*When I build,* I have investors that follow me all over." Erasing all doubt, an August 2007 newsletter to condo buyers, which Trump signed, listed him as one of the developers. The developers claimed they had spent $25 million of the victims' deposits of

$32.5 million and settled the lawsuit for $7.25 million; Trump contributed an undisclosed amount to the settlement. There was a similar lawsuit involving the condos at Trump SoHo in Manhattan, where buyers sued to get their money back, claiming they had been deceived by Trump's misrepresentations. Here, also, Trump claimed he was the brander, not the developer. (As Trump's partners in the deal had relationships with organized crime, I relate the Trump SoHo story in chapter 6, dealing with Trump and the Mob.)

In the 1980s, Trump was on an ego trip. He owned buildings and franchises, beauty contests and casinos, as well as interests in other businesses. He lusted, however, for the quintessential trophy—ownership of a National Football League (NFL) team with the possibility of winning a Super Bowl ring and a photo with the coach holding the Lombardi Trophy. There were only two problems for Trump: he lacked the financial substance to pass muster with the NFL, and the NFL would not permit owners to own gambling casinos. So Trump decided to try to sue his way in with litigation, his aim being to get an NFL team at a bargain-basement price.

In 1984 he bought the New Jersey Generals, one of 12 teams in the fledgling United States Football League (USFL). The purchase price was said to be $9 million. There was glitter to his purchase. The Generals had signed 1982 Heisman Trophy–winning running back Herschel Walker as the team sparkplug. The USFL was organized to attract owners who could not afford the multimillion-dollar price tag attached at the time to the venerable NFL franchises. The USFL's strategy was to play springtime and summer football rather than compete with the impregnable market position the NFL had established in the fall season over its 65-year history.

The USFL slowly sought to develop its brand through organic growth. Trump had a different strategy. If he sued the NFL under the antitrust laws, he might achieve a settlement through which the USFL and the NFL could merge, and he would become an NFL owner through the back door. He had a precedent. In 1966, after the American Football League (AFL) unsuccessfully brought an earlier antitrust suit against the NFL, the NFL agreed to merge with and absorb the AFL—creating its present structure. His strategy was devilishly clever; the only problem was it didn't work.

In October 1984, after his first season as owner of the Generals, Trump and Roy Cohn held a press conference at New York's fabled 21 Club, kicking off a suit by the USFL against the NFL seeking treble damages under the antitrust laws. The USFL lost nearly $200 million in the first three years of its existence. The NFL argued in court papers that this was the result of a flawed business plan. Trump said the USFL wanted to move from a spring schedule to a fall schedule beginning in 1986. But because, as he claimed, the NFL prevented the USFL from securing a network television contract for that season, it folded. So what to do? You sue. Trump said the NFL was "petrified of the suit," declaring, "We have an excellent lawsuit," and "we're going to win."

The USFL brought Trump's suit against the NFL, alleging that the NFL attempted to monopolize the television network market in violation of section 2 of the Sherman Antitrust Act. The Complaint sought threefold the amount of actual damages, which were not less than $440 million in the aggregate ($1.32 billion when trebled). In the joint pretrial order, the USFL increased its demand, as it was entitled to do, seeking "threefold the amount of actual damages," which were more than $567 million (in excess of $1.7 billion when trebled). In a statement reminiscent of his mentor Joe McCarthy, Cohn said the NFL had appointed a "secret committee" to block competition from the USFL. NFL commissioner Pete Rozelle denied the existence of such a committee, and there was no proof at trial that there ever was one.

On October 17, 1984, Cohn signed and filed the USFL complaint. When the case came to trial in the spring of 1986 in the Southern

District of New York before Judge Peter K. Leisure and a jury, Cohn was dying of AIDS. So Trump designated as his trial counsel Harvey Myerson, a "pit bull" of the Bar. Myerson was totally lacking, however, in antitrust experience. In his closing argument, he begged the jury balefully, "Please, God, find for us." If God bestowed a blessing, it wasn't on the USFL; the jury found that the NFL had violated section 2 of the Act, but only awarded the USFL a humiliating one dollar in damages trebled. The check for three dollars was never cashed—it must be preserved somewhere as a collector's item. So Trump won three dollars, but it was a Pyrrhic victory.

The jury rejected the USFL's primary argument that the NFL had denied the USFL access to the much-needed resource of network television. Trump didn't get his NFL team, the USFL was out of business, and Trump lost $22 million on his football kamikaze. If there was any lesson to be learned from the case, it was that litigation is not a get-rich-quick scheme to be substituted for methodical, painstaking investment in a business plan over the long term. It was a lesson totally lost on Donald Trump. "It was a nice experience," Trump recalled to filmmaker Michael Tollin in an interview for the 2009 ESPN documentary *Small Potatoes: Who Killed the USFL?* "It was fun. We had a great lawsuit." Trump's statement reflects an intriguing attitude more in tune with a Hollywood producer or talent manager. Plaintiffs in a lawsuit typically don't do it for the fun; they do it to redress a supposed wrong. There's nothing fun about it. Only someone who enjoyed "litigation for lunch" would make such an outrageous statement.

Like the AFL, the USFL lost the case, but for Trump there was no NFL franchise at the end of the litigation rainbow.

As an aside, Harvey Myerson was convicted in 1992 in federal court of fraudulently overbilling his clients. The sentencing judge found that Myerson had engaged in a "consistent pattern of fraudulent conduct" and sentenced him to a 70-month term of imprisonment. Myerson died shortly after his release from prison.

Trump was up to his ears in contentious confrontation with regulators. While many in business routinely find themselves at the receiving end of a regulatory inquiry, Trump seemed to have a propensity to skirt the law and ignore legal requirements. You might blame this on bad lawyering except that he had the advice of the best available. Trump got into so much trouble with regulators because, if his business practices were not illegal, he himself was antilegal, i.e., determined to circumvent laws that limited his business activity.

Trump was no stranger to the federal money-laundering statutes. ("Money laundering" is the generic term used to describe the process by which criminals disguise the origin and ownership of the fruits of criminal conduct by making such proceeds appear to have been derived from a legitimate source.)

In 1998, the Financial Crimes Enforcement Network (FinCEN) of the U.S. Treasury assessed a $477,700 civil fine against the Trump Taj Mahal for currency transaction reporting violations. Casinos handling large sums of cash, possibly representing laundered funds, are required by law to keep meticulous records and watch out for "red flags" evidencing suspicious transactions. The Taj Mahal was a continuing violator of the anti–money laundering statutes. Federal examiners found violations at the Taj during the three-year period from 2010 to 2012. The Taj failed to police such suspicious transactions as patrons exchanging large sums of cash for gambling chips or paying large cash sums for other goods or services. Trump failed to get the message.

Years later, Trump was still in trouble with FinCEN over his Atlantic City casinos. In 2015, the Taj admitted that it had failed to support and implement an effective anti–money laundering program. "Trump Taj Mahal received many warnings about its deficiencies," said Jennifer Calvery, the then FinCEN director. "Like all casinos in the country, Trump Taj Mahal had a duty to protect our financial system from being exploited by criminals, terrorists, and other bad actors." The violations, the details of which are unknown, must have been egregious. FinCEN said that the conduct of the Taj Mahal "left . . . our financial system unacceptably exposed."

In March 2015, three months before Trump announced his candidacy for president, FinCEN imposed a $10 million civil fine on the Trump Taj Mahal for "willful and repeated violations of the Bank Secrecy Act," notably a failure to report millions of dollars in suspicious transactions, properly file currency transaction reports, and keep proper records. The agency noted the long history of Taj violations of the money-laundering statutes, going back to the 1990s, when it opened. The fine was the largest in history for violation of the Bank Secrecy Act. It involved a staggering 106 violations. The Taj had filed for bankruptcy in 2014, and the bankruptcy court approved the settlement the following year. No one was ever charged with criminal conduct.

———————

Trump's golf course enterprises virtually drowned in litigation. In 1992, he made a bundle settling a case he couldn't win in court. He sued Palm Beach County for failing to figure out a way to muffle the loud noises coming from Palm Beach International Airport. The glide path of planes landing and taking off from the airport was directly over Mar-a-Lago. He actually sued the county four times. None of the first three suits carried the day, but his last suit, for $5 million, struck gold. The county had 215 acres of undeveloped land just south of the airport, near the county jail. They didn't know what to do with it, so Trump took it on a long-term lease, offering an annual rental of $438,000. The county had already racked up $1.1 million in legal fees fighting Trump's noise abatement suits, so they accepted the bargain-basement offer in return for Trump's partially dropping the litigation. Remaining unsettled was Trump's $100 million lawsuit against the county over continuing airport noise, which he dropped after he became president. No reason to keep it going; the Secret Service moved the airport glide path away from Mar-a-Lago. Being president has its perks.

Trump had something in mind for the 215 acres. In 1999, he developed the property for a new golf course, Trump International Golf Club, as an adjunct to his Mar-a-Lago Club. The Trump Organization website Trump Golf advertises that Trump International is only a five-minute drive from Mar-a-Lago. In fact, it takes 15 minutes on a good day without traffic. I have done it.

Initially, the initiation fee was $250,000, and in the financial crisis of 2008, memberships went begging. So Trump lowered the fee to $100,000, and often less. It was effectively a Ponzi scheme. The initial members subsidized the new members, and were understandably angered when they encountered newcomers in the locker room who paid less than they did to get in. After Trump became president, the price of a golf club membership soared to $450,000.

In 2011, Trump absurdly sued the government of Scotland over the Trump International Golf Links in Aberdeen. Trump said that Scotland, the country of his mother's birth, had assured him that a planned offshore wind farm would never be constructed, so he built the golf course and made plans for a neighboring hotel. When the wind farm was built, Trump resorted to the British courts for relief. He ultimately lost the case after appealing fruitlessly to the Supreme Court of the United Kingdom. The British court ordered Trump to pay Scotland's court costs and legal fees in an undisclosed amount.

Trump played fast and loose with taxing authorities whenever he could. In 2008, he opened the Trump National Golf Club Los Angeles—a jewel of a course picturesquely overlooking the Pacific from the Palos Verdes Peninsula. Trump's valuations for the 100 acres of pristine Pacific coastline wavered from $250 million to $50 million, depending on whether he sought to impress someone or wanted more favorable tax treatment.

He received significant tax breaks by reason of a "conservation easement," which he deeded to the Rancho Palos Verdes municipality, forgoing his purported right to construct luxury houses on a portion of the land. He valued the easement at $26 million. Giving away the rights cost Trump nothing since the coastland was unstable and unsuitable for development. Moreover, the valuation of $26 million for the undeveloped part of the property was questionable, as he had paid $27 million for the whole ball of wax. Trump then tried to develop the land anyway, but the city of Rancho Palos Verdes put its foot down. So, shortly after he opened the golf course, Trump sued Rancho Palos Verdes for $100 million, five times its annual budget, telling the *Los Angeles Times*, "I've been looking forward for a long time to do this. The town does everything possible to stymie everything I do." He settled the case four years later with the terms sealed by court order. The land remains undeveloped. It's used as a driving range.

Another case involved the Trump National Golf Club in Jupiter, Florida. Trump had bought the golf course from Ritz-Carlton in 2012. Members wishing to resign from the club accused Trump of sharp practice in failing to refund their initiation fees while at the same time barring them from the club. They sued Trump in federal court for their refunds, which amounted to some $6 million. Club members had paid initiation fees ranging from $40,000 to $200,000 with an agreement that if they resigned, the initiation fee was refundable. There was a lag time on the refund, however, while departing members waited for new members to take their spots.

Before Trump bought the golf course, a departing member was entitled to pay dues and continue to use the club. Trump, however, took the position that resigning members' dues would accrue and be netted against the initiation fee and that while they were waiting they would be barred from using club facilities even though their dues were being charged against the initiation deposit. The court held against Trump and for the members. It reasoned that the club's barring members from club facilities who were paying dues out of their initiation fees "revoked or canceled their memberships" and entitled them to full refunds within 30 days. Trump settled the case with the dissident members for $5.4 million.

And wait until you hear this one, really a Trump golf classic. Trump offered to pay $1 million to anyone hitting a hole in one during a 2010 golf tournament at the Trump National Golf Club in Briarcliff Manor, New York. Martin Greenberg, CEO of Sterling Commodities, made his hole in one, teeing off from the thirteenth hole. Greenberg felt lucky, until Trump refused to pay. Angered over the refusal, he sued. But the fine print in Trump's written rules of engagement was that the shot had to travel at least 150 yards. It would have been impossible to win the prize. The hole on the thirteenth green, like all the par threes on the course, happened to be just short of 150 yards from the farthest tee.

Trump settled the case with Greenberg for $158,000, and funded the settlement not out of his own pocket but *from the Donald J. Trump Foundation.*

This was not the only time Trump illegally manipulated his own foundation. A $10,000 portrait of Donald Trump paid for by the Trump Foundation greeted visitors to the Trump National Doral hotel and golf facility in Miami. The portrait remained in place until after he was president. The *Washington Post* reported that Trump illegally poured out at least $258,000 from his charitable foundation to make political contributions or settle lawsuits against his businesses, which were part of the Trump Organization. The hole-in-one lawsuit contributed to the total.

Trump was ever vigilant in protecting the commercial value of his eponymous brand—even when it did not involve a competing business or even a business he dreamed of conducting. There is a story about Otto Kahn, the legendary German Jewish financier and one of the founding partners of the investment-banking powerhouse Kuhn, Loeb & Co.

Kahn was walking in a certain neighborhood and passed a small tailor shop. In the window was a sign that read: "Joe Kahn, Tailor (Otto Kahn's Cousin)." Kahn stormed into the shop and demanded that the tailor, who was not his cousin, remove the sign. Two weeks later, Kahn passed the tailor shop and viewed the signage. It read: "Joe Kahn, Tailor (Formerly Otto Kahn's Cousin)."

In 1989, like Otto Kahn, Trump became irritated at Claudia Rabin-Manning and her father, who owned a small travel agency operating out of a tiny storefront in Baldwin, Long Island, called "Trump Travel & Tours." The agency had existed since 1985. Trump, who had never been in the travel business, sued for trademark infringement. Trump Travel never claimed to be related to Donald Trump. It chose the name "Trump" from the card game bridge, perhaps because people enjoyed playing bridge on tour boats or to indicate high quality, something like "Ace Hardware." "The existence of Donald J. Trump . . . played no role in the adoption of the trademark 'Trump Travel and Tours,'" stated Rabin-Manning's lawyer in court papers. "I was just annoyed," the defendant told a reporter. "To this day I have no idea why he would go after a small businesswoman on Long Island. He cost me a lot of money to defend myself"—almost $10,000, she estimated. "I wondered, 'Am I going to lose my business?' I was so upset. All my customers knew it by that name."

Trump alleged that "the name and mark TRUMP has been associated with the most celebrated of recent New York City construction projects. The TRUMP name is synonymous with the very best, and projects goodwill of enormous value. Trump has become a celebrity. A day rarely passes that a magazine or newspaper does not carry an article about him." The case, of course, was settled. Rabin-Manning kept the name, but had to include the legend on all her signage, "Not Affiliated with Donald Trump or the Trump Organization." Said Rabin-Manning, "It's a bit ironic that nowadays, the disclaimers help Trump Travel more than they help Trump." Later, Trump tried to sue again, but the case was thrown out because it had already been settled. Trump got a new lawyer who tried to sue in 2005 under the settlement agreement, complaining that the font on the disclaimer was "virtually microscopic," a position that resonated with the government's argument in the race discrimination case discussed in chapter 1. Rabin-Manning increased the size of the font and heard nothing further.

Then there is the story of two brothers, Jules and Edmond Trump, who sought to buy a chain of drug stores using the name "the Trump Group." Jules and Eddie were sons of a Jewish South African tailor named Willie Trump. They had no financial or familial ties to Donald. Over the course of 30 years in business, the Trump Group had built a multibillion-dollar empire based on luxury real estate development in South Florida. Jules and Eddie had branched out into a men's clothing chain called Bond's, the Pay 'n Save chain of discount drug stores, bowling alleys, a substantial auto supply business, and the Manhattan branch of Elite Modeling, which gave us Claudia Schiffer and Cindy Crawford. They were the real package.

What sparked the suit was an innocent letter sent to the Trump Organization on September 11, 1984, from the trade paper *Drug Store News*. "Welcome to the chain drug store industry," the letter began, going on to invite "Mr. Trump" to become a subscriber. The problem was that they had the wrong Trump. Donald Trump had no interest in the chain drug store industry. Jules and Eddie Trump, on the other hand, had recently bid $360 million to buy Pay 'n Save and were obviously the intended recipients of the solicitation from *Drug Store News*.

The letter somehow enraged the sensibilities of Donald Trump. Circa 1984, he was flying high as a real estate developer, casino operator, and owner of a professional football team. So presumably he saw chain drug stores as beneath him. The next day, Roy Cohn demanded that the Trump Group change its name by the following day or they would face "consequences."

When the brothers did not agree to Trump's terms, he sued them in New York State court, alleging they were "immigrants," parasites on his good name. Trump's complaint alleged that he and his family "have used the Trump name for 40 to 50 years in the New York area. More recently, the Trump Organization has come to stand for respectability and success across the United States"—surely a debatable proposition. The complaint went on: "The defendants are South Africans whose recent entrance in the New York area utilizing the name 'the Trump Group' can only be viewed as a poorly veiled attempt at trading on the goodwill, reputation and financial credibility of the plaintiff."

The brothers, who were far wealthier than Trump, didn't accept Trump's assessments of the facts, contending that their name was "widely publicized and acclaimed." Indeed, they cited a *Forbes* article about their business empire that was published in 1976, well before the public became aware of Donald Trump. They also claimed that in 1982, before registering "the Trump Group" name, they had conducted a search to learn whether other businesses were using the name "Trump." They discovered a few companies selling toilet paper, nut candy, and molluscicides—nothing else.

The case gathered dust in the New York State courts for nearly five years. Eventually, in 1989, a judge rang down the curtain on the absurd controversy, ending Donald Trump's quest to prevent the brothers from using their own name. "The court will concede the name 'Trump' is well-recognized in the New York City real estate development community, but the court does not think this is the same as being 'unique' or 'distinctive,'" he wrote.

As for Jules and Eddie Trump, they have gone on for decades running their businesses under the Trump Group flagship, successfully developing valuable properties around the world.

————————

The key to Trump's survival in business may reside in the offshore files of Deutsche Bank. Trump's relationship with the bank arose in the late 1990s, when no other major bank would touch Trump following his business disasters with the Trump Shuttle and the Atlantic City casinos. The Shuttle defaulted on its bank loans and ran out of cash in 1990, one year after Trump bought the carrier out of the Eastern Airlines bankruptcy.

Trump and Deutsche Bank forged a strange history. In 2004 in connection with a loan application, the bank concluded that Trump was worth $788 million. Then, in 2005, the real estate department of Deutsche Bank loaned Trump $640 million to finance construction of Trump International Hotel and Tower in Chicago. After the 2008 global financial crisis, Trump defaulted on the loan. Deutsche Bank then sought payment from Trump of $40 million that he personally guaranteed in order to pay down the loan. When Trump refused payment, Deutsche Bank filed suit to obtain the $40 million.

In court, Trump denied liability, alleging that the financial crisis was a *force majeure* event that Deutsche Bank had aided and abetted. This meant in layman's terms that he claimed he was prevented from fulfilling his contract by the financial crisis, as if it were like some act of God beyond his reasonable control. Pure applesauce! Trump had the money. In 2008, in connection with his proposed golf course in Scotland, he told the Scottish press: "The world has changed financially and the banks are all in trouble, but the good news is that we are doing very well as a company, and we are in a *very, very strong* cash position."

With a startling temerity, he asserted that Deutsche Bank owed *him* money and counterclaimed for $3 billion, alleging lender liability for undermining the project, predatory practices, and damage to his reputation.

Trump explained his cavalier strategy in his 2007 book *Think Big and Kick Ass in Business and Life*, in which he said, "Turn it back on the banks.... I figured it was the bank's problem, not mine."

Steven Molo, an attorney for Deutsche Bank, wrote a devastating letter to the New York court, contrasting Trump's longtime vaunted personal wealth and his disingenuous defense to the bank's suit for payment. Molo's letter totally refuted Trump's claim of *force majeure*:

Trump proclaims himself "the archetypal businessman, a deal-maker without peer." Trump has stated in court he is worth billions of dollars. In addition to substantial cash, personal investments and various other tangible assets, he maintains substantial interests in numerous extraordinary properties in New York and around the country.

The court dismissed Trump's counterclaim. Oddly, two years after Molo's letter, the parties settled and extended the loan term for another five years. Meanwhile, the private wealth department of the bank continued to do business with Trump. Since the 1990s, Deutsche Bank has been Trump's personal cash register, providing him with $3.5 billion in loans.

There was something rotten in the relationship between Trump and Deutsche Bank. From that point until the time of Trump's election, the bank continued with Trump as a customer and kept him afloat, although they knew his loans were nonperforming and he was prone to sue them. Trump now owes Deutsche Bank roughly $300 million. New York's attorney general has subpoenaed Trump's account records from Deutsche Bank. It is unknown what will come of the attorney general's review.

Many of the lawsuits Trump brought were not to get a judgment, but to punish. You might call them spite suits.

In 1993, Chuck Jones was a press agent for Marla Maples, Trump's second wife and mother of their daughter Tiffany. Jones had his employment terminated because Trump wanted to take over as her personal manager. Jones evidently had a foot fetish. He was arrested and convicted in New York for burglary and other crimes after he broke into Maples's apartment, where he allegedly took various personal items belonging to Maples, notably, her shoes. Jones brought lawsuits against Maples and Trump, alleging that Trump was responsible for searches of his Connecticut residence and New York office, defamation in the

New York Post and other news media, malice behind the New York criminal prosecution, and breach of contract. While damages on the other claims were unspecified, Jones demanded an astronomical sum for breech of contract that amounted to roughly 10 percent of Trump's purported net worth. Since no reputable lawyer would take such a case, Jones appeared *pro se*—meaning that he acted as his own attorney, always an undesirable practice.

Jones's lawsuit unleashed a cascade of litigation. Trump and Maples counterclaimed for $35 million. They charged Jones with extortion, theft, fraud, and harassment. "The only stalking that I'm aware of was when Marla Maples was stalking somebody else's husband," Jones said at the time. His suit was dismissed. Trump eventually dropped the counterclaim.

In 2013, after Trump said he would donate $5 million to charity if President Obama would release all of his personal documents to the public, Bill Maher appeared on *The Tonight Show* and joked that he would give Trump $5 million if he could prove that his father was not an orangutan. Trump sent Maher a copy of his birth certificate. When Maher didn't pay up, in surely the most ridiculous claim ever to clutter the halls of justice, Trump sued him for the $5 million. He eventually dropped the case. Joke contracts are unenforceable.

In 1992, Trump sued his ex-wife Ivana for $25 million for blabbing about his finances. He had an agreement with her that she would never discuss the details of their marriage, and she did. Trump accused Ivana of fraud and "willful, deliberate and surreptitious disclosure" of sensitive financial information, despite her having signed an agreement that she wouldn't talk publicly about their relationship.

Trump's business history has been earmarked by a course of conduct engaged in by few other real estate developers or entrepreneurs on the way up. Defying all norms, he litigates at the drop of a hat. He litigates when he has not been damaged. He can afford to do this because if he loses, he stiffs his lawyers on their fees.

He uses lawsuits to improve his brand or to defend his name or to torment his enemies. He sues journalists and their newspapers that criticize his buildings' architecture, even though such an action will not stand up in court. He skirts the law as though it does not exist. He opposes regulation, and he is sued by regulators. He is frequently charged with fraud. He sues the banks that have lent him money. He sues to shoot his way into a professional football league that doesn't want him, claiming damages that do not exist. He builds his Trump-branded golf courses and then chisels on real estate taxes, claiming low valuations for tax purposes that contradict higher valuations he has stated in filings under penalty of perjury. He insists that the Trump name is a trademark even when there is no confusion about his having anything to do with it. He insists that the mark "Trump" covers every conceivable kind of business, whether he is competing in it or not. He borrows from banks, defaults on loans, and then sues them to get an edge.

In the mind of Trump, what is false is true, the incontestable is thrown into doubt, criticism is fake news, wrongful conduct is to be engaged in and then denied, empty threats are the best defense, and morality is irrelevant. At the end of the day, whatever the outcome, the battle ends with preposterous and exaggerated claims of victory.

He enjoys litigation for lunch. If it is one man's poison, it is Trump's meat and drink.

EMPTY THREATS

_____

HOW TRUMP USED THE THREAT OF LITIGATION TO INTIMIDATE HIS FOES

_____

> *The supreme art of war is to subdue the enemy*
> *without fighting.*
>
> —Sun Tzu, *The Art of War*,
> one of the few books Donald Trump
> has professed to have read

Donald Trump could have written a book called *The Art of the Threat.* Mostly, he threatened litigation, and didn't sue because he didn't need to. The threat was enough. If he did sue to make a point, he often dropped the case. Few, if any, of the lawsuits he brought ever went to judgment. Though he denied it, most of the suits he was involved in were settled.

Trump is a castle surrounded by a moat of threats. He has been threatening people since the time of Roy Cohn. He threatened people and they gave way, even though the threats violated every moral norm. A Google search on May 19, 2019, for "Trump threatens suit" came up with 36,600,000 hits. What is interesting is comparing how many times he has threatened suit with how many times he went ahead and filed papers in the courthouse. The threats have it.

In the world of lawfare that he created, Trump's approach, more often than not, was to threaten a suit and not go through with it. There is a place for threats. Often they avoid needless litigation. The threat may bring about a desired settlement and spare the parties protracted litigation. But blurred lines often exist between threatening legitimate litigation, which is acceptable, and extortion and blackmail, which are not. There is also the ethical issue of using threats to strong-arm someone into an unfair settlement.

The ploy became his second nature. Threatening worked for him much of the time. No one wanted to litigate with Trump. He would lawyer you to death with discovery, motion practice, and delaying tactics. He would run up a legal bill that you couldn't afford. Years of litigation with nothing to show for it. Better to pack your bag and move on. So, faced with a Trump threat, many of his adversaries caved or apologized or settled or hunkered down, hoping he would go away. Few had the financial resources or the will to face him down.

The threat was a tactic he learned from Roy Cohn. Author Ken Auletta, who followed Cohn closely, wrote of him, "His standard technique is to dispatch a threatening letter on behalf of a client—'Hey, mister. This is now the eleventh hour before the monster strikes!' is how Roy puts it." Trump himself has acknowledged that threat of suit was a Cohn approach that often worked. "The mere sending of a letter from Roy Cohn has saved us a lot of money," he told Auletta for a 1978 *Esquire* piece. "When people know Roy is involved, they'd rather not get involved in the lawsuit and everything else that's involved."

There are stories that when a vendor whose bill he had rejected came to his office, Trump would open his desk and show him an 8-by-10 picture of Roy Cohn, his legal assassin. That's all he needed to do; the man would leave cowering in fright. "We just tell the opposition Roy Cohn is representing me, and they get scared," Mr. Trump told guests at a birthday party he gave for Cohn in the atrium of Trump Tower.

And, in an interview with *Vanity Fair*'s Marie Brenner, Trump revealed: "All I can tell you is he's been vicious to others in his protection of me. . . . He's a genius. He's a lousy lawyer, but he's a genius."

Throughout his litigation history, Trump repeatedly threatened to sue people, often on Twitter. His history is replete with threats to sue those that opposed him: political adversaries, business partners, the press, and others. Trump abused the threat. He took a perverse delight in threatening people. He did so promiscuously, sometimes for publicity, and often as mere entertainment.

In spring 1988, billionaire Leonard Stern sorely displeased him. One of Stern's magazines, *7 Days*, published an article expressing the opinion that resale prices achieved on Trump Tower apartments were below what Trump reported. According to Stern, Trump "went nuts." He lost no time in writing Stern: "I just read a highly inaccurate and biased story in *7 Days* by an obvious Trump hater—it is a disgrace." One of his pet pejoratives, "disgrace," reflects the "us against the hating-us world" attitude imbued in him by his father and developed by Roy Cohn. Trump then wrote to the president of the magazine announcing a mass-plaintiff lawsuit, purportedly brought by all or nearly all of the tenants in every Trump property. He claimed he himself was reluctant to bring suit, but he could not hold back the flood of apartment owners who wanted to sue.

Trump dropped the threat when a subsequent *7 Days* article had a good word for Ivana's redecoration of the Plaza Hotel. All was well until Stern financed an unflattering documentary about him. We can only speculate who then planted stories in the gossip columns that Stern's beautiful wife, Allison, was trying to date him. He confirmed these stories, saying, "We spoke. I wasn't interested." Allison Stern publicly dismissed the dating story as "absurd" and the "product of a juvenile mind."

In the summer of 2004, ABC showed a promotional segment in which billionaire investor Mark Cuban, starring in the ABC reality show *The Benefactor*, stated that it was easier for him than Trump to raise $1 million since Trump's casinos had fallen on hard times. Trump's lawyers wrote to Cuban threatening to sue over the remark. They never did.

The United States Golf Association caved to a Trump threat. It had committed to hold the U.S. Women's Open in July 2017 at Trump National Golf Club in Bedminster, New Jersey. Two years earlier, it had expressed a desire to move the event, after Trump's presidential aspirations began to materialize. Trump said he would sue if they tried to move it. "We can't get out of this," USGA executive director Mike Davis reportedly told members of his executive committee. "He's going to sue us." The event went forward as originally planned.

Some of the threats ripened into lawsuits that overhung Trump's campaign. While campaigning for president, he was distracted by 75 lawsuits affecting his business. Many of these lawsuits he initiated himself. On June 16, 2016, he suspended campaigning to testify on deposition in one of his two lawsuits against celebrity chefs Geoffrey Zakarian and José Andrés after they refused to go forward with a deal to open a restaurant at the Trump International Hotel in Washington. The pair backed out because of Trump's remarks about Mexican immigrants. Trump testified that the media had distorted his remarks. Then he said, "I think, you know, most people think I'm right." The pair settled their litigation with the Trump Organization in April 2017, with the terms designated by the court as confidential.

In 2011, the rapper Mac Miller (now deceased) released a song called "Donald Trump," which included the lyrics "Take over the world when I'm on my Donald Trump shit / Look at all this money, ain't that some shit." Trump tweeted at Miller threatening a lawsuit: "I'm now going to teach you a big boy lesson about lawsuits and finance. You ungrateful dog!" Miller responded, "I'm not trying to put any negative energy into the world. Let's be friends."

In addition, Trump threatened to sue each of the 19 or more women who accused him during the 2016 presidential campaign of unwanted sexual contact. Only one of the women, Summer Zervos, filed suit against him (more on her in chapter 7).

Trump threatened to sue some 26 persons in the course of the campaign. Christianna Silva, blogging for the political website Five-ThirtyEight on October 24, 2016, compiled a box score of the more than 20 times Trump threatened to sue someone over a 16-month period. All but two of these threats were not carried out, but they may have imposed a chilling effect on their targets. Among them were the following:

- **Univision**, the Mexican television station, for dropping the Miss USA pageant. He sued, and the case was settled on undisclosed terms.

- **The National Hispanic Media Coalition** after it called one of his speeches a "bigoted, racist, anti-Latino rant."

- **StopTrump.us**. They were selling anti-Trump shirts.

- **The Culinary Workers Union** and **the Bartender Union** for publishing that he spent the night at the unionized Treasure Island Hotel & Casino in Las Vegas instead of his own nonunionized hotel. He sued, got nowhere, and dropped the case.

- **John Kasich**. When Kasich spent $2.5 million on an ad campaign unfavorable to Trump, Trump said sadistically, "Watch Kasich squirm. If he is not truthful in his negative ads, I will sue him just for fun."

- **New Day for America** (a super PAC) because it ran negative ads.

- **Mike Fernandez**, a Jeb Bush donor, over negative ads.

- **The *Washington Post***, in January 2016, for libel over a piece they ran on how his Atlantic City casinos filed for bankruptcy in the early 1990s. He warned the *Post*, "This was not personal. This was a corporate deal. If you write this one, I'm suing you." The *Post* ran the story. He never sued. In an interview with the *Post* in May 2016, Trump said, "I will be bringing more libel suits as people—maybe against you folks. I don't want to threaten, but I find that the press is unbelievably dishonest."

- **Ted Cruz** over voter fraud in the Iowa caucuses for "not being a natural born citizen" (Cruz was born in Canada) and for attack ads. When Cruz questioned Trump's use of litigation or threatened litigation to deflect criticism, Trump responded, "I have wonderful lawyers; I like to send letters."

- **The Republican Party** over an issue about Louisiana delegates.

- **The Associated Press** for publishing an article about a Trump-branded condo development in Panama.

As the campaign proceeded, Trump intensified his drumroll of threats:

- In April 2016, Trump called Pulitzer Prize–winning investigative journalist **David Cay Johnston** at home. Johnston had written *The Making of Donald Trump*. Johnston said Trump told him he would sue "if he doesn't like what I report." Trump knew well that the Supreme Court had placed strict limitations on public figures suing for libel. "I know I'm a public figure," he told Johnston, "I will sue you anyway." He never did.

- In July 2016, Trump threatened to sue his former ghostwriter **Tony Schwartz** for "defamatory" statements Schwartz made to the *New Yorker* in which Schwartz claimed that Trump did not write a word of *The Art of the Deal*, and that much of what is in there is misleading or untrue.

- Trump threatened to sue the *New York Times* for publishing one piece about Trump's tax returns and another about two women who accused Trump of sexual assault.

- Trump threatened to sue 11 women who claimed he had made unwanted sexual advances.

And there were plenty more outlandish and empty threats I found in the course of my research. None resulted in litigation.

- When journalist Michelle Fields claimed Trump's campaign manager, Corey Lewandowski, had assaulted her, Trump was quick to react. "I am sure there will be a counter-claim coming down the line," he said. No one sued.

- When Club for Growth, the conservative PAC, spent $1 million to highlight liberal positions he had taken, Trump threatened a multimillion-dollar lawsuit. No suit here either.

- He threatened to sue Wayne Barrett in 1978. The *Village Voice* journalist was working on what would become a series of stories that Trump feared might be unflattering. Barrett's eventual story was headed, "LIKE FATHER, LIKE SON—ANATOMY OF A YOUNG POWER BROKER." (Timothy O'Brien, interestingly enough, whom Trump would eventually sue for libel, later became Barrett's research assistant.) While Barrett was poring over some files, the phone rang. It was Trump. "Wayne," said Trump, "I hear you're doing a story on me." Barrett understood the call to be a calculated attempt to head off the story. Later, Trump threatened to sue Barrett. According to Barrett, Trump also subtly hinted at a bribe, telling Barrett that he could get him a nice midtown apartment and relocate him and his wife out of the Brownsville, Brooklyn, home where they lived.

- He threatened to sue the satirical online news site The Onion over an article.

- Someone purporting to act for Trump threatened to sue the artist Illma Gore over a satirical cartoon depicting Trump with a micropenis. Had he sued, one can only speculate what discovery would have looked like, since in a defamation case, truth is a complete defense.

- In 2012, he threatened Amazon founder and *Washington Post* owner Jeff Bezos with tax audits.

- In 2012, Trump threatened legal action against Angelo Carusone, president of the liberal watchdog organization Media Matters for America, who had organized a petition to force Macy's to stop selling Trump-branded products. Trump didn't sue. Macy's cut ties with Trump.

- In an April 6, 2015, tweet, he threatened both *Rolling Stone* and the Huffington Post: "As dishonest as @RollingStone is I say @HuffingtonPost is worse. Neither has much money—sue them and put them out of business!"

- In 2006, Trump threatened to sue Rosie O'Donnell, then a co-host on *The View*, after she said he was bankrupt. Trump retaliated in an interview with *The Insider*, labeling O'Donnell "disgusting, both inside and out." He told *People*, "Rosie will rue the words she said. I'll most likely sue her for making those false statements—and it'll be fun. Rosie's a loser. A real loser. I look forward to taking lots of money from my nice fat little Rosie." The two had been feuding since 20-year-old Miss USA winner Tara Conner faced losing her crown in 2006 because of tabloid reports that she had been seen drinking, using drugs, and kissing a woman. Trump publicly forgave Conner at a televised news conference at Trump Tower. O'Donnell went out of her way to trash Trump on *The View* as a hypocrite for his profession of forgiveness. She combed over his marital history, his hairdo, his six corporate bankruptcies, and his record of stiffing those who worked for him. Trump threatened to sue. He went on TV to call Rosie "disgusting," a "slob," as someone with a "fat ugly face. . . . We're all a little chubby," he said, "but Rosie is just worse than most of us." When Rosie came out as a lesbian, he went on David Letterman and called her a "degenerate." He never sued, and ultimately they seemed to make peace. In 2012, after O'Donnell suffered a heart attack, Trump tweeted to tell her to "get better fast. I'm starting to miss you!" She replied, "well thank you donald—i must admit ur post was a bit of a shock . . . r u trying to kill me? xx"

- In April 2016 he threatened to sue the Associated Press over a story that ran in October 2015 about a movement at the Trump Ocean Club in Panama City to oust a management team put in place by the Trump family.

- In mid-September 2016, Trump was angered when the *New York Times* reported that he gave a last-minute speech in South Carolina to a room only about two-thirds full. He claimed that a third of the chairs were empty because people rushed the stage, which the *Times* said was untrue. He tweeted: "My lawyers want to sue the failing @NYTimes so badly for irresponsible intent. I said no (for now, but they are watching). Really disgusting." There is no concept in the law known as "irresponsible intent." Trump may not have sued the *Times* for libel for two reasons: he is a public figure, and, as he well knew, it is difficult for a public figure to prove a libel case. Also, he may have taken to heart the advice of his teacher Roy Cohn. In his book *How to Stand Up for Your Rights and Win!*, Cohn reflects on the merits of starting a libel suit. Indeed, he devotes an entire chapter to it. Cohn writes that "whether to sue or not may be a difficult decision. If you don't bring suit . . . your failure to do so may encourage a general belief that the [defamation] is true. . . . Still, caution is advised: I would venture to say that there are thousands of pages of false and defamatory statements about me in print. Yet I have sued only twice. A libel suit can be very messy; if they've got a shot at proving the case, you may get hurt, and in any event the suit will generate publicity. On the other hand, if you've been slandered without cause, fight back! You might well win big." He then concluded, "But don't forget the old maxim: *'Don't sue for libel: they're liable to prove it.'*"

- According to testimony before Congress, Trump directed Michael Cohen during the 2016 campaign to threaten lawsuits against the high school and colleges he attended if they publicly released his grades or SAT test scores.

What to do? Change the libel laws. Trump's surreal statement on the subject came in February 2016, when he said he was "going to open up our libel laws so when they write purposely negative and horrible and false articles, we can sue them and win lots of money. We're going to open up those libel laws. So when the *New York Times* writes a hit piece which is a total disgrace, or when the *Washington Post*, which is there for other reasons, writes a hit piece, we can sue them and win money instead of having no chance of winning because they're totally protected."

There has been no institution in our society that Trump has threatened more than the mainstream media. Trump's disdain for a free press is well known. In September 2016, he had a reporter arrested outside one of his campaign events where Trump blamed the New York terrorist bombings on "freedom of the press."

In October 2016, after the *New York Times* ran a story on how he had taken almost a billion dollars of losses that sheltered from taxation income reported on his tax returns, he threatened "prompt initiation of appropriate legal action." This was at least the eleventh time Trump had threatened to sue a news organization in the course of the campaign. The *Times* stuck with its story.

When he realized that threatening libel suits against the media didn't work, and indeed only engendered more criticism, Trump reached for stronger medicine—threatening NBC's "license." NBC News had reported a leak that over the summer of 2017 Trump had astonished military leaders by saying he wanted to rebuild the nation's nuclear stockpile to its peak level of the late 1960s—a tenfold increase that would violate international agreements the U.S. has adhered to since the 1980s. Trump's proposal for such an expansion reportedly prompted then secretary of state Rex Tillerson to call Trump a "moron." For this remark, which he denied making, Tillerson was almost fired. Later, he was.

On October 11, 2017, Trump launched tweets equating his two favorite TV piñatas:

Fake @NBCNews made up a story that I wanted a "tenfold" increase in our U.S. nuclear arsenal. Pure fiction, made up to demean. NBC = CNN!

With all of the Fake News coming out of NBC and the Networks, at what point is it appropriate to challenge their License? Bad for country!

Later, at a news conference on October 11, 2017, sitting alongside Canadian prime minister Justin Trudeau, Trump seized the opportunity to continue his attack on NBC, stating, "It's frankly disgusting the way the press is able to write whatever they want to write, and people should look into it."

In a tweet launched later that day, he said, "Network news has become so partisan, distorted and fake that licenses must be challenged and, if appropriate, revoked." He threatened to revoke the broadcast "license" of NBC, something that he didn't have the power to do. NBC, the network, does not even have a broadcast license. Only the individual stations do. And only the FCC, an independent agency, can revoke a station's broadcast license, and they can do it only when the station lacks requisite "character," which in practice means the station has been convicted of a felony. Nixon tried such a threat in the 1970s, seeking unsuccessfully to revoke the broadcast licenses of the *Washington Post* over its Watergate coverage.

In November 2017, when NBC fired *Today Show* host Matt Lauer for inappropriate sexual behavior, Trump couldn't resist crowing. In an early-morning November 29 tweet he wrote:

Wow, Matt Lauer was just fired from NBC for "inappropriate sexual behavior in the workplace." But when will the top executives at NBC & Comcast be fired for putting out so much Fake News. Check out Andy Lack's past!

Andrew Lack is the chairman of NBC News and MSNBC. To date, no allegations of past impropriety have been made against him.

6

TRUMP AND THE MOB

TRUMP'S TIES TO THE MAFIA

It's strictly business.
— "Michael Corleone" in Mario Puzo's *The Godfather*

Trump's business history, both in real estate and gambling, was replete with links to infamous mobsters—most of which he flatly denied or professed not to recall. To be fair, businessmen in both fields swam in Mob-infested waters and were confronted with a choice—to deal or not to deal with the Mob, which had a brooding omnipresence in the unions representing construction workers and Teamsters as well as in the world of casino gambling. Some chose not to deal. Trump's choice was to deal.

When judges charge juries in organized crime cases they tell them that in America we believe that guilt is personal, and that guilt by association is alien to our traditions. However, in terms of drawing conclusions based on patterns of behavior, deep ties to mobsters are to a criminal investigator what contacts between suspected terrorists are to the CIA. One need only connect the dots.

As the man said, "It's all about the money." In a report issued in the late 1980s, the New York State Organized Crime Task Force concluded that mobsters and labor racketeers have mined the veins of the building trades for decades. They do this not by subverting legitimate business but by partnering symbiotically so that "everybody makes money."

By the 1980s, crime families had infiltrated all aspects of the New York contracting industry, including the Teamsters Union, which controlled the delivery, and necessary removal, of building materials from construction sites.

Trump had three construction projects going virtually at once in the New York City of the 1980s: the renovation of the Commodore Hotel, discussed in chapter 2; Trump Plaza, a 36-story cooperative apartment and retail building on East 61st Street; and Trump Tower on Fifth Avenue and East 56th Street. Most of the major private and public cement contracts for new construction in Manhattan were with a mobster-owned cartel consisting of four companies operating as two separate joint ventures: Dic-Underhill, which supplied the concrete for Trump Tower, and Nasso-S&A, supplying the concrete for the other two Trump projects.

At that time, Mob kingpin Paul Castellano and his partner in crime, Anthony "Fat Tony" Salerno, the cigar-chomping underboss of the Genovese crime family, the most powerful Mafia group in New York, ruled the roost over the poured concrete cartel. The Teamsters Union controlled delivery of the cement to the construction sites. Few builders dared to take on the Mob cartel and refuse their offer of poured concrete at grossly inflated prices.

On December 16, 1985, just before Christmas, four gunmen approached Castellano at about 5:30 p.m. on a busy midtown New York side street. Dressed in long white trench coats and black Russian hats, the shooters drew semiautomatic weapons, and Castellano, head of the Gambino crime family, went down in a hail of bullets, shot six times in the head and body. Castellano was out on bail, as he was standing trial in federal court on charges of racketeering and murder. Also murdered was Thomas Bilotti, Castellano's bodyguard. John Gotti, known as "the Dapper Don" for his impeccable taste in designer suits and garishly patterned ties, eagerly waited around the corner to make sure all went well. Gotti had orchestrated the hit. He was waiting in the wings to succeed Castellano as head of the Gambino family.

The succession would have little noticeable effect on Trump's business. Trump had strong ties to Gotti through Roy Cohn. Cohn represented John "Junior" Gotti when he was charged with murder. Gotti was acquitted.

In 1987, U.S. attorney Rudy Giuliani (later one of Trump's lawyers in the Mueller investigation) brought to trial in the Southern District of New York eight mobster defendants on 51 counts of federal racketeering charges. All were convicted. The defendants included Salerno and the top leaders of the "commission" that ruled the U.S. Mafia.

The indictment charged, among other things, that from 1978 to 1981, approximately 70 percent of the major private and public cement contracts for new construction in Manhattan were maintained by the Mob-owned cartel. The government presented evidence that the defendants had participated in a scheme to rig the contracts for concrete superstructure work on high-rise buildings in Manhattan where the value of the concrete work was over $2 million. Cohn at various times represented some of the defendants in the case, including Salerno.

Dic-Underhill was a concrete firm that Fred Trump had used years before to build Trump Village in Coney Island. Its president, Joe De-Paolo, had alleged Mob associations. DePaolo's brother owned a carting company that did the hauling. When the Trump Tower job began, the carting company and the Dic accounts were sold to Carmine Persico, who was given a 139-year prison sentence for racketeering and died in prison on March 7, 2019. Persico (known as "the Snake") was boss of the notorious Colombo crime family. Federal prosecutors named Dic principals as unindicted co-conspirators in the 1987 indictment of Salerno, and other mobsters, who testified as government witnesses. The awarding of an $8 million contract for Trump Plaza to S&A made up a count in the federal indictment.

In addition to their control of a number of illegal businesses, Castellano and Salerno were the secret owners of S&A. Two companies,

Transit Mix Company and Certified Concrete Company, both owned by another Mob-connected Cohn client, Edward J. "Biff" Halloran, produced almost 100 percent of the reinforced concrete used in Manhattan. Halloran's company poured the concrete for Trump at the Grand Hyatt.

After the verdict, chief prosecutor Michael Chertoff (later secretary of Homeland Security in the George W. Bush administration) told the judge that the cartel was "the largest and most vicious criminal business in the history of the United States." The sentences for the eight defendants ranged from 40 to 100 years. Sentenced to a term of 100 years in January 1987, Salerno died in prison in 1992.

No builder could pour concrete for a New York project of over $2 million without the sanction of the Mafia cartel. Master builder Sam LeFrak told John Cody, notorious boss of Teamsters Local 282 and a very close associate of the Gambino crime family, that he would use prefabricated concrete and structural steel at his Battery Park City project rather than poured concrete, and that it would be trucked in by non-Teamster employees. Cody and LeFrak worked out a settlement. LeFrak and other builders spoke out publicly against the cartel, telling the New York Times that to avoid dealing with Cody's threatened work stoppages, he had used a more expensive type of concrete that cost him an estimated $10 million extra. "Concrete is a monopoly in this town," said LeFrak. "There are a few guys and they are working hand and glove with the unions."

Trump's connection to the Mob was Roy Cohn. Village Voice journalist Wayne Barrett, who followed Trump and Cohn for decades, related that both Castellano and Salerno were clients of Cohn and met with the lawyer frequently at his townhouse offices at 39 East 68th Street.

Cohn represented a number of Mob figures. Writer Ken Auletta, who followed Cohn for many years, reported that Cohn had the private telephone numbers of several Mafia dons on his speed dial. He advised them about their business affairs and many of the legitimate fronts they used in their illegal operations.

Cohn also represented Horace Mann classmate and close friend Generoso Pope Jr. from the Bronx, who founded the supermarket tabloid the *National Enquirer* in 1952 with a $75,000 loan from the godfather, mobster Frank Costello. After Pope died in 1988, a group led by David Pecker, also from the Bronx, eventually acquired the *Enquirer* for $850 million. Pecker was—and is—a close friend of Donald Trump. They forged a relationship in the 1990s when Trump was coming off his casino failures and became the frequent subject of tabloid gossip. Both Cohn and Trump found their relationships with the *Enquirer* to be of lasting value, both in planting stories that would smear their enemies and in killing stories that would be embarrassing. Pecker struck an immunity deal with prosecutors over hush money payments to certain women linked to Trump.

In many respects, Cohn was a Mob consigliere. Mob meetings took place in his townhouse because Cohn knew judges would be reluctant to authorize wiretaps on a lawyer's office. In 1977, Cohn used a unique defense to win a jury disagreement for Salerno on tax evasion charges. The government's theory of tax evasion was that Salerno had spent more than he had earned over a four-year period. "It's not a crime in this country to spend more money than you earned," Cohn told the jury in summation. Cohn later admitted to *New York Times* journalist Sam Roberts that Salerno was "technically guilty," but justified the outcome by maintaining that "truth is hardly ever an absolute. There are so many elements."

Beyond his association with Cohn, Trump's own ties with the Mob ran deep, both in New York and in Atlantic City where he operated his casinos. For unknown reasons, Trump wanted Trump Tower to be built using reinforced concrete, more expensive than the steel girder construction used in most New York skyscrapers—and not the labor-saving precast concrete that Sam LeFrak chose. By choosing ready-mix concrete, as Wayne Barrett noted, he put himself "at the mercy of a legion of concrete racketeers."

Cohn also introduced Trump to Teamsters president John Cody, convicted in 1982 on federal charges of racketeering and tax evasion.

Prosecutors contended that Cody had lined his pockets with cash obtained by extortion and kickbacks. He also accepted valuable services from corporations employing rank-and-file members of his local. According to Barrett, Cohn even orchestrated a meeting between Trump and Salerno at his Upper East Side townhouse during the construction of Trump Tower. Although a Cohn staff member who was present confirmed the meeting to Barrett, Trump flatly denied it ever happened. Barrett recounted the meeting that did not take place in his fascinating 2016 book, *Trump: The Greatest Show on Earth; The Deals, the Downfall, the Reinvention.*

Trump paid $8 million to S&A for concrete at his Trump Plaza project at what a federal indictment of Salerno later concluded were inflated prices. Irving Fisher, the general contractor who built Trump Tower, testified that "goons" once entered his office and held a knife to the throat of his switchboard operator to send a message that the Mob meant business. The Mob always means "business." The problem was perhaps ameliorated by payment of inflated prices for concrete.

Through Cohn, Trump met, fraternized with, and did business with others with Mob ties. Teamsters boss Cody was tied closely to Biff Halloran. One of Halloran's employees, Louis Ambrosio, was Cody's chauffeur. Federal law prohibits an employer from giving anything of value to an official of a union with which they have collective bargaining agreements. Yet Halloran's company paid a bill for Cody's 10-day stay in 1978 at the elite Jockey Club in Miami, and officials of Cody's union were "comped" at his Halloran House hotel on Lexington Avenue. Halloran was convicted along with Salerno on federal bid-rigging and extortion charges and served four years in prison. A federal prosecutor told the jury, "Biff Halloran, ladies and gentlemen, . . . was a full associate of the Genovese family." Halloran was last seen in August 1998 driving his Rolls Royce Silver Cloud down to Florida; he then suddenly vanished and was not seen again. He was the man who knew too much.

Cody described Cohn as "a pretty good friend" and sometime legal adviser. Trump worked with Cody through Cohn, as Trump thought

Cody was a "bad guy and I didn't deal with him almost at all because I knew the kind of guy he was. He was a very bad cookie." But Trump later contradicted himself, suggesting to the *Wall Street Journal* that he did deal with Cody. "I was never going to run for office. . . . I'd go by the lowest bid and I'd go by their track record, but I didn't do a personal history of who they are."

Cody was a labor racketeer. He was so joined at the hip with the Mob that Carlo Gambino, the "boss of bosses" of the Mafia, attended his son's 1973 Long Island wedding. To intimidate the developers, Cody worked with the Gambinos and later Castellano. Cody had on his rap sheet eight arrests, including one for attempted rape, and three convictions, one for armed robbery. In 1982, while Trump Tower was under construction, he was convicted on federal racketeering charges involving $160,000 in kickbacks and sentenced to five years in federal prison. At his sentencing, prosecutors said that he had links to "high-echelon members of organized crime."

It was illegal for Cody to accept money from employers at construction sites. Such conduct would implicate the RICO laws applicable to extortion and labor racketeering, since the receipt of anything of value from a contractor would be the equivalent of a cash payoff.

So Cody tried to end-run the law, among other means by shaking down developers for rent-free apartments for his female friends. He had done this in North Shore Towers, a Queens apartment house where his mistress Marilyn Taggart was luxuriously ensconced. And he did this at Trump Tower.

He was considered the construction industry's most powerful union leader. As it turned out, in 1982 when Cody was calling a citywide Teamsters strike, Trump got an early heads up and obtained the assistance of Cody in finishing the final floors of Trump Tower despite the strike. When the Tower officially opened in 1983, with Cohn posing for a "cutting-the-ribbon" photo op with Trump and Trump's mother, and Mayor Koch and former New York governor Hugh Carey making speeches, none of the politicians seemed to notice that the concrete work was delivered without incident in the middle of a Teamsters strike. How did Trump achieve labor peace at Trump Tower? Wayne Barrett cited "FBI sources" for his assertion that "he did it through Cohn."

The construction of Trump Tower had a special problem. Construction access to the site at Fifth Avenue and 56th was available only through the 56th Street side, and the concrete trucks had to make deliveries at predetermined times throughout the day. Ready-mix concrete is manufactured at a cement plant and then poured into the familiar barrel-shaped trucks in which it is churned into concrete. The concrete must be delivered to the construction site within an hour or it will spoil. Any delays might prove disastrous, and even imperil completion of the project. It was common for the Teamsters to use this leverage against construction projects in process such as Trump Tower in order to exact concessions from the developer, who would be at their mercy. Cody's son, Michael, told journalists in 2016 that Trump "wasn't going to build Trump Tower without having these connections. Every builder in New York had to do it at the time."

Trump lied to investigators, implausibly claiming he was able to complete the project by threatening Cody with the prospect of hiring private concrete dealers. Trump was hardly in a position to threaten Cody with anything. Subpoenaed by the Organized Crime Task Force, which looked into the matter, Trump flatly denied he had promised Cody an apartment at Trump Tower to secure labor peace, and the investigators strangely took him at his word.

What the investigators missed was that six prime apartments on two of the penthouse floors of Trump Tower had been purchased by a "friend" of Cody's called Verina Hixon. The apartments were on floors just below the posh triplex where Trump lived with Ivana.

Wayne Barrett, in *Trump: The Greatest Show on Earth*, describes Hixon, 37 at the time, as a "strikingly beautiful Austrian divorcée with no visible income." Her lawyer said that she lived off the "skin of the city," a variant of Tennessee Williams's deathless expression "the kindness of strangers." When asked at a deposition how she subsisted, her answer was: "That's a good question." Barrett writes that she had "shoulder-length blond hair, a melting smile and an international jet set lifestyle." The lifestyle included an ample wardrobe of designer clothes and intimate *dinners* à *deux* at the finest New York restaurants.

It is not clear just what the relationship was between Cody and Hixon. Trump thought they were romantically involved, and Barrett uncovered that they traveled together to Florida. Whatever the facts, it is clear they were joined at the hip, and it is easy to conclude that the apartments were a payoff to Cody for labor peace at the project.

In the closing months of 1982, Hixon had signed contracts to purchase the connected suite of apartments for roughly $10 million. Her plan was to renovate the six units by creating separate apartments, some of which could then be sold off to finance the acquisition. As for the financing, when the proceeds of Hixon's purchase money mortgage turned out to be $3 million less than what was needed, Cody turned to Trump to broker a suitable mortgage. According to Hixon, the bank never asked for financials, a loan application, or any of the paperwork normally required in such a transaction. Hixon moved in, and Cody stayed there whenever it suited him.

When estimated costs for the renovation soared from $850,000 to $2 million, Cody dipped into a Swiss numbered account to "loan" Hixon $500,000 to help cover the shortfall. She never repaid the loan. Hixon's story was that Cody said he might want some of the apartments if the appeal from his racketeering conviction was successful (it wasn't) or else after he served his five-year sentence. Meanwhile, Cody's impregnated girlfriend (not Hixon) stayed in one of the apartments from time to time. Sometimes he stayed with her. While the Swiss account easily funded the $500,000 loan for Hixon, Cody told the federal court that he was unable to pay the $700,000 fine that accompanied his sentence for racketeering.

Hixon still needed more money for the renovation so Cody found a new underwriter for her in Nick Auletta, president of a Mob-owned concrete company that supplied concrete for Trump buildings. Auletta, who also would do time for racketeering, advanced another $100,000. The Auletta loan was supposedly secured by a diamond ring belonging to Hixon, but no one has ever found the facts on that one.

Hixon visited Cody in prison in 1983 to keep him abreast of the problems with the renovation. On one occasion, Cody called Trump from the federal jail in Danbury, Connecticut, to complain about an issue or two. The renovation proceeded. At one point, Hixon wanted the telephone wiring in her apartment to go to the central switchboard, but Trump wanted otherwise. So Cody put a "man from the union" at Verina's door to keep Trump's people out.

Cody, although in prison, continued to play a vital role in Trump's businesses. His power enveloped all deliveries at Trump job sites, not just concrete. But in mid-1984, the Teamsters stripped Cody of his presidency, and Trump cracked down on Hixon, suing her for $250,000 that he claimed she owed him for the alterations. Taking a leaf from Trump's playbook, she counterclaimed for $20 million for defective workmanship, and alleged that Trump had received a 10 percent kickback from the architect. She contended that this and other kickbacks could "be the basis of a criminal proceeding requiring an attorney general's investigation" into Trump's business. Trump quickly and quietly settled the case, exacting from Hixon a nondisclosure agreement. Sound familiar?

There were other strange tenants at Trump Tower. A number had Mob ties or criminal records. Tenants who lived on the fringe of the underworld wanted to launder ill-gotten gains in a purchase price readily wired from an offshore LLC. The roster of initial tenants was a veritable rogues' gallery. These included Roberto Polo, an Italian fraudster who later went to jail; Sheldon and Jay Weinberg, father and son, convicted in a $16 million Medicaid scam, said to be the largest in history; David Bogatin, alleged to be a high-level Russian mobster (Trump attended the closing in 1984 on five Tower apartments purchased by Bogatin for $6 million); and Robert Hopkins, who ran a considerable gambling operation out of his Trump Tower suite of apartments. Roy Cohn represented Hopkins, in connection with the 1981 deal where

Hopkins acquired the apartments for $2 million. Hopkins was a Lucchese crime family associate arrested at Trump Tower for ordering a hit on a competitor. The murder charge was dismissed; the gambling charge stuck.

Trump's dealings with shady characters were legion. In 1985, two years after Trump Tower opened, Joseph Weichselbaum ran Trump's helicopter service, transporting high rollers between Manhattan and Atlantic City. Weichselbaum had a considerable criminal rap sheet. His first recorded offense was grand theft auto in 1965. In 1979, he pleaded guilty to two counts of embezzlement, and was ordered to return $135,000 to an employer for whom he had worked for ten years.

Most businessmen would not want to be seen as dealing with known criminals, and as a casino owner Trump stood to lose his license for such associations. Nevertheless, he paid Weichselbaum for helicopter services, and continued to pay his company after Weichselbaum's conviction for drug dealing. Journalist David Cay Johnston relates that Weichselbaum was not the only criminal Trump engaged to provide helicopter services. There was Dillinger Charter Services, owned in part by John Staluppi, identified by law enforcement as a made member of the Colombo crime family.

In 1985, an Ohio federal grand jury charged Weichselbaum with possession of dealer quantities of marijuana and cocaine. New Jersey gambling regulators were aware of this, but did nothing about it. Weichselbaum pleaded guilty to the Ohio charges; for sentencing, his case was strangely transferred to the United States District Court for New Jersey, where Trump's sister Maryanne Trump Barry was to preside over the case. I say, "strangely," because New Jersey had nothing to do with the case. Barry shortly thereafter recused herself, giving the explanation that she and her husband had flown in Weichselbaum helicopters.

Barry handed off the case to a new judge who read a letter from Trump imploring the court for leniency. The letter stated that the drug dealer was "a credit to the community ... conscientious, forthright and diligent." Minor figures in the Ohio case received stiff sentences of up to 20 years. Weichselbaum, the kingpin, got three years and served 18 months. The whole affair had an aroma.

Upon release from prison, Weichselbaum moved to Trump Tower (where else?) where he and his girlfriend had bought two adjoining apartments. The sales price was $2.4 million. Trump has never offered any explanation for his relationship with Weichselbaum. Indeed, the significance of their strange connection remains shrouded in mystery. Trump told David Cay Johnston that he "hardly knew" Weichselbaum. He told casino regulators that his only contact with Weichselbaum was to see him in the building—a statement he omitted to make to the New Jersey federal court when he praised Weichselbaum as a "credit to the community."

In 1984, Trump launched his casino empire in Atlantic City when he opened Harrah's at Trump Plaza, the first of three casinos he acquired. Atlantic City, which had a depressed economy, was eager to have him. Casinos, unlike real estate, are a highly regulated business, particularly because of the danger of Mob involvement. Regulators are always concerned about any relationship between casino owners and organized crime. In 1981, FBI agents had warned Trump about Mob influence in the dark world of casino gambling, and that he was swimming in Mob-infested waters.

The FBI documents its investigations in internal memorandums called Form 302s. An FBI memorandum written by Supervising Agent Damon T. Taylor records an FBI meeting with Trump dated September 22, 1981. The 302 is available on the Smoking Gun website. It states the following:

> Trump advised Agents that he had read in the press media and had heard from various acquaintances that Organized Crime elements were known to operate in Atlantic City. Trump also expressed at the meet-

ing the reservation that his life and those around him would be subject to microscopic examination. Trump advised that he wanted to
build a casino in Atlantic City but he did not wish to tarnish his family's
name. Agents advised Trump that he should carefully think over his
decision to build in Atlantic City, and carefully prepare not only
methods of securing employees' honesty, but also corporate integrity.

Then Trump asked one of the agents his personal opinion regarding whether he should build in Atlantic City, and according to the FBI
memorandum, the agent replied as follows:

[I] advised Trump, on a personal level, not as a matter of policy, that . . .
[I] thought there were easier ways that Trump could invest his money.

Trump forged ahead anyway. Roy Cohn told Trump that he ought
to persuade then New Jersey attorney general John Degnan to complete
the background check in six months instead of the normal 18. Degnan,
who was interested in running for governor, made a special exception
for Trump in the interest of having him invest in economically distressed
Atlantic City. Concerned that Trump might someday open a casino at
the Grand Hyatt in Manhattan, which would have adversely affected Atlantic City's gaming industry, Degnan bowed to Trump's request.

Trump appeared to keep his end of the bargain. He vociferously opposed gambling anywhere in the East. He of course did not include
Atlantic City—a position that mollified Degnan but at the same time
protected Trump's fledgling casino business. In any event, Trump assured Degnan that he was "clean as a whistle." At age 35, he argued, he
was too young to have had criminal associations.

It was all a prevarication. The DGE casino application required Trump
to disclose whether he had been the subject of any government investigation "for any reason." Trump's application was woefully deficient. It
omitted at least four governmental investigations into Trump's conduct, some of which were pending at the time. For example, it omitted a

pending federal grand jury probe, begun in 1979, into how he had acquired an option to buy the Penn Central railroad yards on Manhattan's
West Side. Federal agents twice informed Trump he was a subject and a
target of the investigation. In the end, Trump was never charged. John
Martin, the U.S. attorney in Manhattan, had investigated Trump in 1980
about his deal to acquire the old Commodore Hotel, which became the
Grand Hyatt. The subject again was the Penn Central yards, which
along with the Commodore were part of the Penn Central bankruptcy.
Martin later dropped the case. Nor did Trump disclose the pending
FBI inquiry into the benefits Teamster czar John Cody may have received at Trump Tower in return for labor peace.

The DGE application form also called upon Trump to disclose any
civil misconduct. Candor would have required Trump to disclose the
Justice Department housing case charging racial discrimination. The discrimination case was settled in 1975 but revived in 1978, and it remained unresolved. Yet, Trump omitted reference to the matter. In a
footnote to its 120-page report to the New Jersey Casino Control Commission, the DGE said that Trump had "volunteered" the requested information, much of which had been reported in the press, as though
volunteering information is a substitute for full disclosure on an official application form, presumably submitted under penalty of perjury.
Trump's past certainly would have merited further inquiry, but the
DGE rushed through his application in a record five months.

The initial casino project was a joint venture between Trump and
Harrah's, a subsidiary of Holiday Inn. The financing pattern paralleled
the one Trump had used successfully in New York: a minimal early
investment, government concessions in a depressed economy, and an institutional partner as the source of finance.

Daniel Sullivan was a giant of a man—a barrel-chested Irishman
standing six feet, five inches and weighing close to 300 pounds. Sullivan
would become one of Trump's initial partners in Atlantic City. Sullivan
was at the same time a "Mafia associate," FBI informant, and labor nego-
tiator. A "Mafia associate" in FBI-speak is someone controlled by the

Mob, but not a "made man." Sullivan's FBI connection was a hope on his part that the Bureau would protect him in his illegal operations. When I was a federal prosecutor in Manhattan, there were raised eyebrows when the FBI protected informants who continued to benefit from their illegal operations. One such informant, Herbert Itkin, testified at the trial of Carmine DeSapio that he received a cash payoff (which he called "green") in bank currency wrappers, pocketed the cash, initialed and dated the wrappers, and turned the wrappers over to the FBI as evidence.

Sullivan had a long rap sheet. He was a hardened criminal. He had been arrested on assault charges and served time for larceny. He had a weapons violation. He'd had a storied career on the docks of New York as a union enforcer. One day, after a truck driver declined to follow union rules, Sullivan decided to drive the recalcitrant driver's semi into the river. In 1966, Sullivan was the last person to see a labor lawyer named Abraham Bauman before he disappeared. Later, he openly discussed his ties to Teamsters president Jimmy Hoffa, who disappeared in 1975. He said he knew where the body was buried.

Trump told the media he continued his business relationship with Sullivan only after the FBI gave Sullivan a clean bill of health. That was untrue. A September 22, 1981, FBI memorandum recites that agents "have *repeatedly* told Trump that they were not references for [Sullivan] and cannot speak for [his] business dealings."

Trump's casino required the acquisition of land, and Sullivan, who had been in the trash-hauling business, knew of just the right site. The owner of the property, who was $800,000 in arrears on the mortgage, sought Sullivan's financial help. Sullivan gave the owner $325,000 for a one-third share in the property and said he planned to find two other partners. On June 26, 1980, the three partners closed the deal. The three were Sullivan, Trump, and Kenny Shapiro. The sale price was $2.7 million. Before the deal was even consummated, the partnership leased the property to the casino for 98 years.

Shapiro, a Philadelphia scrap metal dealer, partnered with Trump in at least three Atlantic City real estate deals. Like Sullivan, Shapiro had

deep ties to organized crime. He was the principal financier for the Philadelphia Scarfo crime family, and law enforcement officers described
him as Scarfo's "agent" in Atlantic City. Nicodemo "Little Nicky" Scarfo
was boss of the Scarfos. He was responsible for over two dozen murders,
including that of a judge who did not see things his way. Scarfo died in
prison in 2017. His concrete company, Scarf, Inc., made money in Atlantic City as it intimidated casino owners, including Trump, into buying
from them. Other subcontractors for the casino were thick with the
Scarfo family. One, Robert Winzinger, was eventually indicted. Scarfo
personally visited Winzinger on the Trump Plaza site. Another one, concrete subcontractor Joseph Feriozzi, was said to have evaded questions
before the State Commission of Investigation about why he awarded jobs
to two dodgy firms. Feriozzi's firm was involved with the construction of
the Taj Mahal, the Trump Plaza, and the Trump's Castle casinos. Trump's
lawyer, brought in from New York for the occasion to handle the unions,
was Paul Viggiano, also known as Paul Victor. Victor, a Mob lawyer, was
a Bronx political crony of Cohn's partner Stanley Friedman.

Sullivan and Trump agreed to partner on another venture, a drywall
company known as Circle Industries. There was also to be a third investor in Circle, most certainly Shapiro. Drywall, a board made of several
plies of fiberboard, paper, or felt bonded to a hardened gypsum plastic
core, becomes a wallboard used to make interior walls and ceilings. Drywall is essential to the construction industry. The drywall industry was
under FBI investigation. When Trump agreed to acquire Sullivan's interest, Circle was one of the firms swept up in the prosecution dragnet
involving a racketeering scheme with the carpenters' union and the
Genovese crime family. The grand jury indicted the president of the
union, Theodore Maritas, who disappeared before trial and was not
seen again. Aware that his deepening relationship with Sullivan and
Shapiro might end up getting him banned from the casino business,
Trump withdrew from the drywall deal.

Trump had his Grand Hyatt Hotel in New York retain Sullivan as a
"labor consultant" to negotiate the hotel's new union contract with the

hotel workers. As we have seen, Trump also had obtained Sullivan's assistance when he had trouble with undocumented Polish workers who were demolishing the Bonwit Teller building in Manhattan to make way for Trump Tower. Sullivan and Trump had a falling out in the mid-1980s and went their separate ways. Sullivan died of a heart attack in 1993.

Trump helped arrange New York political contributions to mobbed-up Atlantic City mayor Mike Matthews, with whom Trump had extensive dealings. Matthews subsequently pleaded guilty to federal extortion charges and was sentenced to 15 years in prison. A casino owner could not legally make campaign contributions to local politicians controlling zoning and signage permits. Shapiro testified before a federal grand jury that he had illegally channeled for Trump thousands of dollars in cash contributions to the mayor (Trump was barred from contributing because of his casino ownership). Trump flatly denied the story.

In statements both under oath and otherwise, Trump bobbed and weaved over having ties to the Mob.

In the fall of 1999 on *Meet the Press*, at a time when he announced he was running for president on the Reform Party ticket, Trump had the following exchange with Tim Russert:

Russert: Another book written suggested that because you are in the construction business, because you're in the casino business, you've had relations with members of organized crime.

Trump: False. I mean—you know, the funny thing about the casino business, in particular in Atlantic City, as an example, you have to go through a very brilliant casino control system. Every check you write, every deal you make, even outside of Atlantic City. I'm talking if I build a building in New York I send in papers as to who's building it, who's the concrete people, etc., etc. Everything I do is under scrutiny. And one of the things different, I think, about me is that my life has been, Tim, a very, very open book. More so than virtually any politician that you interview on Sundays.

Russert hammered away:

Russert: But you've never had to meet with, to do business with any organized [crime] figure in order to build buildings or do—

Trump: I never have had to, and, to be honest with you, being a celebrity at a very high level is a good thing. Because they sort of—and they're—I'm not saying the Mob doesn't exist. But they want to keep it low. They want to really keep it low. The last thing they want to do is meet with Donald Trump and have 500 paparazzi taking pictures. The answer is no. And I think, in that way—and I must tell you, I think, in that way, celebrity has been a positive for me.

In 2003, however, Trump admitted to journalist Timothy O'Brien that he believed Sullivan and Shapiro, who gave him his start in Atlantic City, had ties to organized crime:

Trump: They were tough guys. In fact, they say that Dan Sullivan was the guy that killed Jimmy Hoffa. I don't know if you ever heard that. . . .

O'Brien: What I heard about both of them, and that anybody who wanted to get anything done down there [in Atlantic City], that if you wanted to deal with labor you had to deal with Sullivan, if you wanted to deal with politics you had to deal with Shapiro. . . .

Trump: Yeah, it was really bullshit. *But, but they were tough guys. And not good guys.*

O'Brien: How do you handle people like that? . . .

Trump: I wasn't worried because I felt I could handle it, but I felt I'd get a partner. But getting a partner wasn't easy. And reputational, I didn't want to have anything to do with those guys because I had heard bad, I had heard good and bad. Sullivan was like a con man and he would convince you that he's virtually working for the FBI. You know, he'd always, and ultimately he was sent to jail on income tax evasion and it was the FBI that testified against him.

O'Brien: What was Shapiro like?

Trump: He was like a third-rate, local, real estate Mob guy. Nothing spectacular.

So Trump tells O'Brien that he heard Sullivan was connected with the Hoffa murder and Shapiro was a "Mob guy." But he testified before state regulators that Shapiro and Sullivan were "well thought of." And though Trump told O'Brien that he wanted to distance himself from Sullivan, he considered investing in a drywall company with him.

After the New Jersey Division of Gaming Enforcement granted Trump his casino license in 1982, they compelled him to buy the property he had leased from Shapiro and Sullivan. Trump eventually paid $8 million for the property. New Jersey regulators later banned Sullivan and Shapiro from the gaming industry.

Trump persisted in telling journalists that he did no business with the Mob. As he told the *Wall Street Journal* in September 2016,

If people were like me, there would be no Mob, because I don't play that game. I am the cleanest guy there is.

Trump also disclaimed recollection of other organized crime figures with whom he had certainly been involved. One was mobster Robert LiButti, who had close ties to John Gotti. LiButti had referred to Gotti on a law enforcement tape as "my boss." Because of that connection, LiButti was eventually banned from all New Jersey casinos.

Trump and LiButti had a long and sometimes stormy relationship. Trump flew LiButti on his private helicopter from New York to Atlantic City so LiButti could gamble at one of his casinos. Trump Plaza executive Jack O'Donnell said of their relationship,

It isn't like [Trump] saw LiButti once or twice—he spent time with him, saw him multiple times.

LiButti gambled heavily in Trump's casino. He was a high roller, their biggest customer. Between 1986 and 1989 his gambling losses totaled $11 million. It was illegal in New Jersey for casino owners to give cash gifts to high rollers. Regulators fined Trump Plaza for giving LiButti $1.65 million in expensive cars, which LiButti sold for cash. LiButti claimed Trump once paid him $250,000, which if true would have cost Trump his casino license. The casino regulators refused to credit LiButti and accepted Trump's denial.

LiButti and his attractive daughter Edith partied and hung out on Trump's yacht. They even had a deal for Trump to buy a thoroughbred racehorse LiButti owned named Alibi, which Trump wanted to rename "DJ Trump." The price was an inflated $500,000. Trump backed out of the deal when Alibi came up lame. It has been suggested that LiButti, a horse breeder, sold other horses to Trump at inflated prices to disguise cash payments being made to a high roller mobster. There is a video of Trump standing next to LiButti at a 1988 *WrestleMania* match in Atlantic City. Nearby was *Wheel of Fortune* hostess Vanna White.

Trump hit on LiButti's daughter. Not a good idea. According to David Cay Johnston, who followed Trump for 30 years, LiButti confronted Trump about it and said, "Donald, I'll fucking pull your balls from your legs." Not something one would forget!

Trump told Yahoo! News in an email in early 2016,

During the years I very successfully ran the casino business [the casinos went bankrupt], I knew many high rollers. I assume Mr. LiButti was one of them, but I don't recognize the name.

And, referring to LiButti, in February 1991, Trump told the *Philadelphia Inquirer*,

I have heard he is a high roller, but if he was standing here in front of me, I wouldn't know what he looked like.

But Edith Creamer, the mobster's daughter, told investigative reporter Michael Isikoff that Trump and her father knew each other quite well:

He's a liar. Of course he knew him. I flew in the helicopter with Ivana and the kids. My dad flew it up and down [to Atlantic City]. My 35th birthday party was at the Plaza and Donald was there. After the party, we went on his boat, his big yacht. I like Trump, but it pisses me off that he denies knowing my father. That hurts me.

Later, in 2016, he told the *Wall Street Journal,* "LiButti was a high roller. I found him to be a nice guy. But I had nothing to do with him."

Nothing to do with him? Trump must have known that LiButti was fond of loudly expressing racist and sexist slurs as he gambled at the Trump Plaza casino in Atlantic City. He also loudly swore like a sailor. Trump gave LiButti a private room to play in from which black and female employees were excluded. Trump was never noted for meticulousness when it came to tolerating race or sex discrimination. State investigators fined Trump $200,000 for what happened at his casino with LiButti.

So which was it? He didn't know LiButti, but he was a "nice guy." LiButti died in 2014, denying to the end that he had links with the Mob.

In 2008, the Trump SoHo hotel opened its doors. It was a 46-story, 391-unit glass tower condominium hotel in lower Manhattan. Trump partnered on the construction and development of the project with the Bayrock Group, consisting of partners Tamir Sapir, Felix Sater, and

Tevfik Arif. Sapir was a Russian billionaire oligarch whom Trump called a "great friend." He had a $5 million apartment in Trump Tower. Trump had partnered with Sapir in various real estate projects aside from Trump SoHo.

Trump showcased the project in 2007 on *The Apprentice*. The plan was to sell the 391 units with the proviso that the same person could occupy a unit for no more than 29 days in a 36-day period or for more than 120 days a year. When not occupied by the condominium owner, Trump SoHo could rent out the apartment to hotel guests.

Felix Sater, one of Bayrock's partners, was a convicted felon with ties to organized crime. The son of a Russian mobster, he had offices in Trump Tower. In 1993, before he met Trump, Sater did prison time for thrusting a shattered margarita glass stem into the face of a commodities broker over an argument in a bar. In 1998, Sater was also the subject of a federal money-laundering and stock-manipulation complaint, which was filed under seal, where it remains. One of his friends told the *New York Times* in December 2007 that Sater pleaded guilty to the 1998 complaint and was cooperating with prosecutors. The complaint arose out of a $40 million stock manipulation scheme involving 19 stockbrokers and organized crime figures from four Mafia families.

According to a March 2000 federal indictment, which was part of the original investigation, Sater was an "unindicted co-conspirator." It charged that he was a key figure in the $40 million stock scam involving a brokerage firm he operated "for the primary purpose of earning money through fraud involving manipulation of the prices of securities." The naming of such a key figure as an unindicted co-conspirator supports the *Times* story that Sater indeed had "flipped" and turned state's evidence.

Sater occupied space at Trump Tower two floors below Trump's offices, and he negotiated deals on Trump's behalf to put his name on buildings and get equity in hotel projects, such as the Trump SoHo condos in New York City and the Trump International Hotel & Tower in Fort Lauderdale. At the 2007 launch party for the Trump SoHo, Trump praised the greatness of the project. Standing beside him in the kickoff photograph was Felix Sater. As late as 2010, after Trump admitted he knew of Sater's criminal past, Trump issued business cards to Sater, giving as his title "Senior Adviser" to Donald Trump. It was Sater who, after Trump announced for president in 2015, gleefully sent an email to his longtime pal Michael Cohen that said in part, "We will get this done, I will get Putin on this program and we will get Donald elected," and "I know how to play it . . . our boy can become president of the USA and we can engineer it. *I will get all of Putin's team to buy in on this.*"

Sater escorted Ivanka and Don Jr. around Moscow in 2006 when their father was scouting real estate in Russia. They stayed for several days at the Hotel National Moscow opposite the Kremlin, according to the *New York Times.*

A lawsuit brought in 2010 against Sater and his partner Tevfik Arik alleged that "for most of its existence [Bayrock] was substantially and covertly mob-owned and operated," engaging "in a pattern of continuous, related crimes, including mail, wire, and bank fraud; tax evasion; money laundering; conspiracy; bribery; extortion; and embezzlement."

Sater is a force field of a person, a very likable con man. I ran into him at a cocktail party in the Hamptons, where we stood no more than 50 feet away from Bill and Hillary Clinton, who were also guests. Sater was proud of a selfie he had just taken of himself with Bill Clinton. (Yes, *mes amis*, in the Hamptons things like this happen.) He told me that Trump is the first president in U.S. history to host a reality TV show from 1600 Pennsylvania Avenue. And so he is.

Trump SoHo was engulfed in controversy. Both the SoHo Alliance and the Greenwich Village Society for Historic Preservation opposed the project because they believed the building was not in keeping with the neighborhood's character. It stuck out like a sore thumb. There were fatal accidents at the jobsite. Workers at the site died or sustained serious injuries because of allegedly unsafe working conditions. The Department of Buildings issued four violations and a stop-work order. Work did not resume for seven months. Structural engineers determined that the wooden framework of the building did not meet industry standards.

Trump frequently made misrepresentations to get customers into the store, and the Trump SoHo was no exception. In August 2009, buyers of ten condos, including French soccer star Olivier Dacourt, commenced an action in Manhattan federal court against Trump SoHo, claiming there had been "fraudulent misrepresentations and deceptive sales practices" by inflating the number of purchases to attract more buyers. It was a standard Trump promotional technique. He invented paid members to get more members into his Trump National Mar-a-Lago golf club. In November 2011, Trump settled with the Trump SoHo plaintiffs by refunding 90 percent of their deposits, a whopping $3.16 million. Prior to the settlement, Trump had tried to scam other condo owners by offering them partial refunds of up to 50 percent if they did not join in the pending suit. The scam was so close to the chalk that as part of the settlement deal plaintiffs had to agree not to cooperate with prosecutors unless they were subpoenaed. The condo owners' lawyers were required to write a letter to the New York County district attorney stating that defendants had not violated the criminal laws. It would be the province of the district attorney to make this determination—not the victims—but DAs always take into account such statements before deciding whether or not to prosecute. In November 2017, the Trump Organization announced it would sever all ties with the Trump SoHo property by the end of the year.

The Trump SoHo reeked of criminal activity, and the aroma of fraud was everywhere. According to the *Financial Times*, an alleged Kazakh money-laundering operation channeled millions through apartment sales. Although Trump showcased the Trump SoHo on *The Apprentice* in 2007 as another member of the Trump family of enterprises, Trump tried to distance himself from it when the project began to sail into stormy waters, stating that he did not own the property but merely managed it under a licensing deal with the Russians. But whether owner, developer, apparent owner, or licensor, Trump was in the Trump SoHo up to his eyeballs. His partners were mobsters, and his fingerprints were everywhere.

In 2012, the New York County district attorney's office was reportedly about to indict Ivanka and Don Jr. over alleged misrepresentations made to investors about the value of the Trump SoHo hotel. District Attorney Cy Vance decided not to bring criminal charges against Trump's children. Eyebrows raised when it came out that Trump's attorney Marc Kasowitz had donated $25,000 to Vance's re-election campaign before he met with Vance to discuss the possible prosecution. Vance returned the money before the meeting, but less than six months later, after he decided not to prosecute, Kasowitz donated $32,000 to Vance's campaign and helped raise an additional $18,000. This time, the money was returned only when journalists inquired about it.

Another Trump Mob connection, perhaps more peripheral, was Russian organized crime figure Vyacheslav Ivankov, who moved his operations to the United States in 1992. The FBI had been trying to find him for three years before he turned up living in a luxury apartment in Trump Tower. Ivankov, a major player at the Trump Taj Mahal casino in Atlantic City, was extradited to Russia in 2004, where he stood trial for murder. The trial ended in his acquittal. In 2009, as Ivankov walked to his car from lunch at a Moscow Thai restaurant, an unknown sniper perched on a rooftop shot him in the stomach. He died less than three months later of the single gunshot wound.

Long as the list of criminal associations and business dealings with mobsters has been, Trump fell all over himself with implausible denials. His testimony about Robert LiButti and Felix Sater was reminiscent of the denials of Alger Hiss at his confrontation with Whittaker Chambers.

In a deposition conducted in 2011, Trump testified that he spoke to Sater "for a period of time." Yet at another deposition, conducted two years later, using the same phraseology he used for LiButti, Trump testified about Sater: "If he were sitting in the room right now, I really wouldn't know what he looked like."

Asked by a reporter about Sater, he responded, "Felix Sater, boy, I have to even think about it. I'm not that familiar with him."

He apparently forgot the photograph of himself standing next to Sater at the 2007 launch party for the Trump SoHo.

If you are in the casino business or the president of the United States, however, criminal associations count. Yet despite the immutable evidence of his sordid underworld connections—Castellano, Salerno, Cody, Halloran, Sullivan, Shapiro, Winzinger, LiButti, Weichselbaum, Sater, and the Russian Mob—Trump never got his story straight. Either he flatly denied Mob dealings, even under oath, or failed to identify criminals like Robert LiButti or Felix Sater, whom he had been photographed standing next to. It was all part of his aversion to shame and disgrace. He had to construct an alternative universe in which he was blameless.

Trump continued to repeat his flat denial of Mob association even in sworn testimony. At a deposition in a libel action that he brought against Timothy O'Brien for claiming that his wealth was overstated, Trump was asked this question under oath:

Q: Have you previously associated with individuals you knew were associated with organized crime?

A: I haven't.

At a deposition in a Bayrock matter involving Felix Sater, he testified as follows:

Q: Other than "this situation," have you ever before associated with individuals you knew were associated with organized crime?

A: Not that I know of.

But in February 1999, when Trump visited the small Ozark resort town of Branson, Missouri, which was hosting the Miss Universe pageant, he sang a different song. Perhaps in an unguarded moment, he made a statement that undercuts all of these protestations, sworn and unsworn:

> Usually, I build buildings. *I have to deal with the unions, the Mob, some of the roughest men you've ever seen in your life.* I come here and see these incredible beauties. It's a lot of fun.

Why would Trump, a major real estate player, successful brander, and gifted promoter have had such extensive dealings with the Mob, any more than he needed to involve the Russians in his campaign for the presidency? What did they bring to the table? Was it all about the money? Or did he have a screw loose somewhere? Many entrepreneurs find themselves doing business with crooks. Sometimes they have no choice. The Swedish economist Anders Aslund, an expert on how Russia became a market economy, whom author Craig Unger interviewed for his book *House of Trump, House of Putin*, said, "Crooks have two big advantages. First, they're prepared to pay more money than honest people. And second, they will always lose if you sue them because they are known to be crooks." These advantages would surely have appealed to Trump.

"No other occupant of the White House has anything close to Trump's record of repeated social and business dealings with mobsters, swindlers and other crooks," wrote David Cay Johnston for Politico in 2016.

Was Trump married to the Mob? It certainly would appear they dated, slept together, or were possibly engaged. Most of those who know the intimate details are dead.

7

TRUMP AND HIS WOMEN

TRUMP'S MISOGYNY

You have to treat 'em like shit.
—Donald Trump, speaking of his attitude toward women,
reported in *New York* magazine, November 9, 1992

Trump's history with women is heavily earmarked by sex, lies, videotape—and litigation.

In the 1970s, when Trump was in his twenties, he frequented Le Club, a darkened, boozy disco where married men on the dance floor nuzzled blonde women festooned in sparkling jewelry. As he later wrote in *The Art of the Deal*, "[Le Club's] membership included some of the most successful men and the most beautiful women in the world. It was the sort of place where you were likely to see a wealthy 75-year-old guy walk in with three blondes from Sweden."

As noted earlier, it was at Le Club that Trump met Roy Cohn. Cohn also represented Ian Schrager and Steve Rubell, who owned Studio 54, on the West Side. Studio 54 was really the "room where it happens," its portals guarded by burly bouncers. The nightclub had its own connections to the Mob. A raid by federal agents in December 1978 sought documents showing ties with organized crime figures. Schrager's father, Louis, alias "Max the Jew," was the legendary chief of the Williamsburg, Brooklyn, loan shark and racketeering operations. Louis, a convicted felon, was an associate of Meyer Lansky.

Cocaine, the drug of choice among the rich and famous, was ubiquitous. Recreational drugs were plentiful, gays performed sex acts in the men's room, and half-naked busboys cleaned up the remains of the evening. Studio 54 attracted city leaders, Hollywood stars, and a Technicolor cross-section of other revelers, straight, gay, and bisexual. The nightclub achieved some cachet when Jackie O turned up with her sister one night, along with a host of other celebrities.

Trump remembered seeing a couple "getting screwed" on a sofa. "I saw things happening there that to this day, I have never seen again," Trump told Timothy O'Brien. "I would watch supermodels getting screwed, well-known supermodels getting screwed on a bench in the middle of the room. There were seven of them and each one was getting screwed by a different guy. This was in the middle of the room."

If anyone taught Trump that it was legally possible to treat women like shit, it was Cohn. In 1977, Trump told Cohn he planned to marry a Canadian model, Ivana Zelnickova, who said she was a former member of the Czech ski team. Cohn insisted that they sign a prenuptial agreement. Cohn professed an expertise in marriage. In *How to Stand Up for Your Rights and Win!*, he wrote,

While there are things that each of us wouldn't do for love or money, marriage is an act often undertaken for either motive, or both.... Accordingly, the odds of success in marriage are likely to be increased if both agree mutually, before marrying, what it is that each expects to put into the relationship and what each expects to get out. It's difficult to imagine ... that the flush of the moment may become the flush of the toilet as the relationship goes down the tubes.

Speaking of prenups, Trump said, "If you're a person of wealth, you have to have one." Trump wanted to qualify as a "person of wealth." He told Larry King, "I am a great prenup believer. You have to have them even though they are nasty documents." Cohn found just the right lawyer to represent Ivana in connection with the agreement. The lawyer had a lucrative association with Cohn on at least one case and had been a fixture passenger on Cohn's yacht, the *Defiance*. Cohn drew the prenup—a stingy contract that gave Ivana only $20,000 a year.

In 1987, on Cohn's advice, Trump renegotiated the deal preemptively. Cohn knew the original deal was so niggardly that it could not withstand judicial scrutiny. By then, Ivana had borne Trump three children. Trump now agreed, in the event of a divorce, to give Ivana a $10 million lump sum payment plus $350,000 a year as alimony.

The "renegotiation" was a setup. Trump had known for some time that he was going to divorce Ivana. In the late 1980s he had taken a mistress, a ravishing 26-year-old model, actress, and former Miss Georgia named Marla Maples. Initially, Maples lived in the shadows, hiding behind a secret code name and sequestering herself either in a Trump friend's Southampton beach house or aboard his *Trump Princess* yacht. Eventually, Trump became recklessly exhibitionistic in sporting his liaison with Maples under the eye of the press and the nose of Ivana. Maples herself made headlines when she told the *New York Post* that Trump gave her "the best sex she ever had."

"He had taken to unfurling a giant poster of . . . [Maples] and showing it to businessmen," wrote Wayne Barrett in his 1991 book. "He had even run the risk in 1988 of storing her furniture and other personal items with the storage company Ivana and he used for the Trump Tower apartment during its second reconstruction. She was the heart of his double life, and he began slipping off to see her in the middle of his workday, even ducking key staff meetings."

When Trump's increasingly public relationship with Maples made the marriage untenable, Ivana sued for divorce, alleging adultery, as well as "cruel and inhuman treatment" in that he had publicly flaunted his relationship with Maples during the time they were married. For his part, Trump suggested that had he not been caught cheating, the adulterous relationship would have continued. He said in a 1994 interview with ABC's *Primetime Live*: "My life was so great in so many ways. The business was so great . . . a beautiful girlfriend, a beautiful wife, a beautiful everything. Life was just a bowl of cherries."

It has been said that the 1980s, the decade of excess, ended with the Drexel bankruptcy and the Trump divorce. By 1990, their marriage was on the rocks. Ivana had become, Trump thought, overly involved with his businesses, mainly the Plaza Hotel in New York and the Trump's Castle casino in Atlantic City. Trump had bought the Plaza in 1988 for $407.5 million, mostly with borrowed funds. It was the most money ever paid for a hotel. Ivana was responsible for redecorating the trophy property, and she did so in what many thought were vulgarly garish tones proclaiming a neo–gilded age of opulence and over-the-top excess. He grew to resent Ivana's role. Deflecting the real reason for the divorce, his desire to marry Marla Maples, he wrote in his 1997 book *The Art of the Comeback* that he regretted having allowed Ivana to run his businesses:

> My big mistake with Ivana was taking her out of the role of wife and allowing her to run one of my casinos in Atlantic City, then the Plaza Hotel. The problem was work was all she wanted to talk about. When I got home at night, rather than talking about the softer subjects of life, she wanted to tell me how well the Plaza was doing, or what a great day the casino had.

That February he told columnist Liz Smith, "I have had it with Ivana. She has gotten to be like Leona Helmsley."

Ivana and Donald were divorced in 1992 after a 15-year marriage. They split largely under the terms of the 1987 postnuptial agreement. In the end, Ivana got royally screwed. The 1987 postnup required, among other things, that she return all of his gifts in the event of a split—cars, furs, jewelry, and anything else of value. He blamed the harsh treatment on his lawyer. Ivana later testified in their 1992 divorce proceeding that Trump apologized and said, "It's just one of those Roy Cohn numbers." Interesting claim since Cohn died in 1986!

Seeking to sort it all out, the *New York Times* brought suit to unseal the Trump divorce papers residing in the court files. They lost. In New York, the papers in a matrimonial action are shrouded in secrecy by court order because of their frequently salacious nature. In the final divorce, Trump reportedly paid Ivana $25 million, but she may have been able to up the ante even further. Claiming she had been lied to in the settlement negotiations, she sued Trump after the divorce was final for fraudulently misleading her lawyers about the true value of his holdings. Trump settled the case. Because the fraud case was not a matrimonial action, the papers should have been publicly available in the court records, but the files revealing the details mysteriously disappeared from the archives of the New York County Clerk.

No wonder Ivana appeared in *The First Wives Club* in 1996, with the line, "Ladies, you have to be strong and independent. And remember: don't get mad, get everything." In her 1995 "survival guide," *The Best Is Yet to Come: Coping with Divorce and Enjoying Life Again*, she gave women advice she didn't give herself. To women who cannot tolerate infidelity, she said, "Get yourself a great settlement, and before you do, take his wallet to the cleaners." Her postnup with Trump, however, made sure she would wind up with something short of that.

The saga of the first Trump divorce is riddled with mistreatment of Ivana. In his fascinating 1993 book *Lost Tycoon: The Many Lives of Donald J. Trump*, journalist Harry Hurt III described a night in 1989 when an enraged Trump was said to have "raped" Ivana. She had told the story under oath in a deposition given in the 1990s, in the matrimonial litigation. In Hurt's account, Trump was furious that a "scalp reduction" operation he had undergone to eliminate a bald spot had been unexpectedly painful. Ivana had recommended the plastic surgeon. In retaliation, Hurt wrote, Trump yanked out a handful of his wife's hair, and then forced himself on her sexually. Afterward, according to the book, she spent the night locked in a bedroom, crying. In the morning, Trump asked her, "Does it hurt?" Trump has denied both the rape allegation and the suggestion that he had a scalp-reduction procedure.

Trump, who has a very selective memory, did not forget Hurt. In a 2015 tweet, Trump denounced Hurt as a "dummy dope," a "failed writer" who had written a "failed book." Hurt said that the incident, which is detailed in Ivana's deposition, was confirmed by two of her friends. Trump's lawyers insisted that Hurt's publisher, W. W. Norton, place in the front of each book a statement from Ivana in which she qualified the accusation. In the course of "marital relations," she said, she "felt violated, as the love and tenderness, which he normally exhibited toward me, was absent." She added that during the deposition, "I stated that my husband had raped me. I referred to this as a 'rape,' but I do not want my words to be interpreted in a literal or criminal sense." Ivana pulled away from the sensational allegation to secure the divorce settlement, which guaranteed her $25 million in cash. Hurt characterized Ivana's statement as a "non-denial denial."

Trump was so incensed at Hurt that in 2016, when Hurt sought to reprint his book online 23 years after its initial publication, he had his lawyer, Michael Cohen, threaten Hurt: "You write a story that has Mr. Trump's name in it and the word 'rape,' and I'm going to mess your life up, for as long as you're on this frickin' planet." Hurt re-published the book.

In December 2016, Trump evicted Hurt from his Trump International Golf Club in West Palm Beach. As Hurt relayed in a Facebook post, he had gone to the club with two friends as the guest of David Koch, a billionaire industrialist and Trump Club member. Koch is a reliably heavy contributor to Republican and conservative causes. Hurt, a scratch golfer, is known for his colorful vintage golfing attire. Waiting for his tee time, Hurt walked over to Trump on the course to congratulate the president-elect on his victory.

According to Hurt, he said: "Congratulations, sir," and extended his hand. Trump lashed out at him, saying: "You were rough on me, Harry. Really rough. That shit you wrote." Hurt looked Trump straight in the eye. "It's all true," he said. "Not the way you wrote it," Trump replied. He then told Hurt it was "inappropriate" for him to play at the club, and had his security detail escort Hurt, Koch, and the two friends to the parking lot. "We played Emerald Dunes [a nearby golf club where Koch also belonged] instead." Hurt observed that Emerald Dunes is a "much better golf course than Trump International."

When the Daily Beast in July 2015 alleged that Ivana testified during the divorce proceedings that Trump had raped her during the marriage, Trump threatened to sue the Daily Beast. Of course, he quite sensibly never did. Michael Cohen called the Daily Beast and improperly advised that "you cannot rape your spouse. And there's very clear case law."

As a lawyer, Cohen should have known better—spousal rape has been for some time unlawful throughout the United States—and he later corrected himself, terming his remarks "inarticulate."

In the early 1990s, after the divorce and settlement, Trump sued Ivana for $25 million for writing a fictionalized account of their 15-year marriage. Titled *For Love Alone*, it's a spicy story about a beautiful model who marries a tycoon only to lose him to another woman. Trump claimed that the book violated a nondisclosure clause in their separation agreement. He also sought a gag order to stop publication of the book.

Trump prevailed in the New York appellate court on the gag order, which upheld its validity. Trump's lawyer, Jay Goldberg, said Trump might also sue to retrieve the multimillion-dollar divorce settlement Trump paid Ivana, which had been, at least in part, for her silence. The case was eventually settled, but the terms are under seal. *For Love Alone* is still being offered on Amazon. Trump's hardball approach only helped Ivana publicize her book. It's a lesson he seems not to have learned in the White House, as his intemperate tweets have caused books by James Comey, Michael Wolff, and Omarosa Manigault to soar onto the bestseller lists.

After the divorce, Trump married Maples, who was already preg-

nant with his fourth child, Tiffany. The wedding occurred in 1993 at
the Plaza Hotel. The social pages reported there was "not a wet eye in
the house." The marriage lasted three and a half years. A clause in the
prenup agreement said Marla would get a paltry $2.5 million, subject
to escalation after a certain number of years of marriage. To avoid the
escalator, Trump had to give timely notice of intention to divorce. He
did, and Marla was history. Trump's lawyer, Jay Goldberg, said the prenup
was "solid as concrete."

Marla hired Ivana's lawyer to try to upset the prenup, but Trump
promised to play "hardball," as Marla in the meantime had acquired another love interest. Trump has said that he was married to "two wonderful women" and blames the collapse of his first two marriages to his
devotion to business. "It is unfair being married to Donald Trump," he
spinned it, "since business comes first."

There is also a story that before they were married, he pressured Maples to pose nude for *Playboy*. Journalist Glenn Plaskin reported in August 1990 for the Tribune Media Services, "Trump himself was on the
phone negotiating the fee," remembers a top *Playboy* editor. "He wanted
her to do the nude layout. She didn't." ("I'm thankful for my body, but
I didn't want to exploit it," Marla said. "How would I ever be taken seriously?") A *Washington Post* article published in January 2018 puts the
Playboy offer at $2 million.

Maples was not the first woman in his life that he wanted to pose
nude. According to Wayne Barret's *Trump: the Greatest Show on Earth*,
written in 1991, he wanted his female staffers to do a spread in *Playboy*
called "The Girls of Trump." He offered *Playboy* everything from full
nudes to breasts to "wet lip" shots. Trump evidently had a one-track
mind. In a bizarre interview with Marla on Robin Leach's *Lifestyles of
the Rich and Famous* in 1994, he described their one-year-old daughter
Tiffany as follows:

Leach: Donald, what does Tiffany have of yours and what does
Tiffany have of Marla's?

Trump: I think that she's got a lot of Marla, she's a really beautiful baby. She's got Marla's legs. We don't know whether or not she's got this part yet [Trump cupping his hands under his chest]. But time will tell.

Trump was first, last, and always a womanizer. Even while married to Ivana and Marla, he took in the club scene with great relish. His lust for women over the years seemed to morph into unwanted sexual encounters. At the time Trump took office, there were at least 16 complaints brought by women who charged him with sexual misconduct of some kind, ranging from groping to sexual assault. There is no telling how many other claims Trump has settled with six-figure payments papered over with nondisclosure agreements.

White House press secretary Sarah Huckabee Sanders said that Trump's official stance on the sexual assault accusations is that "every single one of the women is lying." According to veteran journalist Bob Woodward in his 2018 book *Fear: Trump in the White House*, Trump expressed his approach as follows: "You've got to deny, deny, deny and push back on these women," he said. "If you admit to anything and any culpability, then you're dead." This was the very approach that Don McGahn, the White House counsel, fed to Trump's Supreme Court nominee Brett Kavanaugh, who was threatened by claims of sexual impropriety that nearly capsized his confirmation to the Supreme Court.

Trump was for many years the proprietor of the annual Miss Universe international beauty pageant. It airs in more than 190 countries worldwide and is seen by more than half a billion people annually. Along with Miss World, Miss International, and Miss Earth, Miss Universe is one of the "big four" international beauty contests. Trump savored his connection with the pageant. It brought him celebrity, glitz, access to beautiful women, and the chance to make international contacts that might be sources of finance for his business. It was the 2013 Miss Universe contest in Moscow that led him to visit Russia for the first time.

A number of former Miss USAs and Miss Teen USAs accused him of entering their dressing rooms while they were in stages of undress.

Still more charged him with groping and other inappropriate behavior. Trump told Howard Stern in a 2005 radio interview that he could "get away with things like that."

What follows is a partial list of the women who have complained about Trump's conduct. I have limited myself to those making the most plausible claims, in cases where litigation is pending or threatened. There were many more who kept incidents to themselves. Many of the allegations, other than those indicated, have rested undenied to this day. Gloria Allred, the high-profile feminist lawyer who specializes in sexual harassment and sexual misconduct cases, represented four of the women; only one of them, Summer Zervos, filed suit. Later, for unexplained reasons, Allred withdrew as Zervos's attorney. (Allred represented 33 of the women who accused Bill Cosby of drugging and raping them. Trump despises Allred. In 2012, Trump called in to TMZ, the celebrity news website, and offered to show defense attorney Allred his penis. "I think Gloria would be very, very impressed with it," bragged Trump.)

Jessica Leeds, a New York businesswoman, claimed that in the early 1980s she sat next to Trump in the first-class section of a flight from the Midwest. She said that about 45 minutes after takeoff, Trump began touching her breasts and tried to put his hand up her skirt. "He was like an octopus," she said. "His hands were everywhere. It was an assault." Trump denied her allegation and implied she was not attractive enough. "Believe me," he said, "she would not be my first choice," a flippant reference to her appearance. Trump's denial was a litigation ploy known as the "negative pregnant." In his denial, he implied he was not above such behavior.

Jill Harth and her husband were Trump's disgruntled business associates in the world of beauty pageants and contests. In 1997 she commenced a federal lawsuit for $125 million against Trump, alleging, among other things, sexual assault, sexual harassment, and attempted rape. She subsequently withdrew the suit "without prejudice" about the same time that her husband's company settled a separate breach of contract suit against Trump arising out of its work on an Atlantic City beauty contest. The terms of the settlement are under seal. During the 2016 campaign, Harth emailed Trump seeking work as a makeup consultant. Trump's personal attorney Michael Cohen, who would manage other sex claims against Trump, issued a statement in February 2016 stating that Harth "would acknowledge" that the sexual allegations were false and there was "no truth to the story." Harth would acknowledge nothing of the kind. She responded that the purported denial was made without her permission and that she basically sticks to her story.

Temple Taggart McDowell was the 21-year-old Miss Utah in 1997. She said Trump introduced himself to her at a rehearsal by forcibly kissing her on the lips—she knew he was married to Marla Maples at the time. This was not the only occasion that Trump treated her this way, she said. She told the *New York Times* in March 2016 that she knew of other contestants he kissed on the mouth. Trump denied her charges and said that he is a germophobe and does not kiss strangers on the lips. Trump threatened to sue her after the election. McDowell promised to countersue him if he did. "Enough is enough. I feel like he is trying to bully and frighten us into silence. Mr. Trump, that is not going to work with me."

Summer Zervos, the only one of the women to have sued Trump, met him in 2005 when she became a contestant on *The Apprentice*. Zervos alleged that she was "ambushed by Mr. Trump on more than one occasion." In 2007 she claimed she contacted Trump about a job. Accordingly, she claimed, he invited her to his New York office, where he twice kissed her on the mouth, making her "feel uncomfortable, nervous, and embarrassed." Subsequently, he asked her to meet him at the Beverley Hills Hotel, where he occupied a suite of rooms. She said that Trump was sexually aggressive during the meeting, French kissing her, groping her breast, and thrusting his genitals against her. Trump denied the allegations, claiming that Zervos had continued contact with him as late as 2016, when she invited him to visit her restaurant. He called Zervos a liar. She in turn sued for defamation in New York State Supreme Court three days before he took office, claiming he had defamed her when he stated she had lied about her allegations.

Trump sought dismissal of the Zervos case, claiming that a sitting president cannot be sued in a civil action in state court and that the First Amendment protects his comments about Zervos in that he stated they were opinions. He also sought a stay of action for the duration of his presidency to avoid "a private witch-hunt that could threaten to interfere with the operations of the executive branch and the federal government." A hurdle to Trump's argument was the U.S. Supreme Court ruling that had allowed Paula Jones's suit against Bill Clinton to proceed while Clinton was still in office. After all, if the president refuses to pay his American Express bill or his dentist, can he be sued in a civil action? Of course he can. In our country, needless to say, even the president is not above the law.

The New York State Supreme Court judge denied Trump's motion to dismiss, holding that Trump's repeated denials that he had groped Zervos were assertions of fact, not opinions. Trump appealed the decision, arguing that his statements about Zervos were "opinions made in quintessentially political forums during a political campaign." The appellate judges affirmed the lower court, both as to this contention that he was merely expressing an opinion and the claim of presidential immunity in a civil action. Zervos's case now proceeds to discovery and trial.

Zervos subpoenaed Trump and the Trump campaign for documents that might evidence similar complaints that he "subjected any woman to unwanted sexual touching and/or sexually inappropriate behavior." In October 2018, the court quashed the subpoena to the extent it compelled Trump to answer questions related to *other women* who claimed he made unwanted sexual advances. The court restricted the inquiry to Zervos's allegation that he inappropriately kissed and touched *her* on two occasions. The court said, however, that Trump would also have to give discovery as to whether he had a policy as to how he should respond to other women's allegations of sexual misconduct and name any "fixers" who might have assisted him in dealing with those charges.

The alleged defamation, according to Zervos's complaint, is that Trump "knowingly, intentionally and maliciously threw" Zervos, as well as other women, "under the bus, with conscious disregard of the impact that repeatedly calling them liars would have upon their lives and reputations." Strangely, Zervos seeks in the suit only $2,914 in damages for lost business at her restaurant plus unquantified damages for emotional distress, leading some to wonder whether the suit might be some kind of political stunt. Why did she sue for defamation rather than for the unwanted sexual contact? Most probably because the sexual misconduct claims date back 10 years prior to the complaint and may be barred by the applicable statute of limitations. New York has a one-year statute of limitations on libel, and the time bar would not apply to the alleged defamation, which occurred in 2016.

Ironically, Trump also argued in the Zervos case that the freedom of speech clause of the First Amendment protects his statements, allowing him to slander a private individual in the course of a heated political campaign. This position ignored the landmark 1964 Supreme Court case *New York Times v. Sullivan*, making it difficult under the First Amendment for public figures to sue for libel. Trump has said he wants to sue the *New York Times*, CNN, and other mainstream media organizations for defamation and "fake news," but he concedes that he would have an uphill fight under *Sullivan*. Trump has called upon the Supreme Court to overrule *Sullivan* so he can more easily sue the mainstream media. *Sullivan*, however, is not at all relevant in the Zervos case. The Supreme Court never dealt in *Sullivan* with the unfettered right of private citizens to sue public officials for defamation.

Trump's instinctive response to the Zervos suit and subpoena was his characteristic denial and counterattack, to try the case in the court of public opinion: "All I can say is it's totally fake news. It's just fake. It's fake. It's made-up stuff, and it's disgraceful, what happens, but that happens in the—that happens in the world of politics."

Trump's lawyers will have to decide whether it is just too dangerous for him to litigate the Zervos case. He will not want to risk perjury in testifying about the facts at issue over a suit for $2,900 in lost restaurant revenues. The jury is out on that one.

Alva Johnson. Finally, there is the only accuser to come forward since Trump took office, and the only one to claim inappropriate behavior during the campaign. Alva Johnson, a former Trump campaign worker, has sued Trump, claiming he tried to kiss her on the mouth as he exited a recreational vehicle outside a Tampa rally on August 24, 2016. The recreational vehicle was used as a mobile office as the campaign traveled the state. Johnson has alleged she told her boyfriend, stepfather, and mother about Trump's attempt to steal a kiss on the day it happened. She shortly thereafter confided the story to a lawyer specializing in representing sexual abuse victims, as well as to a psychotherapist. Florida attorney general Pam Bondi, an ardent Trump supporter, and Karen Giorno, director of Trump's Florida campaign, are alleged to have been present inside the vehicle, as well as Stephanie Grisham, who was Trump's press director. All three women have denied seeing the alleged incident.

———————

And then there were stories that suspiciously never saw the light of day. Karen McDougal, a *Playboy* centerfold model, alleged that she had had a yearlong extramarital affair with Trump in 2006 and 2007 while he was married to his incumbent wife, Melania. Through a spokesperson, Trump denied the relationship. On August 5, 2016, just three months before the election, McDougal sold her story exclusively to American Media, Inc., owner of the *National Enquirer*. As noted earlier, American Media's CEO and guiding spirit, David Pecker, was a longtime friend of Trump's.

The relationship between Trump and the *National Enquirer* could not have been closer. David Hughes, an American Media board member, spent many years as an executive in Trump's casino business. *Enquirer* board meetings were frequently held at Mar-a-Lago, Trump's opulent Palm Beach estate. An executive even acknowledged to the *New York Times* that American Media made broad efforts to suppress information that might prove damaging to Trump.

American Media entered into a "catch-and-kill" contract with

McDougal wherein, in exchange for $150,000, she granted the tabloid in perpetuity "exclusive life rights to any relationship she has had with a then married man." Many lawyers believe that in the era of Harvey Weinstein, catch-and-kill contracts are unenforceable. In a written statement, American Media at first claimed it did not pay McDougal to hush up her relationship with Trump, but to acquire two years of her fitness columns and magazine covers. Later, under a no-prosecution agreement with the U.S. attorney's office, American Media admitted that it had paid the "hush money" to McDougal in concert with Trump's presidential campaign. It acknowledged that its principal purpose in making the payment was to buy McDougal's silence lest she make "damaging allegations" about Trump on the eve of the presidential election.

McDougal signed an engagement letter with attorney Keith Davidson, the same lawyer who, as will be seen, represented Stormy Daniels. The engagement letter defined the scope of representation as "claims against Donald Trump and/or assisting client in negotiating a confidentiality agreement and/or life rights related to interactions with Donald Trump and/or negotiating assignment of exclusive press opportunities regarding same." McDougal has since sued American Media for a declaratory judgment invalidating the catch-and-kill agreement.

Davidson is a California lawyer who has made his way peddling dirt on Hollywood celebrities, including wrestler Hulk Hogan, *Austin Powers* actor Verne Troyer, and former *Playboy* model and MTV host Tila Tequila. The FBI had quizzed Davidson in 2012 about possible extortion in the Hulk Hogan case. When Davidson cuts a catch-and-kill deal for a client, he gets a contingency fee of as much as 60 percent of the sales price. According to the *New York Times*, the California State Bar suspended his law license for 90 days in 2010 on four counts of professional misconduct. Davidson reported to Michael Cohen that the catch-and-kill deal between McDougal and the *Enquirer* had gone down. Cohen gave Davidson a ringing endorsement: "He has always been professional, ethical, and a true gentleman." You may wonder whether Davidson was somehow working for Trump to facilitate the agreement. There is no evidence of this. Most probably, he was just a lawyer interested in a fee. He got paid when the money changed hands. It was Cohen who secretly recorded conversations with Trump documenting that Trump knew of the $150,000 payoff to McDougal and that he considered buying the rights from the *Enquirer* with cash or a check emanating from a secret slush fund. Criminal proceedings against the *Enquirer* arising out of the McDougal affair resulted in a plea bargain, which may be upended as a result of the *Enquirer*'s alleged attempted extortion of Amazon's Jeff Bezos.

There are other stories of catch-and-kill involving Trump, the *Enquirer*, and a compromising Trump tape that never got published. The *Enquirer*, it is said, outbid celebrity news site TMZ for the tape, which never surfaced again.

Davidson happened to double as the first lawyer to represent Stephanie Clifford, a porn star known professionally as "Stormy Daniels." In October 2016, Clifford contacted ABC's *Good Morning America* about telling her story of an extramarital affair with Trump beginning in 2006, the year after he married Melania, and continuing into 2007. Abruptly, Stormy broke off negotiations with ABC and never told her story. Michael Cohen managed a $130,000 payment to Clifford in order to buy her silence. Cohen initially claimed that he had made the payment out of personal funds, a position that raised questions as to whether he had violated election law as well as ethical rules prohibiting a lawyer from lending financial assistance to a client in a contemplated litigation. It was Cohen who said in 2016, "It is not like I just work for Mr. Trump. I am his friend, and I would do just about anything for him and also his family." Since Trump claimed he had no knowledge of Cohen's deal with Stormy, Cohen could not admit that the $130,000 was Trump money, since that would run afoul of another ethical rule, covering a lawyer's duty to keep the confidences of his client. Later, Cohen changed his story and admitted that the money had come from Trump. Trump's signed 2017 financial disclosure filing revealed that he had "fully reimbursed" Cohen for an amount between $100,001 and $250,000 in 2017. And Rudy Giuliani told reporters in May 2018 that Trump had personally reimbursed Cohen for the $130,000 payment made to Stormy Daniels under her nondisclosure deal with Trump.

Cohen had Stormy enter into a nondisclosure agreement (NDA) dated October 28, 2016, just days before the presidential election. The agreement between Stormy and Essential Consultants LLC, a shell entity created by Cohen as a vehicle for the funds necessary to consummate the deal, provided for $130,000 in hush money to seal Stormy's lips about her affair with Trump. He styled the agreement a "Non-disparagement Agreement," words sugarcoating the true nature of the agreement—to prevent disclosure of a meretricious relationship. To read the NDA is to wonder what Trump thought she didn't have on him. The NDA provides, among other things, that Stormy is not to "directly or indirectly, verbally or otherwise, publish, disseminate, disclose, post or cause to be published, disclosed, or posted . . . any Confidential Information or Tangible and/or Intangible Confidential information created by or relating to [David Dennison]." David Dennison was the contractual alias for Donald Trump. In the NDA, "Confidential Information" is defined to include "information pertaining to [Trump] and/or his family (including but not limited to his children or any alleged children or any of his sexual partners, alleged sexual actions or related matters), and/or friends learned, obtained or acquired by [Stormy], including . . . information contained in letters, e-mails, text messages, agreements, documents, audio or images recordings, electronic data and photographs." Pretty broad language. Everything but the kitchen sink.

In office, Trump continued to litigate. In March 2018, a year and two months into his term, Stormy Daniels sued Trump in California federal court for a declaration that her nondisclosure agreement was null and void. After Trump retaliated by suing her for $20 million in damages, claiming $1 million for each of the 20 times she had allegedly violated the nondisclosure agreement, Stormy amended her complaint to add a claim for libel over his tweet that her story about the threat on her life was a "con job." He had at first flatly denied knowing of or funding the $130,000 payment to Stormy, and then his new-to-the-case attorney Rudy Giuliani acknowledged Trump had known all the time.

Every lawyer I have talked to agrees that the $1 million for each of the 20 violations is unenforceable. Liquidated damages must be a reasonable pre-estimate of damages that will be incurred in situations where it is difficult to calculate with certainty what those damages are. Here, Trump had no damages. What has Stormy damaged by disclosing the affair? Trump's reputation as a loyal husband? He has no reputation to destroy. He is an admitted adulterer. The liquidated damages clause was not a reasonable pre-estimate but an illegal penalty that no court would enforce. And, as a practical matter, there is no way that Stormy had $20 million. Why Trump sued is simply baffling.

The nondisclosure agreement is invalid for another reason. Lawyers say that no court will enforce an agreement to cover up disclosure of an immoral act such as adultery, which is a crime in 20 states, including New York, or a violation of the election laws, or to silence information relevant to the qualifications of a candidate to occupy the office of president on the very eve of a presidential election. The court stayed proceedings in the California civil cases between Stormy and Trump pending the outcome of Cohen's criminal matter in New York. After Cohen pleaded guilty there, he offered to "rescind" the nondisclosure agreement, perhaps to eliminate the possibility that he and Trump might have to testify about the subject matter on deposition.

On March 25, 2018, Anderson Cooper interviewed Stormy Daniels in what had to be the lowest-energy interrogation of all time. Instead of focusing on the money and the contract, Cooper seemed to be more interested in the details of the sexual encounter. A lawyer would have certainly asked trenchant questions such as:

- What did you understand to be Essential Consultants LLC, the entity with which you entered into the contract?

- Whom did you understand Michael Cohen to be representing?

- Did you understand that Trump would sign the nondisclosure agreement and become a party to the agreement?

- Who did you understand was paying you $130,000?

- What did you understand the payment was for?

- You entered into the nondisclosure agreement 10 years after your alleged liaison with Trump on the eve of the presidential election. Why did you think they wanted to buy your silence after so many years?

- Were you told that the contract had something to do with the presidential election, which was ten days off?

- If you agreed to accept money in return for silence, why are you coming forward now?

Instead, Cooper decided to explore the more salacious aspects. For example, he asked about the love play that supposedly started when Stormy spanked Trump on the fanny over his undershorts or the disgusting assertion that Trump said Stormy reminded him of his daughter Ivanka. Cooper, a soft interviewer, ignored the most significant parts of Stormy's story.

During the Cooper interview, Stormy claimed she had been physically threatened. She also asserted she had been pressured by Michael Cohen to enter into the NDA. "They can make your life hell in many different ways," she said she was told.

Glenn Kessler of the *Washington Post* uncovered three additional cases of Trump engaging in sexual violence, which Kessler found convincing because the alleged victims confided the incidents to corroborating witnesses at or about the time they occurred, and long before 2015.

When the *New York Times* published a piece that featured two women claiming Trump had touched them inappropriately, Trump threatened suit and demanded a retraction. "Your article is reckless, defamatory and constitutes libel per se," Trump's lawyer Marc Kasowitz wrote to the *Times*. "It is apparent from, among other things, the timing of the article, that it is nothing more than a politically motivated effort to defeat Mr. Trump's candidacy." The *Times* stood by its story. The stirring letter responding to Kasowitz, dated October 13, 2016, written by *Times* vice president and deputy general counsel David McCraw, was for a time the "most emailed" and "most viewed" on nytimes.com:

Dear Mr. Kasowitz:

I write in response to your letter of October 12, 2016 to Dean Baquet concerning your client Donald Trump, the Republican Party nominee for President of the United States. You write concerning our article "Two Women Say Donald Trump Touched Them Inappropriately" and label the article as "libel per se." You ask that we "remove it from [our] website and issue a full and immediate retraction and apology." We decline to do so.

The essence of a libel claim, of course, is the protection of one's reputation. Mr. Trump has bragged about his non-consensual sexual touching of women. He has bragged about intruding on beauty contestants in their dressing rooms. He acquiesced to a radio host's request to discuss Mr. Trump's own daughter as a "piece of ass." Multiple women not mentioned in our article have publicly come forward to report on Mr. Trump's unwanted advances. Nothing in our article has had the slightest effect on the reputation that Mr. Trump, through his own words and actions, has already created for himself.

But there is a larger and much more important point here. The women quoted in our story spoke out on an issue of national importance—indeed, an issue that Mr. Trump himself discussed with the whole nation watching during Sunday night's presidential debate. Our reporters diligently worked to confirm the women's accounts. They provided readers with Mr. Trump's response, including his forceful denial of the women's reports. It would have been a disservice not just to our readers but to democracy itself to silence their voices. We did what the law allows: We published newsworthy information about a subject of deep public concern. If Mr. Trump disagrees, if he believes that American citizens had no right to hear what these women had to say and that the law of this country forces us and those who would dare to criticize him to stand silent or be punished, we welcome the opportunity to have a court set him straight.

Sincerely,
David McCraw

While one reader demanded that McCraw be disbarred, the positive response to the letter was overwhelming. One reader wrote, "Sending you the highest of fives." A couple in California said they had opened a bottle of wine and toasted the letter. A New Yorker said he wanted to be the "289,000th human being to say thank you." McCraw's favorite was one that ended: "As my sister put it, 'I've never wanted to hang a paragraph from a lawyer on my fridge before.'"

In May 2016, reporters Michael Barbaro and Megan Twohey of the *New York Times* interviewed some 50 women over a six-week period who'd had some contact with Trump over the past four decades in the workplace, at beauty pageants, or socially. Their conclusions were startling:

Their accounts—many relayed here in their own words—reveal unwelcome romantic advances, unending commentary on the female form, a shrewd reliance on ambitious women, and unsettling workplace conduct, according to the interviews, as well as court records and written recollections. The interactions occurred in his offices at Trump Tower, at his homes, at construction sites and backstage at beauty pageants. They appeared to be fleeting, unimportant moments to him, but they left lasting impressions on the women who experienced them.

What emerges from the interviews is a complex, at times contradictory portrait of a wealthy, well-known and provocative man and the women around him, one that defies simple categorization. Some women found him gracious and encouraging. He promoted several to the loftiest heights of his company, a daring move for a major real estate developer at the time.

He simultaneously nurtured women's careers and mocked their physical appearance. "You like your candy," he told an overweight female executive who oversaw the construction of his headquarters in Midtown Manhattan. He could be lewd one moment and gentlemanly the next.

Trump has condoned sexual harassment. He defended disgraced Fox News harasser Roger Ailes, trashed Ailes's accusers, and then engaged Ailes as an adviser. While the sins of the son can't be visited upon the father, Donald Trump Jr. interestingly said that women who can't handle workplace sexual harassment "should go maybe teach kindergarten."

Trump has never apologized to any of the women. Rather, he has flatly denied their allegations. He has also used shopworn techniques of counterattack—threatening litigation, paying hush money, smearing his attackers, and big-lie approaches—all from the playbook of Roy Cohn, his political mentor.

Allegations of sexual misconduct are often hard to prove because they are usually word against word, and the alleged incident often takes place in private, where there would be no witnesses. Such allegations are always more credible when there is a similarity of acts or when the women have confided their story to others at or about the time of the event. In Trump's case, the convincing contemporaneous communications would have necessarily occurred long before he announced he was running for office. The contemporaneous statements remove the claims from the "he said, she said" category of sexual complaint.

During his presidential campaign, Trump was on record leveling sexist remarks and insults about women that should have sunk the candidacy of any mainstream politician of either party. What was Trump's strategy? Counterattack, smear, denigrate Obama, demonize Hillary, and maybe the electorate will forget how crude and insensitive you are.

Aided by the pinky-ringed dirty trickster Roger Stone, Trump produced four women for the presidential debates who alleged the Clintons had mistreated them. Some of the women certainly were paid for their services by the Trump campaign. Trump invited the four to the second presidential debate in St. Louis to sit with his family (eventually, they were seated elsewhere) in a transparent attempt to rattle Clinton and deflect attention from Trump's own censorable sexual conduct.

Trump appeared with the four women at a video "press conference" the day before the debate. The public knew three of the four women: Paula Jones, Juanita Broaddrick, and Kathleen Willey. Jones and Broaddrick had previously claimed that Bill Clinton initiated unwanted sexual conduct with them before he became president.

The only "new" story was that of the fourth woman, Kathy Shelton. Shelton had received $2,500 in cash from "Super PAC Stone" to come forward with a story that kept changing.

Shelton claimed that her 41-year-old cousin Thomas Taylor had raped her in 1975 when she was 12. The court assigned Hillary Clinton, then a law professor in Fayetteville, Arkansas, to defend Taylor, who had requested a female lawyer. Shelton claimed that Hillary had attacked her character, asked explicit sexual questions, and subjected her to polygraph tests and a humiliating psychiatric examination. The record showed no connection between Hillary and polygraph tests administered to Shelton. Apparently she failed one and passed another. Hillary did apply for psychiatric examination. Her affidavit to the court, filed July 28, 1975, stated that "I have been informed that the complainant is emotionally unstable with a tendency to seek out older men and to engage in fantasizing." Hillary got Taylor off on a reduced charge. Shelton's GoFundMe website originally featured both the polygraph tests and the psychiatric examination claims, which she subsequently took down, since she could not prove Hillary's involvement in either.

In 2007, Shelton had said she had no problem with Hillary, who was "just doing her job." But in 2014, after it was clear that Hillary was going to make a run for the White House, Shelton strangely claimed that Hillary "took me through hell." Strange because until a *Newsday* reporter informed her in 2007 that Clinton was the lawyer in the case, Shelton had no idea that Hillary Clinton had even been involved.

That Trump could pay for and seize upon such a flimsy story to deflect attention from his own history with women profanes every concept of fairness. His women were silenced with money in two cases just before the election. The Clintons' women, however, were paraded before the nation. It is an example of the old Roy Cohn/Roger Stone/Donald Trump technique that if you fling enough mud at the wall, some of it just might stick.

THE PROFESSOR OF FRAUD

TRUMP UNIVERSITY AND OTHER FRAUDS

Another of those sickening financial frauds which so sadly memorialize the rapacity of the perpetrators and the gullibility, and perhaps also the cupidity, of the victims.

—Judge Henry Friendly,
in *United States v. Benjamin*,
328 F. 2d 854 (2d Cir. 1964)

In 2004, a management consultant called Michael Sexton approached Trump with the idea of licensing his name for online real estate education courses. The concept quickly morphed into face-to-face seminars featuring professors purportedly handpicked by Trump himself. Sexton's only experience with real estate was owning his own home.

The two eventually made a deal in which Trump would own a 93 percent stake in the business that would become Trump University, and Sexton would receive an equity interest of 4.5 percent and a salary of $250,000 per year to be its president. Trump "felt this was a very good business," Sexton would later testify on deposition, "and he wanted to put his own money into it." Trump initially invested $2 million to get things started.

Why Trump, a professed billionaire real estate mogul, would go for such a small-potatoes venture is a matter of speculation. We may assume that his ego got in the way of his judgment. Trump wanted to tell the world how he had made his money. Arrogance shrieked in his principal books: *The Art of the Deal* (1987), *The Art of the Comeback* (1997), *How to Get Rich* (2004), *Trump 101* (2006), and *Think Big and Kick Ass* (2008).

It is not known how much Trump made from Trump University, since he has failed to disclose his tax returns for the relevant years, but New York's attorney general estimated the figure at $5 million. Deposition testimony was that Trump repaid himself what he invested and took out $5 million more in capital distributions.

What we do know is that over 5,000 individuals, mainly retirees and widows, paid an estimated $40 million to take courses under the supposed direction of Donald Trump when Trump would personally have little or nothing to do with the teachers, the curriculum, or the lesson plans. The courses were essentially worthless.

November 2016 was the "best of times and the worst of times" for Donald Trump. On November 8, he was elected president of the United States. But on November 18, he was set to go to trial in California federal court in a lawsuit charging him with consumer fraud arising out of his failed Trump University "success course."

Founded as a for-profit enterprise at the height of the real estate boom, Trump University purported to give courses in real estate management, entrepreneurship, and wealth creation. It offered to instruct students in Trump's "insider" success secrets and his tried-and-true real estate investment techniques. Its promise to students was to make them rich—rich in real estate, maybe even as rich as Donald Trump. Trump said he organized it because he had "a real passion for learning." It didn't quite turn out that way.

Trump University was a fraud from start to finish. It wasn't a "university" at all. Most universities are accredited institutions. Although Trump let on that Trump University was an accredited academic institution, even featuring a school crest, it was not. No one accredited it except Donald Trump.

Trump University never obtained the license required by the New York Education Law before it could advertise or transact business using the name "university." Licensure required that it comply with rigorous standards set by the state's Board of Regents. There is no way that Trump could have made the case. The State Education Department warned Trump in 2005 to drop the term "university" or not offer seminars in New York. Despite the repeated warnings that he was doing business illegally, Trump continued to operate the business as Trump University between 2005 and 2010. Ultimately, he stopped using the term "university" following a 2010 order from New York regulators, who called Trump's use of the word "misleading and even illegal." He changed the name to "The Trump Entrepreneur Initiative." Justice Cynthia Kern of the New York State Supreme Court held Trump personally liable for noncompliance with state licensing laws applicable to Trump University. "It is undisputed that Mr. Trump never complied with the licensing requirements," the court stated.

Trump University's sales techniques were replete with the kind of misrepresentation, salesmanship, and predatory pitches dramatized in David Mamet's Pulitzer Prize–winning play *Glengarry Glen Ross*. Beginning in 2007, consumers were invited to a 90-minute "Free Preview" of an orchestrated marketing campaign. There was a signed letter from Donald Trump offering "my *handpicked* instructors and mentors [who] will show you how to use real estate strategies." Victims were exposed to ads touting how they could "learn from Trump's *handpicked experts*." He boasted in one, "I can turn anyone into a successful real estate investor, including you." Students would be able to "learn from the master. It's the next best thing to being his apprentice." They would garner "inside success secrets from Donald Trump."

It is marketing 101 to give away free samples, but the free ride didn't last for long. At free introductory seminars, victims were offered a three-day "Fulfillment Seminar" for $1,495. Trump's salesmen, however, strongly urged students to take the premium "Gold Elite" program for one year of interactive support for up to $35,000, which promised unlimited mentoring for a year.

Trump testified that he reviewed and approved all the advertising. He was Trump University's promoter in chief. Among the most deceptive of his statements was the video played at the beginning of each Free Preview, in which Trump stated,

> We're going to have professors and adjunct professors that are absolutely terrific. Terrific people, terrific brains, successful . . . The best. We are going to have the best of the best and honestly if you don't learn from them, if you don't learn from me, if you don't learn from the people that we're going to be putting forward—and these are *all* people *that are handpicked by me*—then you're just not going to make it in terms of the world of success. . . . We're going to teach you better than the business schools are going to teach you, and I went to the best business school.

Michael Sexton testified in one of the class action suits that in truth and in fact, "none of the professors at the live events" were handpicked by Trump. Under oath, moreover, Trump acknowledged a lack of close involvement with mentors and students. In December 2015, a lawyer representing the class plaintiffs asked Trump on deposition, "Did you do anything personally to confirm the expertise of any of the Trump University mentors?" "No I didn't," he answered.

Trump sold 7,611 tickets of admission to Trump University programs; 6,000 of these were for the Fulfillment Seminar. For his efforts to bring customers into the store—a broadcast infomercial, a signed letter, and an introductory video—Trump received a personal cut of every seat sold, defrauding his victims of millions of dollars in fees for services that were misrepresented, of dubious value, or nonexistent.

A Trump University sales manager, Ronald Schnackenberg, testified that his superiors chided him for not pushing harder for a financially challenged couple to take the $35,000 package. Schnackenberg watched in horror as a fellow salesman persuaded the couple to enlist in the program. "I believe that Trump University was a fraudulent scheme," he said, "and that it preyed upon the elderly and uneducated to separate them from their money."

Corinne Sommer, employed as an events manager for Trump University from May to October 2007, recounted in a sworn declaration that she had attended the first live event in Florida in May and the second in California in June. She said that the emphasis was on making sales rather than providing quality educational services.

According to Sommer, the events were designed to lure consumers into the initial free course based on the name and reputation of Donald Trump. If students subscribed for a low-priced package and asked for additional information, the instructors were trained not to answer the question but to pressure them into buying the high-priced package. Trump University even exploited the homeless, encouraging them to open up multiple credit card accounts so they would not be maxed out to pay for classes that many of them could not afford. "It's okay, just max out your credit card," she recalled a salesman saying.

Sommer said that the speakers, instructors, and mentors lacked real estate backgrounds. Many did not own their own homes, and none had experience in buying or selling real estate. David Stamper, whose work experience was as a jewelry salesman, became a Trump "instructor" after a year of selling the Trump University course to consumers.

Jason Nicholas, a sales executive, testified to the deception that Trump would be "actively involved" in students' education to lure them in. "This was not true," he said, "Donald Trump was not actively [involved] in Trump University as far as I could tell." When confronted in his deposition with the names and photographs of Trump University instructors and mentors, Trump disclaimed recollection some 35 times and could not identify a single one. A chart outlining the boiler-room-style sales pitch elaborated phases in a "roller coaster of emotions" the sales force was to instill in their targets: the "Blast"—"giving your clients hope again" (a near ancestor of "Make America Great Again");

the "Probe," which must "slowly bring the client back down to reality"; "talk about the target's finances [and] figure out if they have room for it on their credit cards"; and "Goals"—reminding the mark of their hopes and dreams with the instruction that if there was hesitation: "Let me ask you, is everything Donald Trump does the BEST? He wouldn't put his name on this if it weren't, right?"

Trump was heavily involved in marketing but not designing the program. He signed letters used to spur students to take advantage of a downturn in the housing market to earn a fast buck. "How would you like to 'market-proof' your financial future?" Trump rhetorically inquired in one brochure. The pitch smacked of Bernie Madoff. "You can't lose money"—until you do.

Trump University went out of business in 2011, leaving students dissatisfied with the program they had bought into. Over 3,700 students filed claims that they had been defrauded. Trump victimized the unwary, the greedy, the vulnerable, and, most pathetically, the disabled and the elderly concerned about financing their retirement.

In April 2010, Tarla Makaeff, a Trump University student who did not attend the Free Preview but who on the recommendation of a friend purchased the Fulfillment Seminar in August 2008 and later the Gold Elite program, brought a class action in federal court in San Diego in which she charged consumer fraud and other related claims against Trump University and Donald Trump in connection with the Trump University marketing program. The Makaeff case was consolidated with cases brought against Trump by Florida and New York citizens making similar claims and invoking the laws of their own states applicable to financial elder abuse, false advertising, "deceptive acts and practices, . . . and unjust enrichment." Trump was a named defendant in all of the cases.

The court later consolidated the class action plaintiffs with a case brought in 2013 by New York attorney general Eric Schneiderman that accused Trump, Trump University, and its president, Michael Sexton, of defrauding 5,000 New Yorkers of $40 million on the Trump University program. Schneiderman's complaint alleged violation of New York's General Business Law, which outlaws "deceptive acts or practices in the conduct of any business." Schneiderman sought restitution and an injunction. The three cases were consolidated for trial.

Schneiderman said that evidence of the fraud perpetrated by Trump University is "pretty straightforward." "It [was] a bait-and-switch scheme," he told CNN, defending his and other lawsuits against the school. "He did ads saying my handpicked instructors will teach you my personal secrets. You just copy what I did and get rich." The fact is, as Schneiderman observed, Trump played no part in writing the curriculum or selecting the instructors. "Mr. Trump used his celebrity status and personally appeared in commercials making false promises to convince people to spend tens of thousands of dollars they couldn't afford for lessons they never got," Schneiderman said.

Trump launched a blitzkrieg media campaign against the lawsuit. He claimed a 98 percent approval rating for the program and set up a website to prove it called 98percentapproval.com. He said, "If you go to Wharton or Harvard, they didn't have a 98 percent approval rating. People loved the school. The school was terrific." He said that Trump University would teach them better than the best business school. It was a grift. Nothing could be further from the truth.

Refunds to dissatisfied consumers were few and far between. Bob Guillo, a retired paralegal from Manhasset, Long Island, and his son Alex attended the Trump Free Seminar and the three-day $1,500 course. At the time in his mid-70s, Guillo then signed up for the Trump Gold Elite program for $35,000. He was told that the package entitled him to be part of a privileged "in-the-know group" who would be invited into Trump-sponsored real estate deals. In a sworn affidavit, Guillo stated that he was led to believe he would have a chance to purchase a condominium in a Trump building and then flip it at a profit.

The first day of the Gold Elite program, Guillo knew he'd been had.

The information he was getting came not from Trump but from prominent real estate websites such as Trulia.com and the IRS's website, which he already knew about. As he took further doses of Trump University blather, he realized that "I had been truly scammed." Guillo conceded he had initially given the program good marks in response to questionnaires, and Trump in a May 27 campaign speech called him out for this after Guillo appeared in campaign attack ads paid for and approved by Marco Rubio. But Guillo said Trump University instructors pressured him to give them and their courses good marks. An instructor hovered over him, saying, "OK, if you don't rate me a five, I'm not going to come back here, and I've got a wife and kids." Guillo never dreamed that Trump would use his answers to defend himself against the lawsuits. In August 2011 he wrote to the Trump Organization demanding a refund. What he got was the offer of a better mentor, which Guillo declined. He would have to wait for his money.

Former students recounted high-pressure tactics from instructors wanting them to give the highest possible approval ratings, including threats of withholding graduation certificates. In fact over 25 percent of the students requested refunds.

Trump would later claim that he was not involved in the day-to-day management of the school. How would he know then that people loved it or that the "school was terrific"? Schneiderman countered by offering 46 negative affidavits from students who felt they were bilked. The Trump team was unmoved. "When you take into account the fact that [Schneiderman has] . . . been looking at this for what, two-plus years, 46 [negative] affidavits is [nothing]," said Alan Garten, in-house counsel for the Trump Organization.

It meant nothing for Trump to claim that 98 percent of the students approved. The issue was, were students defrauded? As for the probative force of approval ratings, the Ninth Circuit Court of Appeals stressed,

As the recent Ponzi-scheme scandals involving one-time financial luminaries like Bernard Madoff and Allen Stanford demonstrate, victims of con artists often sing the praises of their victimizers until the moment they realize they have been fleeced.

———————

Although he lost in the New York courts in his effort to get Schneiderman's suit dismissed, Trump went on a public relations counterattack, claiming that Schneiderman's suit was politically motivated and corrupt. He called Schneiderman a "sleazebag," a "political hack trying to get publicity," "not respected in New York," "doing a terrible job," "not electable," a "lightweight," and a "gross incompetent."

After Schneiderman filed his suit in New York in late August 2013, Florida's Republican attorney general, Pam Bondi, considered joining forces with Schneiderman and bringing her own suit against Trump University. Schneiderman alleged that 827 Trump University programs had been sold in Florida. Florida has a sizable elderly population, many of whom were targeted by the offending marketing practices. It ranked second among states in purchases of the Trump University product with 950 transactions, and third in sales at $3.3 million. On September 13, 2013, Bondi's office confirmed to the *Orlando Sentinel* that it was reviewing Schneiderman's New York lawsuit. According to the *Sentinel*, the review was to "determine whether Florida should join the multi-state case." No one knows precisely when Bondi's internal review of Trump University began or whether Trump was made aware of it before the piece appeared in the *Sentinel*.

On September 9, 2013, four days *before* the *Sentinel* report, with the Florida investigation of the allegations against Trump University pending, Trump signed a check for $25,000, payable to Bondi's reelection PAC "And Justice for All" on behalf of the Trump Foundation. Under the law, a charitable foundation is absolutely prohibited from contributing to a political campaign. Trump had founded the Trump Foundation to distribute his profits from *The Art of the Deal*. The contribution was illegal, since the nature of the contribution was not charitable but political, and Trump, who claimed it was all a big mistake, had to reimburse the foundation and pay a $2,500 excise tax as a penalty. The Trump Foundation concealed the nature of the contribution on its tax return, listing the money as going to a Utah charity called "And Justice for All." That statement was false. The Utah charity received nothing from the Trump Foundation.

Many of Trump's political contributions were to Florida candidates. Trump has golf courses and other business interests throughout the state. Records show that, according to the *New York Times*, he contributed at least $375,000 to state and federal candidates in Florida since 1995, accounting for about 19 percent of the $2 million he had given to campaigns nationwide.

No one has established whether Trump actually knew of the Florida investigation at the time he *agreed* to make the contribution or on September 9, when he cut Bondi the check. Surely he and his lawyers would have reasonably anticipated that Bondi might follow Schneiderman's lead and piggyback onto his suit. Not one, but two attorneys general charging him with fraud, including the attorney general of his favorite red state, Florida, could not be good for Trump's possible presidential bid. Bondi received the $25,000 check on September 17, four days after the *Sentinel* report. By that time, Trump had already contributed $500 to Bondi's campaign on July 15; Ivanka contributed $500 on September 10.

What we do know is that in October 2013, Bondi's office told the *Miami Herald* that she had decided not to join in Schneiderman's suit. The story they told was that Florida victims would be compensated if Schneiderman were successful. Trump maintained that his decision to contribute to Bondi's campaign had nothing to do with Trump University. Tell me another one!

In March 2014, Trump hosted a $3,000-a-plate fundraiser for Bondi at Mar-a-Lago. The fundraiser reportedly yielded at least $50,000. It was only five months after she decided not to sue him over Trump University. In early 2016, when the presidential campaign of Florida's native son Marco Rubio began to founder, Bondi announced her endorsement of Donald Trump for president. She would later serve on his drug abuse transition team.

———————

Trump went to town on one of the class plaintiffs, Tarla Makaeff. He targeted Makaeff because she "completed multiple surveys rating Trump University's three-day seminar 'excellent.'" She also "praised Trump University's mentorship program in a glowing five-minute-plus video testimonial." This was before it dawned on her that she had been had.

Not content to smear Makaeff and threaten her financially at a deposition, Trump had to assert his signature counterclaim for defamation: he sought $1 million in damages. A counterclaim sets the adverse party back on her heels, runs up the legal fees, deflects attention from the main event, and makes the plaintiff rue the day she brought the action in the first place. He learned all about counterclaims in the 1970s, when he counterclaimed against the government for $100 million in the Fair Housing Act race-discrimination case. He used counterclaims promiscuously when sued throughout his business career. Often, they worked.

Beginning in the fall of 2009, Makaeff published a number of disparaging statements on the internet and elsewhere about Trump University, including the following, saying that Trump University engaged in "'fraudulent business practices,' 'deceptive business practices,' 'illegal predatory high pressure closing tactics,' 'personal financial information fraud,' 'illegal bait and switch,' 'brainwashing scheme[s],' 'outright fraud,' 'grand larceny,' 'identity theft,' 'unsolicited taking of personal credit and trickery into [sic] opening credit cards,' 'fraudulent business practices utilized for illegal material gain,' 'felonious teachings,' 'neuro-linguistic programming and high pressure sales tactics based on the psychology of scarcity,' 'unethical tactics,' 'a gargantuan amount of misleading, fraudulent, and predatory behavior,' and business practices that are 'criminal.'"

Her explanation for this is contained in a letter she sent to her bank suggesting that her goal was to protect other consumers from dealing with Trump University:

I am contacting the Better Business Bureau (BBB), the Federal Trade Commission (FTC), Bureau of Consumer Protection and the FDIC as well as posting the facts of my highly negative experience on a wide variety of Internet sites to ensure that this organization at some point is stopped from defrauding others with its predatory behavior. I am also contacting the media to give them a statement of facts so that they can expose this scam and am willing to go to whatever lengths necessary to obtain my money back including taking legal action at the state and federal levels for this crime that has been committed to [sic] thousands of students nationwide who have been preyed on and victimized as I know I am one of many.

These statements got under Trump's skin and formed the basis for his counterclaim against Makaeff for defamation. He hoped to pressure her into going away. But this time the counterclaim gambit blew up in his face. In 2014, California—like 29 other jurisdictions, including New York—enacted some extraordinary protections against an abuse of process. The protections became known as the Strategic Lawsuit Public Participation civil action and were intended to punish counter-claimants suing to "deter ordinary people from exercising their political or legal rights or to punish them for doing so." Lawyers like to use acronyms, so this particular legal procedure became known as a "SLAPP." Trump's counterclaim for defamation fit the definition of a SLAPP quite neatly.

What Trump didn't calculate was that he was about to get slapped or, should we say, anti-SLAPPed for his counterclaim. California's SLAPP law features an anti-SLAPP motion, furnishing the possibility of fast-track pretrial dismissal of SLAPP actions, such as Trump's counter-claim, that "masquerade as ordinary lawsuits." The SLAPP law enabled

Makaeff to make a special motion to strike the counterclaim, which she did. Trump never expected to collect $1 million or anything like it. His sole motive in mounting the counterclaim was to put pressure on Makaeff.

Makaeff's road to SLAPP recovery was tortuous. Even more interestingly, in light of Trump's verbal attacks on Mexicans during the campaign, a troika of Mexican American judges would decide the SLAPP motion.

The matter initially came before Judge Irma Gonzalez in the Southern District of California. President George H. W. Bush appointed Gonzalez to the federal bench in 1992. She was the first Mexican American woman to be appointed to the federal court—and the first of three Hispanic judges Trump would draw in the course of this litigation. Unlike with Judge Gonzalo Curiel, whom he later lambasted as being hopelessly biased against him by virtue of his Mexican background, Trump never uttered a word of criticism about Gonzalez or her ethnicity. She handed him a short-lived victory when she dismissed Makaeff's anti-SLAPP motion.

Makaeff appealed Gonzalez's decision to the Ninth Circuit. In reversing Gonzalez, the Court of Appeals readily perceived that Makaeff was exercising her free speech rights in that her statements were "made in connection with a public issue or an issue of public interest." Makaeff's statements, it held, provided "consumer protection information," a warning to other potential victims that Trump University was a bad actor and that they should steer away from buying its programs.

The appeals court stressed that with its vigorous advertising campaigns featuring videos of Donald Trump touting the virtues of the school, Trump University voluntarily exposed itself to increased risk of injury from defamatory falsehood. Its ad campaign, moreover, gave it special access to avenues of communication not enjoyed by mere mortals.

The court stated,

To be clear: Trump University is not a public figure because Donald Trump is famous and controversial. Nor is Trump University a public figure because it utilized Donald Trump as a celebrity pitchman. Trump University is a limited public figure because a public debate existed regarding its aggressively advertised educational practices.

The Ninth Circuit opinion was the work of a Clinton appointee, Judge Kim McLane Wardlaw, whose mother was a Mexican American. Wardlaw was the first Hispanic woman to be appointed a United States circuit judge. The appellate panel reversed the case and sent it back to Judge Gonzalez.

Judge Gonzalo Curiel took over when Judge Gonzalez retired in October 2013. Curiel is a U.S. district judge in California appointed by Barack Obama. He was born in Indiana, and like Mike Pence obtained his law degree from Indiana University. His parents, who became American citizens, were immigrants from Mexico. Included in his impressive resume is a stint as a federal prosecutor during which he went after drug dealers. In the course of one case, involving a Mexican drug cartel, one of the defendants threatened Curiel's life, and Curiel lived for a time under federal protection.

Curiel dismissed Trump's counterclaim on June 17, 2014. Makaeff, thanks to SLAPP, was able to turn the tables, and she ended up the victor, collecting nearly $1 million from Trump. Trump lost this one, and lost it big time.

Even though she won the anti-SLAPP motion and Curiel had denied Trump's motion for summary judgment, Tarla Makaeff was so unnerved by Trump's attacks that she moved in February 2016 to withdraw from the case. She claimed she had been "put through the wringer," grilled for more than 15 hours on deposition, "and had endured health problems, family loss and financial troubles" since the case began. She said that when she brought the suit, she knew Trump was a celebrity but had no idea that "he would become a viable presidential candidate and a 24/7 media obsession."

But Trump would not let Makaeff off the hook. He became obsessed with her. He vindictively opposed her motion to withdraw, claiming he wanted her to remain in the case so he could skewer her when she took the stand. "Make no mistake," stated Trump's legal brief, "Makaeff is *the* critical witness in this case," adding that she was a "disastrous witness."

On March 6, 2016, Trump tweeted using his favorite pejorative imputing shame and disgrace: "The primary plaintiff in the Trump University suit wants to abandon the case. Disgraceful."

Nonsense. If Makaeff was so important to him, he was free to call her as a witness at the trial or read her deposition into the record if he thought she had helpful testimony, whether she was in the case or not.

Trump smeared Makaeff's character. He painted her as a loser. "Despite her education, Makaeff failed to achieve success in real estate," states the Trump brief. "Discovery has confirmed . . . she simply did not put in the time, work and perseverance necessary to achieve success. In fact, in the one real estate investment she made, where she used her mother's money to invest in a deal in Las Vegas, Makaeff backed out of it and demanded her money back. As Makaeff later learned, if she had . . . stuck with the investment, it would have yielded a $35,000 profit."

Trump and his lawyers finessed the obvious point that Makaeff was suing individually *and* as a representative of a class. Makaeff's individual suit was for only $35,000; the class claim was for millions. Makaeff's departure from the case changed nothing. Members of the class all had the same lawyer. Over Trump's strident objection, Judge Curiel allowed Makaeff to withdraw from the case, and another class member, Sonny Low, a retired State Department officer who had paid $25,000 for the Gold Elite program, picked up the fallen standard.

In February 2014, Curiel certified a class of victims who had alleged that Trump University was "a basically fraudulent endeavor," and he accepted residents of three states as members of that class.

During the presidential campaign, when his opponents, casting doubt on Trump's claims of business success, called him to task over the Trump University scandal, Trump exploded with a vicious attack on Curiel. He claimed that any judge other than Curiel would have dismissed the class actions on summary judgment. Curiel, he said, was "biased."

There was no basis for the claim of bias—only mean-spiritedness on Trump's part. On February 15, 2016, Trump moved for summary judgment dismissing the *Low v. Trump University* case, as the Makaeff case came to be known, and separately for summary judgment the following March in *Cohen*, the companion RICO case that other class members brought against Trump. Summary judgment is a preliminary tool to ascertain whether there is a genuine issue for trial. The motion is not designed to close the curtain on trial but to "[enable] the court to determine if the 'curtain' should be raised at all."

Curiel made a perfectly reasonable judgment in the class actions before him when he determined there were controverted issues of fact pertaining to the alleged fraud, which only the jury could resolve. Had he granted Trump summary judgment, he surely would have been reversed on appeal. Fewer than 10 percent of federal court cases between 1975 and 2000 were resolved on summary judgment.

Trump erupted almost immediately, telling Fox News that Curiel was personally biased against him because of his tough immigration posture and his campaign promise to build a wall along the U.S./Mexican border. "He has been extremely hostile to me," Trump declared without any support. "Now, he is Hispanic, I believe." He told the *Wall Street Journal* that Curiel could not fairly preside because of his "Mexican heritage," explaining, "I'm building a wall; it's an inherent conflict of interest."

Trump continued to denounce Curiel in campaign speeches and interviews, saying three times for emphasis that he had "a judge who was a hater of Donald Trump, a hater. He's a hater." Trump claimed Curiel's rulings were unfair and referred to the Indiana-born judge as "Mexican." He further suggested taking some kind of action against Judge

Curiel: "They ought to look into Judge Curiel, because what Judge Curiel is doing is a total disgrace. Okay?"

On May 30, 2016, Trump tweeted:

I should have easily won the Trump University case on summary judgement but have a judge, Gonzalo Curiel, who is totally biased against me.

Sigmund Freud placed great emphasis on the words people choose to express themselves, since words often give clues to unconscious longings. "Disgrace" is one of the recurrent words in Trump's limited vocabulary. A psychoanalyst might say there is a revealing insight here into certain Trump character traits. Does his frequent use of words like "disgraceful" and "shameful" indicate a deep sensitivity and aversion to feelings of shame? This might reflect the deep-seated emotions acquired in childhood of a son desperately needing the approval of a distant father but somehow ashamed of his failure to earn it. Only others can be disgraceful or shameful. In Trump's head, he can do no wrong.

Trump never moved to disqualify Judge Curiel. Indeed, after Curiel rendered a ruling favorable to Trump on a procedural issue, Daniel Petrocelli, Trump's lead lawyer, complimented him and said, "The judge is doing his job." Famed civil libertarian Nat Hentoff wrote that Curiel had ruled in Trump's favor far more often than not, including granting his motion to delay the trial until after the 2016 presidential election because of concerns about a "media frenzy" that might improperly influence the jury. Hentoff concluded, "Donald Trump has an odd way of showing his appreciation for a trial judge who, as Trump's attorney admitted, is just 'doing his job.'"

Curiel undoubtedly chafed at Trump's attacks and wrote in court papers that Trump had "placed the integrity of these court proceedings at issue." He was forbidden, however, from responding publicly in light of ethical rules against extrajudicial comment by judges on active cases.

On June 7, 2016, Trump, responding to charges in the campaign of attempts to subvert the judiciary with bigoted slurs on the judge's ethnicity, issued an opaque statement saying that his criticism of Curiel had been "misconstrued" and that his concerns about Curiel's impartiality were not based on ethnicity alone but also on rulings in the case. What rulings? Curiel never passed on the merits of the Trump University controversy. That was a matter left for trial.

The cases before Judge Curiel alleged fraud, but there was a difference. The *Low* plaintiffs sued under the consumer protection laws of three states, a garden-variety class action lawsuit. The *Cohen* plaintiffs, however, charged Trump University under the RICO Act, and sought an award of treble damages and attorneys' fees.

Trump also urged Curiel to dismiss the RICO claims, contending there was a "pervasive abuse of civil RICO." It was a classic case of the pot calling the kettle black. As we have seen, Trump was a great fan of civil RICO in 1993 when he sued the Pritzkers, his Commodore Hotel partners, and in the 1970s when he sued the law firm representing the Central Park South tenants. In the Trump University case, he argued, "Indeed, if this case is allowed to proceed, it would represent an unprecedented and unprincipled expansion of civil RICO and transform every alleged violation of consumer protection laws into a civil RICO claim."

Curiel held a hearing on the RICO case in July 2016. In August, noting that the Supreme Court had interpreted civil RICO broadly, he denied Trump summary judgment, holding that "ultimately, while Defendant may believe that, as a policy matter, civil RICO ought not be extended to consumer class action cases . . . it is not for this Court to effectuate Defendant's policy preferences in contravention of the settled approach of the higher courts."

Trump University became a burning issue in the 2016 primaries. Trump had vowed never to settle the case, falsely claiming that the Better

Business Bureau had approved Trump University. Here is his March 2016 exchange with Marco Rubio on the subject at the Republican presidential debates:

Rubio: Well, he did, and that's why Trump University . . . is so relevant here. I saw this video last week where he's sitting in front of a camera saying we're going to hire the best people, and I'm going to handpick them. There are going to be handpicked instructors, the best instructors in the world. One of them, by the way, was the manager at a Buffalo Wild Wings. And that's who they hired to do this, and people borrowed money, and they signed up for this fake university. And these people owe all this money now, and they got nothing in return for it, but you are willing to say whatever you had to say to get them to give you their money. . . .

Trump: . . . And, by the way, just so you understand. This is a case I could have settled very easily, but I don't settle cases very easily when I'm right. Ninety-eight percent approval rating, we have an "A" from the Better Business Bureau—

Rubio: That's false. . . .

Trump: . . . *We have a 98 percent approval rating from the people who took the course.* We have an "A" from the Better Business Bureau. And, people like it. Now, he's saying they didn't learn. We have many, many people that will be witnesses. Again, *I don't settle cases. I don't do it because that's why I don't get sued very often, because I don't settle, unlike a lot of other people.* We have a situation where we will win in court. . . . But many of the people that are witnesses did tremendously well, and made a lot of money—

Rubio: That's false. . . .

Trump: . . . By taking the course . . . You're going to see, you don't know. . . .

Rubio: . . . The Better Business Bureau gave it a "D-minus."

Trump: You're going to see, you're going to see.

We didn't see! The Better Business Bureau responded by saying that it never gave Trump University an "A" rating and had in fact received "many consumer complaints" about the program.

Trump's claim, moreover, to a 98 percent approval rating was a bald-faced lie. As Steven Brill sized it up in a November 2015 investigative piece written for *Time*,

> Trump's director of operations Mark Covais . . . declared that the satisfaction percentages were taken from "about 10,000" surveys of Trump University customers. Yet in the same affidavit Covais said that there were 7,611 tickets sold to Trump University programs. . . . How could Trump have 10,000 "rave" surveys from paying customers if there were only 7,611 paying customers? . . . The more apparent inconsistency is that Covais . . . declared that the company had issued 2,144 refunds to 6,698 attendees of the $1,495 three-day program, or 32%. That a third of the customers demanded refunds is hard to reconcile with a claimed 98% satisfaction rate. . . . Similarly, the refund rate for the $34,995 program, which according to the lawsuits was tougher on giving money back, was 16%. If at least 31% [*sic*] of one group and 16% of the other were so instantly dissatisfied that they immediately demanded refunds, how could 98% have been satisfied?

And on November 18, 2016, just 10 days after his election, Trump *did* settle the case. He announced a hefty, $25 million settlement that had been reached with Trump University students, refunding to them about 90 cents on the dollar of their paid tuition. Which Judge Curiel termed an "extraordinary amount of recovery." In addition, Trump had to pay $1 million to the State of New York for violating state education laws. Trump's advisers had counseled him strongly that the president of the

United States would have more important things to do than to defend himself in a fraud case. Judge Curiel approved the settlement March 31, 2017. The plaintiffs' law firm, which Trump had called "sleazebags," negotiated the settlement and waived all fees. They had taken the case *pro bono*. He also had called New York attorney general Schneiderman a "sleazebag." It was one of his favorite pejoratives, reserved for anyone who would dare take him on.

Stories are out there that Trump settled the case at the urging of one of his close friends, Thomas Barrack, a Los Angeles billionaire who had found Trump his lawyer in the case. There is even the suggestion that the settlement was secretly funded by the Trump Inaugural Committee, of which Barrack was the chair. Barrack was a major contributor to the Trump campaign. Trump and the class plaintiffs struck the settlement deal the day after ethics experts, veterans of Republican and Democratic administrations, sent Trump a letter urging him to settle the case to avoid "embroiling the presidency in litigation." For a sitting president to be in court defending himself in a fraud suit would be unseemly. The ethicists were right.

Barrack was close to Trump politically. In 2016, he recommended Paul Manafort, who for the previous decade had owned a $3.6 million apartment in Trump Tower, to the Trump campaign as "the most experienced and *lethal* of managers." Manafort eventually became Trump's campaign manager, until Manafort's illegal financial dealings made him toxic.

So why did Trump settle a case he says he should have won on summary judgment? His answer came from Alan Garten, general counsel of the Trump Organization:

> While we have no doubt that Trump University would have prevailed at trial based on the merits of this case, resolution of these matters allows President-Elect Trump to devote his full attention to the important issues facing our great nation.

New York attorney general Schneiderman had another take on "the important issues facing our great nation":

In 2013, my office sued Donald Trump for swindling thousands of innocent Americans out of millions of dollars through a scheme known as Trump University. Donald Trump fought us every step of the way, filing baseless charges and fruitless appeals and refusing to settle for even modest amounts of compensation for the victims of his phony university. Today all that changes. Today's $25 million settlement agreement is a stunning reversal by Donald Trump and a major victory for the over 6,000 victims of his fraudulent university.

A brand name often gets customers into the store; in the Trump University case, it brought dissatisfied customers into federal court. So who won, and who lost? Trump lost little. He only had to give back the fees he had stolen from his victims. The victims got some of their money back, as they did in the Madoff bankruptcy. Trump gloated that in the settlement of the Trump University case, as in the settlement of the Fair Housing Act case with the government in the 1970s, he did not admit guilt. In the world of Trump, admitting guilt is shameful. Redemption doesn't come with confession. Confession does not bring expiation. Confession is shameful and disgraceful. It must be avoided at all costs.

THE CLOSING BELL

LIFE IN THE PRESIDENT'S LITIGATION BUNKER

I took a lot of finance courses at Wharton.
First they taught you all the rules and regulations.
Then they taught you that those rules
and regulations are really meant to be broken.

—Donald Trump

The story that began in Jamaica Estates, Queens, moved to the White House. Trump's conduct in office has channeled his conduct as a private citizen. He has managed his presidency straight out of the Roy Cohn "Fuck the law, who's the judge?" playbook. He says he is willing to work with a newly elected Democratic Congress, provided they refrain from investigating him. He blames declines in the stock market on the Democrats or the Federal Reserve, but never on his failed policies. A judge who rules against his immigration policies is an "Obama judge" or a "so-called judge."

Trump has not stopped litigating, has not stopped lying, and has not stopped fighting to protect his name. Fred Trump's son can do no wrong. In his world, the only judge that counts sits in the court of Trumpocracy. He distracts with his feckless and nonsensical policy choices and with lie after lie after lie. He leaks to the press what he wants his base to hear. He has surrogates spin one "truth"; he spins another "truth"—and then he lies again. The Constitution and the rule of law have no meaning for him, not even the constitutional tradition of majoritarianism with protections for minorities. The amazing thing about his approach is that so far it has worked. Where he leaves most Americans outraged or astounded, he satisfies his ruling minority base. They stand solidly behind him, even though, according to the latest polls, they represent less than 40 percent of America.

What is clear in the law becomes contestable for Trump. He appoints an "acting" attorney general without sending his name to the Senate for confirmation. He proposes to revoke birthright citizenship, even though the Constitution's Fourteenth Amendment and 120 years of Supreme Court precedent guarantee the status. He declares a "national emergency" to build a wall unauthorized by Congress, a direct attack on the constitutional separation of powers. An overwhelming number of lawyers, law professors, and political thinkers have objected to this outright trashing of the Constitution. Harvard Law professor Laurence Tribe in an October 12, 2018, tweet wondered whether Trump seeks to dismantle "every potential source of institutional resistance" brick by brick. If we allow Trump to tweet his way past the plain language of the Constitution, what's to stop him from declaring that the First Amendment no longer applies to journalists, because the Framers did not intend it to apply to "enemies of the people"? As for "enemies of the people," he revoked CNN correspondent Jim Acosta's press pass to the White House for asking a trenchant question at a press conference. CNN responded by suing Trump, claiming he had infringed its First Amendment rights.

The American public is deeply divided over Donald Trump. Many of those who agree with most of his policies find his behavior unacceptable and possibly impeachable. His base may be cracking among voters who reside in key electoral states. It is only the Republican Senate, not a national consensus, that keeps him in power.

New York Democratic senator Pat Moynihan, known for working

across the aisle, once said, "You are entitled to your own opinion, but you are not entitled to your own facts." A bitter partisan rift beclouds consensus acceptance of any fact bearing on Trump's conduct and precludes critical judgment. There is little room for common ground, as one lie nourishes the next. Former Carter cabinet member Joseph Califano argues persuasively in a thoughtful book that the partisanship at every level of American society has dangerously damaged our democracy. Or, as Princeton professor Eddie Glaude Jr. puts it, the "country is coming apart at the seams."

Amazingly, the more outrageous and hyperbolic the Trumpian statement, the more the press is willing to publish it, true or false. There are obvious dangers in publishing what he says, and there are dangers in ignoring him. As president, he has found a bully pulpit to ramp up an ugly voice. His pre-presidential propensity to lie is scalable in the White House, and it can be used to confound his critics, delight his base, and, most terrifyingly, evade the requirements of law.

———————

Donald Trump has for the time being faced down the most threatening litigation of his life. A serious inquiry, led by special counsel Robert Mueller, looked into possible ties between his campaign and the Russians who meddled in the 2016 election to help him get elected. Trump is obsessed with Mueller. As of February 14, 2019, he had criticized Mueller or his investigation on more than 43 percent of the days he had been in office. As the nation eagerly awaited the denouement of his inquiry, Mueller produced, in 22 months, a stunning 100 or more criminal counts against 34 people, including 6 Americans once affiliated with Trump's campaign or administration and 26 Russian nationals, and 3 Russian companies. Two people—Michael Cohen, whose connection to Trump needs no elaboration, and lobbyist Sam Patten, a figure tied to Paul Manafort—pleaded guilty to charges leveled by Mueller.

The theory of Mueller's investigation was a possible conspiracy in which Trump lieutenants like Manafort and others traded Russian help in the election in return for the promise that Trump would deliver to Russia, with love, a reset in relations, including a deal to end U.S. pushback over Russian aggression in Ukraine and Crimea and to provide sanctions relief. Russian "help" might include the illegal hacking of John Podesta's emails at the Democratic National Committee by the Russian platform known as Guccifer. Podesta was Hillary Clinton's campaign manager. There was even speculation that, as elaborated in the dossier prepared by Christopher Steele, a retired MI6 officer who had served the intelligence agency's Russian desk, Michael Cohen traveled to Prague to give Trump money to Guccifer for the hack. This, however, Mueller was unable to establish. What we do know is that the fruits of the hack, consisting of stolen DNC emails, were dumped onto Julian Assange's WikiLeaks web platform.

The evidence of "collusion" could not be stronger even if there was no conspiracy. On July 27, 2016, in a Miami, Florida speech, Trump famously exhorted Russia to find Clinton's "missing" emails. He said: "Russia, if you're listening, I hope you're able to find the 30,000 emails that are missing." On October 7, 2016, a month before the election, the *Washington Post* published the bombshell Billy Bush *Access Hollywood* tape in which Trump boasted of his attempt to bed a married woman and bragged that because he was a star, he could grab any woman "by the pussy." The Trump campaign was devastated. About one-third of the Republican Senate caucus called on Trump to quit the race. Many members of the Republican House caucus followed suit. Then came a stunning reversal of fortune. One hour after the *Access Hollywood* tape went public, WikiLeaks released 2,000 emails hacked from the servers of John Podesta. The release of the emails was brilliantly synchronized. It drowned out the tale of the tape and breathed new life into the foundering Trump campaign. Michael Cohen testified before Congress on February 27, 2019, that Trump knew in advance that WikiLeaks planned to publish the emails hacked by Russia from the Democrats.

As CIA director, Mike Pompeo called WikiLeaks a "hostile

intelligence service" that "will take down America any way they can." And Assange, shadowy guiding spirit of WikiLeaks, is the subject of a federal indictment. He was arrested in London after residing for seven years in the Ecuadorian embassy, where he had sought temporary asylum.

Trump's indicted trickster pal Roger Stone is the only person known to have had contact with both Guccifer and WikiLeaks. It was Stone, now facing federal criminal charges, who prophesied the WikiLeaks dump as an "October surprise." Trump proclaimed during the campaign, "This WikiLeaks is like a treasure trove. . . . It's been amazing what's come out on WikiLeaks. . . . Now, this just came out," he went on, holding up some papers à la McCarthy. "WikiLeaks! I love WikiLeaks." In fact, he mentioned WikiLeaks 137 times in speeches during the last month of the campaign.

Then there was the Trump Tower meeting with the Russians attended by campaign chairman Paul Manafort, Donald Trump Jr., and Trump's son-in-law, Jared Kushner. Trump Jr. admitted he pressed for and solicited "dirt" on Hillary Clinton from the Russians and relished the prospect of receiving it. Cohen testified before Congress that Trump personally OK'd the meeting. There is Trump's central role in the payoffs to Stormy Daniels and Karen McDougal to buy their silence on the eve of the election. Other possible wrongdoings in the glare of the investigative spotlight were obstruction of justice, fraud, money laundering, and false campaign and other federal filings, as well as a host of financial and other improprieties. The Mueller inquiry beclouded the very legitimacy of Trump's presidency, and Mueller would not be put off with Roy Cohn–style attacks.

Mueller's appointment on May 17, 2017, was the unintended consequence of Trump's firing of FBI director James Comey a week before. Mueller, a Republican straight shooter, was a career prosecutor from whom Trump had nothing to expect but the worst. Upon first learning of Mueller's appointment, Trump slumped back in his chair and bemoaned, "Oh my God. This is terrible. This is the end of my presidency.

I'm fucked." Mueller scarcely had time to hang his hat in his new office before Trump tweeted the following day, "This is the single greatest witch-hunt of a politician in American history!" It was not the first time Trump would use the McCarthy-era phrase "witch-hunt" in an effort to discredit Mueller's investigation. And it would not be the last.

Trump defended himself against Mueller in the brazenly antilegal way he defended cases his entire professional life. As we have seen, he learned from Roy Cohn that he must attack, counterattack, and deflect. He must leak, tweet, and spin to the press his side of the story, replete with lies and wild conspiracy theories of "spygate" and the "deep state." Trump redefined truth. In 2016, the *Oxford English Dictionary* added the word "post-truth" to the lexicon, referring to "circumstances in which objective facts are less influential in shaping public opinion than appeals to emotion and personal belief"—the more outlandish the better. Casper Grathwohl, the president of Oxford University Press's dictionaries division, predicted that the term could become "one of the defining words of our time." Trump's attorney Rudy Giuliani publicly acknowledged that undermining Mueller is the centerpiece of their defense strategy, and he has repeatedly channeled his client in making post-truth claims. Giuliani's infamous assertion, made on *Meet the Press* on August 19, 2018, that "truth isn't truth" topped the *Yale Book of Quotations* list as the most notable quote of that year.

In October 2017, campaign worker George Papadopoulos would plead guilty to lying to the FBI the previous January about his contacts with Russian agents, and come over to Mueller's side of the table. Trump's former national security adviser Michael Flynn would also plead guilty in December 2017 to lying to the FBI; he too cut a plea deal with Mueller, since the scope of possible crimes he had committed expanded well beyond false statements about his conversations with the Russians. In December 2018, Mueller presented a sentencing memorandum to federal district court judge Emmet Sullivan that noted Flynn's "substantial cooperation" and recommended no jail time in fulfillment of the plea deal. The memorandum was heavily redacted, apparently to shield sensitive information relative to Flynn from public view. Sullivan, describing his "disgust" that President Trump's national security adviser had sought to deceive FBI agents while "on the premises of the White House," even wondered whether Flynn could have been charged with treason. Threatening jail time for Flynn, Sullivan adjourned the sentencing to consider the matter further.

On February 16, 2018, Mueller indicted 16 Russia-related individuals and business organizations for conspiring to influence the election improperly. With the filing of the indictment, national security adviser H. R. McMaster said the evidence of Russian interference in the election was "incontrovertible"—a statement with which Trump took sharp issue. McMaster's conclusion channeled findings of the intelligence community (CIA, DNI, and NSA), which Trump questioned. The Republican-majority Senate Intelligence Committee, after 14 months of investigation, also accepted the conclusion that it was the Russians who interfered in the election, not, as Trump once speculated, a guy from "New Jersey sitting on the bed who weighs 400 pounds." From there on in, McMaster's days in the White House were numbered. Trump announced his departure on March 22, 2018.

The February 16 indictment was not the end of the story. On July 13, 2018, Mueller's grand jury indicted 12 Russian intelligence operatives alleged to be involved in the hack of the Clinton campaign and the DNC, as well as other cyberattacks on the United States calculated to bring about the election of Donald Trump. In *Fire and Fury*, Michael Wolff writes: "It was clear where Mueller and his team were going, said [Trump adviser Steve] Bannon: they would trace a money trail through Paul Manafort, Michael Flynn, Michael Cohen, and Jared Kushner and roll one or all of them on the President."

Mueller's inquiry is said to have comprehended, among other things, Russian money swimming around in Trump's various business ventures, evidence of Russian and other foreign offers of assistance to his campaign, and the possibility of blackmail, which the KGB called kompromat. The details of these aspects of the investigation may have been in the materials Mueller treated but were then redacted from the eventual report.

Mueller also took a deep dive into whether Trump had tried to head off any inquiry into Russian collusion by firing FBI director James Comey, conduct that smacked of obstruction of justice. Obstruction of justice requires a corrupt endeavor, such as taking extrajudicial action to try to protect oneself from prosecution. Bribing or threatening a witness, a juror, a judge, or a prosecutor would be classic textbook obstruction. The Congress that enacted the obstruction of justice statute could not have even remotely conceived that a president might obstruct justice by trying to subvert the director of the FBI—or, for that matter, his own attorney general.

Trump sought to throttle Mueller's investigation from day one. Initially, he wanted his first attorney general, Jeff Sessions, to take charge of the Russia probe, even though he had recused himself. When Sessions refused to do so, Trump eventually fired him, after rhetorically asking White House counsel Don McGahn, "Where's my Roy Cohn?" Trump eventually ordered McGahn to fire Mueller, but according to Mueller's investigation, McGahn, fearing that to do so would amount to an obstruction of justice, refused to carry out the executive mandate. The Justice Department regulation governing the appointment of Mueller states that a special counsel can be fired only for "misconduct, dereliction of duty, incapacity, conflict of interest, or for other good cause." No accident that Trump made a veiled threat that he might fire Mueller for "conflict of interest" in his tweet of March 19, 2018: "A total WITCH-HUNT with massive conflicts of interest!"

It is ironic that Trump would use the very phrase, "witch-hunt," that Cohn's enemies used to describe his tactics and those of Joseph McCarthy during the 1950s Red Scare. When the FBI executed a search warrant at the home and office of Trump's fixer and personal lawyer, Michael Cohen, Trump again called the prosecution a "witch-hunt." He told reporters on April 9, 2018, something that no lawyer ever would have said: that the raid was "an attack on our country, what we all stand for." On April 10 he tweeted that "attorney-client privilege is dead," and a minute later tweeted that the raid was "a total witch-hunt," ignoring that the raid was approved by three Trump-appointed lawyers and a federal judge in accordance with a strict Justice Department regime governing raids on lawyers' offices. After former federal judge Barbara Jones, acting as a court-appointed special master, screened the seized documents for privilege—thousands of pages of Cohen documents—federal judge Kimba Wood turned them over to the prosecutors in the Southern District of New York.

The heat in Washington on August 21, 2018, was just too much for Donald Trump. That day, Cohen pleaded guilty to eight counts of tax evasion, fraud, and breaking campaign finance laws. Cohen told a federal judge that he paid a total of $280,000 in hush money to two women "at [Trump's] direction" in order to scotch damaging stories just before the 2016 election. Further investigation has uncovered a total of $420,000 transmitted from the Trump Organization to Michael Cohen in connection with his efforts to silence women who claimed they had had sexual relationships with Donald Trump. For the first time, Trump faced the ugly possibility of an indictment charging that he broke the law to further his candidacy. While the plea agreement did not specify that Cohen would cooperate, it would only be a matter of time before Cohen began talking to Mueller. The same day, a federal jury in Alexandria, Virginia, convicted Paul Manafort on five counts of tax fraud, two counts of bank fraud, and one count of failure to disclose a foreign bank account.

Trump hates "flippers." He's said he knows all about them. From where? Queens? New York? Atlantic City? He claims he knows the ropes of how the game is played in conspiracy cases. On August 23, 2018, using the vocabulary of a mob boss in a grade-B gangster movie, he told Ainsley Earhardt on *Fox and Friends*, "I've had many friends involved in this stuff," adding an acknowledgment that it's hard to imagine any other president making:

I know all about flipping. For 30, 40 years, I've been watching flippers. Everything's wonderful, and then they get 10 years in jail and they flip on whoever the next highest one is—or as high as you can go.

Earlier, when there was talk about Cohen flipping, Trump had launched this tweet:

I feel very badly for Paul Manafort and his wonderful family. "Justice" took a 12 year old tax case, among other things, applied tremendous pressure on him and, unlike Michael Cohen, he refused to "break"— make up stories in order to get a "deal." Such respect for a brave man!

Of course, Manafort did plead guilty in federal district court on September 14 to all pending federal charges, and in formal papers he promised to cooperate with Mueller. But it was a fake flip. Instead of telling the truth, he spun a web of lies, and Mueller promptly voided the agreement, stating he would seek further charges.

In entering into a cooperation agreement with a defendant who might turn state's evidence, prosecutors are too smart to buy a pig in a poke. Normally they get a written proffer from defense counsel in advance as to what the witness will say, and they test the veracity of those statements against any corroborative facts they have already gathered. Then the prosecutors can grill the witness to discover what he would say if called to testify. Only when they are satisfied that the witness will give them new and reliable information do they offer a cooperation agreement with a reduced charge or ameliorative sentencing recommendation. The witness must agree to cooperate fully and give the prosecutor truthful evidence of criminal activity to the best of his knowledge, information, and belief, not just evidence about the surrounding circumstances of the crimes to which he will plead guilty.

But there was more to Manafort's purported cooperation than met the eye. He had decided to become a mole deep in the caverns of

Mueller's office. Hoping for a pardon, he instructed his lawyers to tell Trump's lawyers what Mueller was asking him about, opening both himself and his lawyers to obstruction-of-justice charges. There is no Justice Department regulation preventing the indictment of *the lawyers* for a sitting president.

How long Manafort will stay in jail following his volte-face remains to be seen. He certainly knows all that is knowable about domestic involvement in Putin's plot to influence the election, as well as Trump's financial involvement with the Russians.

The story of Paul Manafort remains to be told. He is the man who knows too much. He may prefer to remain in jail rather than face the possibility of being murdered by the Russians. He served as Trump's campaign chairman for only two months, from June to August 2016, but was a major voice in the campaign both before and after he occupied that position. Besides being Roger Stone's partner, Manafort had been retained by the pro-Putin Party of Regions in Ukraine to help elect Viktor Yanukovych president. Driven from office, Yanukovych later fled in disgrace to Russia. Another star in the Manafort firmament is the Russian Konstantin Kilimnik, whom prosecutors have tied to a Russian intelligence service. It was Kilimnik who allegedly obtained polling data from Manafort about the 2016 election just before Putin began the social media blitz intended to help Trump win the White House.

Trump calls Manafort a "brave man" and says he is so sad about the way he has been treated. But Mueller sees Manafort as a "hardened criminal" who "repeatedly and brazenly violated the law"—the underboss of the Trump crime family. Regardless, Manafort's convictions were a total home run for Mueller. His guilty plea surgically gutted the witch-hunt argument. All Trump and Giuliani could manage to stammer by way of comment was that Manafort's convictions weren't about the president.

The majority of the American people—polls say as much as 57 percent as of December 2018—supported Mueller. They wanted to know the truth about Trump and the Russians, to the extent that the truth is knowable, with 81 percent believing that Mueller's report should be made public. As of this writing, we don't have all of the facts that Mueller has unearthed, but the die is cast.

As Mueller proceeded, the president and many of his men lawyered up. There has been an unusual amount of turnover among Trump's lawyers. A number resigned or were marginalized. Chief counsel John Dowd resigned. After Dowd left, Trump announced that legal talking head Joe diGenova and his wife, Victoria Toensing, would join the legal team, only to say days later that they wouldn't. Marc Kasowitz, Trump's perennial legal spokesman, appears to have been pushed off to the side. Seasoned DC impeachment lawyer and former Scalia clerk Emmet Flood replaced Ty Cobb. Don McGahn, the highly regarded White House counsel, spilled his guts to Mueller. An announcement that he was leaving the White House followed, as he disagreed with Trump about how to manage Mueller's inquiry. Rudy Giuliani has been dusted off for the occasion. How long he will last is anybody's guess—he's already made a number of damaging admissions against Trump's interest.

Steve Bannon, in a position to know, predicted that Trump's son-in-law, Jared Kushner, was "trying to find a parachute" and would resign. Kushner wisely retained Abbe Lowell, a seasoned Washington criminal lawyer, to safeguard his interests. Kushner's security clearance application was Swiss cheese. He revised the application several times before it was approved, adding over 100 previously omitted foreign contacts that he could not possibly have forgotten. One of those added was the mysterious Russian lawyer Natalia Veselnitskaya, who later admitted she had close ties to the Kremlin. Kushner met Veselnitskaya at the June 2016 powwow at Trump Tower. Other Russians were there as well.

Kushner's business links to hostile foreign powers were riddled with conflicts of interest. Just one month before the election, his real estate company finalized a $285 million loan as part of a refinancing package for a troubled Times Square property. The cast of characters involved in the loan included some of the Russians who attended the Trump Tower meeting. The lender was Deutsche Bank, which at the time was dickering with regulators to settle charges involving a possible Russian money-laundering scheme.

And then there are Kushner's financial ties in the Middle East. In August 2018, Brookfield Asset Management, a Canadian concern, announced a 99-year lease on 666 Fifth Avenue, a troubled Midtown tower near Rockefeller Center. Kushner had paid a whopping $1.8 billion for the building in 2007, but it had underperformed since its acquisition. The building was 30 percent vacant, and its largest tenant planned to leave at the expiration of its lease. Kushner was in desperate need of a bailout. The deal with Brookfield would ease pressure on Kushner, whose mortgage on the property for $1.4 billion was due in February 2019. Brookfield paid $1.1 billion in rent up front. The second-largest owner of Brookfield is the Qatar Investment Authority, one of the world's largest sovereign wealth funds.

Jared Kushner's remit in the White House includes the Middle East. The bailout struck many as astonishing since Kushner had backed a Saudi- and UAE-led blockade of Qatar. Is it an emolument for the president when a foreign power rescues his financially troubled son-in-law? I leave this one to the ethicists and the law professors.

———————

As for the august Deutsche Bank, why did it stay with a litigious borrower with such a bad credit history as Trump? Was it that, in the eyes of the bank, Trump was "too big to fail"? Or is there somehow a connection with the fact that Deutsche Bank was at the same time laundering $10 billion in dirty Russian money in a "mirror trading scheme" for which regulators in New York and London fined the bank almost $700 million?

Mueller surely subpoenaed relevant records of Deutsche Bank, particularly records linked to Michael Flynn and Paul Manafort. Those records may have included Trump's tax returns. The lurking question is whether the Russians bailed Trump out of his financial woes with money laundered by his kept bankers at Deutsche Bank. Former MI6 head Richard Dearlove put it this way in an interview with *Prospect*: "What lingers for Trump may be what deals on what terms he did after the financial crisis of 2008 to borrow Russian money when others in the West would not lend to him."

One report suggested that Deutsche Bank may have sold Trump debt to the Russian state development bank VEB, now under U.S. and EU sanctions. Holders of such debt might have great leverage over Trump now that he is in office. The chairman of VEB's supervisory board is none other than Vladimir Putin. Meanwhile, Trump told the *New York Times* in a July 2017 interview that any investigation by Mueller into his family finances would cross a "red line," leading to his firing Mueller. As Obama learned with regard to his Syrian policy, it is undesirable for presidents to lay down red lines, as later events may give rise to agonizing reappraisal. According to Michael Wolff, when Steve Bannon read the interview, he exploded. It is always dangerous to tell prosecutors where not to look, he said.

———————

While Trump has hired and fired a series of attorneys, some of whom, unlike Roy Cohn, took notes, he has often acted as his own lawyer. Cohn titled one of his books *A Fool for a Client*, riffing on the shopworn maxim that "a man who is his own lawyer has a fool for a client." Of course, in his own trial Cohn defied conventional wisdom, summed up in his own behalf, and he won.

What Trump failed to learn from his life in court is that a lawsuit is about truth, not an exercise in name-calling, hyperbolic characterization, or sweeping denials. It is not a psychological pathway to winning a father's approval. A litigator may strike hard blows, but not cheap shots. The advocate in court should attack partisan ideas and reasoning, not people. His tools should be reason, not lies.

The leader of a self-governing democracy, like a litigator, must have the facts. No judge would permit crude character assassination of the kind Trump engages in. He had no reasonable basis to say, as he did during the 2016 campaign and afterward, that Chris Christie actually *knew* about Bridgegate, that George W. Bush actually *knew* there were no weapons of mass destruction in Iraq, that Obama was born in Kenya or was a Muslim, or that the execution of a search warrant by his own Justice Department was an attack on America. But certain people believed those things, and it worked for them. And those who didn't totally buy in nodded their heads and laughed, as though they were watching an episode of *All in the Family*. Someone was finally saying something politically incorrect that they all had felt but were reluctant to say.

Trump is not about the truth. David Frum observes in *Trumpocracy: The Corruption of the American Republic*, "No American president in history—no national political figure of any kind since at least Senator Joe McCarthy—has trafficked more in untruths than Donald Trump." McCarthy, of course, gave birth to McCarthyism, the strain of right-wing extremism that spawned the John Birch Society in 1958. The *Washington Post*'s Fact Checker team keeps a running tally of Trump's lies since entering office. As of Monday, April 29, 2019, it had documented 10,000 false or misleading claims in the 828 days since he took the oath of office. *That's an average of over 12 false claims a day.* Flamboyant former White House communications director Anthony Scaramucci, who was fired six days after he was hired, told CNN on April 5, 2019, that Trump lies so much "because it's fun."

Trump is responsible for what the RAND Corporation in a 324-page report aptly calls "truth decay" in American political discourse. RAND defines truth decay as "increasing disagreement about facts and analytical interpretations of facts and data; a blurring of the line between opinion and fact; an increase in the relative volume, and resulting influence, of opinion and personal experience over fact; and lowered trust in formerly respected sources of factual information."

Trump has conflated fact and opinion just as he did in his libel suit against Paul Gapp, the *Chicago Tribune* critic who didn't like his idea for a skyscraper. In many cases, Trump simply lies about the facts, and then lies about or strangely fails to remember what he has just said. His most recent assertion may contradict an assertion he uttered moments before. Trump's counselor, Kellyanne Conway, said, "[We] gave alternative facts."

None of that appears to matter to Trump's electoral base. Digital billboards appearing in Missouri and Texas in advance of the 2018 midterm elections suggested that Trump is the second coming of Jesus Christ. Other supporters have maintained he deserves the Nobel Peace Prize. And perhaps it's true that the Democrats are really the "devil"—a word Trump used in the 2018 midterm campaign, which was carefully orchestrated to resonate with elements of his evangelical Christian base—but the real question is, why do thinking people in a democratic society put up with being repeatedly lied to?

————————

Lawyers disagree about whether a sitting president may be indicted for wrongful conduct occurring either before or after he took office. Nothing in the Constitution gives the president immunity from indictment, and the Supreme Court has made clear that the president is not above the law. But the specter of a sitting president standing trial in a criminal courtroom is so horrific that many constitutional scholars say it just cannot happen. Trump's damaged Supreme Court justice Brett Kavanaugh appeared to acknowledge in an article that a sitting president was not immune from subpoena, indictment, and prosecution. He said he didn't like this and called on Congress to change the law so that the president could be assured of getting on with his job without the distraction of a criminal proceeding.

The sole remedy for serious presidential misconduct may be impeachment. Rudy Giuliani has argued that Trump may not be indicted while he occupies the Oval Office. The basis for this is a Justice Department memorandum stemming from the Nixon era that suggests the DOJ will not indict a sitting president. The Constitution, however, states that a president may be indicted *after* he leaves office. Indicted for what? Crimes in office? How about crimes *before* taking office? The Supreme Court made clear in the case of Bill Clinton and Paula Jones that a president could be sued civilly on pre-inauguration facts. So why can't the prosecutor indict a sitting president on pre-inauguration non-impeachable offenses to stop the running of the five-year statute of limitations and ask the court to stay the trial until after his term so that the president may be free to perform his constitutional duties? This legal question remains unanswered. The distraction argument is unconvincing. If a president is impeached, he must stand trial in the Senate, and that is certainly distracting. And, if Trump, as of February 18, 2019, could find the time to play golf on 172 occasions while in office, he could certainly find the time to stand trial in a criminal case.

The Mueller investigation raised enough fascinating legal hypotheticals to fill a law school textbook. On June 4, 2018, Trump tweeted the following: "As has been stated by numerous legal scholars, I have the absolute right to PARDON myself, but why would I do that when I have done nothing wrong?"

Rudy Giuliani argued that Trump could pardon himself, even if he murdered James Comey in the White House, but he would then face a nearly certain impeachment. Chris Christie agrees. Legal scholars are not so certain that Trump could pardon himself. Contrary to the Trump/Giuliani contention, the weight of legal authority is that the president cannot self-pardon. No president has ever attempted self-pardon, any more than any pope has attempted self-canonization.

The Justice Department advised Nixon that he couldn't self-pardon on the basis of a venerable principle of natural law, *nemo iudex in sua causa* (no man shall be the judge in his own case). Brett Kavanaugh disingenuously testified that he hadn't thought about the point. What lawyer has not since Trump took office? James Madison, one of the principal Framers of the Constitution, picked up this principle in *Federalist* No. 10 when he wrote, "No man is allowed to be a judge in his own cause, because his interest would certainly bias his judgment, and, not improbably, corrupt his integrity."

If Trump's "numerous" unnamed "legal scholars" actually exist, they're just wrong. No self-pardon. The Constitution expressly states that the president's pardon power does not extend to a case of his own impeachment. It also makes clear that if the president is convicted after impeachment, he "shall nevertheless be liable and subject to indictment, Trial and Punishment according to law." If he could pardon himself, this clause of the Constitution would be a snare and a delusion.

So if Trump can't self-pardon, could he pardon or commute the sentences of former associates against whom charges have been brought, such as Manafort, Gates, Papadopoulos, Stone, or Flynn? Could he preemptively pardon friends and family against whom no charges have been brought, such as Don Jr. or Jared Kushner? Could he pardon old political cronies or witnesses or potential witnesses who might cooperate with Mueller? You bet he could.

The pardon power is of course limited in the Constitution to "offenses against the United States." So state crimes in most instances could still be prosecuted after a presidential pardon. Accordingly, Manhattan district attorney Cyrus R. Vance Jr. is reportedly preparing state criminal charges against Paul Manafort, irrespective of whether he receives a presidential pardon. Manafort, who turned 70 in April 2019, is already facing a possible life sentence in two federal cases in which he stands convicted of tax and bank fraud, as well as conspiracy. Everyone agrees that a president can't pardon someone for future crimes, but there is ample precedent for presidents pardoning for past federal crimes before any charges are brought or the trial takes place. The pardon power is very broad. George H. W. Bush pardoned Caspar

Weinberger just ten days before his Iran-Contra trial was to begin, and Jimmy Carter pardoned all Vietnam draft evaders whether they had been charged or not. As for family members, Clinton pardoned his brother. Most famously, Ford pardoned Nixon for crimes he "committed or may have committed or taken part in" while in office "from January 20, 1969, through August 9, 1974."

But legalities aside, how would it look politically? There could be a constitutional crisis if Trump was seen to be abusing the pardon power, and the matter would have to be resolved in the courts. Or there might be a drumroll of political pressure on Congress to proceed with a bill of impeachment.

There is also the issue of the previously obscure Emoluments Clauses of the Constitution, under which Trump, based on what we know today, may be most vulnerable to impeachment. The Foreign Emoluments Clause, Article I, section 9, clause 8, provides in pertinent part:

> No Title of Nobility shall be granted by the United States: And no Person holding any Office of Profit or Trust under them, shall, without the Consent of the Congress, *accept of any present, Emolument, Office, or Title, of any kind whatever, from any King, Prince, or foreign State.*

There is also the lesser-known Domestic Emoluments Clause, Article II, section 1, clause 7, which provides in pertinent part:

> The President shall at stated Times receive for his Services, a Compensation, which shall neither be increased or diminished during the Period for which he shall have been elected, and he shall not receive within that Period any other Emolument from the United States, *or any of them.*

I have italicized the most relevant words. There is a dearth of legal precedent on the proper interpretation of the Emoluments Clauses because nothing like Trump has ever come up before, since the dawn of the republic. Suffice it to say, courts have interpreted the Emoluments Clauses as "broad anti-corruption provisions" designed to prevent improper domestic or foreign influence on the president.

Watchdog groups have sued under the Emoluments Clauses to stop Trump or his family from receiving any money from a foreign state or from any of the United States. They argue that any receipt of money for services violates the Constitution. The federal district courts have split over whether the issue can even be decided by judges, since the Constitution requires there to be a "case or controversy." Courts often use this requirement to avoid deciding difficult issues, dismissing them as a "political question." Trump has simply stonewalled the allegations.

But in fact Trump has shredded the Emoluments Clauses. He has more conflicts of interest than any other president in history. For example, he opened the Trump International Hotel in Washington in October 2016. Foreign diplomats and state officials are frequently guests of the hotel when they visit Washington at the invitation of the president. The hotel may also rent them private rooms for events. According to the *Wall Street Journal*, room rates at the Trump International have climbed by 50 percent since Trump's election. They are as much as 15 percent higher than those at comparable luxury hotels in Washington. Is the spread above market rates an "emolument"? Would the receipt of moneys of any kind from a foreign or state government be an "emolument" even at market rates?

The Founding Fathers looked askance at the diamond-studded snuffbox Benjamin Franklin received from Louis XVI when Franklin was America's first ambassador to France, but that was a gift, not a fee for services. Franklin had to receive approval for the gift both from President Thomas Jefferson and from Congress. Franklin received the gift before the ratification of the Constitution; during the debates, Virginia's Edmund Randolph pressed the point that a president's acceptance of emoluments from a foreign power would be an impeachable offense.

One of the biggest tenants in New York's Trump Tower is a Chinese state-owned enterprise, the Industrial and Commercial Bank of China

(ICBC). ICBC is the world's biggest lender by assets. In kicking off his presidential campaign in 2015, Trump said, "I love China. The biggest bank in the world is from China. You know where their United States headquarters is located? In this building, in Trump Tower."

ICBC has occupied 25,000 square feet on the twentieth floor, over 11 percent of Trump Tower's office capacity. Its rental rate of $95.48 per square foot is more than that paid by any other major office tenant in the building, so China pays Trump roughly $2 million annually for the space. (ICBC has announced plans to reduce its Trump Tower space when its current lease runs out in October 2019.) Whether that rate represents the market may be difficult to ascertain, and it may be the subject of conflicting expert opinion. Stay tuned on this one.

Instead of soft-pedaling his business relationship with the China bank, Trump has featured it as an accomplishment of his presidency. When the *Washington Post* asked in March 2016 about the aspirations of China in the South China Sea, Trump answered, "I do deals with them all the time. The largest bank in the world, 400 million customers, is a tenant of mine in New York, in Manhattan." "I have a great relationship with China," Trump told Breitbart in early 2016. "I'll do fine with China—we'll do much better with China than we do now, and China [will] like us better than they do now." Last I looked, we were embroiled in a trade war with China.

Certain of Trump's acts in office have appeared to be irrational. Trump signaled an abandonment of the "one-China policy" elaborated by eight presidents going back to Nixon's 1972 Shanghai Communiqué. The one-China policy states that the United States does not challenge the Chinese position that Taiwan is a part of China. On December 2, 2016, Trump and Taiwanese president Tsai Ing-wen conducted a short phone call regarding "the close economic, political and security ties between Taiwan and the U.S." On December 6, a few days after the call, Trump said that the United States is not necessarily bound by the one-China policy. Trump then reversed that stance on February 9, 2017, when he and President Xi Jinping of the People's Republic of China had a lengthy telephone conversation. The two leaders discussed numerous topics, and President Trump agreed to honor the one-China policy. What a time to rock the boat! And why?

Or maybe Trump's purported rethink of the one-China policy and then his abrupt reversal of course was not so irrational after all. Shortly thereafter, Ivanka Trump received valuable intellectual property rights from China, covering her brands of jewelry, bags, and spa services. China had denied her trademark applications before Trump took office. The day she won the approval, she and Jared Kushner dined with Xi and his wife at Mar-a-Lago.

And this was not all with Ivanka and China. In May 2018, out of the blue, Trump removed sanctions on the Chinese state-owned technology firm ZTE, which traded with both Iran and North Korea. The executive order rescued ZTE from the jaws of bankruptcy. He acted without any interagency consultation. He said his astounding move would save *Chinese* jobs. At a talk I heard him give to the Pilgrims of the United States, former Canadian prime minister Jean Chrétien quipped sarcastically that Trump's trade policy was: "Make China Great Again!" He was not the only one to say it.

A little more than a year before the ZTE affair, in March 2017, China granted Ivanka provisional approval for 38 additional products bearing the Trump name, covering branded spas, massage parlors, golf clubs, hotels, insurance, finance and real estate companies, retail shops, restaurants, bars, and bodyguard and escort services—though it's unclear whether any such businesses will actually materialize in China. The rights may well be worth millions to the Trump family. Then there is Trump's questionable conduct in the Philippines. Trump has said emphatically that the United States will not enter into regional free trade agreements. He said, however, that he is open to free trade with the Philippines. During his November 2017 Asia trip, he made no mention of human rights when he cozied up to Philippine dictator President

Rodrigo Duterte, an unabashed human rights violator. "Human rights are, in essence, an international agreement," said John Sifton, director of Asia advocacy for Human Rights Watch. Talking about trade that way suggests that Trump "doesn't hold the multilateral legal system in very high regard—and that's frightening."

In his November 2017 Asia trip, Trump, wearing the traditional Philippine *barong tagalog*, exchanged toasts with Duterte. What was Trump saluting—a U.S.-Philippines relationship or a Trump-Duterte business relationship that would reap him millions in licensing fees from the Philippine state? It is astounding that Trump didn't pressure Duterte on human rights. Trump's clinking of glasses with Duterte symbolizes a departure from the strong pro–human rights stance that is mainstream U.S. foreign policy. When he toasted Duterte, was Trump saluting shared interests between the two countries? Or was he thinking of his deal with Philippine partners who would construct a $150 million, 57-story luxury housing tower known as Trump Tower Manila, which, coincidentally, was scheduled to open in November 2017? Trump's business partner in Manila is Jose E. B. Antonio, whom Duterte appointed as special envoy for trade, investment, and economic affairs. Just before Trump's inauguration, Antonio met with Trump's sons to discuss new ventures.

Duterte achieved infamy on the world stage with his authorization of extrajudicial killings of some 7,000 suspected drug dealers and users. Like Trump, Duterte likes to brag. He told a group of businessmen in December 2016 that as mayor of Davao, he personally executed suspects, saying, "I used to do it personally—just to show to the guys that if I can do it, why can't you?"

When Trump took office in 2017, he announced a plan to turn over management of the Trump Organization to his children, seemingly to deflect any criticism over his many business dealings with foreign or state governments. Legal ethicists say this does not go far enough to insulate him from conflict of interest, as it falls far short of the traditional blind trust.

The Trump Organization has since brought at least nine new lawsuits against state and local taxing authorities across the country, seeking breaks on local property taxes. Such claims, if established, would seem to violate the Domestic Emoluments Clause. To defeat taxes, the Trump Organization has claimed that Trump's holdings are worth far less than the assessed valuations, although on other occasions and for other purposes Trump had priced the properties for far more. Here is a selection.

- Trump claimed his Chicago mixed-use skyscraper is worth less than he said before because its retail space is a failure and is virtually worthless. Trump has negotiated lower Chicago tax bills by over $145 million over the years. Dissatisfied with those breaks, Trump has brought five suits against Cook County, seeking about $34 million more in tax refunds.

- He bought the Trump National Westchester Golf Club in 1996 for $7.5 million and put in $40 million for renovations. The course features a 75,000-square-foot clubhouse, a 101-foot artificial waterfall, and a nest of condos overlooking the fairway. He valued the asset for financial disclosure purposes at $50 million. When the Town of Ossining assessed the property at $15 million, Trump sued, claiming the golf course was worth only $1.5 million. At stake is more than $32 million in refunds Trump claims are due, which will come out of strained local school budgets. The litigation is ongoing. The Town of Ossining situation is an embarrassment. Presidents should not be chiseling with local officials about their tax bills. Asked how he felt about being embroiled in litigation with a sitting president, the Ossining town supervisor uttered an oxymoronic sentence worthy of Yogi Berra: "It's certainly uncomfortable at best."

And there is more:

- In Manhattan, Trump filed six lawsuits over assessments for Trump Tower, Trump Park Avenue, and certain of his other buildings. These lawsuits are pending.

- He valued the Trump National Golf Course in Jupiter, Florida, at $50 million on his financial disclosure forms, but he claims in a lawsuit that Palm Beach County's $19.5 million assessment "exceeds the market value of the course" by over $5 million. He refused to pay taxes based on the assessed valuation for five straight years. Commenting on the lawsuit, journalist David Cay Johnston, author of the Trump-themed book *It's Even Worse Than You Think*, said, "Trump tells voters his properties are hugely valuable but claims they are worth far, far less for property tax purposes, which unfairly shifts to others the burdens of government."

There is a consistent theme to Trump's approach to federal, state, and local taxing authorities: he manipulates valuations. As Lee-Ford Tritt, a University of Florida law professor and leading expert in tax law, told the *New York Times*, "They play around with valuations in extreme ways. There are dramatic fluctuations depending on their purpose." One egregious example, according to the *Times* investigation, was the valuation of 886 rental apartments in two buildings at Trump Village, a complex in Coney Island. Trump claimed in 1995 for gift tax purposes that they were worth less than zero—negative $5.9 million. These were the very 886 units that the city valued that year at $38.1 million and that bank appraisers in 2004 would put at $106.6 million.

And in an astounding statement, giving the term "fake news" new meaning, Trump lied once again about his undeniable conflicts of interest, complaining to reporters that being president had cost him a fortune.

In June 2018, following a two-year investigation, New York State attorney general Barbara Underwood filed a 40-page verified petition in New York State Supreme Court against Trump, his three oldest children—Donald Jr., Ivanka, and Eric—and the Donald J. Trump Foundation alleging persistent violations of state and federal law governing charitable foundations. Lawyers call this "charity fraud." Anyone else but Trump might have been indicted for the conduct alleged in the complaint. Because her charges might also implicate violations of federal statutes, including federal criminal law, Underwood referred the matter as well to the Department of Justice, the IRS, and the Federal Election Commission for further action. At the moment, the alleged conduct is only the subject of a civil complaint in a state court.

According to Underwood's pleading, Trump used his foundation as a piggy bank to fund his personal and business expenses and for strategic political contributions designed to finance his campaign for president. The action sought to dissolve the foundation, enjoin the Trumps from future service as directors on not-for-profit boards, and obtain $2.8 million in restitution and penalties.

The pleading elaborated that the Trumps, "for more than a decade," had illegally caused the foundation to engage in prohibited political activity designed, among other things, to influence the outcome of the 2016 election. Trump, who was the sole signatory on the foundation's bank accounts, approved all grants and other disbursements from the foundation. Accounting staff for the Trump Organization had responsibility for issuing checks from the foundation, and did so based solely on Trump's approval before presenting the checks to Trump for signature. What Trump did, according to the complaint, was to use foundation money to make donations to select veterans' groups as a means of enhancing Trump's status with Republican voters in Iowa. The donations were featured using enlarged checks, which Trump brandished at campaign rallies. This amounted to in-kind contributions to the campaign.

Also referenced in the complaint was an unlawful $25,000 contribution from the foundation to the reelection campaign of Florida attorney general Pam Bondi, who, as mentioned earlier in chapter 8, was pondering a complaint against Trump in the Trump University imbroglio. Trump initially attempted to conceal the true nature of this payment. Only when a watchdog organization uncovered the truth about the Bondi contribution did Trump refund the money to the foundation and pay a federal excise tax as a penalty. The complaint also alluded to a series of false IRS filings on IRS Form 990, routinely signed by Trump under penalty of perjury, in which he represented that the foundation had not engaged in political activity.

The New York attorney general also alleged, among other things, misuse of charitable assets for Trump's personal and business benefit, in that the foundation had accomplished self-dealing transactions and settled legal claims against Trump's various businesses instead of using its funds for charitable pursuits. These included purchasing a $10,000 portrait of Trump to hang in one of his golf clubs, as well a second portrait (Michael Cohen also told Congress he arranged for the 2013 purchase of a third, previously unreported Trump portrait via a straw man bidder, whom Trump reimbursed with $60,000 from the coffers of the Trump Foundation, although Trump kept the portrait for himself); funding the $158,000 settlement in the 2012 action by Martin Greenberg to obtain his million-dollar prize for making a hole-in-one at the Trump National Golf Club; using $100,000 in foundation money to fund his settlement with the Town of Palm Beach over the flagpole flap at Mar-a-Lago; and paying various expenses and legal obligations of the Trump hotels. All this from a man who is supposed to be a multi-billionaire.

Underwood's lawsuit was perhaps too little too late: the *Washington Post* had revealed during the campaign how Trump was playing fast and loose with his charitable foundation. But seeing it all together in a complaint filed in court underscored how close to the chalk Trump had played his game. True to form, Trump almost immediately trashed the complaint as an attempt by "sleazy New York Democrats" to damage him. And he vowed never to settle the case. Where have we heard that one before? It was a vow Trump often made, more honored in the breach than in the observance.

In December 2018, Underwood announced a settlement, which provided that Trump would shutter the foundation under judicial supervision. Meanwhile, the attorney general's office would pursue a damage remedy against the foundation, Trump, and his three eldest children.

Because Trump hasn't released his tax returns or made known the full extent of his personal involvements with foreign governments, and has refused to put his assets in a credible blind trust, there is a pattern of conduct suggesting conflict of interest, making money from the public trust, and accepting emoluments from a foreign state—conduct that might give rise to an impeachable offense. Congress has subpoenaed Trump's tax returns perhaps to lay the basis for an Emoluments Clause violation. The bad behavior, the tax evasion, the charity fraud, the stonewalling, the manipulation of the media with lies and finely spun conspiracy theories, the shredding of constitutional norms, and the overall antigovernment approach are all extensions of deep-seated patterns of behavior that Trump has pursued throughout his business history. It all goes back to Fred Trump and how he played the game. And it all goes back to Roy Cohn as well.

On March 22, 2019, the long-awaited Mueller report, 448 pages in length, landed on the desk of Trump-appointed attorney general William Barr. Barr summarized the report's "principal conclusions" for Congress in a four-page handout but was criticized for putting a political spin on Mueller's findings, which were at the time embargoed. Mueller complained to the attorney general in a letter that Barr's four-page memo to Congress in March "did not fully capture the context, nature, and substance" of the special counsel's findings about possible obstruction of justice by President Trump, a development that led to calls for Barr's resignation.

One incontestable fact emerged from the exercise. In our constitutional architecture, when the president and his close associates are the subject of serious criminal inquiry, the executive branch cannot investigate itself in a way that will command public confidence. Why is this so? Because nothing like Donald Trump was ever contemplated by James Madison or Alexander Hamilton when they framed the Constitution in 1789. We, the people, simply cannot rely on the presidentially appointed Department of Justice to cleanse political corruption at the summit of the executive branch, even when serious crimes have been committed.

On April 18, Barr met with the press, just hours before releasing the redacted report. Barr had previously advised on March 24 of Mueller's cryptic conclusion on obstruction: "The Special Counsel states that 'while this report does not conclude that the President committed a crime, it also does not exonerate him.'" Or, as Mueller put it in his report:

> If we had confidence after a thorough investigation of the facts that the President clearly did not commit obstruction of justice, we would so state. Based on the facts and the applicable legal standards, however, we are unable to reach that judgment. . . . Accordingly, while this report does not conclude that the President committed a crime, it also does not exonerate him.

Mueller stressed that the obstruction laws apply to the "President's corrupt exercise of the powers of office," which accords with the constitutional principle that, in our country, "no person is above the law." His report, concluding a nearly two-year investigation into Trump's relationship with the Russians, was said to be based on an impressive 500 interviews, 500 search warrants, and 2,800 subpoenas. Mueller concluded that a Russian hacking and social media campaign "coincided with a series of contacts between Trump Campaign officials and individuals with ties to the Russian government." And he determined that the Trump campaign "expected it would benefit electorally from information stolen and released through Russian efforts." Yet, despite the incriminating circumstantial evidence, he found no domestic conspiracy or coordination with the Russians, who on multiple occasions offered campaign assistance. The charge, repeatedly trumpeted in the media, echoing assertions by retired intelligence officers, that Trump was or is a Russian agent or "asset," Mueller concluded, was without foundation.

Obstruction of justice, however, was another matter. The evidence Mueller accumulated was damning. Even though there was no underlying crime, Mueller noted correctly that it was not necessary to establish one to make out an obstruction offense. Trump's corrupt motive in throttling an investigation that questioned the very legitimacy of his election was self-evident. Mueller neatly laid out at least ten documented instances of obstructive Trumpian conduct consistent with the cynical, antilegal "Fuck the law, who's the judge?" attitudes this book is all about and which Trump had studiously developed with Roy Cohn long before taking office.

Mueller cited the instances of outright obstruction, including the web of needless public lies and deceit; the witness tampering and intimidation; the firing of FBI director James Comey after demanding "loyalty"; the attacks on the intelligence community; the repeated undermining of Mueller's investigation as a "witch-hunt" and a "hoax"; the effort to limit the scope of Mueller's investigation to exclude the president's conduct; the direction to White House counsel Don McGahn to fire Mueller and then lie about it; the trashing of witnesses, such as his longtime lawyer and fixer Michael Cohen, whose character he had earlier praised; and the intimation of pardons for Manafort and Stone, indicted associates who might "flip" and testify truthfully against him. Then there were the troubling answers of a man who bragged he had "one of the greatest memories of all time" yet disclaimed recollection more than 30 times when prosecutors asked him about key events. The tactic was straight out of the Roy Cohn playbook. As we have seen earlier, Cohn was fond of telling his mobster clients facing inquiry that "it is no crime not to remember."

Only long-standing Justice Department policies against indicting a sitting president prevented Mueller from concluding that Trump was guilty of obstruction offenses. Name Trump as an unindicted co-conspirator, as special prosecutor Leon Jaworski did with Nixon in June 1974? Courts have since criticized prosecutors filing indictments that name individuals as "unindicted co-conspirators," because it is unfair—the reputations of those people are sullied, but they have no forum or procedural opportunity to defend themselves.

For this reason, Mueller concluded he could not formally accuse Trump of a crime in his report when he knew Barr would not approve an indictment against the president. As previously noted, Mueller did report that he could have cleared Trump of obstruction of justice, but on these facts he could not do that either.

Barr, who called the shots, said in his four-page summary on March 24 that he would not prosecute Trump for an obstruction offense because of the legal and policy considerations against indicting a sitting president. He went further and stressed the "difficult issues" of law and fact in proving the elements of motive and corrupt intent, where Mueller had concluded that there was no underlying crime.

But, under the law, there did not have to be an underlying crime to establish motive and corrupt intent. Barr ignored Mueller's key finding:

> As described in Volume I, the evidence uncovered in the investigation did not establish that the President or those close to him were involved

in the charged Russian computer-hacking or active-measure conspiracies, or that the President otherwise had an unlawful relationship with any Russian official. But the evidence does indicate that a thorough FBI investigation would uncover facts about the campaign and the President personally that the President could have understood to be crimes or that would give rise to personal or political concerns.

On May 6, 2019, more than 375 former federal prosecutors, who had served both Republican and Democratic administrations, signed an open letter, which they posted online, in which they protested Barr's reasons for declining prosecution:

> Each of us believes that the conduct of President Trump described in Special Counsel Mueller's report would, in the case of any other person not covered by the Office of Legal Counsel policy against indicting a sitting President, result in multiple felony charges for obstruction of justice. . . .
>
> We emphasize that these are not matters of close professional judgment. . . . But, to look at these facts and say that a prosecutor could not probably sustain a conviction for obstruction of justice—the standard set out in Principles of Federal Prosecution—runs counter to logic and our experience.

Notwithstanding the ten instances of potential obstruction of justice by Trump that Mueller documented, Barr saw "difficult issues" of law and fact relative to whether the president's actions and intent could be viewed as obstruction. Prosecutors have unfettered discretion to decline criminal prosecution even where, as here, the proof is very strong. Barr's decision not to prosecute dismayed Trump's critics; Trump had lived to fight another day.

Trump characteristically overreached his Pyrrhic victory, crowing in a March 24 tweet: "No Collusion, No Obstruction, Complete and Total EXONERATION." And on April 18, he repeated the misleading claim in a tweet backdropped by an eerie *Game of Thrones* logo: "NO COLLUSION. NO OBSTRUCTION. FOR THE HATERS AND THE RADICAL LEFT DEMOCRATS—GAME◆OVER."

The game is not really over; it is still afoot. The Mueller report is but the first lap around the track. Trump-related criminal proceedings continue, and their details were exquisitely redacted from the Mueller report. Democrats in Congress are not finished picking over the investigation. They have subpoenaed Mueller's unredacted report and its underlying documents. They also seek to question Mueller himself in congressional hearings and have him explain his conclusions. They will want to question McGahn, now out of the White House; his cooperation with Mueller, with Trump's consent, surely waives any claim of executive privilege. Doubtless, they will also want, among other things, to plow the fertile ground of Roger Stone's relationship with the Russians, who accomplished the hack and the dump of the Democrats' emails on Julian Assange's WikiLeaks. Barr said he saw nothing illegal in Roger Stone or possibly others in the Trump campaign dealing in the stolen documents turned over to WikiLeaks, but that does not make such conduct any less reprehensible.

All this gives rise to consideration of the *i*-word: *impeachment*.

When Congress has digested the full Mueller report and held further hearings, nothing except a political calculus in the run-up to the 2020 election would preclude finding that Trump may be impeached for high crimes and misdemeanors, based on his links to the Russians and the subsequent obstruction of justice—the offensive conduct Barr excused. Prosecution decisions do not necessarily resolve questions of presidential ethics or impeachability. Verdicts rendered in the court of public opinion, the acts of Congress, and the final judgments of history will not turn on Attorney General Barr's decision not to indict a sitting president.

What are the legal standards for impeachment, and on what grounds could Trump be impeached? At the constitutional convention of 1787, Charles Pinckney, of South Carolina, and Pennsylvania's Gouverneur Morris sought to eliminate a narrowly worded draft provision that the president could be removed "on impeachment and conviction for malpractice or neglect of duty." Morris thought that if a president committed crimes, he wouldn't be reelected. George Mason, of Virginia, found this argument untenable. "Shall any man be above justice?" Mason mordantly inquired: "Above all shall that man be above it, who can commit the most extensive injustice?" It was Mason, arguing for a broader definition of impeachable offense, who coined the compromise formulation that carried the day: "high Crimes and Misdemeanors." Beyond this, the history of the Constitution sheds little light.

As we gauge whether there are grounds to impeach President Trump, Article II, section 4 of the Constitution sets the essential legal test:

> The President, Vice President and all civil Officers of the United States, shall be removed from Office on Impeachment for, and Conviction of, Treason, Bribery, or other high Crimes and Misdemeanors.

The use of the words "treason" and "bribery" in the text suggests that the "other high crimes and misdemeanors" referred to must be a corrupt act of the same kind as treason or bribery. But the Constitution is silent on what other crimes might possibly be "high." In his 1833 *Commentaries on the Constitution*, Supreme Court Justice Joseph Story, a great legal scholar, said that impeachment is of a "political character" and is appropriate when there is "gross neglect or usurpation or habitual disregard of the public interests, in the discharge of the duties of political office."

For an impeachment to proceed, a bill of impeachment must be brought in the House of Representatives. A trial in the Senate follows, with the chief justice presiding to rule on questions of evidence. Conviction is by a supermajority, a two-thirds vote of the senators. Impeachment proceedings involving a sitting president have been preferred only twice in American history (Andrew Johnson and Bill Clinton) and seriously contemplated on one other occasion (Richard Nixon).

If Trump is to be impeached, the question lurks: impeached for what? Carl Bernstein, who helped expose Watergate, said on CNN that he found "a consensus developing in the military, at the highest levels in the intelligence community," that Trump "is unfit to be the president." Fifty-six percent of voters, according to Quinnipiac polls, have shared this view. Despite a buoyant economy, a booming stock market, low inflation, and low unemployment, Trump's approval ratings sank to around 37 percent following the release of the Mueller report, making him perhaps the most unpopular president since polling began. But this is clearly not enough.

Another exquisitely interesting question is whether a president may be impeached for crimes committed before he took office. The articles of impeachment drawn up against Nixon related to the Watergate burglary and the cover-up, all matters that occurred during his presidency. The articles drawn up against Bill Clinton related to Monica Lewinsky and perjury, which also occurred while he was president.

Could Trump be impeached if he shot someone on Fifth Avenue, which he bragged in 2016 he could do with impunity? The Constitution prescribes no statute of limitations on high crimes and misdemeanors. Therefore, can Congress go back in time beyond the general five-year period of limitations applicable to federal crimes? Could they include in a bill of impeachment charges arising out of the old race discrimination case, or the allegations of mob involvement in the construction of Trump Tower, or his alleged crimes against women? Can they go into the Trump University scandal or the charity fraud involving the Trump Foundation (including, among other things, its illegal $25,000 political contribution to Florida attorney general Pam Bondi)? Could Congress include information from his tax returns? Could they consider possible money laundering in concert with Manafort? On this, leading constitutional lawyers may differ, but the weight of scholarly authority is that the president may be impeached only for conduct in office, and pre-presidential conduct is out of bounds.

There is, however, a minority view, held by Allan Lichtman, a professor of politics at American University. As precedent, Lichtman points to the situation in 2010 in which Congress impeached and removed from office a Louisiana federal judge named Thomas Porteous. Porteous's alleged misconduct included corrupt acts before he took office. Leading the charge that Porteous's prior misconduct was relevant to impeachment was Jeff Sessions, then a senator, who argued that if Porteous took bribes to fix cases as a state court judge before he took office, he was impeachable as a federal judge after he took office.

Of course, if a president's wrongful conduct during the campaign occurred with the intention of illegally bringing about his election, most legal scholars agree that there would be grounds for impeachment. This could include the illegal payment of hush money on the eve of a close presidential election to buy the silence of Stormy Daniels, Karen McDougal, and possibly other women with whom he allegedly dallied. It might also include welcoming help from a hostile foreign power, which hacked the Democrats (a digital-age version of the Watergate burglary), and profiting from the fruits of the hack. This might be a subversion of the political process serious enough to warrant impeachment.

Collusion with the Russians may not amount to a criminal conspiracy, but it still may amount to an impeachable offense. If the House of Representatives concludes that there is sufficient evidence of a symbiotic relationship or conscious parallelism between the Trump campaign, Russian efforts to rig the very election whereby the president attained office, some of the wrongful conduct that occurred before

January 20, 2017, and some that took place after, it might charge him with an impeachable offense. If after investigation the House found that the Russian hacking, disinformation, targeted ads, and synchronized dumping of the stolen emails that took place in 2016 was done in anticipation of future acts by Flynn, Manafort, or Trump related to Russian sanctions relief, then there would be apparent grounds for impeachment.

And while it would be hard for Congress to prove, if it concludes that while in office Trump has neglected to defend the country against future Russian or Chinese election interference because he believes it has been helpful to him in the past and would certainly be helpful to him in the future, that would certainly be a slam-dunk basis for impeachment.

In the last analysis, because impeachment is a political process, not a legal one, there are no cases on the books to point the way as to what is an impeachable offense and what is not. There is no appeal to the courts, even though Trump fatuously threatened that if the Congress moved to impeach him, he would ask the Supreme Court to intervene. In short, the reality of what may be charged as "high crimes and misdemeanors" is what a majority of the House says it is, and what conduct may warrant removal of a president from office is what two-thirds of the Senate says it is at any point in history, and that is that.

Now that the House has flipped Democratic, it must weigh the imponderables. It might vote out a bill of impeachment based on what has come out of the Mueller report. Even if it does so, it is unlikely that two-thirds of the Senate will vote to convict. Knowing that they can't convict in the Senate, the House Democratic leadership may think it an exercise in futility to impeach in the House. Alternatively, they may feel obligated to impeach as a matter of principle to vindicate the rule of law, or they may conclude, as Speaker Nancy Pelosi has intimated, that impeachment would backfire politically and only further divide the country. Most Americans, polls show, do not want to see an impeachment. In 2020, the American people may find Trump's conduct

in office so grotesquely repugnant to presidential norms that they refuse to return him to power. In the last analysis, If Trump is to be impeached, the American people must impeach him at the ballot box.

———————

The Trump presidency has become an international embarrassment.
It takes a lot for the United States to antagonize the Canadians, but
Trump managed to do it. We all watch anxiously for the next shoe to
drop, the next salacious fact to emerge, the next dollar to be wired to or
from an LLC bank account, the next multilateral agreement to be repu-
diated, the next traditional ally to be trashed, the next cabinet member
to be fired or hired or the next "great" deal to be announced only to
find that there is no deal at all.

Trump is not about to change his orange colors at age 73. Just as he
has not stopped tweeting, he has not stopped litigating. His administration is drowned in controversy, a legal battlefield as much as it is a
political one. In our system, it is lawyers who wage legal contests, and
there is no shortage of lawyers in Washington to represent him. Days
after release of the Mueller report, Trump, his two sons, and the Trump
Organization were back in court, suing Congress to block access to his
tax returns and to relevant financial records in the files of Deutsche
Bank and Capital One. Let the games begin. The House Committee on
Financial Services and the Permanent Select Committee on Intelligence soon intervened in the suit to prevent Trump's attempt to suppress the records. Trump most probably has no standing to do this
under the law. These are records that belong to the banks or to the IRS,
not to Trump. If these routine subpoenas are sustained by the courts,
and there is every reason to believe they will be, one can only wonder
what dark tales of skullduggery will be revealed.

Litigation is a contest, with a judgment the goal. The scurrilous conduct of the Trump campaign, the links to the Russians, and the obstruction of justice all remain as storm clouds over the Trump presidency.

Much of the public distrusts his every word and deed. If he makes a bad deal with North Korea or China or if he authorizes an attack on Syria or Iran, there is the reasonable suspicion it is a "wag the dog" scenario, much as Shakespeare's King Henry IV on his deathbed counseled his son, Prince Hal, to "busy giddy minds with foreign quarrels" as a way to look good or distract his political enemies from making trouble at home.

What's next? What will be Trump's future in public life? Will he be reelected? Will he be impeached? Will he resign from office, as did Nixon? Surely time will tell. Tyrants are inherently unstable; history teaches us they don't last very long.

Trump's "antic disposition" has significantly harmed our foreign relations, our diplomacy, the Constitution, and the rule of law. I hope the situation is not irremediable. However he leaves office, he will be judged by history on the degree to which he has destabilized public confidence in legal norms. We will have to discover whether he has indelibly damaged America's reputation as a world leader and a reliable, stable, and consistent player on the global stage.

Like most of us, I have marveled at how events in Washington and New York have proceeded, and am mindful that further relevant facts will surface after the publication of this book that I would have included if I had known of them. I can only say that Trump's bunker mentality, his bullying character traits, his antilegal attitudes, his erratic and irrational behavior, his lack of clarity, and his unbridled propensity to lie are ingrained in the double helix of his DNA, and these patterns are unlikely to change. But whenever or however this enfant terrible leaves office, this story of his 3,500 lawsuits and his outsized litigious character will continue to be relevant to the historical record.

April 18, 2019, the date the Mueller report was issued, was a great day for Trump, but a dark day for the justice system and the rule of law.

Trump may have cheated the hangman for the time being as far as criminal prosecution for conspiracy or obstruction of justice are concerned, but the real jury is still out on this "plaintiff in chief." History and the court of public opinion remain to render the final verdict on Donald Trump, with the only handwriting on the wall being what Trump's mentor Roy Cohn shrewdly observed in his autobiography, "No public man can remain indefinitely at the center of controversy."

ACKNOWLEDGMENTS

This book is the product of three years of hard work. I began following Trump shortly after he announced his candidacy in 2015. I found myself deeply offended by his antilegal approach to the Constitution, the courts, and the rule of law, institutions to which I had devoted my entire professional life. His wild statements cut against the grain of everything about the American judicial system I had taken as an article of faith. "What to do about Trump?" I asked myself. "Write something," came the answer from my inner self.

A look at Trump's considerable "litigation for lunch" history, I found, furnished chilling clues to his character. I quickly realized that with him, as with so many things, the past is prologue, and his 3,500 or more lawsuits furnished an accurate prediction as to how he would react in office. He has not disappointed, and it has not been a pretty picture.

Many who crossed Trump's path in one way or another have been helpful in the course of this journey, freely rendering stories, giving encouragement, or expressing opinions. A large number did not want to be acknowledged by name, perhaps fearing reprisals.

Thanks at the outset to my friends Jeffrey Rosen and his wife, Marjorie, who gave me the germ of an idea, suggesting I write a biography of Roy Cohn, the dark political sorcerer to whom Trump served as apprentice. Cohn's unethical behavior is essential to a complete understanding of Trump's character.

The brave, who had good Trump/Cohn stories to tell, perceptive insights, or else just provided necessary encouragement, included Cindy Adams, Michael Armstrong, Ken Auletta, Tom Baer, Marie Brenner, Peter Dougherty, John Doyle, John Eastman, Peter Georgescu, Ryan

Goodman, Garrett Graff, Samuel Issacharoff, Ben Lambert, Marty London, Andrew J. Maloney, Jim Marlas, Vanessa Mouner, Tom Pulling, John Rosenwald, Alan Schwartz, Peter Solomon, Katrina vanden Heuvel, and Frank Wisner. I owe thanks to them all.

There are others who have been the *sine qua non*. I give special thanks to my best conceivable agent, Peter Bernstein, who found a home for the idea and then valiantly guided my hand with invaluable editorial advice, and to my best conceivable editor, Adam Bellow, at St. Martin's Press, along with his colleagues Kevin Reilly, Alan Bradshaw, and Ryan Masteller, who meticulously waded through the manuscript and responded wisely with creative and valuable ideas that helped immeasurably in molding and shaping the book.

Most importantly, I express deep gratitude for the support and help of my wife, Marlene Hess, who plowed through successive drafts of the manuscript, made many excellent suggestions, and generously gave me the time I needed for my work. With apologies to Michael Bennett, "What she did for love!" It only remains for me to express my love for her, and for our sustaining family, without whom this book could not exist.

As the reader can readily observe, I enjoy quoting others. One of my favorite people to quote is Winston Churchill. Of writing a book, he famously said:

> Writing a book is an adventure. To begin with it is a toy and an amusement. Then it becomes a mistress, then it becomes a master, then it becomes a tyrant. The last phase is that just as you are about to be reconciled to your servitude, you kill the monster and fling him to the public.

Here, I trust, I have "killed the monster."

NOTES

PROLOGUE

ix "take care that the laws be faithfully executed": U.S. Constitution, art. II, § 3.

ix "a riddle, wrapped in a mystery": Winston Churchill, radio broadcast, October 1, 1939.

x *violation of all norms:* David Brooks, "Donald Trump's Lizard Wisdom," *New York Times*, May 10, 2018, https://nyti.ms/2KQczul.

xi "float like a butterfly": Muhammad Ali before his fight with Sonny Liston, February 25, 1964.

xii *3,500 lawsuits:* Nick Penzenstadler and Susan Page, "Exclusive: Trump's 3,500 Lawsuits Unprecedented for a Presidential Nominee," *USA Today*, June 1, 2016, https://www.usatoday.com/story/news/politics/elections/2016/06/01/donald -trump-lawsuits-legal-battles/84995854/. See also, Stephen Kotkin, "American Hustle," *Foreign Affairs*, May 21, 2019, https://www.foreignaffairs.com/articles /2019-05-21/american-hustle?utm.

xii *the American Bar Association counts 4,000:* In 2016, the American Bar Association commissioned a report by media lawyer Susan Seager that placed the number at 4,000, aside from cease-and-desist letters he sent journalists. The ABA then refused to publish the report in fear that Trump might file a lawsuit over its contents. Susan Seager, "The ABA Wouldn't Run a Piece Calling Trump a 'Libel Bully.' Here It Is," *Vox*, October 26, 2016, https://www.vox.com /the-big-idea/2016/10/26/13408060/aba-libel-law-trump-abuse-times; Adam Liptak, "Fearing Trump, Bar Association Stifles Report Calling Him a 'Libel Bully,'" *New York Times*, October 24, 2016, https://www.nytimes.com /2016/10/25/us/politics/donald-trump-lawsuits-american-bar-association .html.

xii *1,300 suits since 2000:* On April 25, 2016, Bloomberg reported that Trump had been sued 72 times in federal court since 2000. The 72 cases include only federal lawsuits against Trump himself, not those filed against his companies. Include them—along with the many lawsuits Trump and his businesses have filed against others—and all together Trump and his companies have either sued or been sued at least 1,300 times since 2000. Records on earlier suits, according to Bloomberg's research, are unavailable. https://www.bloomberg.com /graphics/2016-trump-lawsuits/.

xv *160 federal lawsuits:* Rachel Stockman, "We Investigated, Donald Trump Is
Named in at Least 169 Federal Lawsuits," Law & Crime, February 16, 2016,
https://lawandcrime.com/high-profile/we-investigated-donald-trump-is
-named-in-at-least-169-federal-lawsuits/.

xvi *Trump's abnormal breaches:* Editorial Board, "Donald Trump's Guide to
Presidential Etiquette," *New York Times*, May 25, 2018, https://www.nytimes
.com/interactive/2018/05/25/opinion/editorials/Donald-Trumps-Guide-To
-Presidential-Etiquette.html?action=click&pgtype=Homepage&clickSource
=story-heading&module=opinion-c-col-right-region&region=opinion-c-col
-right-region&WT.nav=opinion-c-col-right-region.

xvii "Trump tends to think of things in terms of real estate law": Editorial Board,
"President Trump, Please Read the Constitution," *New York Times*, November 11, 2017, https://www.nytimes.com/interactive/2017/11/11/opinion
/editorials/President-Trump-Please-Read-the-Constitution.html.

xviii *originally Roy Cohn:* Marie Brenner, "How Donald Trump and Roy Cohn's
Ruthless Symbiosis Changed America," *Vanity Fair*, June 28, 2017, https://
www.vanityfair.com/news/2017/06/donald-trump-roy-cohn-relationship.

xxi "If America has a claim to glory": Speech of Roger Nash Baldwin on receiving
the Presidential Medal of Freedom from Jimmy Carter on January 16, 1981,
quoted in William vanden Heuvel, *Hope and History: A Memoir of Tumultu-
ous Times* (Ithaca, NY: Cornell University Press, 2019), 19.

CHAPTER 1: THE FIRST LAWSUIT

1 *In October 1973, the government:* Complaint in United States v. Trump,
73 C. 1529 (E.D.N.Y. 1973), https://www.clearinghouse.net/chDocs/public
/FH-NY-0024-0005.pdf.

1 *Trump's father, a multimillionaire:* See Michael Kranish and Robert O'Harrow Jr.,
"Inside the Government's Racial Bias Case Against Donald Trump," *Washington Post*, January 23, 2016, https://www.washingtonpost.com/politics/inside
-the-governments-racial-bias-case-against-donald-trumps-company-and-how
-he-fought-it/2016/01/23/fb90163e-bfbe-11e5-bcda-62a36b394160_story.html.
See also Counsel Order in United States v. Trump, filed July 10, 1975 (U.S. Dist.
Ct. East Dist. N.Y.).

1 *The community groups handed:* Ibid.

2 "immediately rent either one": Ibid.

2 *There was also evidence that:* Ibid.

2 *Investigative journalist Wayne Barrett:* Wayne Barrett and Jon Campbell,
"How a Young Donald Trump Forced His Way from Avenue Z to Manhattan," *Village Voice*, July 20, 2015, https://www.villagevoice.com/2015/07/20
/how-a-young-donald-trump-forced-his-way-from-avenue-z-to-manhattan/.

3 *Donald Trump grew up in:* Jason Horowitz, "For Donald Trump, Lessons
from a Brother's Suffering," *New York Times*, January 2, 2016, https://www

.nytimes.com/2016/01/03/us/politics/for-donald-trump-lessons-from-a
-brothers-suffering.html.

3 "the first ethnic family to move": Ibid.

3 *Trump's grandfather, Friedrich Drumpf:* Gwenda Blair, *The Trumps: Three Generations of Builders and a President* (New York: Simon & Schuster, 2000; reprinted 2015); Nina Burleigh, *Golden Handcuffs: The Secret History of Trump's Women* (New York: Gallery Books, 2018).

4 "thousands of homes for the middle class": Tracie Rozhon, "Fred C. Trump, Postwar Master Builder of Housing for Middle Class, Dies at 93," *New York Times*, June 26, 1999, http://www.nytimes.com/1999/06/26/nyregion/fred-c -trump-postwar-master-builder-of-housing-for-middle-class-dies-at-93.html.

5 "Beach Haven is Trump's Tower": Woodie Guthrie, "Old Man Trump," 1954, never recorded, available at the Woodie Guthrie Center, Tulsa, OK.

5 *In 1927, the Ku Klux Klan:* Philip Bump, "In 1927, Donald Trump's Father Was Arrested After a Klan Riot in Queens," *Washington Post*, February 29, 2016, https://www.washingtonpost.com/news/the-fix/wp/2016/02/28/in-1927 -donald-trumps-father-was-arrested-after-a-klan-riot-in-queens/?utm_term= .372b40bc4095.

5 *Asked in 2015 by the* New York Times: "First Draft: In Interview, Donald Trump Denies Report of Father's Arrest in 1927," *New York Times*, September 22, 2015, https://www.nytimes.com/politics/first-draft/2015/09/22/in-interview -donald-trump-denies-report-of-fathers-arrest-in-1927/.

5 *But when Trump's parents were married:* Mike Pearl, "All the Evidence We Could Find About Fred Trump's Alleged Involvement with the KKK," Vice, May 10, 2016, https://www.vice.com/en_us/article/mvke38/all-the-evidence -we-could-find-about-fred-trumps-alleged-involvement-with-the-kkk.

5 *Donald Trump dismissed the press reports:* Jason Horowitz, "First Draft: In Interview, Donald Trump Denies Report of Father's Arrest in 1927," *New York Times*, September 22, 2015, https://www.nytimes.com/politics/first-draft/2015 /09/22/in-interview-donald-trump-denies-report-of-fathers-arrest-in-1927/.

6 "Denies $4 Million FHA Profit": UP, "But Trump Has That Much Surplus in the Bank," *Brooklyn Daily Eagle*, Late News edition of July 13, 1954, https:// www.newspapers.com/image/54414987.

6 *The story concerned Fred Trump's extraordinary testimony:* Hearings before the Committee on Banking and Currency, United States Senate, 83rd Congress, second session, pursuant to S. Res 229. July 12, 1954, pp. 395–420, https:// www.washingtonpost.com/wp-stat/graphics/politics/trump-archive/docs /fha-investigation-1954-part-1.pdf.

7 "untold damage to my standing": Ibid.

7 *For example, four decades later:* Isaac Stanley-Becker, "The Family Feud Behind the Trump-Cuomo Battle: 'Sometimes You Have to Hold a Grudge,'" *Washington Post*, August 20, 2018, https://www.washingtonpost.com/news /morning-mix/wp/2018/08/20/the-family-feud-behind-the-trump-cuomo

-battle-sometimes-you-have-to-hold-a-grudge/?noredirect=on&utm_term=
.e592487b2de7.

8 *"I began screaming"*: Donald Trump, *Trump: How to Get Rich: Big Deals from the Star of* The Apprentice (New York: Random House, 2004).

8 "Whenever I see Mario at dinner": Stanley-Becker, "The Family Feud Behind the Trump-Cuomo Battle."

8 "political career is over": Jacqueline Thomsen, "Trump Knocks Cuomo's 'Blunder': 'His Political Career Is Over!'" *The Hill*, August 17, 2018, https:// thehill.com/homenews/administration/402416-trump-knocks-cuomos -blunder-on-america-his-political-career-is-over.

8 *One of his business partners*: Special Interview before the Federal Housing Authority, Washington, D.C., June 18, 1954, transcript at 284, https://www .washingtonpost.com/wp-stat/graphics/politics/trump-archive/docs/1954 -06-18-senate-interview-of-fred-trump.pdf; Tomasello v. Trump, 30 Misc. 2d 643 (1961), https://www.leagle.com/decision/196167330misc2d6431542; Sidney Blumenthal, "A Short History of the Trump Family," *London Review of Books* 39, no. 4 (February 16, 2017), https://www.lrb.co.uk/v39/n04/sidney -blumenthal/a-short-history-of-the-trump-family.

9 *In 1936, he married Mary Anne MacLeod*: Nina Burleigh, *Golden Handcuffs: The Secret History of Trump's Women* (New York: Simon & Schuster, 2018).

9 *Donald's older brother, Fred Jr.*: Horowitz, "For Donald Trump, Lessons from a Brother's Suffering."

9 "For me, it worked out very well": Ibid.

9 *Freddy's bad luck was his legacy*: Heidi Evans, "Inside Trumps' Bitter Battle: Nephew's Ailing Baby Caught in the Middle," *New York Daily News*, December 19, 2000, https://www.nydailynews.com/archives/news/trumps-bitter-battle -nephew-ailing-baby-caught-middle-article-1.888562.

9 "other than [those of] my son": Rebecca Kheel, "Trump Helped Draft Will That Excluded His Brother's Children," *The Hill*, January 2, 2016, https:// thehill.com/blogs/ballot-box/presidential-races/264579-report-trump -helped-draft-will-that-excluded-his-brothers.

10 "I was so angry because they sued": Horowitz, "For Donald Trump, Lessons from a Brother's Suffering."

10 *Donald was a problem child*: Alisa Chang, "This Is Where Donald Trump Played by the Rules and Learned to Beat the Game," NPR, November 10, 2015, https://www.npr.org/2015/11/10/455331251/this-is-where-donald-trump -played-by-the-rules-and-learned-to-beat-the-game.

10 "I was a wise guy": Mark Fisher, "'Grab that Record': How Trump's High School Transcript Was Hidden," *Washington Post*, March 5, 2019, https:// www.washingtonpost.com/politics/grab-that-record-how-trumps-high -school-transcript-was-hidden/2019/03/05/8815b7b8-3c61-11e9-aaae -69364b2ed137_story.html?utm_term=.6c174d8d1dba.

10 *One of his neighbors, Laura*: Jason Horowitz, "Donald Trump's Old Queens Neighborhood Contrasts with the Diverse Area Around It," *New York Times*,

September 22, 2015, https://www.nytimes.com/2015/09/23/us/politics/donald
-trumps-old-queens-neighborhood-now-a-melting-pot-was-seen-as-a
-cloister.html.

11 "first in his class": Alden Whitman, "A Builder Looks Back—and Moves Forward," *New York Times*, January 28, 1973, https://www.nytimes.com/1973/01
/28/archives/a-builder-looks-backand-moves-forward-builder-looks-back
-but-moves.html.

11 "bone spurs in his heels": Steve Eder, "A Foot Doctor's 'Favor' May Have Helped
Trump Avoid Vietnam," *New York Times*, December 26, 2018, https://www
.nytimes.com/2018/12/26/us/politics/trump-vietnam-draft-exemption.html.

11 "personal Vietnam": Donald Trump, interview with Howard Stern, 1997, audio
at   http://www.dailymail.co.uk/news/article-3451452/Trump-says-sex-eighties
-personal-Vietnam-Howard-Stern-interview-1997.html. Stern said, "You're
braver than any Vietnam vet because you're out there screwing a lot of women."
Trump replied, "Getting the Congressional Medal of Honor in actuality."

12 *He died in June 1999:* Tracie Rozhon, "Fred C. Trump, Postwar Master Builder
of Housing for Middle Class, Dies at 93," *New York Times*, June 26, 1999,
https://www.nytimes.com/1999/06/26/nyregion/fred-c-trump-postwar
-master-builder-of-housing-for-middle-class-dies-at-93.html.

12 *$51.8 million, some 23 percent more:* Laura Davison, Lynnley Browning, and
David Voreacos, "Trump Family Tax Story Tests New IRS Chief on Second
Day in Office," Bloomberg, October 4, 2018, https://www.bloomberg.com
/news/articles/2018-10-04/trump-family-tax-report-tests-new-irs-chief-on
-2nd-day-in-office.

12 *The most significant asset reported:* David Barstow, Susanne Craig, and Russ
Buettner, "Trump Engaged in Suspect Tax Schemes as He Reaped Riches
from His Father," *New York Times*, October 2, 2018, https://www.nytimes
.com/interactive/2018/10/02/us/politics/donald-trump-tax-schemes-fred
-trump.html.

12 *The gift tax returns:* Ibid.

13 *estimates of between $1 million and $60.7 million:* Kevin Breuninger, "Trump
Claimed He Turned a 'Small' $1 Million Loan from His Father into an Em-
pire. The New York Times Says It Was More Like $60.7 Million in Loans,"
CNBC, https://www.cnbc.com/2018/10/02/trumps-small-loan-from-his-father
-was-more-like-60point7-million-nyt.html4. See also Barstow, Craig, and
Buettner, "Trump Engaged in Suspect Tax Schemes."

13 "I was never intimidated by my father": Donald Trump and Tony Schwartz,
The Art of the Deal (New York: Random House, 1992), 71.

13 "hero, role model and best friend": Kaitlin Menza, "16 Things You Didn't
Know About Donald Trump's Father, Fred," *Town & Country*, April 5, 2017,
https://www.townandcountrymag.com/society/money-and-power/g9229257
/fred-trump-facts.

13 "learned more from [him] than anyone else": Horowitz, "Donald Trump's
Old Queens Neighborhood."

13 "talked right past each other": Gwenda Blair, *The Trumps: Three Generations That Built an Empire* (New York: Simon & Schuster, 2000), 296.

13 "That's why I'm so screwed up": Donald J. Trump and Bill Zanker, *Think Big and Kick Ass in Business and Life* (New York: HarperCollins, 2007), 302.

13 "They all said, 'You have a good case'": Ken Auletta, "Don't Mess with Roy Cohn," *Esquire*, December 1978, https://www.esquire.com/news-politics /a46616/dont-mess-with-roy-cohn.

14 *It owned and managed 37 apartment complexes:* Complaint in United States of America v. Trump, 73 C. 1529 (E.D.N.Y., filed October 15, 1973), https://www.clearinghouse.net/chDocs/public/FH-NY-0024-0005.pdf; File Memorandum dated December 17, 1977, from Frank E. Schwelb, Chief, Housing and Credit Section, Civil Rights Division, United States Department of Justice, https://www.clearinghouse.net/chDocs/public/FH-NY-0024 -0039.pdf.

14 *Trump rental agents told the FBI:* Michael Kranish and Robert O'Harrow Jr., "Inside the Government's Racial Bias Case Against Donald Trump's Company, and How He Fought It," *Washington Post*, January 23, 2016, https:// www.washingtonpost.com/politics/inside-the-governments-racial-bias-case -against-donald-trumps-company-and-how-he-fought-it/2016/01/23 /fb90163e-bfbe-11e5-bcda-62a36b394160_story.html.

14 "Tell them to go to hell": Anthony Haden-Guest, "Donald Trump's Nights Out at Le Club with Roy Cohn," *Daily Beast*, January 30, 2016, https://www .thedailybeast.com/donald-trumps-nights-out-at-le-club-with-roy-cohn.

14 "Oh, you'll win hands down!": Auletta, "Don't Mess with Roy Cohn."

14 "Roy had a whole crazy deal going": Robert O'Harrow Jr. and Shawn Boburg, "The Man Who Showed Donald Trump How to Exploit Power and Instill Fear," *Washington Post*, June 17, 2016, https://www.washingtonpost.com /investigations/former-mccarthy-aide-showed-trump-how-to-exploit-power -and-draw-attention/2016/06/16/e9f44f20-2bf3-11e6-9b37-42985f6a265c _story.html.

14 *In his heyday, Roy Cohn:* Auletta, "Don't Mess with Roy Cohn"; Arnold Lubasch, "Cohn Is Acquitted with 2 Associates in Bus Probe Case," *New York Times*, December 13, 1969, https://timesmachine.nytimes.com/timesmachine/1969/12 /13/78548035.html.

16 *One of Cohn's clients was media mogul "Si" Newhouse:* Peter Robison and Mark Schoifet, "Without Si Newhouse, There Might Never Have Been a President Trump," Bloomberg, October 2, 2017, https://www.bloomberg.com /news/articles/2017-10-02/without-newhouse-there-might-never-have-been -a-president-trump.

16 *When Newhouse died in September 2017:* Jonathan Kandell, "S. I. Newhouse Jr., Who Turned Condé Nast into a Magazine Powerhouse, Dies at 89," *New York Times*, October 1, 2017, https://www.nytimes.com/2017/10/01 /obituaries/si-newhouse-dead.html.

16 "Roy Cohn Barter and Swap Exchange": Nicholas von Hoffman, *Citizen Cohn* (New York: Doubleday, 1988), 15.

16 "Lawyers are supposed to learn rules": Ibid.

17 "You knew when you were in Cohn's presence": Marie Brenner, "How Donald Trump and Roy Cohn's Ruthless Symbiosis Changed America," *Vanity Fair*, June 28, 2017, https://www.vanityfair.com/news/2017/06/donald-trump-roy-cohn-relationship.

17 "He really amazed me": Hoffman, *Citizen Cohn*, 457.

17 "I expected to hate him": O'Harrow and Boburg, "The Man Who Showed Donald Trump."

17 "It was always hard for some folks": Sidney Zion, *The Autobiography of Roy Cohn* (New York: Lyle Stuart, 1988), 11.

18 *Cohn's mobster clients included:* Selwyn Raab, "Galante Is Buried After Brief Private Rites," *New York Times*, July 17, 1979, http://www.nytimes.com/1979/07/17/archives/galante-is-buried-after-brief-private-rites-killed-in-brooklyn.html.

18 "with a thick New York accent": Jason Leopold, "If You Keep Fucking with Mr. Trump, We Know Where You Live," BuzzFeed News, May 1, 2017, https://www.buzzfeednews.com/article/jasonleopold/if-you-keep-fucking-with-mr-trump-we-know-where-you-live.

19 "It was a fetid place": Brenner, "How Donald Trump and Roy Cohn's Ruthless Symbiosis Changed America."

19 *Cohn's partner Thomas A. Bolan:* Sam Roberts, "Thomas A. Bolan, Understated Force in New York Law, Dies at 92," *New York Times*, May 16, 2017, https://www.nytimes.com/2017/05/16/nyregion/thomas-bolan-dead-roy-cohn-law-partner.html.

19 "character neurosis": United States v. Driscoll, 399 F. 2d 135 (2d Cir. 1968), available at https://law.justia.com/cases/federal/appellate-courts/F2/399/135/346849/.

20 "Isn't Roy wonderful?": William Lambert, "The Hotshot One-Man Roy Cohn Lobby," *Life*, September 5, 1969, 30.

20 "Trump lost his moral compass": Brenner, "How Donald Trump and Roy Cohn's Ruthless Symbiosis Changed America."

21 *In the McCarthy years, Cohn revitalized:* The concept of a particular style in American politics that is characterized by "heated aggression, suspiciousness, and conspiratorial fantasy" was laid out by Richard Hofstadter in "The Paranoid Style in American Politics," *Harper's*, November 1964, https://harpers.org/archive/1964/11/the-paranoid-style-in-american-politics.

21 "Only a fool pays more taxes": Roy Cohn, *How to Stand Up for Your Rights and Win!* (New York: Simon & Schuster, 1981), 301.

21 *Trump learned at the feet of the master:* Steve Rosenthal, "The Art of the Dodge: Trump's $916 Million of Net Operating Losses," *Forbes*, November 1, 2016, https://www.forbes.com/sites/beltway/2016/11/01/the-art-of-the-dodge-trumps-916-million-of-net-operating-losses/#452bff2f128f.

22 *Sandy Lindenbaum commanded high fees:* David W. Dunlap, "Samuel H. Lindenbaum, Dean of New York Zoning Lawyers, Dies at 77," *New York Times*,
August 21, 2012, https://www.nytimes.com/2012/08/22/nyregion/samuel-h
-lindenbaum-lawyer-to-major-new-york-developers-dies-at-77.html.

22 "Roy charged less": Wayne Barrett, *Trump: The Greatest Show on Earth: The
Deals, the Downfall, and the Reinvention* (New York: Regan Arts, 2016), 252.

22 *diamond-encrusted cufflinks in a Bulgari box:* Carl Campanile and Kate
Sheehy, "Trump Has Been Giving Out Fake Diamond Cufflinks for Years,"
New York Post, June 21, 2016, https://nypost.com/2016/06/21/trump-has-been
-giving-out-fake-diamond-cuff-links-for-years.

23 "conflicted prosecutor gone rogue": John Wagner, "Trump Calls Mueller a
'Conflicted Prosecutor Gone Rogue,'" *Washington Post*, November 27, 2018,
https://www.washingtonpost.com/politics/trump-calls-mueller-a-conflicted
-prosecutor-gone-rogue/2018/11/27/cbb1ba7a-f234-11e8-80d0-f7e1948d55f4
_story.html.

23 "What if he's a loser?": Ivana Trump, *Raising Trump* (New York: Gallery
Books, 2017), 63.

24 "I don't feel I insult people": O'Harrow and Boburg, "The Man Who Showed
Donald Trump."

24 "I just look at him and see Roy": This and the subsequent quote from Barrett
are in O'Harrow and Boburg, "The Man Who Showed Donald Trump."

24 "not only Donald's lawyer": Howard Blum, "Trump: The Development of a
Manhattan Developer," *New York Times*, August 26, 1980, https://timesmachine
.nytimes.com/timesmachine/1980/08/26/111281145.pdf.

24 "Roy was more than his personal lawyer": O'Harrow and Boburg, "The Man
Who Showed Donald Trump."

24 "Donald calls me 15 to 20 times a day": Brenner, "How Donald Trump and
Roy Cohn's Ruthless Symbiosis Changed America."

24 "That bravado, and if you say it aggressively and loudly enough": Jonathan
Mahler and Matt Flegenheimer, "What Donald Trump Learned from Joseph
McCarthy's Right-Hand Man," *New York Times*, June 20, 2016, https://www
.nytimes.com/2016/06/21/us/politics/donald-trump-roy-cohn.html.

25 "Roy was brutal": Marcus Baram, "Eavesdropping on Roy Cohn and Donald
Trump," *New Yorker*, April 14, 2017, https://www.newyorker.com/news/news
-desk/eavesdropping-on-roy-cohn-and-donald-trump.

25 "When an autocratic, paranoid, narcissistic ruler": Stephen Greenblatt,
Tyrant: Shakespeare on Politics (New York: W. W. Norton, 2018), 124.

25 *According to journalist Sam Roberts:* Quoted in Martin Longman, "The Story
of Roger Stone, Paul Manafort and Donald Trump," *Washington Monthly*,
February 23, 2018, https://washingtonmonthly.com/2018/02/23/the-story-of
-roger-stone-paul-manafort-and-donald-trump.

25 "The place settings were astronomical": Hoffman, *Citizen Cohn*, 376.

26 *His legal career ended in 1986:* Matter of Cohn, 118 A.D. 15 (N.Y. App. Div.
1st Department 1986), https://www.leagle.com/decision/1986133118ad2d151131.

26 *Trump testified as a character witness:* Alexandra Hutzler, "Barr Draws Comparisons to Donald Trump's Former Personal Attorney and Loyal Fixer," *Newsweek*, April 11, 2019, https://www.newsweek.com/roy-cohn-william-barr -donald-trump-attorney-1393150.

26 "stood in the back of the room silently": Marc Fisher, "Trump, Cohen and Cohn: When 'My Attorney' Becomes Just 'One of My Lawyers,'" *Washington Post*, https://www.washingtonpost.com/politics/trump-cohen-and-cohn -when-my-attorney-becomes-just-one-of-my-lawyers/2018/04/18 /03c3bcd2-4255-11e8-ad8f-27a8c409298b_story.html?utm_term= .894bcb581270.

26 *Cohn's 68th Street townhouse:* Arnold H. Lubasch, "Town House Used by Cohn Is Purchased," *New York Times*, October 17, 1987, https://www.nytimes .com/1987/10/17/nyregion/town-house-used-by-cohn-is-purchased.html.

26 *A "visibly agitated" Trump told Pirro:* Maggie Haberman, Glenn Thrush, and Peter Baker, "Inside Trump's Hour-by-Hour Battle for Self-Preservation," *New York Times*, December 9, 2017, https://www.nytimes.com/2017/12/09/us /politics/donald-trump-president.html.

26 "Where's my Roy Cohn?": Michael S. Schmidt, "Obstruction Inquiry Shows Trump's Struggle to Keep Grip on Russia Investigation," *New York Times*, January 4, 2018, https://www.nytimes.com/2018/01/04/us/politics/trump -sessions-russia-mcgahn.html.

27 "If Roy were here": Author interview with Cindy Adams.

27 "such outrageous lies": Kranish and O'Harrow, "Inside the Government's Racial Bias Case."

28 "The idea of settling drove me crazy": Trump and Schwartz, *Art of the Deal*, 98.

28 "What we didn't do was": Josh Gerstein, "FBI Releases Files on Trump Apartments' Race Discrimination Probe in '70s," *Politico*, February 15, 2017, https://www.politico.com/blogs/under-the-radar/2017/02/trump-fbi-files -discrimination-case-235067.

28 *Trump and Cohn announced with great fanfare:* United States v. Trump, filed December 12, 1973, available at https://www.clearinghouse.net/chDocs /public/FH-NY-0024-0013.pdf; transcript of hearing in United States v. Trump on February 28, 1974, before Judge Edward Neaher, p. 12, available at https://www.clearinghouse.net/chDocs/public/FH-NY-0024-0019.pdf.

29 *Trump moved to cite Goldstein:* This account is based on the following: affidavit of Frank E. Schwelb, Esq., sworn to August 2, 1974, in United States v. Trump (para. 2), https://www.clearinghouse.net/chDocs/public/FH-NY-0024 -0047.pdf; affidavit of Roy M. Cohn, Esq., sworn to July 29, 1974, in support of motion to find Donna F. Goldstein in contempt of court, in United States v. Trump (paras. 3–7), https://www.clearinghouse.net/chDocs/public/FH-NY -0024-0022.pdf; affidavit of Roy M. Cohn, Esq., sworn to July 29, 1974, in support of motion to find Donna F. Goldstein in contempt of court, in United States v. Trump (para. 1), https://www.clearinghouse.net/chDocs/public/FH -NY-0024-0022.pdf; handwritten statement of Carol Falcone, dated July 19,

1974, attached to the Cohn affidavit; affidavit of Donna F. Goldstein, sworn to August 2, 1974, in United States v. Trump (para. 2), https://www.clearinghouse .net/chDocs/public/FH-NY-0024-0046.pdf; sworn statement of Thomas Miranda, dated July 22, 1974, exhibit 2 to the Cohn affidavit; affidavit of Elyse S. Goldweber, Esq., sworn to August 5, 1974, in United States v. Trump (para. 5), https://www.clearinghouse.net/chDocs/public/FH-NY-0024-0002.pdf; testimony of Thomas Miranda at hearing before Judge Edward Neaher in United States v. Trump, held October 24, 1974 (transcript pp. 86–90), https://www .clearinghouse.net/chDocs/public/FH-NY-0024-0041.pdf.

30 "I find no evidence in the record": Ruling by Judge Neaher on October 24, 1974, denying Trump's motion to hold government attorney in contempt (transcript pp. 111–13), https://www.clearinghouse.net/chDocs/public/FH-NY -0024-0041.pdf.

31 "a long series of delaying tactics": File Memorandum from Frank E. Schwelb, Chief, Housing and Credit Section, Civil Rights Division, United States Department of Justice, dated December 17, 1977, https://www.clearinghouse.net /chDocs/public/FH-NY-0024-0039.pdf.

31 *The consent decree between Trump and the government:* The following passage is based on the consent order filed June 10, 1975, in United States v. Trump, https:// www.clearinghouse.net/chDocs/public/FH-NY-0024-0034.pdf; transcript of hearing before Judge Neaher on the consent order held June 10, 1975 (pp. 34, 42), https://www.clearinghouse.net/chDocs/public/FH-NY-0024-0036.pdf.

31 "compel the Trump Organization": Joseph P. Fried, "Trump Promises to End Race Bias," *New York Times*, June 11, 1975, https://www.nytimes.com/1975/06 /11/archives/trump-promises-to-end-race-bias-realty-management-concern -reaches.html.

33 "qualified blacks and Puerto Ricans": Kranish and O'Harrow, "Inside the Government's Racial Bias Case."

33 "In the end the government couldn't prove its case": Trump and Schwartz, *Art of the Deal*, 99.

33 *But it didn't end there:* Letter dated January 23, 1978, from Assistant Attorney General Drew S. Days to Roy M. Cohn, https://www.clearinghouse.net /chDocs/public/FH-NY-0024-0038.pdf; motion of the United States for supplemental relief, filed March 7, 1978, https://www.clearinghouse.net/chDocs /public/FH-NY-0024-0037.pdf.

34 "nothing more than a rehash": "Trump Charged with Rental Bias," *New York Times*, March 7, 1978, http://www.nytimes.com/1978/03/07/archives/trump -charged-with-rental-bias.html.

CHAPTER 2: TRUMP TAKES MANHATTAN

36 "It was good for me": Michelle Kapusta, "Who Was Fred Trump? What We Really Know About Donald Trump's Father," Cheat Sheet, October 3, 2018,

https://www.cheatsheet.com/entertainment/who-was-fred-trump-what-we
-really-know-about-donald-trumps-father.html.

37 "altered some cadences": Jonathan Greenberg, "Trump Lied to Me About
His Wealth to Get onto the Forbes 400. Here Are the Tapes," *Washington
Post*, April 20, 2018, https://www.washingtonpost.com/outlook/trump-lied
-to-me-about-his-wealth-to-get-onto-the-forbes-400-here-are-the-tapes
/2018/04/20/ac762b08-4287-11e8-8569-26fda6b404c7_story.html.

37 "over $10 billion": David Barstow, Susanne Craig, and Ross Buettner, "Trump
Engaged in Suspect Tax Schemes as He Reaped Riches from His Father,"
New York Times, October 2, 2018, https://www.nytimes.com/interactive/2018
/10/02/us/politics/donald-trump-tax-schemes-fred-trump.html; "Bloomberg
Billionaires Index: Donald Trump $2.84B," Bloomberg, 2018, https://www
.bloomberg.com/billionaires/profiles/donald-j-trump/; "Billionaires: The Richest People in the World," *Forbes*, March 4, 2019, https://www.forbes.com
/billionaires/#60b10b91251c.

38 *Commodore Hotel*: Robert E. Tomasson, "Deal Negotiated for Commodore,"
New York Times, May 4, 1975, http://www.nytimes.com/1975/05/04/archives
/deal-negotiated-for-commodore-hyatt-would-operate-it-after.html; Max
Rosenthal, "The Trump Files: How Donald Tricked New York into Giving
Him His First Huge Deal," *Mother Jones*, July 11, 2016, http://www.motherjones
.com/politics/2016/07/trump-files-how-donald-tricked-new-york-huge-deal.

38 "Whatever my friends Fred and Donald want": Michael D'Antonio, *Never
Enough: Donald Trump and the Pursuit of Success* (New York: Macmillan,
2015), 90.

40 "systematically looted tens of millions": Diana B. Henriques, "Company News:
Pritzker vs. Trump and Vice Versa," *New York Times*, March 29, 1994, http://
www.nytimes.com/1994/03/29/business/company-news-pritzker-vs-trump
-and-vice-versa.html.

40 *RICO, both a criminal and civil statute:* Hand originally referred to conspiracy as "that darling of the modern prosecutor's nursery" in Harrison v. United
States, 7 F. 2d 259, 263 (2d Cir. 1925).

40 "the rich have a very low threshold for pain": Martin London, "Spiro Agnew
Lawyer: Everyone Has the Right to Criticize the President," *Time*, January 5,
2018, time.com/5089028/donald-trump-steve-bannon-cease-desist.

40 "if you want to see what kind of partner": Diana B. Henriques, "Trump Sues
Pritzker as a Feud Goes Public," *New York Times*, July 29, 1993, http://www
.nytimes.com/1993/07/29/business/trump-sues-pritzker-as-a-feud-goes
-public.html.

41 "Every 'i' was dotted": Henriques, "Company News: Pritzker vs. Trump and
Vice Versa."

41 "I see this thing ending": Ibid.

41 *the Pritzkers bought out Trump for $140 million:* Charles V. Bagli, "Trump
Sells Hyatt Share to Pritzkers," *New York Times*, October 8, 1996, http://www

.nytimes.com/1996/10/08/business/trump-sells-hyatt-share-to-pritzkers
.html.

41 *said the Grand Hyatt was "very successful"*: "Conversation with Donald Trump," interview by David Rubenstein at the Economic Club, Washington, DC, December 15, 2014, https://www.c-span.org/video/?323309-1/conversation-donald -trump.

41 Vanity Fair *writer Vicky Ward:* The following account of the GM Building deal draws largely on Vicky Ward, *The Liar's Ball: The Extraordinary Saga of How One Building Broke the World's Toughest Tycoons* (Hoboken, NJ: Wiley, 2014). See also Peter Grant and Joseph T. Hallinan, "Trump's Plan Backfires in Battle with Conseco over GM Building," *Wall Street Journal*, February 15, 2002, https://www.wsj.com/articles/SB1013742503797704000; "Conseco Completes Sale of GM Building," Business Wire, September 26, 2003, https://www.businesswire.com/news/home/20030926005338/en /Conseco-Completes-Sale-GM-Building; Charles Bagli, "G.M. Building Sells for $1.4 Billion, a Record," *New York Times*, August 30, 2003, http:// www.nytimes.com/2003/08/30/nyregion/gm-building-sells-for-1.4-billion -a-record.html.

42 "General Odors Building": Sandra Salmans, "Estee Lauder: The Scents of Success," *New York Times*, April 18, 1982, https://www.nytimes.com/1982/04/18 /business/estee-lauder-the-scents-of-success.html.

42 *The son of a maintenance man:* Evan West, "Dumpster Fire of the Vanities: John Menard, Steve Hilbert, and the Midwestern Nouveau Riche," *Indianapolis Monthly*, February 26, 2016, http://www.indianapolismonthly.com/long form/john-menard-steve-hilbert-dumpster-fire-of-the-vanities.

44 *Zell told journalist Vicky Ward:* Ward, *Liar's Ball*, 104–105.

45 "I felt it was just disloyal of Ben": Ibid., 106.

45 "I couldn't believe it": Ibid., 107.

46 "I made a lot of money": Ibid., 107.

46–47 "the whole thing was a charade": Ibid., 21.

47 *In September 2008, developer Leslie Dick:* Isabelle Clary, "Developer Sues Soros, Cerberus," *Pensions & Investments*, October 9, 2008, http://www .pionline.com/article/20081009/ONLINE/810099993/developer-sues-soros -fortress-cerberus.

47–48 "in every material respect": Samuel Maull, "Investment Firm Says Soros Group Rigged GM Building Bid," *New York Sun*, July 12, 2006, in Leslie Dick Worldwide, LTD. v. George Soros et al., 08 Civ. 7900 ECF (S.D.N.Y 2008), https://www.scribd.com/document/188214877/RICO-ACT-Money -Laundering-Complaint-v-George-Soros-Donald-Trump-Et-Al#.

48 "This is an absurd lawsuit": Helen Peterson, "Soros Rigged Bid on City's GM Building—Suit," *Daily News*, July 12, 2006, https://www.nydailynews.com /archives/news/soros-rigged-bid-city-gm-building-suit-article-1.639770.

48 "poorly written & very boring": Emily Smith, "Trump Still Tearing His Hair Out over GM Building Book," *New York Post*, October 16, 2014, https://

pagesix.com/2014/10/16/donald-trump-still-on-warpath-over-book-about
-gm-building.

49 "This is a great deal for me": Devin Leonard, "Empire State Building Splits
Billionaire Dad from Jet-Set Daughter," *Observer*, April 6, 1998, https://
observer.com/1998/04/empire-state-building-splits-billionaire-dad-from
-jetset-daughter.

50 "One court called it 'frivolous'": Charles V. Bagli, "Partnership in Deal for
Empire State Building," *New York Times*, March 19, 2002, http://www.nytimes
.com/2002/03/19/nyregion/partnership-in-deal-for-empire-state-building
.html. For more on the history of the Empire State Building, see Charles V.
Bagli, "Empire State Building Has a Tangled History," *New York Times*,
May 4, 2013, http://www.nytimes.com/2013/05/05/business/empire-state
-building-has-a-tangled-history.html.

50 *Trump hated real estate powerhouse Leona Helmsley:* Aaron Elstein, "Trump's
Lost Empire: The Deal That Marked the Donald's Turn from New York Real
Estate," *Crain's*, April 17, 2016, http://www.crainsnewyork.com/article/20160417
/REAL_ESTATE/160419898/the-deal-that-marked-donald-trumps-turn-from
-new-york-real-estate-and-led-him-to-find-other-ways-to-remain-in-the-public
-eye.

51 "Leona Helmsley should be ashamed": Dareh Gregorian, "Trump Fails to
Topple Queen of Mean," *New York Post*, December 17, 1999, https://nypost
.com/1999/12/17/trump-fails-to-topple-queen-of-mean.

51 "Like many savvy New York real estate players": Will Parker, "Crossing
Trump: A Deep Dive into the Mogul's NYC Real Estate Litigation Offers a
Unique Window into How He'd Pursue Conflicts as Leader of the Free
World," Real Deal, April 1, 2016, https://therealdeal.com/issues_articles
/crossing-trump.

51 *In 2002, Trump sued New York City:* Charles V. Bagli, "Trump Sues City, Saying Scheme by Assessors Hurt Condo Values," *New York Times*, November 8,
2002, https://www.nytimes.com/2002/11/08/nyregion/trump-sues-city
-saying-scheme-by-assessors-hurt-condo-values.html.

52 *Trump wangled a 17 percent reduction:* Zoe Rosenberg, "Trump's NYC Real
Estate Empire Is Built on Immoderate Tax Breaks," *Curbed New York*, September 19, 2016, https://ny.curbed.com/2016/9/19/12970458/donald-trump
-nyc-real-estate-tax-breaks.

52 "I beat China all the time": Michael Cole, "When Donald Trump Sued Vincent
Lo and Henry Cheng for $1 Bil," Mingtiandi: Asia Real Estate Intelligence,
May 31, 2016, https://www.mingtiandi.com/real-estate/outbound-investment
/when-donald-trump-sued-vincent-lo-and-henry-cheng-for-1-bil.

52 *In 2005, Trump sued:* Trump v. Cheng, 9 Misc. 3d 1120 (Sup. Ct., N.Y. County),
September 14, 2005, https://law.justia.com/cases/new-york/other-courts/2005
/2005-51703.html.

52 *Lo called the lawsuit "a shock":* Farah Stockman and Keith Bradsher, "Donald Trump Soured on a Deal, and Hong Kong Partners Became Litigants,"

New York Times, May 30, 2016, https://www.nytimes.com/2016/05/31/us /politics/donald-trump-hong-kong-riverside-south.html.

52 "the Donald Trump of China": Ryan Swift, "How Vincent Lo Trumped the Donald in New York Project," *South China Morning Post*, March 2017, https:// www.scmp.com/property/hong-kong-china/article/2076696/how-vincent-lo -trumped-donald-new-york-project.

53 *Riverside South:* Timothy L. O'Brien, "How Trump Bungled the Deal of a Lifetime," Bloomberg, January 27, 2016, https://www.bloomberg.com/view /articles/2016-01-27/donald-trump-s-track-record-on-deals; Shawn Tully, "How Donald Trump Lucked into the Most Lucrative Deal of His Career," *Fortune*, April 27, 2016, http://fortune.com/2016/04/27/how-donald-trump-lucked -into-the-most-lucrative-deal-of-his-career.

53 *Trump wrote a letter to Koch:* O'Brien, "How Trump Bungled."

54 *William Zeckendorf Jr. offered:* Ibid.

54 *Judge Richard Lowe:* Anne Urda, "Judge Won't Enter $1.4B Judgment Against Trump," Law 360, January 6, 2009, https://www.law360.com/articles/81793 /judge-won-t-enter-1-4b-judgment-against-trump.

55 *Trump sued the Carlyle Group:* Trump v. The Carlyle Group, Sup. Ct. N.Y. County, opinion by Justice Bransten, March 29, 2010, https://casetext.com /case/trump-v-the-carlyle-group#!.

55 "What, you think [the Chinese are] giving up a billion dollars": Parker, "Crossing Trump."

56 *Trump labeled the top story as "68":* Vivian Lee, "Donald Trump's Math Takes His Towers to Greater Heights," *New York Times*, November 1, 2016, https://www.nytimes.com/2016/11/02/nyregion/donald-trump-tower -heights.html.

56 *Cohen made a cool $3.3 million:* Claudine Zap, "The Real Estate Maneuver- ings of Former Trump Lawyer Michael Cohen," Realtor.com, July 6, 2016, https://www.realtor.com/news/celebrity-real-estate/michael-cohen-real -estate-wheeler-dealer/.

56 *Cohen . . . had a somewhat unsavory background:* William K. Rashbaum, Danny Hakim, Brian M. Rosenthal, Emily Flitter, and Jesse Drucker, "How Michael Cohen, Trump's Fixer, Built a Shadowy Business Empire," *New York Times*, May 5, 2018, https://www.nytimes.com/2018/05/05/business/michael -cohen-lawyer-trump.html.

57 "Michael Cohen has a great insight": Lauren Price, "Upping the Ante," *New York Post*, February 22, 2007, https://nypost.com/2007/02/22/upping-the -ante.

57 "In 2014, he sold four buildings": Rashbaum et al., "How Michael Cohen."

57 *in 1980 he reneged on a promise:* Terence Cullen, "Trump Wants to Save Confederate Statues, but He Didn't Care About the Artwork on His Own Building," *Daily News*, August 17, 2017, http://www.nydailynews.com/news /politics/trump-save-confederate-statues-not-artwork-article-1.3419756.

57 *Trump was involved in at least four lawsuits:* Benjamin Mazzaro, "What Donald Trump Owns—and What He Doesn't—in NYC," *Bisnow,* August 12, 2016, https://www.bisnow.com/new-york/news/economy/how-big-is-trumps -nyc-empire-63995#0; David Margolick, "Top State Court Rules Trump Is Entitled to Tax Break for Trump Tower," *New York Times,* July 6, 1984, https://www.nytimes.com/1984/07/06/nyregion/top-state-court-rules-trump-is -entitled-to-tax-break-for-modtown-tower.html; Parker, "Crossing Trump"; Massimo Calabresi, "What Donald Trump Knew About Undocumented Workers at His Signature Tower," *Time,* August 25, 2016, http://time.com /4465744/donald-trump-undocumented-workers/.

58 "Polish Brigade": Emily Atkin, "The Story Behind Donald Trump's Undocumented Polish Workers," ThinkProgress, February 26, 2016, https://think progress.org/the-story-behind-donald-trumps-undocumented-polish -workers-243a00a77fd8; Charles V. Bagli, "Trump Paid over $1 Million in Labor Settlement, Documents Reveal," *New York Times,* November 27, 2017, https://www.nytimes.com/2017/11/27/nyregion/trump-tower-illegal -immigrant-workers-union-settlement.html.

59 "the only thing I did was sign checks": Court testimony in Diduck v. Trump, 774 F. Supp. 802 (S.D.N.Y. 1991), https://law.justia.com/cases/federal/district -courts/FSupp/774/802/1425921/. See also Calabresi, "What Trump Knew About Undocumented Workers."

59 "Still don't know there were illegal aliens": Dean Baquet, "Trump Says He Didn't Know He Employed Illegal Aliens," *New York Times,* July 13, 1990, https://www.nytimes.com/1990/07/13/nyregion/trump-says-he-didn-t -know-he-employed-illegal-aliens.html.

59 *According to attorney John Szabo:* Bagli, "Trump Paid over $1 Million."

59 "he [Trump] liked the way": Charles V. Bagli, "Donald Trump Paid $1.375 Million to Settle Case Involving Undocumented Polish Workers, Reveal Documents," *The Independent,* November 28, 2017, https://www.independent .co.uk/news/world/americas/us-politics/donald-trump-undocumented -polish-workers-tower-paid-settlement-millions-bonwit-teller-building-new -a8080336.html.

59 *mobster Daniel Sullivan:* Michelle Melnick, Lisa Riordan Seville, and Cynthia McFadden, "Trump Tower Got Its Start with Undocumented Foreign Workers," NBC News, https://www.nbcnews.com/news/us-news/donald-says -controversy-over-his-tower-was-trumped-n397821.

59 "knowingly participated": Diduck v. Kaszycki & Sons Contractors, Inc., 774 F. Supp. 802 (S.D.N.Y. 1991), https://law.justia.com/cases/federal/district -courts/FSupp/774/802/1425921.

60 *Shea & Gould:* George Rush, Joanna Molloy, and Marcus Baram, "Towering Fee Battle Pits Lawyer Against Trump," *Daily News,* October 1, 1997, http:// www.nydailynews.com/archives/gossip/towering-fee-battle-pits-lawyer -trump-article-1.778609.

60 *In 1998, after 15 years of litigation:* Bagli, "Trump Paid over $1 Million."

60 *nine of the properties received huge tax breaks:* Charles V. Bagli, "A Trump Empire Built on Inside Connections and $885 Million in Tax Breaks," *New York Times,* September 17, 2016, https://www.nytimes.com/2016/09/18/nyregion /donald-trump-tax-breaks-real-estate.html.

61 *Trump Shuttle:* Alex Horton, "The Ups and Downs of Trump Shuttle, the President's Long-Defunct Airline," *Washington Post,* January 2, 2018, https:// www.washingtonpost.com/news/retropolis/wp/2018/01/02/the-ups-and -mostly-downs-of-trump-shuttle-the-presidents-long-defunct-airline.

62 *paid an average of $15 million:* Tom Kludt, "Donald Trump's 'Apprentice' Salary Claim a 'Total Lie,' MSNBC host says," *CNN Business,* July 16, 2015, https://money.cnn.com/2015/07/16/media/lawrence-odonnell-donald -trump-salary/.

CHAPTER 3: ATLANTIC CITY TAKES TRUMP

64 *Bally Manufacturing Corporation:* Donald Janson, "Trump Ends His Strug- gle to Gain Control of Bally," *New York Times,* July 2, 1987, https://www .nytimes.com/1987/02/23/nyregion/trump-ends-his-struggle-to-gain -control-of-bally.html.

66 *A further wrinkle on the Bally litigation:* James Rowley, "Trump Agrees to Pay $750,000 Penalty to Settle Antitrust Lawsuit," AP News, April 5, 1988, https://www.apnews.com/54ea0dc590fc97d9e9e86c65336649a1.

66 *he entered the field with mobster partners:* David Cay Johnston, "Just What Were Donald Trump's Ties to the Mob?" *Politico,* May 22, 2016, https://www .politico.com/magazine/story/2016/05/donald-trump-2016-mob-organized -crime-213910; Linda Qiu, "Yes, Donald Trump Has Been Linked to the Mob," *Politifact,* March 2, 2016, https://www.politifact.com/truth-o-meter /statements/2016/mar/02/ted-cruz/yes-donald-trump-has-been-linked-mob /; Peter Grant and Alexandra Berzon, "Trump and His Debts: A Narrow Escape," *Wall Street Journal,* July 4, 2016, https://www.wsj.com/articles /trump-and-his-debts-a-narrow-escape-1451868915; David Cay Johnston, *The Making of Donald Trump* (London: Melville House, 2016), 41, quoted by blogger Isely, "Trump's Most Important Deals," September 26, 2016, https:// isely.wordpress.com/2016/09/26/trumps-most-important-deals/.

66 "eighth wonder of the world": Gillian Blair, "Trump's 'Eighth Wonder of the World' Sells for Pennies on the Dollar," *Jersey Digs,* May 19, 2017, https:// jerseydigs.com/trump-taj-mahal-hard-rock-casino-atlantic-city-sale/.

66 *James M. Crosby:* Joan Cook, "James M. Crosby, 58, Founder of Hotel and Casino Concern," *New York Times,* April 12, 1986, https://www.nytimes .com/1986/04/12/obituaries/james-m-crosby-58-founder-of-hotel-and -casino-concern.html.

67 "I have glitzy casinos": Mark Singer, "Trump Solo," *New Yorker,* May 19, 1997, https://www.newyorker.com/magazine/1997/05/19/trump-solo.

67 *Merv Griffin made a competing bid:* Richard W. Stevenson, "Griffin Wins Resorts in Deal with Trump," *New York Times*, April 15, 1988, http://www.nytimes.com/1988/04/15/business/griffin-wins-resorts-in-deal-with-trump.html.

68 "I'm very happy with the deal": Ibid.

68 *spending $1 million per week on personal expenses:* Celina Durgin, "Trump Spent $1 Million Per Week on Himself While Stiffing Builders," *National Review*, March 8, 2016, https://www.nationalreview.com/corner/donald-trump-taj-mahal-hotel-deal-cheated-builders/.

68 *Atlantic City native Marty Rosenberg:* William Sokolic, "Clinton Blasts Trump's Atlantic City Record in Boardwalk Speech," *The Press of Atlantic City*, July 6, 2016, https://www.pressofatlanticcity.com/currents_gazettes/politics/clinton-blasts-trump-s-atlantic-city-record-in-boardwalk-speech/article_7051667f-772b-5f88-bb70-9b7c6af1ab33.html.

69 *Trump said that the lurid publicity:* Michael Kruse, "The Man Who Beat Donald Trump," *Politico*, April 25, 2016, https://www.politico.com/magazine/story/2016/04/donald-trump-marvin-roffman-casino-lawsuit-213855.

69 "Once the cold winds blow": Roffman's quote from the *Wall Street Journal* of March 20, 1990, is set out in Roffman v. Trump, 754 F. Supp. 411 (E.D. PA. 1990), https://law.justia.com/cases/federal/district-courts/FSupp/754/411/2353559.

69 *Janney fired Roffman:* Diana B. Henriques, "Analyst Who Criticized Trump Is Ousted," *New York Times*, March 27, 1990, https://www.nytimes.com/1990/03/27/business/analyst-who-criticized-trump-casino-is-ousted.html.

69 *the analyst had called "begging" him:* Marie Brenner, "After the Gold Rush," *Vanity Fair*, September 1, 1990, https://www.vanityfair.com/magazine/2015/07/donald-ivana-trump-divorce-prenup-marie-brenner.

70 "the man who beat Donald Trump": Michael Kruse, "The Man Who Beat Donald Trump: How Marvin Roffman Told the Truth, Was Punished for It, and Then Fought Back," *Politico*, April 25, 2006, https://www.politico.com/magazine/story/2016/04/donald-trump-marvin-roffman-casino-lawsuit-213855.

70 *When the newspaper was about to publish:* Nick Penzenstadler, "Trump, Bill Maher and Miss Pennsylvania: The 'I'll Sue You' Effect," *USA Today*, July 11, 2016, https://www.usatoday.com/story/news/politics/elections/2016/2016/07/11/trump-bill-maher-and-miss-pennsylvania-ll-sue-you-effect/85877342/.

70 *New Jersey regulators:* Russ Buettner and Charles V. Bagli, "How Donald Trump Bankrupted His Atlantic City Casinos, but Still Earned Millions," *New York Times*, June 11, 2016, https://www.nytimes.com/2016/06/12/nyregion/donald-trump-atlantic-city.html.

70 *Steve Wynn:* John L. Smith, "Frenemies Donald Trump and Steve Wynn's Long History of 'Outrageous Conduct,'" *Daily Beast*, January 3, 2017, https://www.thedailybeast.com/frenemies-donald-trump-and-steve-wynns-long-history-of-outrageous-conduct.

70 "scumbag": Michelle Brunetti, "Trump v. Wynn, and Other Atlantic City Battles," *The Press of Atlantic City*, June 26, 2016, https://www.pressofatlanticcity .com/trump/trump-v-wynn-and-other-atlantic-city-battles/article_8c6f8d6e -38e7-11e6-830f-9baf784b4d3a.html.

70 "private driveway": "Atlantic City Tunnel 'A Hazard,' Trump Says," *The Press of Atlantic City*, February 26, 1998, https://www.pressofatlanticcity.com /townnews/law/atlantic-city-tunnel-a-hazard-trump-says/article_39604a38 -333c-11e6-80c8-d3a99698d446.html.

70 "taking money from widows and orphans": Olivia Nuzzi, "Donald Trump Sued Everyone but His Hairdresser," *Daily Beast*, July 6, 2015, https://www .thedailybeast.com/donald-trump-sued-everyone-but-his-hairdresser.

70 *Trump spent over $500,000:* John Curran, "Fed Up with Obstructions, Mirage Resorts Sues Trump, Hilton," *Las Vegas Sun*, September 10, 1997, https:// lasvegassun.com/news/1997/sep/10/fed-up-with-obstructions-mirage -resorts-sues-trump.

71 "double agent for Wynn": Smith, "Frenemies Donald Trump and Steve Wynn's Long History"; David Strow, "Private Investigator's Role Detailed in Mirage-Trump Suit," *Las Vegas Sun*, October 18, 1999, https://lasvegassun .com/news/1999/oct/18/private-investigators-role-detailed-in-mirage-trum/.

71 *Vera Coking:* Manuel Roig-Franzia, "In Heat of Legal Fight, Lawyer Says He Got a Shocking Call from Donald Trump," *Washington Post*, March 25, 2016, https://www.washingtonpost.com/politics/in-heat-of-legal-fight-lawyer-says -he-got-a-shocking-phone-call-from-donald-trump/2016/03/25/b8c8d900 -e7c1-11e5-b0fd-073d5930a7b7_story.html.

72 "I mean, the banks call me": State of New Jersey Casino Control Commission, transcript of Testimony of Donald J. Trump, February 8, 1988, https:// archive.org/stream/DonaldTrumpArchive/Atlantic%20City%20casinos%20 %20trump%20doc%20i%20DJT%20Testimony%202-8-88%20AM%20Ses sion_djvu.txt.

73 *The principal financing for the Taj:* Buettner and Bagli, "How Donald Trump Bankrupted."

73 "He's got a point": Personal interview I conducted with one of the Bear Stearns investment bankers who heard the conversation.

74 "the Partnership believes": In *re Donald J. Trump Casino Securities Litigation— Taj Mahal Litigation*, 7 F3d 357 (3d Cir. 1993), https://openjurist.org/7/f3d /357/donald-v-trumps.

75 *buying $3.35 million in chips:* Allan Sloan, "From Father Fred to the Donald Cashing In Chips off the Old Block," *Washington Post*, January 29, 1991, https://www.washingtonpost.com/archive/business/1991/01/29/from-father -fred-to-the-donald-cashing-in-chips-off-the-old-block/40928ac7-ce98 -46b8-b257-b6a5893461fb.

75 *This was later deemed an illegal loan:* Max J. Rosenthal, "The Trump Files: The Shady Way Fred Trump Tried to Save His Son's Casino," *Mother Jones*, September 26, 2016, https://www.motherjones.com/politics/2016/09/trump

-files-fred-trump-funneled-cash-donald-using-casino-chips/; "Trump Is Fined for Illegal Loan," *Tulsa World*, April 10, 1991, https://www.tulsaworld.com /archive/trump-is-fined-for-illegal-loan/article_d57f110a-c582-5eb4-adfd -a3da233a8620.html.

75 *The bondholders sold Trump's Castle:* Buettner and Bagli, "How Donald Trump Bankrupted."

75 *And when in 1990 Trump needed an emergency line of credit:* David Barstow, Susanne Craig, and Russ Buettner, "Trump Engaged in Suspect Tax Schemes as He Reaped Riches from His Father," *New York Times*, October 2, 2018, https://www.nytimes.com/interactive/2018/10/02/us/politics/donald-trump -tax-schemes-fred-trump.html.

75 *In 1996, records show:* Buettner and Bagli, "How Donald Trump Bankrupted."

75 *In 2002, the SEC slapped Trump:* In the Matter of Trump Hotels & Casino Resorts, Inc. SEC Administrative Proceeding File No. 3-10680 (Accounting and Auditing Enforcement Release No. 1499), January 16, 2002, https://www .sec.gov/litigation/admin/34-45287.htm.

76 "There's something not right": Buettner and Bagli, "How Donald Trump Bankrupted."

76 "Leverage is an amazing phenomenon": Jonathan O'Connell, David A. Fahr- enthold, and Jack Gillum, "As the 'King of Debt,' Trump Borrowed to Build His Empire. Then He Began Spending Hundreds of Millions in Cash," *Wash- ington Post*, May 5, 2018, https://www.washingtonpost.com/politics/as-the -king-of-debt-trump-borrowed-to-build-his-empire-then-he-began -spending-hundreds-of-millions-in-cash/2018/05/05/28fe54b4-44c4-11e8 -8569-26fda6b404c7_story.html.

76 "I've seen more people fail": "Warren Buffett on Donald Trump in 1991," *Con- servative Income Investor*, June 20, 2016, https://theconservativeincomeinvestor .com/warren-buffett-on-donald-trump-in-1991.

77 "he was failing in Atlantic City": Buettner and Bagli, "How Donald Trump Bankrupted."

77 "the casinos have done very well": David Hochman, "The 2004 Playboy In- terview with Donald Trump," *Playboy*, October 1, 2004, https://www.playboy .com/read/donald-trump-interview.

78 "The Trump name does not connote": Buettner and Bagli, "How Donald Trump Bankrupted."

78 *William Mays and Louis Buddy Yosha:* Mays and Yosha v. Trump, 255 F. 2d 351 (7th Cir. 2001), https://caselaw.findlaw.com/us-7th-circuit/1305717.html.

79 "tremendous amounts of crime": Nuzzi, "Donald Trump Sued Everyone."

79 *In 1993, he sued the federal government:* Wayne King, "Trump, in a Federal Lawsuit, Seeks to Block Indian Casinos," *New York Times*, May 4, 1993, http://www.nytimes.com/1993/05/04/nyregion/trump-in-a-federal-lawsuit -seeks-to-block-indian-casinos.html.

79 *Trump was on the warpath:* Shawn Boburg, "Donald Trump's Long History of Clashes with Native Americans," video, *Washington Post*, July 25, 2016,

https://www.washingtonpost.com/national/donald-trumps-long-history-of
-clashes-with-native-americans/2016/07/25/80ea91ca-3d77-11e6-80bc
-d06711fd2125_story.html.

80 "obscene, indecent and profane racial slurs": Shawn Boburg, "Donald Trump's Long History of Clashes with Native Americans," article, *Washington Post*, July 25, 2016, https://www.washingtonpost.com/national/donald-trumps-long -history-of-clashes-with-native-americans/2016/07/25/80ea91ca-3d77-11e6 -80bc-d06711fd2125_story.html?utm_term=.d9c4c1dd63fd.

80 *organized crime "is rampant—I don't mean a little bit"*: "'They Don't Look Like Indians to Me,'" video, *Washington Post*, October 5, 1993, https://www .washingtonpost.com/video/politics/they-dont-look-like-indians-to-me -donald-trump-on-native-american-casinos-in-1993/2016/07/01/20736038 -3fd4-11e6-9e16-4cf01a41decb_video.html.

81 "To date there has not been": Boburg, "Donald Trump's Long History of Clashes with Native Americans," article.

81 *the most "irresponsible" testimony*: Ibid.

81 *In 2000, with New York considering*: Ibid.

81 "a factor in my mind": Ibid.

82 *Trump sued the Eastern Pequots*: Jim Adams, "Trump Sues Eastern Pequots," *Indian Country Today*, May 30, 2003, https://indiancountrymedianetwork .com/news/trump-sues-eastern-pequots.

82 "Nobody is more for the Indians": Testimony of Trump before Congress About Indian Gaming Act, October 5, 1993, *Factbase*, https://factba.se/transcript /donald-trump-testimony-congress-indian-gaming-october-5-1993.

82 "the Taj Mahal was a very successful job": Delphine D'Amora, "How Trump's Atlantic City Gamble Went Bust," *Mother Jones*, January 20, 2016, https:// www.motherjones.com/politics/2016/01/mistake-heart-trump-atlantic-city -fiasco.

82 "Atlantic City was a very good cash cow": Buettner and Bagli, "How Donald Trump Bankrupted."

CHAPTER 4: LITIGATION FOR LUNCH

83 *the reported 3,500 lawsuits*: Nick Penzenstadler and Susan Page, "Exclusive: Trump's 3,500 Lawsuits Unprecedented for a Presidential Nominee," *USA Today*, June 1, 2016, https://www.usatoday.com/story/news/politics/elections /2016/06/01/donald-trump-lawsuits-legal-battles/84995854/.

83 "I love to have enemies": Dan Mitchell, "How Donald Trump Became Donald Trump," *Time*, July 23, 2015, http://time.com/3969794/donald-trump -history/. See also Otto Friedrich, "Flashy Symbol of an Acquisitive Age: DONALD TRUMP," *Time*, January 16, 1989, http://content.time.com/time /subscriber/article/0,33009,956733,00.html.

83 "be strategically dramatic": Donald Trump, *Trump: How to Get Rich: Big Deals from the Star of* The Apprentice (New York: Random House, 2004),

quoted in Luke Harding, "Is Donald Trump's Dark Russian Secret Hiding in Deutsche Bank's Vaults?" *Newsweek*, December 21, 2017, https://www.newsweek.com/2017/12/29/donald-trump-russia-secret-deutsche-bank-753780.html.

83 "love[s] to crush the other side": Donald Trump and Bill Zanker, *Think Big and Kick Ass in Business and Life* (New York: HarperCollins, 2007).

83–84 *he advised her to sue the European Union:* "Theresa May: Trump Told Me to Sue the EU," BBC News, July 15, 2018, https://www.bbc.com/news/uk-44838028.

84 *Trump's favorite lawsuit:* Susan E. Seager, "Donald Trump Is a Libel Bully but Also a Libel Loser," *Communications Lawyer*, Fall 2016, https://www.americanbar.org/content/dam/aba/publications/communications_lawyer/fall2016/cl32-3.authcheckdam.pdf; Olivia Nuzzi, "Donald Trump Sued Everyone but His Hairdresser," Daily Beast, July 6, 2015, https://www.thedailybeast.com/donald-trump-sued-everyone-but-his-hairdresser.

84 *Trump threatened to sue people for defamation:* Christianna Silva, "The ~20 Times Trump Has Threatened to Sue Someone During This Campaign," *FiveThirtyEight*, October 24, 2016, https://fivethirtyeight.com/features/the-22-times-trump-has-threatened-to-sue-someone-during-this-campaign/.

84 "like a fine Stradivarius violin": Callum Borchers, "Yes, Donald Trump Is Playing the Media to His Benefit. But It's Not the Media's Fault," *Washington Post*, December 9, 2015.

85 "libel proof": Martin London, "Spiro Agnew Lawyer: Everyone Has the Right to Criticize the President," *Time*, January 5, 2018, time.com/5089028/donald-trump-steve-bannon-cease-desist.

85 *"treasonous" and "unpatriotic":* Michael Wolff, *Fire and Fury: Inside the Trump White House* (New York: Henry Holt, 2018), 255.

85 "dumb as a brick": Ibid.

85 "imminent legal action": David Choi, "Trump Threatens 'Imminent' Legal Action Against Steve Bannon After Disparaging Remarks Surfaced in New Book," LMTOnline, January 3, 2018, https://www.lmtonline.com/technology/businessinsider/article/Trump-attorney-threatens-imminent-legal-action-12472634.php.

86 "spent his time at the White House leaking false information": Peter Baker and Maggie Haberman, "Trump Breaks with Bannon, Saying He Has Lost His Mind," *New York Times*, January 3, 2018, https://www.nytimes.com/2018/01/03/us/politics/trump-bannon.html.

86 "lost his mind": Ibid.

86 "I've broken one writer": Wayne Barrett, "How a Young Donald Trump Forced His Way from Avenue Z to Manhattan," *Village Voice*, July 20, 2015, https://www.villagevoice.com/2015/07/20/how-a-young-donald-trump-forced-his-way-from-avenue-z-to-manhattan/.

86 "total fiction": Interview with Donald Trump, *Washington Post*, June 6, 2016, transcript, 5, https://www.washingtonpost.com/wp-stat/graphics/politics

/trump-archive/docs/donald-trump-interview-with-robert-oharrrow-and
-shawn-boburg-june-6.pdf.

86 "it's no crime not to remember": "Witness Says Cohn Told Him 'It's No
Crime Not to Remember,'" *New York Times*, April 4, 1964, https://www
.nytimes.com/1964/04/04/archives/witness-says-cohn-told-him-its-no
-crime-not-to-remember.html.

86 *In 1985, Trump sued:* Trump v. Chicago Tribune Co., 616 F. Supp. 1434
(S.D. N.Y. 1985), https://www.leagle.com/decision/19852050616fsupp143411833.

86 "one of the silliest things anyone could inflict": Sara Boboltz, "5 Brilliant
Burns from Architecture Critics on the Trumpian Aesthetic," HuffPost, November 8, 2016, https://www.huffpost.com/entry/architecture-critics-burn
-donald-trump_n_581cd91fe4b0aac624843fca.

86 "a skyscraper offering condos": Ibid.

87 "virtually torpedoed": Paul Goldberger, "Architecture View; Can a Critic
Really Control the Marketplace?" *New York Times*, October 14, 1984, https://
www.nytimes.com/1984/10/14/arts/architecture-view-can-a-critic-really
-control-the-marketplace.html.

87 "an atrocious, ugly monstrosity": "Trump's Suit vs. Tribune Is Dismissed,"
Chicago Tribune, September 9, 1985, https://www.chicagotribune.com/news
/ct-xpm-1985-09-09-8503010062-story.html.

87 "men in public life": Trump v. Chicago Tribune Co., 616 F. Supp. 1434
(S.D. N.Y. 1985), https://www.ravellaw.com/opinions/8e3ad3139c144fa939c2
1998ec3e8ccf.

87 *In 2005, Trump threatened a libel suit:* Nuzzi, "Donald Trump Sued Everyone."

87 *he unsuccessfully brought a libel suit for $5 billion:* Ibid. See also "Trump Sues
Writer and Book Publisher," *New York Times*, January 25, 2006, http://www
.nytimes.com/2006/01/25/business/media/trump-sues-writer-and-book
-publisher.html; Trump v. O'Brien, No. A-6141-08T3 (N.J. Sup. Ct. App. Div.
2011), https://law.justia.com/cases/new-jersey/appellate-division-published
/2011/a6141-08-opn.html.

88 *Trump acknowledged he hadn't even read:* David A. Fahrenthold and Robert
O'Harrow Jr., "Trump: A True Story," *Washington Post,* August 10, 2016,
https://www.washingtonpost.com/graphics/politics/2016-election/trump
-lies/?utm_term=.e1bea5dbf73a.

88 *O'Brien's book:* Timothy O'Brien, *TrumpNation: The Art of Being The Donald*
(New York: Business Plus, 2005).

88 "The largest portion of Mr. Trump's fortune": Timothy L. O'Brien and Eric
Dash, "The Midas Touch with a Spin on It," *New York Times*, September 8,
2004, https://www.nytimes.com/2004/09/08/business/the-midas-touch-with
-spin-on-it.html.

88 "egregiously false": "Trump Sues Writer and Book Publisher," *New York
Times*, January 25, 2006, http://www.nytimes.com/2006/01/25/business/media
/trump-sues-writer-and-book-publisher.html.

88 "lowlife sleazebag": Fahrenthold and O'Harrow Jr., "Trump: A True Story."

88 *The two-day deposition:* David A. Fahrenthold and Robert O'Harrow Jr., "Even Under Oath, Donald Trump Struggled with the Truth," *Chicago Tribune,* August 10, 2016, https://www.chicagotribune.com/news/nationworld /politics/ct-trump-truth-20160810-story.html.

91 "spent a couple of bucks": Paul Farhi, "What Really Gets Under Trump's Skin? A Reporter Questioning His Net Worth," *Washington Post,* March 8, 2016, https://www.washingtonpost.com/lifestyle/style/that-time-trump-sued -over-the-size-of-hiswallet/2016/03/08/785dee3e-e4c2-11e5-b0fd -073d5930a7b7_story.html?utm_term=.7613f9a8fa35.

91 "substantially more than $7 billion": Nuzzi, "Donald Trump Sued Everyone."

91 "a beautiful young woman": Ibid.

91 *he claimed that British Petroleum:* Brandy Sadrozny and Tim Mak, "Trump Lawyer Bragged: I 'Destroyed' a Beauty Queen's Life," The Daily Beast, July 31, 2015, https://www.thedailybeast.com/trump-lawyer-bragged-i-destroyed -a-beauty-queens-life.

92 *the arbitrators awarded Trump $5 million:* Colleen Long, "Former Miss USA Has to Pay $5 Million for Defaming Donald Trump's Pageant," *Business Insider,* July 5, 2013, http://www.businessinsider.com/former-miss-usa-has-to -pay-5-million-for-defaming-donald-trumps-beauty-pageant-2013-7.

92 "When I stated my opinion": Cavan Sieczkowski, "Beauty Queen Sheena Monnin 'Shocked' by Ruling in Trump Miss USA Lawsuit," HuffPost, December 31, 2012, https://www.huffpost.com/entry/beauty-queen-sheena-monnin -shocked-trump_n_2387906.

92 *Monnin's father later said:* KTVB staff, "Trump, Bill Maher and Miss Pennsylvania: The 'I'll Sue You' Effect," KTVB.com, July 11, 2016, https://www .ktvb.com/article/news/nation-now/trump-bill-maher-and-miss -pennsylvania-the-ill-sue-you-effect/270161189.

92 *In 2015, Trump sued Univision:* Colin Campbell, "Donald Trump Is Locked in All-Out War with the US' Largest Spanish-Language TV Network," *Business Insider,* June 26, 2015, http://www.businessinsider.com/donald-trump -vs-univision-2015-6.

92 *Trump claimed that an Instagram post:* Ibid.

92 "factually false and legally ridiculous": Brian Stelter, "Donald Trump Settles with Univision over Miss USA Pageant," CNN Business, February 11, 2016, https://money.cnn.com/2016/02/11/media/donald-trump-univision-settle -miss-usa/index.html.

92 *one case in which Trump was himself sued for libel:* Jacobus v. Trump, Sup. Ct. N.Y. County, slip op. No. 153252/16 (January 9, 2017), http://caselaw.findlaw .com/ny-supreme-court/1765946.html.

93 "@CheriJacobus begged us for a job": Donald J. Trump (@realdonaldtrump), Twitter post, February 2, 2016.

93 "Really dumb @CheriJacobus": Donald J. Trump (@realdonaldtrump), Twitter post, February 5, 2016.

93 "virtually incompetent": Donald J. Trump (@realdonaldtrump), Twitter post, December 4, 2015.

93 "failed career": Donald J. Trump (@realdonaldtrump), Twitter post, December 4, 2015.

93 "Privilege protecting the expression of an opinion": Jacobus v. Trump, Sup. Ct. N.Y. County, slip op. No. 153252/16 (January 9, 2017), http://caselaw .findlaw.com/ny-supreme-court/1765946.html.

93 *Justice Jaffe was affirmed on appeal:* Affirmed, Jacobus v. Trump, 2017 NY slip op. 8625-NY: Appellate Div., 1st Dept. 2017 (December 12, 2017), https:// scholar.google.com/scholar_case?case=4836932579157571471&hl=en&as _sdt=6&as_vis=1&oi=scholarr.

93 *One such graphic:* David Martosko, "Republican Consultant Sues Trump and His Campaign Manager in $4 Million Defamation Suit After They Claimed She Criticized The Donald Because He Wouldn't Hire Her," *Daily Mail,* April 18, 2016, https://www.dailymail.co.uk/news/article-3546706 /Republican-consultant-sues-Trump-campaign-manager-4-million -defamation-suit-claimed-criticized-Donald-wouldn-t-hire-her.html.

94 *In the 1970s, he invoked RICO:* Jonathan Mahler, "Tenants Thwarted Donald Trump's Central Park Real Estate Ambitions," *New York Times,* April 19, 2016, https://www.nytimes.com/2016/04/19/us/politics/donald-trump-central -park-south.html.

94 *The plaintiff's lawyer framed a copy of Trump's check:* Martin London, *The Client Decides* (Eastlake Press, 2017).

94 *In 2006, the town of Palm Beach cited him:* Nuzzi, "Donald Trump Sued Everyone." See also Mary Jordan and Rosalind S. Helderman, "Inside Mar-a-Lago, Trump's Palm Beach Castle, and His 30-Year Fight to Win Over the Locals," *Tampa Bay Times,* November 16, 2015, https://www.tampabay.com /news/politics/stateroundup/inside-mar-a-lago-trumps-palm-beach-castle -and-his-30-year-fight-to-win/2254128.

95 "a smaller flag and pole": Nuzzi, "Donald Trump Sued Everyone."

95 "The flag is not going anywhere": Jonathan Lemire, "Fort Trump: The Donald Isn't Ducking in Fight over Giant Banner," *New York Daily News,* November 2, 2006, https://www.nydailynews.com/archives/news/fort-trump-donald-isn -ducking-fight-giant-banner-article-1.631813.

95 *donated $100,000:* Frank Cerabino, "Trump's War with Palm Beach," *Politico,* September 5, 2015, https://www.politico.com/magazine/story/2015 /09/trumps-war-with-palm-beach-213122; Nuzzi, "Donald Trump Sued Everyone."

95 *When she discovered that Trump:* Danny Hakim, "New York Attorney General Sues Trump Foundation After 2-Year Investigation," *New York Times,* June 14, 2018, https://www.nytimes.com/2018/06/14/nyregion/trump-foundation -lawsuit-attorney-general.html.

96 *In 2013, Trump settled with more than 250 hopeful condo buyers:* Unless otherwise noted, information through this section has been taken from

Michael Finnegan, "Trump's Failed Baja Condo Resort Left Buyers Feeling Betrayed and Angry," *Los Angeles Times*, June 27, 2016, http://www.latimes .com/politics/la-na-pol-trump-baja-snap-story.html. See also Stuart Pfeifer, "Donald Trump Settles Lawsuit over Baja Condo Resort That Went Bust," *Los Angeles Times*, November 27, 2013, http://www.latimes.com/business/la -fi-mo-donald-trump-settles-baja-mexico-condo-resort-lawsuit-20131127 -story.html.

96 *The individual deposits were for $50,000 and up*: Finnegan, "Trump's Failed Baja Condo Resort."

96 *The developers claimed they had spent $25 million*: Ibid.

97 *the condos at Trump SoHo in Manhattan*: Mike McIntire, "Real Estate Lawsuit, and a Criminal Case Was Closed," *New York Times*, April 5, 2016, https://www.nytimes.com/2016/04/06/us/politics/donald-trump-soho -settlement.html.

97 *So Trump decided to try to sue his way in*: For an overview of this lawsuit, see Michael Janofsky, "USFL Loses in Antitrust Case; Jury Assigns Just $1 in Damages," *New York Times*, July 30, 1986, http://www.nytimes.com/1986/07 /30/sports/usfl-loses-in-antitrust-case-jury-assigns-just-1-in-damages.html.

97 *The purchase price was said to be $9 million*: Ben Terris, "And Then There Was the Time Donald Trump Bought a Football Team," *Washington Post*, October 19, 2015, https://www.washingtonpost.com/lifestyle/style/and-then -there-was-the-time-donald-trump-bought-a-football-team-/2015/10/19 /35ae71ca-6dd6-11e5-aa5b-f78a98956699_story.html?utm_term= .67f20c79c05b.

98 *"petrified of the suit"*: Michael Janofsky, "Charges Fly from U.S.F.L.," *New York Times*, October 19, 1984, http://www.nytimes.com/1984/10/19/sports /charges-fly-from-usfl.html.

98 *"We have an excellent lawsuit"*: USFL v. NFL CNN Sports. Interview with Trump, YouTube, https://www.youtube.com/watch?v=E-UdK5n0vno.

98 *"we're going to win"*: "Donald Trump, Owner of the New Jersey Generals, said . . . ," UPI, August 6, 1986, https://www.upi.com/Archives/1986/08/06 /Donald-Trump-owner-of-the-New-Jersey-Generals-said/4270523684800/.

98 *"secret committee"*: Janofsky, "Charges Fly from U.S.F.L."

98 *NFL commissioner Pete Rozelle denied the existence*: Ibid.

98 *Cohn was dying of AIDS*: Mary Alice Miller, "*Where's My Roy Cohn?* Digs into One of the 20th Century's Most Evil Men," *Vanity Fair*, January 25, 2019, https://www.vanityfair.com/hollywood/2019/01/wheres-my-roy-cohn -digs-into-one-of-the-20th-centurys-most-evil-men.

98 *a "pit bull" of the Bar*: David Margolick, "Can a Tarnished Star Regain His Luster?" *New York Times*, February 25, 1990, https://www.nytimes.com/1990 /02/25/business/can-a-tarnished-star-regain-his-luster.html.

99 *Myerson was totally lacking, however, in antitrust experience*: Michael Boyd, "Donald Trump Is Filling His Cabinet with Reflections of Himself," HuffPost, January 6, 2017, https://www.huffpost.com/entry/we-now-know-how-donald

-trump-is-selecting-his-cabinet_b_586db579e4b070f5a180d62e?guccounter =1&guce_referrer=aHR0cHM6Ly93d3cuZ29vZ2xlLmNvbS8S&guce_referrer _sig=AQAAAHYOwq8DOZifIK7FD3cMurrEg8LhlOj-MGwYZIk5WSsND 6iDvFCy7Eki_7BF6ojXXCNDRw43VeCyX-Ux_4GvTXpGmvHRSIIGk67e7 Tnm31y-8SjI63XvxALWk7qx4kthbLzWako4Lng-GKZL-pz-zx4H9O2wQz1 KKH4sLvUYiMEE.

99 "Please, God, find for us": Ira Kaufman, "Harvey Myerson, That Self-Avowed Kid from Philadelphia, Turned Preacher . . . ," UPI, July 23, 1986, https:// www.upi.com/Archives/1986/07/23/Harvey-Myerson-that-self-avowed -street-kid-from-Philadelphia-turned/5396522475200/.

99 *The check for three dollars was never cashed:* Boris Kagan, "USFL v. NFL: The Challenge Beyond the Courtroom," *Berkeley Law Review,* https://www .law.berkeley.edu/ . . . /Sports_Stories_USFL_v_NFL__-_Boris_Kogan .pdf.

99 *Trump lost $22 million:* Michael Kruse, "Donald Trump's Art of the Fail," *Politico,* January 31, 2016, https://www.politico.com/magazine/story/2016/01 /donald-trumps-art-of-the-fail-213578.

99 "It was a nice experience": *Small Potatoes: Who Killed the USFL?* dir. Mike Tollin, ESPN Films, 2009.

99 "It was fun. We had a great lawsuit": David Cay Johnston, *The Making of Donald Trump* (London: Melville House, 2016), 57.

99 *Harvey Myerson was convicted in 1992:* Arnold Lubasch, "70 Months for Lawyer in Tax Fraud," *New York Times,* July 30, 1986, http://www.nytimes .com/1992/11/14/nyregion/70-months-for-lawyer-in-tax-fraud.html.

99 "consistent pattern of fraudulent conduct": Ibid.

100 *Trump was up to his ears:* "FinCEN Fines Trump Taj Mahal Casino Resort $10 Million for Significant and Long Standing Anti-Money Laundering Vio- lations," Financial Crimes Enforcement Network, March 6, 2015, https:// www.fincen.gov/news/news-releases/fincen-fines-trump-taj-mahal-casino -resort-10-million-significant-and-long.

100 *Federal examiners found violations:* Ibid.

100 *In 2015, the Taj admitted:* Ibid.

100 "Trump Taj Mahal received many warnings": Ibid.

100 "Like all casinos in the country": Ibid.

100 "left . . . our financial system": Ibid.

101 *FinCEN imposed a $10 million civil fine:* Ibid.

101 "willful and repeated violations": Ibid.

101 *The fine was the largest in history:* Jose Pagliery, "Trump's Casino Was a Money Laundering Concern Shortly After It Opened," CNN Politics, March 22, 2017, https://www.cnn.com/2017/05/22/politics/trump-taj-mahal /index.html.

101 *106 violations:* Ibid.

101 *He sued Palm Beach County:* Information in this section has been taken from Mark Seal, "How Donald Trump Beat Palm Beach Society and Won the

Fight for Mar-a-Lago," *Vanity Fair*, December 27, 2016, https://www
.vanityfair.com/style/2016/12/how-donald-trump-beat-palm-beach-society
-and-won-the-fight-for-mar-a-lago. See also Lisa Gartner, "Donald Trump
Sues Palm Beach Airport over Noise Levels," *Broward Palm Beach New
Times*, July 21, 2010, http://www.browardpalmbeach.com/news/donald-trump
-sues-palm-beach-airport-over-noise-levels-no-youre-fired-puns-youre
-welcome-6454803; Kathleen Walter, "Trump's $100 Million Airport Law-
suit Grounded in Palm Beach County," CBS12.com, November 14, 2016,
http://cbs12.com/news/local/trumps-100-mil-airport-lawsuit-grounded-in
-palm-beach-county; and Frank Cerabino, "Trump's War with Palm Beach,"
Politico, September 5, 2015, https://www.politico.com/magazine/story/2015
/09/trumps-war-with-palm-beach-213122.

102 *The Trump Organization website:* https://www.maralagoclub.com/Default
.aspx?p=dynamicmodule&pageid=100099&ssid=100114&vnf=1.

102 *Initially, the initiation fee was $250,000:* Seal, "How Donald Trump Beat
Palm Beach."

102 *So Trump lowered the fee to $100,000:* Jim Disis, "Trump's Mar-a-Lago Is
Getting More Exclusive," CNN Money, January 26, 2017, https://money.cnn
.com/2017/01/26/news/trump-mar-a-lago-hotels/index.html.

102 *the price of a golf club membership soared to $450,000:* Anita Kumar,
"Trump Personally Pockets Club Membership Fees, Breaking with Industry Norms," *McClatchy*, July 7, 2017, https://www.mcclatchydc.com/news
/politics-government/white-house/article159988019.html.

102 *In 2011, Trump absurdly sued:* Trump International Golf Club Scotland v.
The Scottish Ministers, UKSC 74 (2015), https://www.supremecourt.uk/cases
/uksc-2015-0160.html.

102 *Trump said that Scotland . . . had assured him:* Glenn Campbell, "Trump and
Scotland: The People Who Hit Back at the President," BBC News, July 14,
2018, https://www.bbc.co.uk/news/resources/idt-sh/Trump_and_Scotland.

102 *Trump played fast and loose:* For information on how Trump sued for tax
breaks in Florida, New York, and Illinois, see "Trump's Company Is Suing
Towns across the Country to Get Breaks on Taxes," WNYC Studios, April 11,
2018, https://www.wnycstudios.org/story/trump-inc-podcast-trump-company
-suing-towns-tax-breaks/?utm_source=Newsletter%3A+WNYC+Daily+Ne
wsletter&utm_campaign=3d033083ee-Daily_Brief_July_4_20141_26
_2014&utm_medium=email&utm_term=0_edd6b58c0d-3d033083ee
-68864137&mc_cid=3d033083ee&mc_eid=bb8af1594d.

102 *Trump's valuations for the 100 acres:* Gene Maddaus, "Donald Trump's Palos
Verdes Golf Course Has Holes in It," *Variety*, June 9, 2016, https://variety
.com/2016/biz/news/donald-trump-national-golf-club-palos-verdes-golf
-course-value-1201791482/.

102 *He received significant tax breaks:* Victoria Kim, "Trump Sues City for $100
Million," *Los Angeles Times*, December 20, 2008, http://www.latimes.com
/politics/la-pol-ca-donald-trump-sued-rancho-palos-verdes-golf-course

-story.html. Information on the lawsuit against the city of Rancho Palos Verdes is from this source.

103 "I've been looking forward for a long time": Ibid.

103 *Trump National Golf Club in Jupiter, Florida:* Information in this section has been taken from Andy Reid, "Trump Golf Club Fighting Millions in Reimbursements to Former Members," *South Florida Sun Sentinel,* August 8, 2017, http://www.sun-sentinel.com/local/palm-beach/fl-pn-trump-golf-lawsuit -appeal-20170808-story.html.

103 *accused Trump of sharp practice:* Anita Kumar, "Trump personally pockets club membership fees, breaking with industry norms." *McClatchy,* July 7, 2017, https://www.mcclatchydc.com/news/politics-government/white-house /article159988019.html.

103 –104 "revoked or canceled their memberships": Reid, "Trump Golf Club Fighting Millions."

104 *$5.4 million:* Jonathan Stempel, "Trump Company Settles Lawsuit over Disputed Golf Club Deposits," Reuters, February 23, 2018, https://www.reuters .com/article/us-usa-trump-golf/trump-company-settles-lawsuit-over -disputed-golf-club-deposits-idUSKCN1G802L.

104 *Trump offered to pay $1 million:* Information in this section is from Pete Madden, "Donald Trump Stiffed Winner of $1M Hole-in-One Contest, Report Says," Golf.com, September 21, 2016, https://www.golf.com/tour-and -news/donald-trump-stiffed-winner-1m-hole-one-contest-report-says.

104 *But the fine print:* Ibid.

104 *A $10,000 portrait of Donald Trump:* Ewan Palmer, "Donald Trump's Charity Had to Buy $10,000 Portrait of Him at Auction Because No One Else Wanted It," *Newsweek,* October 26, 2018, https://www.newsweek.com/donald -trumps-charity-had-buy-10000-portrait-him-auction-because-no-one-else -1188734.

104 *The* Washington Post *reported:* David A. Fahrenthold, "Trump Uses $258,000 from His Charity to Settle Legal Problems," *Washington Post,* September 20, 2016.

104 *There is a story about Otto Kahn:* A story, probably apocryphal, reported by Warren Bordson, "Otto H. Kahn's Cousin," *Jewish Standard,* October 22, 2009, https://jewishstandard.timesofisrael.com/otto-h-kahns-cousin/.

104 *Trump became irritated at Claudia Rabin-Manning:* Information for the section on Trump Travel & Tours is from Gersh Kuntzman, "Donald Trump Was a 'Bully' When He Sued a Tiny Travel Agency in 1989," *New York Daily News,* May 19, 2016, http://www.nydailynews.com/news/politics/donald-trump -bully-sued-tiny-travel-agency-article-1.2641738.

106 *Then there is the story of two brothers:* James Barron, "How Donald Trump Tried to Protect His Name from Others Who Shared It," *New York Times,* January 31, 2016, https://www.nytimes.com/2016/02/01/nyregion/how -donald-trump-tried-to-protect-his-name-from-others-who-shared-it .html.

106 *Jules and Eddie were sons:* Sally Apgar, "The Other Trumps," *The Real Deal*, July 1, 2009, https://therealdeal.com/issues_articles/the-other-trumps/.

106 *multibillion-dollar empire:* In February 2013, ABC News reported that Wealth-X, a Singapore company compiling data on the world's wealthiest, placed the net worth of Eddie Trump, co-founder of the Trump Group, at $96 billion. Donald Trump was nowhere to be found on a list of the 50 Most Influential Networking Tycoons beginning with Bill Gates and ending with Paul Allen. Susanna Kim, "The 50 Most Influential Networking Tycoons," ABC News, February 1, 2013, https://abcnews.go.com/Business/50-influential-ultra-high-net-worth-individuals-world/story?id=18375014. *Forbes* put Trump's net worth in 2019 at $3.1 billion: "The 50 Most Influential Networking Tycoons," *Forbes*, 2019, https://www.forbes.com/profile/donald-trump/#498129b47bdb.

106 *Jules and Eddie had branched out:* Apgar, "The Other Trumps."

106 *What sparked the suit:* Barron, "How Donald Trump Tried to Protect His Name."

106 *had recently bid $360 million:* Aaron Elstein, "The Notorious Case of The Donald vs. Trump," *Crain's New York Business*, August 6, 2015, https://www.crainsnewyork.com/article/20150806/BLOGS02/150809914/the-notorious-case-of-the-donald-vs-trump.

106 *the next day Roy Cohn demanded:* Ibid.

106 *"immigrants," parasites on his good name:* Ibid.

106–107 "have used the Trump name": Ibid.

107 "The defendants are South Africans": Ibid.

107 *who were far wealthier than Trump:* "The 50 Most Influential Networking Tycoons," *Forbes*.

107 "widely publicized and acclaimed": Elstein, "The Notorious Case of The Donald vs. Trump."

107 *Indeed, they cited a* Forbes *article:* Ibid.

107 *they also claimed that:* Ibid.

107 *Eventually, in 1989:* Ibid.

107 "The court will concede": Ibid.

107 *Trump's relationship with the bank:* Allan Smith, "Trump's Long and Winding History with Deutsche Bank Could Now Be at the Center of Robert Mueller's Investigation," *Business Insider*, December 8, 2017, http://www.businessinsider.com/trump-deutsche-bank-mueller-2017-12.

108 *The Shuttle defaulted:* Richard D. Hylton, "Company News: $1.1 Million Loan Payment Missed by Trump on Shuttle," *New York Times*, September 21, 1990, https://www.nytimes.com/1990/09/21/business/company-news-1.1-million-loan-payment-missed-by-trump-on-shuttle.html.

108 *In 2004 in connection with a loan application:* Matt Stieb, "Report: Trump Repeatedly Inflated His Net Worth in Deals with Deutsche Bank," *New York Magazine*, March 19, 2019, http://nymag.com/intelligencer/2019/03/report-trump-repeatedly-inflated-assets-in-deutsche-deals.html.

108 *In 2005, the real estate department of Deutsche Bank:* Smith, "Trump's Long and Winding History with Deutsche Bank."

108 *After the 2008 global financial crisis:* Harding, "Is Donald Trump's Dark Russian Secret?"

108 *In court, Trump denied liability:* Smith, "Trump's Long and Winding History with Deutsche Bank."

108 "The world has changed financially": Harding, "Is Donald Trump's Dark Russian Secret?"

108 *he asserted that Deutsche Bank owed* him: Ibid.

108 *alleging lender liability:* Dealbook, "Trump Sees Act of God in Recession," *New York Times*, December 5, 2008, https://dealbook.nytimes.com/2008/12 /05/trump-sees-act-of-god-in-recession/.

108 "Turn it back on the banks": Harding, "Is Donald Trump's Dark Russian Secret?"

109 "Trump proclaims himself": Ibid.

109 *Oddly, two years after:* Ibid.

109 *extended the loan term:* Vijay Prashad, "Trump and a Scam," *Frontline*, May 11, 2018, https://frontline.thehindu.com/world-affairs/trump-and-a-scam /article10107260.ece.

109 *Since the 1990s, Deutsche Bank has been:* Bob Dreyfuss, "Maxine Waters Connects the Dots on Trump, Deutsche Bank and Russia," *The Nation*, December 19, 2017, https://www.thenation.com/article/maxine-waters-connects -the-dots-on-trump-deutsche-bank-and-russia/.

109 *Trump now owes:* Harding, "Is Donald Trump's Dark Russian Secret?"; and Ben McLannahan, Kara Scannell, and Gary Silverman, "Donald Trump's Debt to Deutsche Bank," *Financial Times*, August 30, 2017, https://www.ft .com/content/8c6d9dca-882c-11e7-bf50-e1c239b45787.

109 *In 1993, Chuck Jones:* "Marla Maples' Ex-Publicist Convicted in Shoe Fetish Case," UPI, February 16, 1994.

109 *Jones brought lawsuits:* See, e.g., Jones v. Trump, 919 F. Supp. 583 (D. Conn. 1996), available at https://law.justia.com/cases/federal/district-courts/FSupp /919/583/1580713/; Jones v. Trump, 971 F. Supp. 783 (S.D.N.Y. 1997).

110 *Jones demanded an astronomical sum:* Jones v. Trump, 919 F. Supp. 583 (D. Conn. 1996).

110 *Jones appeared* pro se: Ibid.

110 *Trump and Maples counterclaimed:* Nuzzi, "Donald Trump Sued Everyone."

110 "The only stalking that I'm aware of": Ibid.

110 *Bill Maher appeared on* The Tonight Show: Eriq Gardner, "Donald Trump Withdraws Bill Maher Lawsuit," *Hollywood Reporter*, April 3, 2013, https:// www.hollywoodreporter.com/thr-esq/donald-trump-withdraws-bill-maher -432675.

110 *Trump sent Maher a copy:* Joseph Ax, "Trump Withdraws 'Orangutan' Lawsuit Against Comic Bill Maher," Reuters, April 2, 2013, https://www.reuters.com /article/entertainment-us-usa-trump-lawsuit-idUSBRE9310PL20130402.

110 *Trump sued him for $5 million:* Gardner, "Donald Trump Withdraws Bill Maher Lawsuit."

110 *In 1992, Trump sued his ex-wife Ivana:* Nuzzi, "Donald Trump Sued Everyone."

110 *He had an agreement:* "Trump Can Sue Ivana for Violating Gag Order," UPI, June 30, 1992, https://www.upi.com/Archives/1992/06/30/Trump-can-sue -Ivana-for-violating-gag-order/7036709876800/.

110 "willful, deliberate and surreptitious disclosure": Nuzzi, "Donald Trump Sued Everyone."

CHAPTER 5: EMPTY THREATS

112 *A Google search . . . for "Trump threatens suit":* On May 15, 2019, Trump had about 34,900,000 results (0.51 seconds).

112 *What is interesting:* As of June 2016, *USA Today* said Trump was involved in 3,500 lawsuits; hence the title of this book. Nick Penzenstadler and Susan Page, "Exclusive: Trump's 3,500 Lawsuits Unprecedented for a Presidential Nominee," *USA Today,* June 1, 2016. The threats exceeded the lawsuits by an exponential factor. In the first seven months since taking office Trump was sued more than 100 times. Caroline Hallemann, "Here's What You Need to Know About Donald Trump's Lawsuits," *Town & Country,* August 28, 2017, https://www.townandcountrymag.com/society/politics/a9962852/lawsuits -against-donald-trump/.

113 "His standard technique": Ken Auletta, "Don't Mess with Roy Cohn," *Esquire,* July 13, 2016, http://www.esquire.com/news-politics/a46616/dontmess -with-roy-cohn/.

113 "The mere sending": Ibid.

113 *There are stories:* Ibid.

113 "We just tell the opposition": Ibid.

114 "He's been vicious": Ibid.

114 *often on Twitter:* Saeed Ahmed, "10 Times Donald Trump Has Raised the Possibility of Lawsuits on Twitter," CNN, January 4, 2018, https://www.cnn.com /2018/01/04/politics/trump-twitter-lawsuit-threats-list-trnd/index.html.

114 *One of Stern's Magazines:* Mark Alpert, "The Battle of the Billionaires," *Fortune,* September 25, 1989, http://archive.fortune.com/magazines/fortune/fortune _archive/1989/09/25/72502/index.htm.

114 "went nuts": Ibid.

114 "I just read a highly inaccurate": Kurt Eichenwald, "A People's History of Donald Trump's Business Busts and Countless Victims," *Newsweek,* October 18, 2019.

114 *Trump then wrote to the president of the magazine:* Ibid.

114 *Trump dropped the threat:* Ibid.

114 "We spoke": Ibid.

114 "absurd": Ibid.

114 "product of a juvenile": Ibid.

114 *In the summer of 2004:* Stephen Gandel, "Mark Cuban Just Gave a Bizarre Talk Supporting Donald Trump," *Fortune,* May 13, 2016, http://fortune.com /2016/05/12/mark-cuban-donald-trump-2/.

114 *Trump's lawyers wrote to Cuban:* Ibid.

114 *The United States Golf Association:* Information on the USGA responding to Trump from Christine Brennan, "Donald Trump Said to Have Threatened USGA with Lawsuit if It Moved Women's Open," *USA Today,* July 11, 2017, https://www.usatoday.com/story/sports/golf/lpga/2017/07/10/donald-trump -said-have-threatened-usga-lawsuit/465590001/.

115 *he was distracted by 75 lawsuits:* Nick Penzenstadler and John Kelly, "How 75 Pending Lawsuits Could Distract a Donald Trump Presidency," *USA Today,* October 25, 2016, https://www.usatoday.com/story/news/politics/elections /2016/10/25/pending-lawsuits-donald-trump-presidency/92666382/.

115 *On June 16, 2016:* Ibid.

115 "I think, you know, most people think I'm right": Ibid.

115 *The pair settled their litigation:* Keith L. Alexander, "Trump Organization Settles Restaurant Suit with Second Chef, Geoffrey Zakarian," *Washington Post,* April 10, 2017, https://www.washingtonpost.com/local/public-safety/trump -organization-settles-restaurant-suit-with-second-chef-geoffrey-zakarian /2017/04/10/8a8a8f98-1d8f-11e7-ad74-3a742a6e93a7_story.html?utm_term= .8e6f9a5c38df.

115 "I'm now going to teach you": Donald J. Trump (@realdonaldtrump), Twitter post, January 31, 2013, https://twitter.com/realdonaldtrump/status/2970876 13851017216?lang=en.

115 "I'm not trying": Araceli Cruz, "Mac Miller Responds to Donald Trump Threats: 'Let's Be Friends!'" *Fuse,* February 2, 2013, https://www.fuse.tv/2013 /02/mac-miller-responds-to-donald-trumps-threats-let-s-be-friends.

115 *In addition, Trump threatened to sue:* Matt Ford. "The 19 Women Who Accused President Trump of Sexual Misconduct," *The Atlantic,* December 7, 2017, https://www.theatlantic.com/politics/archive/2017/12/what-about-the -19-women-who-accused-trump/547724/.

115 *Only one of the women, Summer Zervos:* Sarah Maslin Nir, "Trump Can Be Sued for Defamation by Summer Zervos, 'Apprentice' Contestant, Court Rules," *New York Times,* March 14, 2019, https://www.nytimes.com/2019/03 /14/nyregion/summer-zervos-trump-defamation-lawsuit.html.

115 *Christianna Silva:* Unless otherwise noted, all information in the bulleted list is from Christianna Silva, "The ~20 Times Trump Has Threatened to Sue Someone During This Campaign," *FiveThirtyEight,* October 24, 2016, https:// fivethirtyeight.com/features/the-22-times-trump-has-threatened-to-sue -someone-during-this-campaign/.

116 *When Kasich spent $2.5 million:* Theodore Schleifer, "Trump Launches Twitter Tirade Against Kasich After Large Super PAC Ad Buy," CNN, November 19, 2015, https://www.cnn.com/2015/11/19/politics/john-kasich-donald -trump-super-pac-new-hampshire/index.html.

116 "Watch Kasich squirm": Trump quoted in ibid.

116 "This was not personal": Joe Otterson, "Donald Trump Threatens to Sue Washington Post," *The Wrap*, January 19, 2016, https://www.thewrap.com/donald -trump-threatens-to-sue-washington-post-over-casino-bankruptcy-story/.

116 "I will be bringing more libel suits": *Washington Post*, transcript of interview with Donald Trump, May 18, 2016, https://www.washingtonpost.com/wp -stat/graphics/politics/trump-archive/docs/donald-trump-interview-with -shawn-boburg-robert-oharrrow-drew-harwell-amy-goldstein-jerry -markon-may-18-2016.pdf.

117 "I have wonderful lawyers": Jonathan Swan, "Trump: 'I Have Wonderful Lawyers; I Like to Send Letters," *The Hill*, February 18, 2016, https://thehill .com/blogs/ballot-box/presidential-races/269974-trump-i-have-wonderful -lawyers-and-i-like-to-send-letters.

117 "if he doesn't like what I report": David Cay Johnston, Twitter post, September 19, 2016, https://twitter.com/DavidCayJ/status/777928062960795648.

117 "I know I'm a public figure": "Q&A with David Cay Johnston," C-SPAN transcript of Brian Lamb interview with David Cay Johnston, August 26, 2016, https://www.c-span.org/video/transcript/?id=53553.

117 "unbelievably dishonest": *Washington Post*, transcript of interview with Donald Trump, May 18, 2016, https://www.washingtonpost.com/wp-stat/graphics /politics/trump-archive/docs/donald-trump-interview-with-shawn-boburg -robert-oharrrow-drew-harwell-amy-goldstein-jerry-markon-may-18-2016.pdf.

117 *"defamatory" statements Schwartz made:* Jane Mayer, "Donald Trump Threatens the Ghostwriter of 'The Art of the Deal,'" *New Yorker*, July 20, 2016, https://www.newyorker.com/news/news-desk/donald-trump-threatens-the -ghostwriter-of-the-art-of-the-deal.

117 "I am sure there will be a counter-claim": Reuters, "Despite Criticism, Donald Trump Stands by His Arrested Manager," *Newsweek*, March 30, 2016, https://www.newsweek.com/corey-lewandowski-michelle-fieldsdonald -trump-arrest-play-down-442243.

118 *When Club for Growth:* See Silva, "The ~20 Times Trump Has Threatened to Sue"; and Alan Rappeport, "Donald Trump Threatens to Sue Club for Growth Over Ad Campaign," *New York Times*, September 22, 2015, https:// www.nytimes.com/politics/first-draft/2015/09/22/donald-trump-threatens -to-sue-club-for-growth-over-ad-campaign/.

118 *He threatened to sue Wayne Barrett:* Information in this section is from Wayne Barrett and Jon Campbell, "How a Young Donald Trump Forced His Way from Avenue Z to Manhattan," *Village Voice*, July 20, 2015, https://www .villagevoice.com/2015/07/20/how-a-young-donald-trump-forced-his-way -from-avenue-z-to-manhattan/.

118 *He threatened to sue the satirical online news:* Morgan Gstalter, "Cohen Threatened The Onion in 2013 over Satirical Trump Article," *The Hill*, May 22, 2018, https://thehill.com/homenews/media/388740-cohen-threatened-the-onion-in -2013-over-satirical-trump-article.

118 *threatened to sue the artist Illma Gore:* Claire Voon, "The Donald Threatens to Sue Artist over Her Trump Micropenis Portrait," *Hyperallergenic*, April 20, 2016, https://hyperallergic.com/292436/the-donald-threatens-to-sue-artist-over-her-trump-micropenis-portrait/.

118 *In 2012, he threatened Amazon founder:* Matthew Yglesias, "Donald Trump Threatens Amazon as Payback for *Washington Post* Articles He Doesn't Like," *Vox*, May 13, 2016, https://www.vox.com/2016/5/13/11669850/donald-trump-threatens-amazon.

119 *In 2012 Trump threatened legal action against Angelo Carusone:* See Angelo Carusone, "Why Macy's Must Stop Selling Donald Trump's Brand," *Daily Beast*, November 21, 2012, https://www.thedailybeast.com/angelo-carusone-why-macys-must-stop-selling-donald-trumps-brand; and Aaron Couch, "Donald Trump Threatens to Sue Macy's Protester for $25 Million," *Hollywood Reporter*, February 18, 2013, https://www.hollywoodreporter.com/thr-esq/donald-trump-threatens-sue-macy-422135.

119 "As dishonest as @RollingStone is": Donald J. Trump (@realdonaldtrump), Twitter post, April 6, 2015, https://twitter.com/realdonaldtrump/status/585260932831453184.

119 "disgusting, both inside and out": Liam Stack, "Donald Trump Keeps Insulting Rosie O'Donnell. Here's How Their Feud Started," *New York Times*, September 28, 2016, https://www.nytimes.com/2016/09/29/us/donald-trump-keeps-insulting-rosie-odonnell-heres-how-their-feud-started.html?module=inline.

119 "Rosie will rue the words": Mark Dagostino and Brian Orloff, "Rosie Slams Trump, The Donald Fires Back," *People*, December 20, 2006, https://people.com/celebrity/rosie-slams-trump-the-donald-fires-back/.

119 "disgusting": Maya Oppenheim, "Rosie O'Donnell Hits Back at Donald Trump After He Stands by 'Fat Pig' Comments," *The Independent*, September 27, 2016.

119 "slob": Ibid.

119 "fat ugly face": Ibid.

119 "degenerate": Ibid.

119 "get better fast": Camille Mann, "Donald Trump Wishes Rosie O'Donnell Well After Heart Attack," CBS News August 22, 2012, https://www.cbsnews.com/news/donald-trump-wishes-rosie-odonnell-well-after-heart-attack/.

119 "well thank you donald": Ibid.

120 *In April 2016 he threatened to sue the Associated Press:* Silva, "The ~20 Times Trump Has Threatened to Sue."

120 "My lawyers want to sue the failing @NYTimes": Donald J. Trump (@realdonaldtrump), Twitter post, September 17, 2016, https://twitter.com/realdonaldtrump/status/777280259875975169?lang=en.

120 "whether to sue or not may be a difficult decision": Roy Cohn, *How to Stand Up for Your Rights and Win!* (New York: Devin-Adair Publishers, 1981), 293.

120 *According to testimony before Congress:* Collin Brinkley, "Cohen Threatened Trump's Schools Not to Share Grades, Scores," *U.S. News and World Report*,

February 27, 2019, https://www.usnews.com/news/politics/articles/2019-02
-27/cohen-threatened-trumps-schools-not-to-share-grades-scores.

121 "going to open up our libel laws": Hadas Gold, "Donald Trump: We're Going
to 'Open Up' Libel Laws," *Politico*, February 26, 2016, https://www.politico
.com/blogs/on-media/2016/02/donald-trump-libel-laws-219866.

121 *In September 2016, he had a reporter arrested*: Callum Borchers, "Why a Reporter Was Just Arrested Outside a Donald Trump Event," *Washington Post*,
September 17, 2016, https://www.washingtonpost.com/news/the-fix/wp
/2016/09/17/a-reporter-was-just-arrested-outside-a-donald-trump-event
-but-theres-more-to-the-story/?utm_term=.52a05711e3da.

121 "prompt initiation of appropriate legal action": Trevor Timm, "Trump's
Many, Many Threats to Sue the Press Since Launching His Campaign," *Co-
lumbia Journalism Review*, October 3, 2016, https://www.cjr.org/first_person
/donald_trump_lawsuit_new_york_times.php.

121 *When he realized that threatening libel suits*: Louis Nelson and Margaret
Harding McGill, "Trump Suggests Challenging NBC's Broadcast License,"
Politico, October 11, 2017, https://www.politico.com/story/2017/10/11/trump
-nbc-broadcast-license-243667.

122 "Fake @NBCNews made up a story": Donald J. Trump (@realdonaldtrump),
Twitter post, October 11, 2017, https://twitter.com/realdonaldtrump/status
/918110279367643137?lang=en.

122 "With all of the Fake News coming out of NBC": Donald J. Trump (@real
donaldtrump), Twitter post, October 11, 2017, https://twitter.com/realdonald
trump/status/918112884630093825?lang=en.

122 "It's frankly disgusting": Nelson and Harding McGill, "Trump Suggests
Challenging NBC's Broadcast License."

122 "Network news . . . has become so partisan": Donald J. Trump (@realdon
aldtrump), Twitter post, October 11, 2017, https://twitter.com/realdonaldtrump
/status/918267396493922304?lang=en.

122 *Nixon tried such a threat*: Nihal Krishan, "Trump Is Not the First President
to Want Media Licenses Revoked Due to Unfavorable Coverage," *Inside
Sources*, October 20, 2017, https://www.insidesources.com/trump-not-first
-president-want-media-licenses-revoked-due-unfavorable-coverage/.

122 "Wow, Matt Lauer was just fired": Donald J. Trump (@realdonaldtrump),
Twitter post, November 29, 2017, https://twitter.com/realdonaldtrump/status
/935844881825763328?lang=en.

CHAPTER 6: TRUMP AND THE MOB

123 *New York State Organized Crime Task Force concluded*: New York State Organized Task Force Report, quoted by Robert O'Harrow Jr. in "Trump Swam
in Mob-Infested Waters in Early Years as an NYC Developer," *Washington
Post*, December 16, 2015, https://www.washingtonpost.com/investigations
/trump-swam-in-mob-infested-waters-in-early-years-as-an-nyc-developer

/2015/10/16/3c75b918-60a3-11e5-b38e-06883aacba64_story.html?utm
_term=.fa66d71a7515.

124 *Most of the major private and public cement contracts:* Selwyn Raab, "Irregularities in Concrete Industry Inflate Building Costs, Experts Say," *New
York Times,* April 26, 1982, http://www.nytimes.com/1982/04/26/nyregion
/irregularities-in-concrete-industry-inflate-building-costs-experts-say.html
?pagewanted=all.

124 *At that time, Mob kingpin Paul Castellano:* David Cay Johnston, "Just What
Were Donald Trump's Ties to the Mob?" *Politico,* May 22, 2016, https://www
.politico.com/magazine/story/2016/05/donald-trump-2016-mob-organized
-crime-213910.

124 *On December 16, 1985:* Information on Castellano's murder from Arnold H.
Lubasch, "Shot by Shot, an Ex Aide to Gotti Describes the Killing of Castellano," *New York Times,* March 4, 1992, http://www.nytimes.com/1992/03/04
/nyregion/shot-by-shot-an-ex-aide-to-gotti-describes-the-killing-of
-castellano.html?pagewanted=all.

124 *shot six times:* Robert D. McFadden. "Organized-Crime Chief Shot Dead
Stepping from Car on E. 46th Street," *New York Times,* December 17, 1985,
https://www.nytimes.com/1985/12/17/nyregion/organized-crime-chief-shot
-dead-stepping-from-car-on-e-46th-st.html?module=inline.

124 *Castellano was out on bail:* Ibid.

125 *In 1987, U.S. attorney Rudy Giuliani:* Arnold H. Lubasch, "2 Convicted of
Racketeering in Mafia Construction Case," *New York Times,* July 18, 1987,
https://www.nytimes.com/1987/07/18/nyregion/2-convicted-of-racketeering
-in-mafia-construction-case.html.

125 *Dic-Underhill was a concrete firm:* Steve Villano, "The Trumps: 'An Incestu-
ous Intertwining with Organized Crime,'" June 3, 2016, *The Medium,* https://
medium.com/@stevevillano/the-trumps-an-incestuous-intertwining-with
-organized-crime-ab65316c2b48.

125 *In addition to their control:* Raab, "Irregularities in Concrete Industry Inflate
Building Costs."

126 *Halloran's company poured the concrete:* Tom Robbins, "Trump and the
Mob—The Budding Mogul Had a Soft Spot (but a Short Memory) for Wise-
guys," The Marshall Project, April 27, 2016, https://www.themarshallproject
.org/2016/04/27/trump-and-the-mob.

126 *"largest and most vicious criminal business":* Arnold H. Lubasch, "U.S. Jury
Convicts Eight as Members of Mob Commission," *New York Times,* November 20, 1986, http://www.nytimes.com/1986/11/20/nyregion/us-jury-convicts
-eight-as-members-of-mob-commission.html?pagewanted=all.

126 *The sentences . . . ranged from 40 to 100 years:* Arnold H. Lubasch, "Judge
Sentences 8 Mafia Leaders to Prison Terms," *New York Times,* January 14,
1987, https://www.nytimes.com/1987/01/14/nyregion/judge-sentences-8-mafia
-leaders-to-prison-terms.htmlhttps://www.nytimes.com/1987/01/14
/nyregion/judge-sentences-8-mafia-leaders-to-prison-terms.html.

126 *Sentenced to a term of 100 years:* Drawn from James Dao, "Anthony (Fat Tony) Salerno, 80, A Top Crime Boss, Dies in Prison," *New York Times,* July 29, 1992, https://www.nytimes.com/1992/07/29/us/anthony-fat-tony-salerno -80-a-top-crime-boss-dies-in-prison.html.

126 *No builder could pour concrete for a New York project:* Roy Rowan, "The Mafia's Bite of the Big Apple," *Fortune,* June 6, 1988, http://archive.fortune .com/magazines/fortune/fortune_archive/1988/06/06/70628/index.htm; also as stated in United States v. Salerno, 937 F. 2d 797 (2d Cir. 1991), available at https://openjurist.org/937/f2d/797/united-states-v-salerno-j -o-j-o.

126 *a very close associate of the Gambino crime family:* Johnston, "Donald Trump's Ties to the Mob?"

126 *he would use prefabricated concrete:* Raab, "Irregularities in Concrete Industry Inflate Building Costs."

126 *"Concrete is a monopoly":* Ibid.

126 *Village Voice journalist Wayne Barrett:* Wayne Barrett, *Trump: The Greatest Show on Earth: The Deals, the Downfall, and the Reinvention* (New York: Regan Arts, 2016), Kindle edition, p. 1948.

126 *Writer Ken Auletta . . . reported:* "Ken Auletta, "Don't Mess with Roy Cohn."

127 *Cohn also represented:* Unless otherwise noted, information on the *National Enquirer* is from Jeffrey Toobin, "The National Enquirer's Fervor for Trump," *New Yorker,* July 3, 2016, https://www.newyorker.com/magazine/2017/07/03 /the-national-enquirers-fervor-for-trump.

127 *$75,000 loan from the godfather:* Chauncey Mabe, "New York Author's Tell-All on Rise of National Enquirer," *South Florida Sun Sentinel,* October 24, 2010, https://www.sun-sentinel.com/entertainment/events/fl-xpm-2010-10-24 -fl-arts-paul-pope-102410-20101024-story.html.

127 *acquired the* Enquirer *for $850 million:* "David Pecker," *Gawker,* November 18, 2010, https://gawker.com/5693569/david-pecker.

127 *Mob meetings took place in his townhouse:* Johnston, "Donald Trump's Ties to the Mob?"

127 *In 1977, Cohn used:* Arnold H. Lubasch, "Mistrial Is Ruled as Jury Mulling Salerno Tax Case Reports Deadlock at 11 to 1," *New York Times,* October 9, 1977, https://www.nytimes.com/1977/10/09/archives/mistrial-is-ruled-as-jury -mulling-salerno-tax-case-reports-deadlock.html.

127 *"It's not a crime in this country":* Ibid.

127 *"technically guilty":* Sam Roberts, *The Brother* (New York: Random House, 2001), 310.

127 *"truth is hardly ever an absolute":* Ibid.

127 *Beyond his association with Cohn:* Details on ready-mix concrete choice from Johnston, "Donald Trump's Ties to the Mob?"

127 *"at the mercy of a legion":* Barrett quoted in ibid. Originally reported by Barrett, *Trump: The Greatest Show on Earth,* Kindle edition, p. 3950.

128 *According to Barrett:* Recounted in Johnston, "Donald Trump's Ties to the Mob?" Originally reported by Barrett, *Trump: The Greatest Show on Earth*, Kindle edition, p. 4086.

128 *One of Halloran's employees:* Raab, "Irregularities in Concrete Industry Inflate Building Costs."

128 *Yet Halloran's company:* Ibid.

128 "Biff Halloran, ladies and gentlemen": Selwyn Raab, "Ex-Hotel Owner with Former Ties to Mobsters Disappears," *New York Times*, October 30, 1998, https://www.nytimes.com/1998/10/30/nyregion/ex-hotel-owner-with -former-ties-to-mobsters-disappears.html.

128 *Halloran was last seen:* Ibid.

128 "a pretty good friend": Barrett, *Trump: The Greatest Show on Earth*, Kindle edition, p. 3975.

129 "bad guy and I didn't deal with him": *Washington Post*, Interview with Donald Trump, June 6, 2016, transcript, p. 12, https://www.washingtonpost.com /wp-stat/graphics/politics/trump-archive/docs/donald-trump-interview -with-robert-oharrrow-and-shawn-boburg-june-6.pdf.

129 "I was never going to run for office": Michael Rothfeld and Alexandra Berzon, "Donald Trump and the Mob," *Wall Street Journal*, September 1, 2016, https://www.wsj.com/articles/donald-trump-dealt-with-a-series-of-people -who-had-mob-ties-1472736922.

129 *He was so joined at the hip:* Selwyn Raab, "Threat by Teamsters Leader Casts Pall on Building Boom," *New York Times*, June 28, 1982, https://www .nytimes.com/1982/06/28/nyregion/threat-by-teamsters-leader-casts-pall -on-building-boom.html.

129 *Cody had on his rap sheet:* Selwyn Raab, "Cody Sentenced to 5-Year Term as a Racketeer," *New York Times*, December 2, 1982, https://www.nytimes.com /1982/12/02/nyregion/cody-sentenced-to-5-year-term-as-a-racketeer.html.

129 *$160,000 in kickbacks:* Barrett, *Trump: The Greatest Show on Earth*, Kindle edition, p. 3954.

129 *In 1982, while Trump Tower was under construction:* Raab, "Cody Sentenced."

129 *$160,000 in kickbacks:* Craig Wolff, "Ex-Teamster Leader Arrested in Death Plot," *New York Times*, May 31, 1991, https://www.nytimes.com/1991/05/31 /nyregion/ex-teamster-leader-arrested-in-death-plot.html.

129 "high-echelon members": Ibid.

129 *So Cody tried to end-run the law:* United States v. Cody, 722 F. 2d 1052 (2d Cir. 1983), available at https://law.justia.com/cases/federal/appellate-courts /F2/722/1052/51299/.

129 *in 1982 when Cody was calling:* Frank J. Prial, "Driver's Strike Halts Work on Major Building Projects," *New York Times*, July 9, 1982, https://www.nytimes .com/1982/07/09/nyregion/driver-s-strike-halts-work-on-major-building -projects.html.

129 *When the Tower officially opened:* Photo by Joan Tedeschi appears in centerfold of Nicholas von Hoffman, *Citizen Cohn* (New York: Doubleday, 1988).

130 *Wayne Barrett, in Trump:* For the accounts of some of Trump Tower's most infamous tenants in the pages that follow, I acknowledge general indebtedness to the dogged investigative work of the late Wayne Barrett of the *Village Voice*, who tells the whole story in his book *Trump: The Greatest Show on Earth*; On Hixson specifically, see Kindle edition, pp. 4082, 4086.

130 "wasn't going to build Trump Tower": Rothfeld and Berzon, "Donald Trump and the Mob."

130 *Trump lied to investigators:* Ibid.

130 *Subpoenaed by the Organized Crime Task Force:* Johnston, "Donald Trump's Ties to the Mob?"

130 *What the investigators missed:* Section on Verina Hixon's involvement with Trump and Cody drawn from Barrett, *Trump: The Greatest Show on Earth*, Kindle edition, p. 3982 *et seq.*

133 *Joseph Weichselbaum ran Trump's helicopter service:* Information on Weichselbaum from Johnston, "Donald Trump's Ties to the Mob?"

133 *his case was, strangely, transferred:* Michael Daly, "Trump, Who Talks About Executing Drug Dealers, Vouched for Two of Them," Daily Beast, March 15, 2018, https://www.thedailybeast.com/trump-who-talks-about-executing-drug-dealers-vouched-for-two-of-them.

133 "a credit to the community": Ibid.

133 *Upon release from prison:* Johnston, "Donald Trump's Ties to the Mob?"

133 "hardly knew": Ibid.

133 *In 1981, FBI agents had warned Trump:* Rothfeld and Berzon, "Donald Trump and the Mob."

134 *An FBI memorandum:* FBI Memorandum to Special Agent in Charge, September 22, 1981, available at "Trump Thought A.C. Venture Could Tarnish Name," The Smoking Gun, March 30, 2004, http://www.thesmokinggun.com/file/trump-thought-ac-venture-could-tarnish-name.

134 "Trump advised Agents that he had read": Ibid.

135 "[I] advised Trump": Ibid.

135 *Roy Cohn told Trump:* Information on Degnan from Johnston, "Donald Trump's Ties to the Mob?"

135 "clean as a whistle": Ibid.

135 *It omitted at least four governmental investigations:* Max J. Rosenthal, "The Trump Files: How Donald Tried to Hide His Legal Troubles to Get His Casino Approved," *Mother Jones*, August 23, 2016, https://www.motherjones.com/politics/2016/08/trump-files-donald-tried-hide-his-legal-troubles-get-his-casino-approved/.

135 *It omitted a pending:* Johnston, "Donald Trump's Ties to the Mob?"

136 *John Martin, the U.S. attorney in Manhattan:* David Cay Johnston, *The Making of Donald Trump*, (London: Melville House, 2016), 43.

136 *The discrimination case:* Johnston, "Donald Trump's Ties to the Mob?"

136 *In a footnote to its 120-page report:* Report of the New Jersey Division of Gaming Enforcement, "In Re the Application of the Trump Plaza Corporation for

a Casino License, etc.," March 15, 1982, p. 91, available at https://www.scribd
.com/doc/301761265/Report-on-Donald-Trump-to-Casino-Control
-Commission.

136 *The initial casino project:* Donald Janson, "Trump and Harrah's Feud Over
Name," *New York Times,* August 13, 1985, https://www.nytimes.com/1985
/08/13/nyregion/trump-and-harrah-s-feud-over-name.html.

136 *Daniel Sullivan was a giant of a man:* Information on Sullivan from Robert
O'Harrow Jr., "Trump's Ties to an Informant and FBI Agent Reveal His
Mode of Operation," *Washington Post,* September 17, 2016, https://www
.washingtonpost.com/investigations/trumps-ties-to-an-informant-and-fbi
-agent-reveal-his-modes-of-operation/2016/09/16/6e65522e-6f9f-11e6
-9705-23e51a2f424d_story.html?utm_term=.6c93f15e1fba.

137 *Shapiro had deep ties to organized crime:* Information on Shapiro and the
Scarfo crime family from Michael Rothfeld and Alexandra Berzon, "Donald
Trump and the Mob," *Wall Street Journal,* September 1, 2016, https://www
.wsj.com/articles/donald-trump-dealt-with-a-series-of-people-who-had
-mob-ties-1472736922.

138 *He was responsible for over two dozen murders:* Information on Nicky Scarfo
drawn from Sam Roberts, "Nicky Scarfo, Mob Boss Who Plundered Atlantic
City in the '80s, Dies at 87," *New York Times,* January 17, 2017, https://www
.nytimes.com/2017/01/17/nyregion/nicky-scarfo-mob-boss-who-plundered
-atlantic-city-in-the-80s-dies-at-87.html.

138 *One, Robert Winzinger:* Information about Winzinger drawn from "Good-
fellas: The Dark Tower and Beyond Part I," *VISUP,* February 11, 2018, http://
visupview.blogspot.com/2018/02/goodfellas-dark-tower-and-beyond-part-i
.html.

138 *Another one, concrete subcontractor Joseph Feriozzi:* Barrett, *Trump: The
Greatest Show on Earth,* Kindle edition, pp. 4871, 4875, 4879.

138 *Victor, a Mob lawyer:* Ibid., p. 4875.

138 *Sullivan and Trump agreed:* Information on their drywall investigation
drawn from O'Harrow Jr., "Trump's Ties to an Informant."

138 *Trump had his Grand Hyatt Hotel:* Information from this paragraph on
Sullivan is from Robbins, "Trump and the Mob."

139 *Trump helped arrange:* Rothfeld and Berzon, "Donald Trump and the Mob."

139 *Matthews subsequently pleaded guilty:* Donald Janson, "U.S. Judge Sentences Ex-Mayor of Atlantic City to 15 Years for Extortion," *New York
Times,* January 1, 1985, https://www.nytimes.com/1985/01/01/nyregion/us
-judge-sentences-ex-mayor-of-atlantic-city-to-15-years-for-extortion
.html.

139 *Shapiro testified:* David Corn, "The Many Times Donald Trump Has Lied
about His Mob Connections," *Mother Jones,* September 23, 2016, http://www
.motherjones.com/politics/2016/09/donald-trump-lies-about-dealings
-mafia-figures/#.

139 *In the fall of 1999 on* Meet the Press: Information from this interview from Tim Russert, *Meet the Press*, October 24, 1999, 18:34–19:42, available at https://www.youtube.com/watch?v=l_joQ1kxxZs.

140 *In 2003, however, Trump admitted:* Transcript of interview with Timothy O'Brien, reported in Corn, "The Many Times Donald Trump Has Lied about His Mob Connections."

141 "well thought of": Johnston, "Donald Trump's Ties to the Mob?"

141 *Trump eventually paid $8 million:* O'Harrow Jr., "Trump's Ties to an Informant."

141 *New Jersey regulators later:* Johnston, "Donald Trump's Ties to the Mob?"

141 "If people were like me": Rothfeld and Berzon, "Donald Trump and the Mob."

141 *Trump also disclaimed recollection:* Unless otherwise noted, information on LiButti is from Corn, "The Many Times Donald Trump Has Lied about His Mob Connections."

141 "my boss": Michael Isikoff, "Video Shows Trump with Mob Figure He Denied Knowing," *Yahoo News*, November 2, 2016, https://www.yahoo.com/news/video-shows-trump-with-mob-figure-he-denied-knowing-090025964.html.

142 "It isn't like [Trump] saw LiButti": Rothfeld and Berzon, "Donald Trump and the Mob."

142 *LiButti and his attractive daughter Edith:* Details on the relationship between Trump and Edith, and the racehorse, from Michael Isikoff, "Trump Challenged over Ties to Mob-Linked Gambler with Ugly Past," *Yahoo News*, March 7, 2016, https://www.yahoo.com/news/trump-challenged-over-ties-to-mob-linked-gambler-100050602.html.

142 *There is a video of Trump:* Ben Mathis-Lilley, "Video Uncovered of Trump Socializing with Mob Figure He's Denied Knowing," Slate, November 2, 2016, https://slate.com/news-and-politics/2016/11/trump-and-mobster-robert-libutti-captured-on-video-at-1988-wwe-event.html.

142 "Donald, I'll fucking pull your balls": Johnston, *Making of Donald Trump*, 195, quoted in Corn, "The Many Times Donald Trump Has Lied about His Mob Connections"; Rich Schapiro, "'The Making of Donald Trump' Reveals How Billionaire's Attempt to Woo Mobster's Daughter Ended When He Told Him He'd 'Pull Your Balls from Your Legs,'" *New York Daily News*, July 31, 2016, http://www.nydailynews.com/news/politics/donald-trump-attempt-court-mobster-daughter-didn-article-1.2732403.

142 "During the years": Quoted in, Michael Isikoff. "Trump Challenged Over Ties to Mob-Linked Gambler," Yahoo News, March 7, 2016, https://www.yahoo.com/news/trump-challenged-over-ties-to-mob-linked-gambler-100050602.html.

143 "I have heard he is a high roller": *Philadelphia Inquirer* quoted in Corn, "The Many Times Donald Trump Has Lied about His Mob Connections."

143 "He's a liar": Isikoff, quoted in Amy S. Rosenberg, "Trump Ties to Mobster, Racist Casino Policies Alleged in New Report," *Philadelphia Inquirer*, March 7,

2016, https://www.inquirer.com/philly/blogs/downashore/Trump-ties-to-mobster
-racist-casino-policies-resurface-in-new-report.html.

143 "LiButti was a high roller": Rothfeld and Berzon, "Donald Trump and the Mob."

143 *Nothing to do with him?*: On LiButti and racism, see Isikoff, "Trump Chal-
lenged over Ties to Mob-Linked Gambler with Ugly Past." This anecdote
also addressed in Corn, "The Many Times Donald Trump Has Lied about
His Mob Connections"; Schapiro, "'The Making of Donald Trump' Reveals";
Mathis-Lilley, "Video Uncovered of Trump Socializing with Mob Figure
He's Denied Knowing"; and Amy S. Rosenberg, "Trump Ties to Mobster,
Racist Casino Policies Alleged in New Report," *Philadelphia Inquirer*, March 7,
2016, http://www.philly.com/philly/blogs/downashore/Trump-ties-to-mobster
-racist-casino-policies-resurface-in-new-report.html.

144 "great friend": Ben Schreckinger, "The Happy-Go-Lucky Jewish Group That
Connects Trump and Putin," *Politico*, April 9, 2017, https://www.politico.com
/magazine/story/2017/04/the-happy-go-lucky-jewish-group-that-connects
-trump-and-putin-215007.

144 *He had a $5 million apartment*: Keren Blankfeld, "The Money Problems of
Manhattan Real Estate Mogul Tamir Sapir," *Forbes*, September 24, 2010,
https://www.forbes.com/forbes/2010/1011/rich-list-10-real-estate-tamir
-sapir-drenched-in-debt.html#6c5a11be7e88.

144 *Trump showcased the project in 2007*: Mike McIntire, "Donald Trump Settled a Real Estate Lawsuit and a Criminal Case Was Closed," *New York Times*,
April 5, 2016, https://www.nytimes.com/2016/04/06/us/politics/donald-trump
-soho-settlement.html.

144 *The plan was to sell*: Craig Karmin, "Trump SoHo Hotel Lender Plans to Put
Property Up for Sale," *Wall Street Journal*, September 16, 2014, https://www
.wsj.com/articles/trump-soho-hotel-lender-plans-to-put-property-up-for
-sale-1410885344.

144 *Felix Sater*: Unless otherwise noted, information on Felix Sater is from
Charles V. Bagli, "Real Estate Executive with Hand in Trump Projects Rose
from Tangled Past," *New York Times*, December 17, 2007, https://www.nytimes
.com/2007/12/17/nyregion/17trump.html.

144 *One of his friends told*: Bagli, "Real Estate Executive with Hand in Trump's
Projects."

144 *Sater occupied space*: Megan Twohey and Steve Eder, "For Trump, Three Decades of Chasing Deals in Russia," *New York Times*, January 16, 2017, https://
www.nytimes.com/2017/01/16/us/politics/donald-trump-russia-business
.html.

144-145 *Standing beside him in the kickoff photograph*: Ibid.

145 *"Senior Adviser" to Donald Trump*: This detail referenced in McIntire, "Don-
ald Trump Settled a Real Estate Lawsuit and a Criminal Case Was Closed";
Bagli, "Real Estate Executive with Hand in Trump Projects"; and Andrew
Rice, "The Original Russia Connection: Felix Sater Has Cut Deals with the
FBI, Russian Oligarchs, and Donald Trump. He's Also Quite a Talker," *New*

York Magazine, August 3, 2017, http://nymag.com/daily/intelligencer/2017
/08/felix-sater-donald-trump-russia-investigation.html.

145 "We will get this done": Matt Apuzzo and Maggie Haberman, "Trump Associate Boasted That Moscow Business Deal 'Will Get Donald Elected,'"
New York Times, August 28, 2017, https://www.nytimes.com/2017/08/28/us
/politics/trump-tower-putin-felix-sater.html?_r=0.

145 "I know how to play it": Ibid.

145 *Sater escorted Ivanka and Don Jr. around Moscow:* Twohey and Eder, "For
Trump, Three Decades of Chasing Deals in Russia."

145 *A lawsuit brought in 2010:* Allan Lichtman, "Here's a Closer Look at Donald
Trump's Disturbingly Deep Ties to Russia," *Fortune*, May 17, 2017, http://
fortune.com/2017/05/17/donald-trump-russia-2/.

145 *He told me that Trump is the first president:* Personal encounter between the
author and Felix Sater in summer of 2018 in East Hampton, NY.

145 *Both the Soho Alliance and the Greenwich Village Society for Historic Preservation:* Sarah Jacobs, "The Craziest Moments in the Sordid History of Trump
Soho, the Five-Star Hotel and Condo Building That Will Lose the Trump
Name," *Business Insider*, November 29, 2017, https://www.businessinsider
.com/trump-soho-has-a-sordid-history-highlights-photos-2017-11.

145 *There were fatal accidents:* Michael Bird, "Donald Trump's Disastrous Relationship with the Dodgy Kazakh Business World," *The Black Sea*, December 16, 2016, https://theblacksea.eu/_old/mirror/theblacksea.eu/indexa277
.html?idT=88&idC=88&idRec=1275&recType=story.

145 *The Department of Buildings:* Carter Horsley, "Buildings Department Permits Work to Proceed at Trump Soho Site," *City Realty*, December 21, 2006,
https://www.cityrealty.com/nyc/market-insight/carters-view/behind-the
-buildings/buildings-department-permits-work-proceed-trump-soho-site
/789.

145 *Structural engineers determined:* Michael Idov, "Trump Soho Is Not an Oxy-
moron," *New York Magazine*, March 28, 2008, http://nymag.com/news/features
/45591/.

146 *In August 2009, buyers of ten condos:* Bird, "Donald Trump's Disastrous Relationship with the Dodgy Kazakh Business World."

146 "fraudulent misrepresentations": Ibid.

146 *He invented paid members to get more members:* Ibid.

146 *In November 2011, Trump settled:* Ibid. See also McIntire, "Donald Trump
Settled a Real Estate Lawsuit and a Criminal Case Was Closed."

146 *Prior to the settlement, Trump had tried:* Craig Karmin, "Trump SoHo Refunds Money," *Wall Street Journal*, November 17, 2010, https://www.wsj.com
/articles/SB10001424052748704312504575618960285850190.

146 *In November 2017, the Trump Organization:* Ben Jacobs, "Trump's Company
Reaches Deal to Cut Ties with Trump Soho Hotel," *The Guardian*, November 22, 2017, https://www.theguardian.com/us-news/2017/nov/22/trump
-organization-hotel-soho-new-york.

146 *Trump tried to distance himself*: Ben Protess, Steve Eder, and Eric Lipton, "Trump Organization Will Exit from Its Struggling SoHo Hotel in New York," *New York Times*, November 22, 2017, https://www.nytimes.com/2017 /11/22/business/trump-organization-soho-hotel.html.

147 *In 2012, the New York County District Attorney's office*: Information on Cy Vance from Sonam Sheth and Natasha Bertand, "Manhattan DA Reportedly Dropped Felony Fraud Case Against Trump's Kids after Donation from Trump's Lawyer," *Business Insider*, October 24, 2017, https://www.businessinsider .com/trump-soho-criminal-fraud-case-ivanka-don-jr-dropped-after -campaign-donation-2017-10.

147 *Another Trump Mob connection*: Information on Vyacheslav Ivankov from Luke Harding, *Collusion: Secret Meetings, Dirty Money, and How Russia Helped Donald Trump Win* (New York: Vintage, 2017), 289–90, 294.

147 "for a period of time": Corn, "The Many Times Donald Trump Has Lied About His Mob Connections."

148 "[I]f he were sitting in the room right now": Ibid.

148 "Felix Sater, boy": Ibid.

148 "Q: Have you previously associated": Timothy L. O'Brien, "My Lawyers Got Trump to Admit 30 Lies Under Oath," *Bloomberg*, June 12, 2017, https:// www.bloomberg.com/opinion/articles/2017-06-12/trump-s-history-of-lies -according-to-biographer-timothy-o-brien.

148 "Q: Other than 'this situation'": Wayne Barrett, "Inside Donald Trump's Empire: Why He Didn't Run for President in 2012," *Daily Beast*, May 26, 2011, https://www.thedailybeast.com/inside-donald-trumps-empire-why-he -didnt-run-for-president-in-2012.

149 "Usually, I build buildings": Corn, "The Many Times Donald Trump Has Lied about His Mob Connections."

149 "Crooks have two big advantages": Anders Aslund quoted in Craig Unger, *House of Trump, House of Putin* (New York: Dutton, 2018), 124.

149 "No other occupant of the White House": Johnston, "Donald Trump's Ties to the Mob?"

CHAPTER 7: TRUMP AND HIS WOMEN

150 *Trump's history with women*: Michael Barbaro and Megan Twohey, "Crossing the Line: How Donald Trump Behaved with Women in Private," *New York Times*, May 14, 2016, https://www.nytimes.com/2016/05/15/us/politics /donald-trump-women.html.

150 *75-year-old guy walk in with three blondes*: Donald Trump with Tony Schwartz, *The Art of the Deal* (New York: Random House, 2015), 95.

150 *raid by federal agents*: Peter Kihss, "I.R.S. Raids Studio 54; 5 Ounces of Cocaine Seized," *New York Times*, December 15, 1978, https://www.nytimes .com/1978/12/15/archives/irs-raids-studio-54-5-ounces-of-cocaine-seized -studio-54-raided-by.html.

151 "I would watch supermodels getting screwed": O'Brien's *TrumpNation*, cited by Igor Bobic, "The Real Donald: Excerpts from Trump's Books on Marriage, Sex and More," Huffington Post, August 19, 2015, https://www.huffing tonpost.com/entry/donald-trump-books_us_55d4a1a7e4b07addcb44 e2e3.

151 *Cohn professed an expertise in marriage:* Roy Cohn, *How to Stand Up for Your Rights and Win!* (New York: Simon & Schuster, 1981).

152 "If you're a person of wealth": Mark Singer, "Trump Solo," *New Yorker*, May 12, 1997, https://www.newyorker.com/magazine/1997/05/19/trump-solo.

152 "I am a great prenup believer": Interview with Larry King, *CNN*, July 23, 1997, https://www.cnn.com/videos/politics/2016/04/11/donald-trump-marriage -advice-prenups-origwx-bw.cnn/video/playlists/celebrity-splits/.

152 *Trump renegotiated the deal preemptively:* Marie Brenner, "After the Gold Rush," *Vanity Fair*, September 1, 1990, https://www.vanityfair.comAlex Wagnert. /magazine/2015/07/donald-ivana-trump-divorce-prenup-marie- brenner.

152 *$10 million lump sum payment:* "At last, Donald and Ivana Trump Officially Settle Their Divorce Deal," *Baltimore Sun*, March 25, 1991, https://www .baltimoresun.com/news/bs-xpm-1991-03-25-1991084035-story.html.

152 *In the late 1980s he had taken a mistress:* Mary H. J. Farrell, "The Trumps Head for Divorce Court," *People*, February 26, 1990, http://people.com /archive/cover-story-the-trumps-head-for-divorce-court-vol-33-no-8/.

152 "He had taken to unfurling a giant poster": Wayne Barrett, *Trump: The Deals and the Downfall* (New York: HarperCollins, 1992).

153 "My life was great in so many ways": Cameron Joseph, "Donald Trump Says If He Wasn't Caught Cheating on His 'Beautiful Wife' Ivana with Girlfriend Marla Maples, Life Would've Stayed a Bowl of Cherries in 1994," *New York Daily News*, October 8, 2016, http://www.nydailynews.com/news/politics /trump-cheating-ivana-marla-beautiful-1994-article-1.2822695.

153 "My big mistake": From *The Art of the Comeback*, quoted in Alex Wagner, "How Long Can Ivanka Trump Defend Her Father?" *The Atlantic*, May 20, 2016, https://www.theatlantic.com/politics/archive/2016/05/ivanka-versus-the -donald/483542/.

153 "I have had it with Ivana": Brenner, "After the Gold Rush."

154 *The* New York Times *brought suit:* Josh Gerstein, "Judge Rejects *New York Times* Request to Unseal Trump Divorce File," *Politico*, September 22, 2016, https://www.politico.com/story/2016/09/donald-trump-divorce-files-nyt -228546.

154 *1995 "survival guide":* Ivana Trump, *The Best Is Yet to Come: Coping with Divorce and Enjoying Life* (New York: Pocket Books, 1995); Georgia Dullea, "At Work With: Ivana Trump; Thinner, Blonder, Wiser," *New York Times*, April 5, 1995.

154 *fascinating 1993 book:* Harry Hurt III, *The Lost Tycoon: The Many Lives of Donald J. Trump* (New York: Norton, 1993).

155 *he had his lawyer, Michael Cohen, threaten Hurt:* Colin Campbell, "Donald Trump's Adviser Apologizes After Saying 'You Cannot Rape Your Spouse' While Raging at Reporter," *Business Insider*, July 28, 2015, http://www.businessinsider.com/donald-trump-lawyer-michael-cohen-apologizes-2015-7.

155 *Trump evicted Hurt:* Hurt, writing in the third person on Facebook; see Kenneth P. Vogel, "Trump Kicks Biographer Off Golf Course," *Politico*, December 31, 2016, https://www.politico.com/story/2016/12/trump-biographer-golf-course-233092.

156 *"you cannot rape your spouse":* Campbell, "Donald Trump's Adviser Apologizes."

156 *Trump sued Ivana for $25 million:* Hillel Italie, "Ivana Trump Writing Memoir About Her Children with Donald," AP, March 15, 2017, https://apnews.com/2dc345709a5b4d80820dd6afc402ca8e. See also "Trump Can Sue Ivana for Violating Gag Order," UPI, June 30, 1992, https://www.upi.com/Archives/1992/06/30/Trump-can-sue-Ivana-for-violating-gag-order/7036709876800/.

157 *paltry $2.5 million:* Salvatore Arena and K. C. Baker, "Marla Caves on Prenup Gives Up Battle over Pact and Takes 2M in Divorce," *Daily News*, June 9, 1999, http://www.nydailynews.com/archives/news/marla-caves-prenup-battle-pact-takes-2m-divorce-article-1.831793; Dareh Gregorian, "Donald & Marla Settle on Divorce Deal," *New York Post*, April 25, 1999, https://nypost.com/1999/04/25/donald-marla-set-to-settle-on-divorce-deal/.

157 *"solid as concrete":* Singer, "Trump Solo."

157 *"It is unfair being married to Donald Trump":* "Larry King Interviews Donald Trump on Larry King Live," CNN, July 23, 1997, https://factba.se/transcript/donald-trump-interview-cnn-larry-king-live-july-23-1997.

157 *pressured Marla to pose nude:* Glenn Plaskin, "The Marla," *Sun-Sentinel*, August 19, 1990, https://www.sun-sentinel.com/news/fl-xpm-1990-08-19-9002090726-story.html; Joanna Rothkopf, "Donald Trump Reportedly Pressured Marla Maples to Pose Nude for *Playboy*," *Jezebel*, August 23, 2016, https://theslot.jezebel.com/donald-trump-reportedly-pressured-marla-maples-to-pose-1785615966; and Carlos Lozada, "Donald Trump: Vain, Greedy and All-American," *Washington Post*, September 11, 2015, https://www.washingtonpost.com/news/book-party/wp/2015/09/11/donald-trump-vain-greedy-and-all-american/?utm_term=.f0e5a9750e85JenHayden.

157 *offer at $2 million:* Helena Andrews-Dyer, "Tiffany Trump Went to a Playboy Party on New Year's Eve, and the Internet Cares," *Washington Post*, January 2, 2018, https://www.washingtonpost.com/news/reliable-source/wp/2018/01/02/tiffany-trump-went-to-a-playboy-party-on-new-years-eve-and-the-internet-cares/?utm_term=.07b241796e93.

157 *"The Girls of Trump":* Lindsey Ellefson, "The Donald Reportedly Wanted Playboy to Do a 'Women of Trump' Spread in the 1990s," Mediaite, August 5,

2016, https://www.mediaite.com/online/the-donald-reportedly-wanted-playboy
-to-do-a-women-of-trump-spread-in-the-1990s/.

158 "She's got Marla's legs": Rothkopf, "Donald Trump Reportedly Pressured
Marla Maples to Pose Nude for *Playboy*"; and "Donald Trump Describing
His Then 1-Year-Old Daughter Is the Most Cringe-Worthy Video of Him
Yet," Daily Kos, April 6, 2016, https://www.dailykos.com/stories/2016/4/6
/1511295/-Donald-Trump-describing-his-then-1-year-old-daughter-is-the
-most-cringe-worthy-video-of-him-yet; and "Trevor Noah Unearths Video
of Donald Trump Describing 1-Year-Old Daughter's Breasts," *Hollywood
Reporter*, April 6, 2016, https://www.hollywoodreporter.com/news/donald
-trump-baby-daughter-breasts-trevor-noah-881406.

158 *16 complaints:* Meghan Keneally, "List of Trump's Accusers and Their Allegations of Sexual Misconduct," ABC News, February 22, 2018, https://
abcnews.go.com/Politics/list-trumps-accusers-allegations-sexual
-misconduct/story?id=51956410.

158 "You've got to deny": Bob Woodward, *Fear: Trump in the White House* (New
York: Simon & Schuster, 2018).

159 "get away with things like that": Stern interview quoted by Rachel Revesz:
"Donald Trump Boasted About Meeting Semi-Naked Teenagers in Beauty
Pageants," *The Independent*, October 12, 2016, https://www.independent.co
.uk/news/world/americas/donald-trump-former-miss-arizona-tasha-dixon
-naked-undressed-backstage-howard-stern-a7357866.html.

159 "I think Gloria would be very, very impressed with it": Gideon Resnick,
"Donald Trump Said in 2012 Gloria Allred Would Be 'Very, Very Impressed'
with His Penis," Daily Beast, October 8, 2016, https://www.thedailybeast
.com/donald-trump-said-in-2012-gloria-allred-would-be-very-very
-impressed-with-his-penis.

159 *Jessica Leeds:* Hayley Peterson, "Woman Says Trump Called Her 'the Worst
Name Ever' 3 Years after Alleged Sexual Assault," *Business Insider*, December 11, 2017, http://www.businessinsider.com/trump-accusers-says-he-called
-her-the-worst-name-ever-2017-12.

159 *Jill Harth:* Rachel Stockman, "Exclusive: Inside the $125 Million Donald
Trump Sexual Assault Lawsuit," Law & Crime, February 23, 2016, https://
lawandcrime.com/high-profile/exclusive-inside-the-donald-trump-sexual
-assault-lawsuit/.

160 *Temple Taggart McDowell:* Hallie Jackson and Alex Johnson, "Miss USA
Contestant Details Unwanted Encounters with Trump," NBC News, October 13, 2016, https://www.nbcnews.com/politics/2016-election/miss-usa
-contestant-details-encounters-trump-n665521.

160 *Summer Zervos:* Adam Liptak, "'A Bit of Divine Justice': Trump Vowed to
Change Libel Law. But Not Like This," *New York Times*, April 2, 2018, https://
www.nytimes.com/2018/04/02/us/politics/trump-libel-lawsuit.html;
James C. McKinley Jr., "New York Judge Is Asked to Toss Defamation Suit

Against Trump," *New York Times*, December 5, 2017, https://www.nytimes.com/2017/12/05/nyregion/zervos-trump-defamation-lawsuit.html.

160 "ambushed by Trump on more": Complaint in Zervos v. Trump, No. 15022/2017, N.Y. Sup. Ct., N.Y. County, filed January 17, 2017, https://www.documentcloud.org/documents/4108743-Zervos-Complaint.html.

160 "feel uncomfortable, nervous, and": Ibid.

161 *Trump sought dismissal of the Zervos case:* McKinley Jr., "New York Judge Is Asked to Toss Defamation Suit Against Trump."

161 "a private witch-hunt that could threaten": Memorandum of support of President Donald J. Trump's motion to dismiss, July 7, 2017, in Zervos v. Trump, No. 15022/2017, N.Y. Sup. Ct., N.Y. County, https://pmcdeadline2.files.wordpress.com/2017/07/trump-zervos-dismissal-motion-july-71.pdf.

161 *A hurdle to Trump's argument:* McKinley Jr., "New York Judge Is Asked to Toss Defamation Suit against Trump."

161 *The New York State Supreme Court:* Ibid.

161 "knowingly, intentionally and maliciously": Complaint in Zervos v. Trump, No. 15022/2017, N.Y. Sup. Ct., N.Y. County, filed January 17, 2017, https://www.documentcloud.org/documents/4108743-Zervos-Complaint.html; Elsie Viebeck, "Trump Agrees to Turn Over His Calendar in Summer Zervos Defamation Suit," *Washington Post*, October 31, 2018, https://www.washingtonpost.com/politics/trump-agrees-to-turn-over-his-calendar-in-summer-zervos-defamation-suit/2018/10/31/4d9a0076-dd25-11e8-b732-3c72cbf131f2_story.html?utm_term=.333d42eab2b0.

162 *Ironically, Trump also argued in*: McKinley Jr., "New York Judge Is Asked to Toss Defamation Suit against Trump."

162 *This position ignored the landmark 1964 Supreme Court case:* Adam Liptak, "Justice Clarence Thomas Calls for Reconsideration of Landmark Libel Ruling," *New York Times*, February 19, 2019, https://www.nytimes.com/2019/02/19/us/politics/clarence-thomas-first-amendment-libel.html.

162 "All I can say is it's totally fake news": Donald Trump, remarks to reporters, October 16, 2017, in Glenn Kessler, "Trump Says Sex Harassment Claims Are 'Fake News,' but There Are Corroborators," *Washington Post*, October 27, 2017, https://www.washingtonpost.com/news/fact-checker/wp/2017/10/27/trump-says-sex-harassment-claims-are-fake-news-but-there-are-corroborators/?utm_term=.90f6aae7b662.

163 *Alva Johnson:* Beth Reinhard and Alice Crites, "Former Campaign Staffer Alleges in Lawsuit That Trump Kissed Her Without Her Consent. The White House Denies the Charge," *Washington Post*, February 25, 2019, https://www.washingtonpost.com/investigations/former-campaign-staffer-alleges-in-lawsuit-that-trump-kissed-her-without-her-consent-the-white-house-denies-the-charge/2019/02/25/fe1869a4-3498-11e9-946a-115a5932c45b_story.html?utm_term=.11d779868002.

164 *Davidson is a California lawyer:* Molly Redden, "How the Hollywood Lawyer for Trump's Mistresses Turns Celebrity Sex Scandals into Cash," *New York*

Magazine, February 16, 2018, http://nymag.com/daily/intelligencer/2018/02 /lawyer-for-trumps-mistresses-turns-sex-scandals-into-cash.html.

164 *According to the* New York Times: Jim Rutenberg, Megan Twohey, Rebecca R. Ruiz, Mike McIntire, and Maggie Haberman, "Tools of Trump's Fixer: Payouts, Intimidation and the Tabloids," *New York Times,* February 18, 2018, https://www.nytimes.com/2018/02/18/us/politics/michael-cohen-trump .html.

164 *Davidson reported to Michael Cohen:* Ibid.

164–165 "He has always been professional": Redden, "How the Hollywood Lawyer for Trump's Mistresses."

165 *It was Cohen who secretly recorded:* Matt Apuzzo, Maggie Haberman, and Michael S. Schmidt, "Michael Cohen Secretly Taped Trump Discussing Payment to Playboy Model," *New York Times,* July 20, 2018, https://www .nytimes.com/2018/07/20/us/politics/michael-cohen-trump-tape.html.

165 *Clifford contacted:* Joe Palazzolo, Nicole Hong, Michael Rothfeld, Rebecca Davis O'Brien, and Rebecca Ballhaus, "Donald Trump Played Central Role in Hush Payoffs to Stormy Daniels and Karen McDougal," *Wall Street Journal,* November 9, 2018, https://www.wsj.com/articles/donald-trump-played -central-role-in-hush-payoffs-to-stormy-daniels-and-karen-mcdougal -1541786601.

165 *Cohen initially claimed:* Max Greenwood, "Cohen Says Stormy Daniels Payment Was Transferred from His Home Equity Line," *The Hill,* March 9, 2018, https://thehill.com/homenews/news/377673-cohen-says-stormy-daniels -payment-was-transferred-from-his-home-equity-line.

165 "It's not like I just work for Mr. Trump": Rutenberg et al., "Tools of Trump's Fixer."

165 *Trump claimed he had no knowledge:* John Kruzel, "Donald Trump's Shifting Explanations for the Stormy Daniels Payment (updated)," *Politifact,* August 23, 2018, https://www.politifact.com/truth-o-meter/article/2018/aug/23/donald -trumps-shifting-explanations-stormy-daniels/.

166 *Trump's signed 2017 financial disclosure:* Kevin Breuninger, "Trump's Financial Disclosure Report Released, Says President 'Fully Reimbursed' Michael Cohen," CNBC, May 16, 2018, https://www.cnbc.com/2018/05/16/trumps -financial-disclosure-report-released.html.

166 *Giuliani told reporters in May 2018:* Ibid.

166 "directly or indirectly, verbally or otherwise": Quoted from "Confidential Settlement Agreement and Mutual Release; Assignment of Copyright and Non-Disparagement Agreement," dated October 28, 2016, between "David Dennison [Donald Trump]" and Peggy Peterson [Stormy Daniels], available at http://tmz.vo.llnwd.net/o28/newsdesk/tmz_documents/stormy-daniels-sues -trump-redacted.pdf.

166 *In the NDA, "Confidential Information":* Ibid.

166 *In March 2018:* See "First Amended Complaint for: Declaratory Relief/Judgment etc. in Stephanie Clifford a.k.a. Stormy Daniels a.k.a. Peggy Peterson

v. Donald J. Trump a.k.a. David Dennison et al. (Case No. 2:18-CV -02217-SJO-FFM), C.D. Cal., filed March 26, 2018, available at https://www .courthousenews.com/wp-content/uploads/2018/03/StormyDaniels Amended.pdf.

167 *On March 25, 2018, Anderson Cooper:* Anderson Cooper, "Stormy Daniels Describes Her Alleged Affair with Donald Trump," full interview transcript, CBS News, August 21, 2018, https://www.cbsnews.com/news/stormy-daniels -describes-her-alleged-affair-with-donald-trump-60-minutes-interview/.

168 *Glenn Kessler of the* Washington Post: Kessler, "Trump Says Sex Harassment Claims Are 'Fake News.'"

169 *When the* New York Times *published:* Alan Rappeport, "Donald Trump Threatens to Sue the Times over Article on Unwanted Advances," *New York Times*, October 13, 2016, including text of letter from McCraw to Kasowitz dated October 13, 2016, https://www.nytimes.com/2016/10/14/us/politics /donald-trump-lawsuit-threat.html.

169 "Dear Mr. Kasowitz": David McCraw, "The Times's Lawyer Responds to Trump," *New York Times*, October 14, 2016, https://www.nytimes.com/interactive/2016 /10/13/us/politics/david-mccraw-trump-letter.html.

170 "Their accounts—many relayed here": Michael Barbaro and Megan Twohey, "Crossing the Line: How Donald Trump Behaved with Women in Private," *New York Times*, May 14, 2016, https://www.nytimes.com/2016/05/15/us /politics/donald-trump-women.html.

171 *He defended disgraced Fox News harasser Roger Ailes:* Michelle Goldberg, "Save the Phony Weinstein Outrage, Republicans," *New York Times*, October 16, 2017, https://www.nytimes.com/2017/10/16/opinion/columnists/weinstein -sexual-harassment-republicans.html.

171 "should go maybe teach kindergarten": Ibid.

172 *Aided by the pinky-ringed dirty:* Seema Mehta, "What You Need to Know About the Four Women Donald Trump Appeared with at a Surprise Pre-Debate Event," *Los Angeles Times*, October 9, 2016, http://www.latimes.com /politics/la-na-trump-clinton-accusers-20161009-snap-story.html.

CHAPTER 8: THE PROFESSOR OF FRAUD

174 *In 2004, a management consultant:* Trump University president Michael Sexton deposition, in Maggie Severns, "Trump University: Teaching Real Estate and Making Money," *Politico*, March 10, 2016, https://www.politico .com/story/2016/03/trump-university-profits-220595.

175 *It's not known how much Trump:* Trump University comptroller Steven Matejeck deposition, in ibid.

175 *What we do know is that:* New York Attorney General's Press Office, "A.G. Schneiderman Sues Donald Trump, Trump University & Michael Sexton for Defrauding Consumers out of $40 Million with Sham 'University,'" press re-

lease, August 25, 2013, https://ag.ny.gov/press-release/ag-schneiderman-sues
-donald-trump-trump-university-michael-sexton-defrauding-consumers.

175 *But on November 18, he was:* Jonathan Berr, "Lawsuit Accuses Donald Trump
of Deceiving Students," CBS News, October 31, 2014, https://www.cbsnews
.com/news/lawsuit-accuses-donald-trump-of-deceiving-students/.

175 "a real passion for learning": Donald Trump, *Trump 101: The Ways to Success*
(New York: Wiley, 2006).

176 *Trump University never obtained:* New York Attorney General's Press Office,
"A.G. Schneiderman Sues Donald Trump," press release; Opinion and Decision of Hon. Cynthia S. Kern in People ex rel Schneiderman The Trump Entrepreneur Initiative LLC (Sup. Ct. N.Y. County), dated October 8, 2014,
https://cases.justia.com/new-york/other-courts/2014-2014-ny-slip-op-32685
-u.pdf?ts=1413837035.

176 "It is undisputed that Mr. Trump": Opinion and Decision of Hon. Cynthia S.
Kern in People ex rel Schneiderman.

176 "my handpicked instructors and mentors": "Special Invitation from Donald J. Trump," in Makaeff v. Trump University LLC, 145 F. Supp. 3d 962 (S.D.
Calif. 2015), https://www.leagle.com/decision/infdco20151119c77.

176 "learn from Trump's handpicked experts": Examples of Trump University
advertisements, as cited in ibid.

176 "I can turn anyone into": Ibid.

176 "learn from the master": Ibid.

176 "inside success secrets from Donald Trump": Ibid.

176 *At the free introduction seminars:* Ian Tuttle, "Yes, Trump University Was a
Massive Scam," *National Review,* February 26, 2016, http://www.nationalreview
.com/corner/432010/trump-university-was-massive-scam.

177 *Trump testified that he reviewed:* Tom Hamburger and Rosalind S. Helderman, "Trump Involved in Crafting Controversial Trump University Ads, Executive Testified," *Washington Post,* May 21, 2016, https://www.washington
post.com/politics/trump-involved-in-crafting-controversial-trump
-university-ads-executive-testified/2016/05/31/f032a488-2741-11e6-ae4a
-3cdd5fe74204_story.html?utm_term=.7d4cd13d2823.

177 "We're going to have professors": Promotional video played at Trump University Free Preview, as quoted in Makaeff v. Trump University LLC, 145 F.
Supp. 3d 962 (S.D. Calif. 2015).

177 "none of the professors at the live events": Tom Hamburger, Rosalind S. Helderman, and Alice Crites, "What Trump Said Under Oath About the Trump
University Fraud Claims—Just Weeks Ago," *Washington Post,* March 3, 2016,
https://www.washingtonpost.com/news/post-politics/wp/2016/03/03/what
-trump-said-under-oath-about-the-trump-university-fraud-claims-just
-weeks-ago/?utm_term=.395ee86e099d.

177 "Did you do anything personally": Transcript of deposition of Donald Trump
taken December 10, 2015, in Cohen v. Trump (S.D. Cal. CLASS ACTION

3:13-cv-02519), p. 45, lines 14–17, https://www.washingtonpost.com/apps/g/page /politics/deposition-of-donald-trump-on-trump-university/1981/?tid=a_inl.

177 *Trump sold 7,611 tickets:* Kevin Drum, "Three Interesting Tidbits About Trump University," *Mother Jones,* June 4, 2016, https://www.motherjones .com/kevin-drum/2016/06/three-tidbits-trump-university/.

178 "I believe that Trump University was a fraudulent scheme": John Cassidy, "Trump University: It's Worse Than You Think," *New Yorker,* June 2, 2016, https://www.newyorker.com/news/john-cassidy/trump-university-its-worse -than-you-think.

178 *Corrine Sommer, employed as an:* Declaration of Corinne Sommer in support of Plaintiff's Motion for Class Certification, executed September 19, 2012, in Makaeff v. Trump University (S.D. Cal. CLASS ACTION 3:10-cv-00940), https://www.documentcloud.org/documents/2850041-Sommer.html.

178 *Jason Nicholas, a sales executive:* Michael Barbaro and Steve Eder, "Former Trump University Workers Call the School a 'Lie' and a 'Scheme' in Testimony," *New York Times,* May 31, 2016, https://www.nytimes.com/2016/06 /01/us/politics/donald-trump-university.html.

178 *When confronted in his deposition:* Transcript of deposition of Donald Trump taken December 10, 2015, in Cohen v. Trump (S.D. Cal. CLASS ACTION 3:13-cv-02519), p. 45, lines 14–17, https://www.washingtonpost.com /apps/g/page/politics/deposition-of-donald-trump-on-trump-university /1981/?tid=a_inl.

178 "roller coaster of emotions": Trump University, "The Art of the Set," sales playbook, available at "An Excerpt from Trump University's 'Sales Playbook,'" *New York Times,* May 31, 2016, https://www.nytimes.com/interactive /2016/06/01/us/politics/playbook-excerpt.html.

179 "is everything Donald Trump does the BEST": Michael Isikoff, "Trump University's Secret 'Playbook': Who Wants to Be a Billionaire?" Yahoo, May 31, 2016, https://www.yahoo.com/news/trump-universitys-secret-playbook-who -wants-to-be-a-billionaire-233032793.html.

179 *Over 3,700 students:* Drew Griffin, Nelli Black, and Curt Devine, "Thousands of Trump University Students File to Get Their Money Back," CNN Money, March 23, 2017, https://money.cnn.com/2017/03/23/news/trump-university -settlement-claims/index.html.

179 "How would you like to 'market-proof'": Barbaro and Eder, "Former Trump University Workers Call the School a 'Lie.'"

179 "deceptive acts and practices": Opinion of Judge Curiel in Makaeff v. Trump (S.D. Cal. November 18, 2015) denying Trump's motion for summary judgment, http://caselaw.lexroll.com/2016/06/10/makaeff-v-trump-university-llc -10-cv-0940-order-re-defendants-motions-summary-judgment/?print=pdf.

179 "deceptive acts or practices in the conduct": New York Consolidated Laws, General Business Law—GBS § 349. Deceptive acts and practices unlawful.

180 "pretty straightforward": Chris Isidore, "Schneiderman: Trump University Fraud 'Pretty Straightforward,'" CNN Money, March 4, 2016, http://money

.cnn.com/2016/03/04/news/companies/donald-trump-eric-schneiderman
/index.html.

180 *He claimed a 98 percent approval:* "New York Attorney General Eric Schneiderman Suing Donald Trump for 'Fraudulent' University," News.com, August 27, 2013, http://www.news.com.au/world/new-york-attorney-general
-eric-schneiderman-suing-donald-trump-for-fraudulent-university/news
-story/235b0c755532c51257cb8cb7e015eaf7.

180 "If you go to Wharton or Harvard": Jose Pagliery, "Trump Defends His
School, Prosecutor Calls It 'a Scam,'" CNN Money, August 26, 2013,
https://money.cnn.com/2013/08/26/news/companies/trump-university
/index.html.

180 *Bob Guillo, a retired paralegal:* Jim Zarroli, "Trump University Customer:
'Gold Elite' Program Nothing but Fool's Gold," NPR, June 6, 2016, https://
www.npr.org/2016/06/06/480948631/trump-university-customer-gold-elite
-program-nothing-but-fools-gold.

181 "OK, if you don't rate me a five": Jim Zarroli,"Trump University Customer:
'Gold Elite' Program Nothing but Fool's Gold," NPR, June 6, 2016, https://
www.npr.org/2016/06/06/480948631/trump-university-customer-gold-elite
-program-nothing-but-fools-gold.

181 *In fact over 25 percent of the students:* Hamburger, Helderman, and Crites,
"What Trump Said Under Oath."

181 "When you take into account the fact": William D. Cohen, "Big Hair on
Campus," *Vanity Fair*, January 2014, https://www.vanityfair.com/news/2014
/01/trump-university-fraud-scandal.

181 "As the recent Ponzi-scheme scandals": Makaeff v. Trump University, 715 F.
3d 254, 271 (9th Cir. 2013), https://scholar.google.com/scholar_case?case
=3007884613426739840&hl=en&as_sdt=6&as_vis=1&oi=scholarr.

182 *He called Schneiderman a "sleazebag":* Donald Trump, speech, Bentonville,
AZ, February 27, 2016.

182 *After Schneiderman filed his suit:* Kevin Sack and Steve Eder, "New Records
Shed Light on Donald Trump's $25,000 Gift to Florida Official," *New York
Times*, September 14, 2016, https://www.nytimes.com/2016/09/15/us/politics
/pam-bondi-donald-trump-foundation.html; "The Trump Foundation-Pam
Bondi Scandal," Report of CREW (Citizens for Responsibility and Ethics in
Washington), November 4, 2016, https://www.citizensforethics.org/trump
-foundation-scandal/.

182 *On September 9, 2013, four days:* Ibid.

183 *Many of Trump's political contributions:* Ibid.

183 *No one has established whether:* Ibid.

183 *What we do know is that:* Ibid.

183 *In March 2014, Trump hosted a $3,000:* Ibid.

184 *He targeted Makaeff because she:* "Donald Trump's Statement on Trump
University," *New York Times*, June 7, 2016, https://www.nytimes.com/2016
/06/08/us/politics/trump-university-statement.html.

184 "fraudulent business practices": Makaeff v. Trump University, 715 F. 3d 254 (9th Cir. 2013), https://cdn.ca9.uscourts.gov/datastore/opinions/2013/04/17/11-55016.pdf.

185 "I am contacting the Better Business Bureau": Tarla Makaeff to the Better Business Bureau and her bank, ibid.

185 "from exercising their political": California's Anti-SLAPP law, CCP § 425.16 (1991), in Ibid.

186 *The matter initially came before:* Ibid.

186 "in connection with a public issue": Ibid.

186 "To be clear: Trump University": Ibid.

187 *Curiel dismissed Trump's counterclaim:* Makaeff v. Trump University LLC, S.D. Cal. (Dkt Nos. 14, 282, 294). Opinion of Judge Gonzalo P. Curiel, filed June 17, 2014, http://www.casp.net/makaeff-v-trump-univerity-llc/.

187 "put through the ringer": Motion in Support of Plaintiff Tarla Makaeff's Motion to Withdraw filed February 28, 2016, in Makaeff v. Trump University (S.D. Cal. 3:10-cv-0940), https://www.scribd.com/doc/302142753/Makaeff-v-Trump-University-motion-to-withdraw-pdf.

188 "Make no mistake": Eriq Gardner, "Donald Trump Tells Judge That Plaintiff Can't Bow Out of Trump University Lawsuit," *Hollywood Reporter*, February 29, 2016, https://www.hollywoodreporter.com/thr-esq/donald-trump-tells-judge-plaintiff-871359.

188 "The primary plaintiff in the Trump": Donald J. Trump (@realdonaldtrump), Twitter post, March 6, 2016, 9:27 a.m., https://twitter.com/realdonaldtrump/status/706531628525428744?lang=en.

188 "Despite her education, Makaeff failed": Gardner, "Donald Trump Tells Judge That Plaintiff Can't Bow Out."

188 *Over Trump's strident objection:* Tribune News Services, "Judge Grants Woman's Request to Quit Trump University Suit," *Chicago Tribune*, March 22, 2016, http://www.chicagotribune.com/news/nationworld/politics/ct-trump-university-lawsuit-20160322-story.html.

189 *He claimed that any judge other:* Matt Ford, "Why Is Donald Trump So Angry at Judge Gonzalo Curiel?" *The Atlantic*, June 3, 2016, https://www.theatlantic.com/politics/archive/2016/06/donald-trump-gonzalo-curiel/485636/.

189 "biased": Donald J. Trump (@realdonaldtrump), Twitter post, May 30, 2016, 5:55 p.m.

189 *On February 15, 2016, Trump:* Opinion of Judge Curiel in Low v. Trump (S.D. Cal. March 31, 2017), https://www.politico.com/f/?id=0000015b-253a-d4bd-a5df-bffb2c450001; Order of Judge Curiel denying Defendant's Motion for Summary Judgment in Cohen v. Trump (S.D. Cal. 3:13-cv-2519), dated August 2, 2016, text of opinion at https://www.scribd.com/document/320016779/Trump-U-MSJ-Order#from_embed.

189 "[enable] the court to determine": Rule 56, Federal Rules of Civil Procedure; Fitzgerald v. Westland Marine Corporation, 369 F. 2d 499 (2d Cir. 1966), https://www.leagle.com/decision/1966868369f2d4991740.xml.

189 *Fewer than 10 percent of federal:* Michelle Ye Hee Lee, "Sorry, Donald Trump, the Trump University Judge Was Just Following the Law," *Washington Post*, June 7, 2016, https://www.washingtonpost.com/news/fact-checker/wp/2016 /06/07/sorry-donald-trump-the-mexican-judge-was-just-following-the-law/ ?utm_term=.7534b0950b86.

189 "He has been extremely hostile to me": Veronica Stracqualursi and Ryan Struyk, "President Trump's History with Judge Gonzalo Curiel," ABC News, April 20, 2017, https://abcnews.go.com/Politics/president-trumps-history-judge -gonzalo-curiel/story?id=46916250.

189 *He told the* Wall Street Journal: Brent Kendall, "Trump Says Judge's Mexican Heritage Presents 'Absolute Conflict,'" *Wall Street Journal*, June 3, 2016, https://www.wsj.com/articles/donald-trump-keeps-up-attacks-on-judge -gonzalo-curiel-1464911442.

189 "a judge who was a hater": Donald Trump, speech, San Diego, May 27, 2016, in Nat Hentoff and Nick Hentoff, "Why Judge Curiel May Be Donald Trump's Best Friend," Cato.org, June 9, 2016, https://www.cato.org /publications/commentary/why-judge-curiel-may-be-donald-trumps-best -friend.

190 "They ought to look into Judge Curiel": Kristine Phillips, "All the Times Trump Personally Attacked Judges—And Why His Tirades Are 'Worse Than Wrong,'" *Washington Post*, April 26, 2017, https://www.washingtonpost .com/news/the-fix/wp/2017/04/26/all-the-times-trump-personally-attacked -judges-and-why-his-tirades-are-worse-than-wrong/?utm_term= .263f423fcd22.

190 "I should have easily won": Donald J. Trump (@realdonaldtrump), Twitter post, May 30, 2016, 2:55 p.m.

190 "The judge is doing his job": Hentoff and Hentoff, "Why Judge Curiel May Be Donald Trump's Best Friend."

190 *Famed civil libertarian Nat Hentoff:* Ibid.

190 *Curiel undoubtedly chafed at Trump's attacks:* Editorial Board, "Donald Trump and the Judge," *New York Times*, May 31, 2016, https://www.nytimes .com/2016/06/01/opinion/donald-trump-and-the-judge.html.

190 *On June 7, 2016, Trump, responding:* Alan Rappeport, "Donald Trump Says His Remarks on Judge Were 'Misconstrued,'" *New York Times*, June 7, 2016, https://www.nytimes.com/2016/06/08/us/politics/trump-university-judge .html.

191 *The* Cohen *plaintiffs, however, charged:* Ford, "Why Is Donald Trump So Angry at Judge Gonzalo Curiel?"

191 *Trump also encouraged Curiel to dismiss:* Ibid.

191 "Indeed, if this case is allowed": Ibid.

191 "ultimately, while Defendant may believe": Cohen v. Trump, 200 F. Supp. 3d 1063 (S.D. CA 2016), https://www.leagle.com/decision/infdco20160803861.

191 *Trump had vowed never to settle:* Christina Wilkie, "Better Business Bureau: Trump Lied about Trump University Rating," Huffington Post, March 8,

2016, https://www.huffingtonpost.com/entry/trump-university-better-business
-bureau_us_56df236fe4b0000de4064879.

192 "Rubio: Well, he did, and that's": "Transcript of the Republican Presidential
Debate in Detroit," *New York Times*, March 4, 2016, https://www.nytimes
.com/2016/03/04/us/politics/transcript-of-the-republican-presidential
-debate-in-detroit.html?_r=2.

193 *The Better Business Bureau responded:* Wilkie, "Better Business Bureau:
Trump Lied."

193 *Trump's director of operations Mark Covais:* Steven Brill, "What the Legal
Battle over Trump University Reveals About Its Founder," *Time*, November 5,
2015, http://time.com/4101290/what-the-legal-battle-over-trump-university
-reveals-about-its-founder/.

193 *And on November 18, 2016:* Steve Eder, "Donald Trump Agrees to Pay $25
Million in Trump University Settlement," *New York Times*, November 18,
2016, https://www.nytimes.com/2016/11/19/us/politics/trump-university
.html.

194 "While we have no doubt": Ibid.

194 *found Trump his lawyer:* Aaron Glantz, "This Slumlord Is Donald Trump's
Good Pal," *The Nation*, June 8, 2017, ttps://www.thenation.com/article
/slumlord-donald-trumps-good-pal/.

194 *secretly funded by the Trump Inaugural Committee:* Frank DiPrima, "What If
the Russia-Funded Inauguration Fund Paid the $25 Million Trump Univ.
Settlement?" Daily Kos, May 13, 2018, https://www.dailykos.com/stories
/2018/5/13/1763837/-What-If-the-Russia-Funded-Inauguration-Fund-Paid
-the-25-Million-Trump-Univ-Settlement.

194 "embroiling the presidency in litigation": "President-elect Agrees to Settle
Trump University Fraud Lawsuits for $25M," *Chicago Tribune*, Novem-
ber 19, 2016, https://www.chicagotribune.com/news/nationworld/politics/ct
-trump-university-settlement-20161118-story.html.

195 "In 2013, my office sued Donald": New York Attorney General's Press Office,
"Statement by A.G. Schneiderman on $256 Million Settlement Agreement
Reached in Trump University Case," press release, November 18, 2016,
https://ag.ny.gov/press-release/statement-ag-schneiderman-25-million
-settlement-agreement-reached-trump-university.

CHAPTER 9: THE CLOSING BELL

197 *Laurence Tribe:* @tribelaw, Twitter post, October 12, 2018, 9:14 a.m.

198 "You are entitled to your own opinion": Timothy J. Penny, "Facts Are Facts,"
National Review, September 4, 2003, https://www.nationalreview.com/2003
/09/facts-are-facts-timothy-j-penny/.

198 *Joseph Califano:* Joseph A. Califano Jr., *Our Damaged Democracy: We the
People Must Act* (New York: Touchstone, 2018).

198 "country is coming apart": @esglaude, Twitter post, February 6, 2019, 11:06 p.m.

198 *43 percent of the days:* Larry Buchanan and Karen Yourish, "Trump Has Publicly Attacked the Russia Investigation More Than 1,100 Times," *New York Times*, February 19, 2019, https://www.nytimes.com/interactive/2019 /02/19/us/politics/trump-attacks-obstruction-investigation.html.

198 *The theory of Mueller's investigation:* Sharon LaFraniere, Kenneth P. Vogel, and Scott Shane, "In Closed Hearing, a Clue About 'the Heart' of Mueller's Russia Inquiry," *New York Times*, February 11, 2019, https://www.nytimes .com/2019/02/10/us/politics/manafort-mueller-russia-inquiry.html.

199 *Michael Cohen testified before Congress:* Matt Zapotosky, Rosalind S. Helderman, Karoun Demirjian, and Rachel Bade, "Cohen Tells Congress Trump Knew About WikiLeaks' Plans, Directed Hush-Money Payments," *Washington Post*, February 27, 2019, https://www.washingtonpost.com/politics/cohen -tells-congress-trump-knew-about-wikileaks-plans-directed-hush-money -payments/2019/02/27/f2784a20-3acd-11e9-a2cd-307b06d0257b_story.html ?utm_term=.9971e7b3c651.

199–200 *"hostile intelligence service":* Martin Matishak, "CIA Director Labels WikiLeaks a 'Hostile Intelligence Service,'" *Politico*, April 13, 2017, https:// www.politico.com/story/2017/04/mike-pompeo-wikileaks-hostile -intelligence-service-237206.

200 *"will take down America any way they can":* Andrew Blake, "WikiLeaks Wants to 'Take Down America Any Way They Can,' says CIA chief," *Washington Times*, July 21, 2017, https://www.washingtontimes.com/news/2017 /jul/21/wikileaks-will-take-down-america-any-way-they-can-/.

200 *Trump's indicted trickster pal Roger Stone:* Ryan Goodman, "How Roger Stone Interacted with Russia's Guccifer and WikiLeaks," *Newsweek*, September 28, 2017, http://www.newsweek.com/how-stone-interacted-russias -guccifer-and-wikileaks-673268.

200 *"This WikiLeaks is like a treasure trove":* "Trump: 'WikiLeaks Is Like a Treasure Trove,'" *Washington Post*, October 31, 2016, https://www.washingtonpost .com/video/politics/trump-wikileaks-is-like-a-treasure-trove/2016/10/31 /07058498-9fb8-11e6-8864-6f892cad0865_video.html?utm_term= .023d5727bbd3.

200 *he mentioned WikiLeaks 137 times:* Gabrielle Healy, "Did Trump Really Mention WikiLeaks over 160 Times in the Last Month of the Election Cycle?" *Politifact*, April 21, 2017, https://www.politifact.com/truth-o-meter /statements/2017/apr/21/jackie-speier/did-trump-really-mention-wikileaks -over-160-times-/.

200 *Trump Jr. admitted:* Zack Beauchamp. "Legal Experts Say Donald Trump Jr Has Just Confessed to a Federal Crime," *Vox*, July 11, 2017, https://www .vox.com/world/2017/7/10/15950590/donald-trump-jr-new-york-times -illegal.

200 *"Oh my God":* Mueller report, I:290. Special Counsel Robert S. Mueller III, "Report on the Investigation into Russian Interference in the 2016 Presidential Election," March 2019, searchable document and index available at

https://www.nytimes.com/interactive/2019/04/18/us/politics/mueller-report-document.html.

201 "This is the single greatest": Donald J. Trump (@realdonaldtrump), Twitter post, May 18, 2017, https://twitter.com/realdonaldtrump/status/865173176854204416?lang=en.

201 "one of the defining words of our time": "Post-Truth, *adjective*," *Oxford Dictionaries*, November 16, 2016, https://www.oxforddictionaries.com/press/news/2016/12/11/WOTY-16.

201 *Rudy Giuliani publicly acknowledged:* Aaron Blake, "Giuliani's Telling Admission: All That Matters Is That Mueller Is Undermined," *Washington Post*, August 28, 2018, https://www.washingtonpost.com/politics/2018/08/28/giulianis-telling-defense-himself-all-that-matters-is-that-mueller-is-undermined/?utm_term=.5e0e5ebe1e78.

201 *In December 2018, Mueller presented:* Dan Mangan and Kevin Breuninger, "Mueller Says Michael Flynn Gave 'Firsthand' Details of Trump Transition Team Contacts with Russians," CNBC, December 4, 2018, https://www.cnbc.com/2018/12/04/robert-mueller-sentencing-memo-for-former-trump-advisor-michael-flynn.html.

202 *Sullivan, describing his "disgust":* Deanna Paul, "A Judge Implied That Flynn Was a 'Traitor' Who Committed 'Treason.' What Does That Actually Mean?" *Washington Post*, December 20, 2018, https://www.washingtonpost.com/politics/2018/12/20/judge-implied-flynn-was-traitor-who-committed-treason-what-does-that-actually-mean/?utm_term=.42bfd06e56b1.

202 *On February 16, 2018, Mueller indicted:* United States v. Internet Research Agency LLC et al. (D.D.C.), available at https://www.politico.com/story/2018/02/16/text-full-mueller-indictment-on-russian-election-case-415670.

202 "incontrovertible": David E. Sanger, "Trump's National Security Chief Calls Russian Interference 'Incontrovertible,'" *New York Times*, February 17, 2018, https://www.nytimes.com/2018/02/17/world/europe/russia-meddling-mcmaster.html.

202 "New Jersey sitting on the bed": Krishnadev Calamur, "Some of the People Trump Has Blamed for Russia's 2016 Election Hack," *The Atlantic*, July 18, 2018, https://www.theatlantic.com/international/archive/2018/07/trump-russia-hack/565445/.

202 *On July 13, 2018, Mueller's grand jury:* United States v. Viktor Borisovich Netysho et al. (D.D.C.), available at https://www.vox.com/2018/7/13/17568806/mueller-russia-intelligence-indictment-full-text.

202 "It was clear where Mueller": Michael Wolff, *Fire and Fury: Inside the Trump White House* (New York: Henry Holt, 2018), 255.

203 "Where's my Roy Cohn?": Michael S. Schmidt, "Obstruction Inquiry Shows Trump's Struggle to Keep Grip on Russia Investigation," *New York Times*, January 4, 2018, https://www.nytimes.com/2018/01/04/us/politics/trump-sessions-russia-mcgahn.html.

203 *refused to carry out the executive mandate:* Rebecca Ballhaus and Alex Leary, "Trump Says He Never Asked McGahn to Fire Mueller—President's Tweet Directly Contradicts Account in Special Counsel's Report," *Wall Street Journal*, April 25, 2019, https://www.wsj.com/articles/trump-says-he-never-asked-mcgahn-to-fire-mueller-115056196379.

203 "misconduct, dereliction of duty": Order appointing Mueller, Order No. 3915-2017, "Appointment of Special Counsel to Investigate Russian Interference with the 2016 Presidential Election and Related Matters," signed by Acting Attorney General Rod J. Rosenstein, May 17, 2017, available at https://www.justice.gov/opa/press-release/file/967231/download; Code of Federal Regulations §600.7 (d), available at https://www.law.cornell.edu/cfr/text/28/600.7.

203 "an attack on our country": Eli Watkins, "Michael Cohen: From Trump Fixer to Prison Inmate," CNN, May 6, 2019, https://www.cnn.com/2019/05/06/politics/gallery/michael-cohen/index.html.

204 *a total of $420,000:* Carol D. Leonnig, "Trump's Company Approved $420,000 in Payments to Cohen, Relying on 'Sham' Invoices, Prosecutors Say," *Washington Post*, August 21, 2018, https://www.washingtonpost.com/politics/trumps-company-approved-420000-in-payments-to-cohen-relying-on-sham-invoices-prosecutors-say/2018/08/21/b6b327fc-a596-11e8-97ce-cc9042272f07_story.html?utm_term=.cfe4421ce364.

205 "I know all about flipping": Stephanie Murray, "After Cohen Flips, Trump Says Deals With Prosecutors 'Almost Ought to Be Outlawed,'" *Politico*, August 23, 2018, https://www.politico.com/story/2018/08/23/trump-michael-cohen-flipping-outlawed-794329.

205 "I feel very badly for Paul Manafort": Dave Boyer, "Trump Says He Feels 'Very Badly' for Paul Manafort After Sentencing," *Washington Times*, March 8, 2019, https://www.washingtontimes.com/news/2019/mar/8/donald-trump-feels-very-badly-paul-manafort-after-/.

206 *Konstantin Kilimnik:* Kenneth P. Vogel and Andrew E. Kramer, "Russian Spy or Hustling Political Operative? The Enigmatic Figure at the Heart of Mueller's Inquiry," *New York Times*, February 23, 2019, https://www.nytimes.com/2019/02/23/us/politics/konstantin-kilimnik-russia.html.

206 "hardened criminal": Rachel Weiner, "Paul Manafort a 'Hardened' and 'Bold' Criminal, Mueller Prosecutors Tell Judge," *Washington Post*, February 23, 2019, https://www.washingtonpost.com/local/legal-issues/paul-manafort-a-hardened-and-bold-criminal-mueller-prosecutors-tell-judge/2019/02/23/690bd33c-3542-11e9-af5b-b51b7ff322e9_story.html?utm_term=.969ca53cc165.

207 "trying to find a parachute": @presidentbannon, Twitter post, May 19, 2017, 4:36 p.m.

207 *Kushner's security clearance application:* Rebecca Savransky, "Kushner Updated Disclosure to Add More than 100 Foreign Contacts," *The Hill*, July 13, 2017, https://thehill.com/homenews/administration/341844-kushner-updated-disclosure-to-add-more-than-100-foreign-contacts.

207 *Russian lawyer Natalia Veselnitskaya:* Michelle Mark, "People Aren't Buying Kushner Lawyers' Explanation for Security Clearance Form Omissions," *Business Insider*, July 14, 2017, https://www.businessinsider.com/kushners -explanation-of-security-clearance-form-omissions-russia-meeting-prompt -skepticism-2017-7.

207 *Kushner's business links:* Bob Dreyfuss, "Trump Associates' Ties to Russian Money Laundering," *The Nation*, December 19, 2017, https://www.thenation .com/article/maxine-waters-connects-the-dots-on-trump-deutsche-bank -and-russia; Michael Kranish, "Jared Kushner's Firm Given $285 Million Deutsche Bank Loan Just a Month Before Election Day," *Chicago Tribune*, June 25, 2017, https://www.chicagotribune.com/news/nationworld/politics /ct-kushner-deutsche-bank-loan-20170625-story.html; Charles V. Bagli and Kate Kelly, "Deal Gives Kushners Cash Infusion on 666 Fifth Avenue," *New York Times*, August 3, 2018, https://www.nytimes.com/2018/08/03/nyregion /kushners-building-fifth-avenue-brookfield-lease.html.

208 "mirror trading scheme": Ed Caesar, "Deutsche Bank, Mirror Trades and More Russian Threads," *New Yorker*, March 29, 2017, https://www.newyorker .com/business/currency/deutsche-bank-mirror-trades-and-more-russian -threads.

209 "What lingers for Trump": Jay Elwes, "Interview: Richard Dearlove—I Spy Nationalism," *Prospect*, April 13, 2017, https://www.prospectmagazine.co.uk /magazine/interview-richard-dearlove-europe-intelligence-mi6.

209 *One report suggested that Deutsche Bank:* Allan Smith, "Trump's Long and Winding History with Deutsche Bank Could Now Be at the Center of Robert Mueller's Investigation," *Business Insider*, December 8, 2017, https://www .businessinsider.com/trump-deutsche-bank-mueller-2017-12.

209 *According to Michael Wolff:* Wolff, *Fire & Fury*, 277. Comment summarized in column by E. Pilkington, "'Bannon May Already Be Cooperating with Mueller': Tell-All Book Shifts Frame of Russia Inquiry," *The Guardian*, January 4, 2018, https://www.theguardian.com/us-news/2018/jan/04/trump-russia -steve-bannon-book-robert-mueller.

210 "No American president in history": David Frum, *Trumpocracy: The Corruption of the American Republic* (New York: Harper, 2018), 104; Fact Checker, "In 828 Days Since Taking Office, President Trump Has Made 10,0000 False or Misleading Claims," *Washington Post*, April 29, 2019, https://www .washingtonpost.com/politics/2019/04/29/president-trump-has-made-more -than-false-or-misleading-claims/?noredirect=on&utm_term=.852993877579; "In 649 Days, President Trump Has Made 6,420 False or Misleading Claims," *Washington Post*, October 30, 2018, https://www.washingtonpost.com/graphics /politics/trump-claims-database/?utm_term=.92c02ee31d60; Glenn Kessler, Salvador Rizzo, and Meg Kelly, "President Trump Made 8,158 False or Misleading Claims in His First Two Years," *Washington Post*, February 17, 2019, https://www.washingtonpost.com/politics/2019/01/21/president-trump-made -false-or-misleading-claims-his-first-two-years/?utm_term=.5f28960fd177.

210 "because it's fun": Bailey Vogt, "Anthony Scaramucci on Trump's Lies: 'He Does It Because It's Fun,'" *Washington Times*, April 5, 2019, https://www .washingtontimes.com/news/2019/apr/5/anthony-scaramucci-donald -trumps-lies-he-does-it-b/.

210 "truth decay": Jennifer Kavanagh and Michael D. Rich, "Truth Decay: An Initial Exploration of the Diminishing Role of Facts and Analysis in American Public Life," RAND Corporation Research Reports, RR-2314-RC, 2018, https://www.rand.org/pubs/research_reports/RR2314.html.

211 "[We] gave alternative facts": Eric Bradner, "Conway: Trump White House Offered 'Alternative Facts' on Crowd Size," CNN, January 23, 2017, https:// www.cnn.com/2017/01/22/politics/kellyanne-conway-alternative-facts /index.html.

211 *Digital billboards:* Bo Gardiner, "Pre-Election Billboard Ads Portray Donald Trump as Second Coming of Jesus," *Friendly Atheist*, November 5, 2018, https://friendlyatheist.patheos.com/2018/11/05/pre-election-billboard-ads -portray-donald-trump-as-second-coming-of-jesus/.

211 *Nobel Peace Prize:* Trump supporters believe Trump's claim that Japan's prime minister, Shinzo Abe, nominated Trump for a Nobel Peace Prize. Abe did make such a nomination, but it was at Trump's request. Chas Danner, "White House Asked Japan for Trump's Nobel Peace Prize Nomination," *New York Magazine*, February 18, 2019, http://nymag.com/intelligencer /2019/02/white-house-asked-japan-for-trumps-peace-prize-nomination .html.

211 *Democrats are really the "devil":* Steve Benen, "'Evil' Becomes Trump's Adjective of Choice for His US Opponents," MSNBC, October 10, 2018, http:// www.msnbc.com/rachel-maddow-show/evil-becomes-trumps-adjective -choice-his-us-opponents.

211 *Brett Kavanaugh appeared to acknowledge:* Bob Bauer and Ryan Goodman, "Setting the Record Straight: Brett Kavanaugh's Views on Criminal Investigation of the President," Just Security, July 12, 2018, https://www.justsecurity .org/59356/setting-record-straight-brett-kavanaughs-views-criminal -investigation-president/.

212 *play golf on 172 occasions:* Golf News Net, "How Many Times Has President Donald Trump Played Golf While in Office?" GNN, May 11, 2019, https:// thegolfnewsnet.com/golfnewsnetteam/2019/02/18/how-many-times -president-donald-trump-played-golf-in-office-103836.

212 *even if he murdered James Comey:* Margaret Hartmann, "Giuliani's New Tactic: Arguing Trump Can Literally Get Away With Murder," *New York Magazine*, June 4, 2018, http://nymag.com/intelligencer/2018/06/why-giuliani -said-trump-could-literally-get-away-with-murder.html

212 *Christie agrees:* Tim Hains, "Chris Christie: If Trump Tried to Pardon Himself, He Would Be Impeached," RealClear Politics, June 3, 2018, https://www .realclearpolitics.com/video/2018/06/03/chris_christie_if_trump_tried_to _pardon_himself_he_would_be_impeached.html.

212 *The Justice Department advised Nixon:* Scott Bomboy, "Explaining the Presidential Self-Pardon Debate," *Constitution Daily,* June 4, 2018, https://constitutioncenter.org/blog/explaining-the-presidential-self-pardon-debate.

213 *Brett Kavanaugh disingenuously testified:* Stephen Collinson and Don Berman, "Kavanaugh Says 'No One Is Above the Law' but Ducks Questions About Trump," CNN, September 5, 2018, https://www.cnn.com/2018/09/05/politics/supreme-court-nomination-hearing-brett-kavanaugh/index.html.

214 *Ford pardoned Nixon:* Text of President Ford's Pardon Proclamation, September 8, 1974, http://watergate.info/1974/09/08/text-of-ford-pardon-proclamation.html.

214 *Emoluments Clauses of the Constitution:* The Supreme Court stated in DaimlerChrysler Corp. v. Cuno, 547 U.S. 332 (2006), "No principle is more fundamental to the judiciary's proper role in our system of government than the constitutional limitation of federal-court jurisdiction to actual cases or controversies." The case-or-controversy requirement of Article III of the Constitution requires plaintiffs to establish their standing to sue. Article III standing law is built on separation-of-powers principles. Its purpose is to prevent the judicial process from usurping the powers of the other two departments of the federal government. The principle may prevent litigation against Trump under the Emoluments Clause. It's hard to say for sure, though, because before Trump, the issue hadn't come up.

215 "broad anti-corruption provisions": Stephen Rohde, "The Emoluments Clause Could Be a Tipping Point in Trump's Downfall," *The American Prospect,* May 13, 2019, https://prospect.org/article/emoluments-clause-could-be-tipping-point-trumps-downfall.

215 *Trump International Hotel:* Alexandra Berzon, "Trump Hotel in Washington Saw Strong Profit in First Four Months of 2017," *Wall Street Journal,* August 11, 2017, https://www.wsj.com/articles/trump-hotel-in-washington-saw-strong-profit-in-first-four-months-of-2017-1502424589.

215 *Industrial and Commercial Bank of China:* Ian Millhiser, "A Bank Controlled by the Chinese Is Helping Make Trump Rich," ThinkProgress, November 18, 2016, https://thinkprogress.org/a-bank-controlled-by-the-chinese-government-is-helping-make-trump-rich-ea5b7c8c77f2.

216 *ICBC has announced plans:* "China's Biggest Bank to Reduce Its Space at Trump Tower," Bloomberg News, January 9, 2019, https://www.bloomberg.com/news/articles/2019-01-09/china-s-biggest-bank-said-to-reduce-space-at-nyc-s-trump-tower.

216 "I do deals with them all the time": "A Transcript of Donald Trump's Meeting with the *Washington Post* Editorial Board," *Washington Post,* March 21, 2016, https://www.washingtonpost.com/blogs/post-partisan/wp/2016/03/21/a-transcript-of-donald-trumps-meeting-with-the-washington-post-editorial-board/?utm_term=.277d29237b3f.

216 "I have a great relationship with China": Matthew Boyle, "Exclusive—Donald Trump: 'I Will Stop China from Taking America to the Cleaners Every

Single Year,'" Breitbart, January 14, 2016, http://www.breitbart.com/big
-government/2016/01/14/exclusive-donald-trump-i-will-stop-china-from
-taking-america-to-the-cleaners-every-single-year.

216 "the close economic, political and security ties": Amy B. Wang, Emily Rau-
hala, and William Wan, "Why People Are Making Such a Big Deal About
the Trump-Taiwan Call," *Washington Post*, December 5, 2016, https://www
.washingtonpost.com/news/worldviews/wp/2016/12/05/why-people-are
-making-such-a-big-deal-about-the-trump-taiwan-call/?utm_term=
.e18d11cc1cb5.

217 *Shortly thereafter, Ivanka Trump received:* Renae Reints, "Ivanka Trump's
Brand Received Five New Trademarks From China This Month," *Fortune*,
January 21, 2019, http://fortune.com/2019/01/21/ivanka-trump-china
-trademarks/; Gary Shih and Jonathan O'Connell, "China Greenlights Large
Batch of Ivanka Trump Trademark Applications," *Washington Post*, November 6, 2018, https://www.washingtonpost.com/world/asia_pacific/china
-greenlights-large-batch-of-ivanka-trump-trademark-applications/2018/11/06
/c085e88c-e1c8-11e8-a1c9-6afe99dddd92_story.html?utm_term=.39b0d1d3efae.

218 "Human rights are, in essence": Mark Landler, "Trump to Asia: Unite on
North Korea, but Go It Alone on Trade," *New York Times*, November 17,
2017, https://www.nytimes.com/2017/11/11/world/asia/trump-asia-danang
-vietnam.html; Russell Goldman, "Rodrigo Duterte on Killing Criminal
Suspects: 'I Used to Do It Personally,'" *New York Times*, December 14, 2016,
https://www.nytimes.com/2016/12/14/world/asia/rodrigo-duterte
-philippines-killings.html; Kurt Eichenwald, "How Donald Trump's Business Ties Are Already Jeopardizing U.S. Interests," *Newsweek*, December 13,
2016, http://www.newsweek.com/2016/12/23/donald-trump-foreign-business
-deals-jeopardize-us-531140.html.

219 *Chicago mixed-use skyscraper; Trump National Westchester Golf Club:* Dees
Stribling, "Trump Organization Pursues Property Tax Breaks by Aggressively Suing Local Municipalities," *Bisnow*, April 12, 2018, https://www
.bisnow.com/national/news/other/trump-organization-pursues-property
-tax-breaks-aggressively-nationwide-87275.

220 *six lawsuits over assessments:* Katherine Sullivan, "Trump's Company Is
Suing Towns Across the Country to Get Breaks on Taxes," *ProPublica*,
April 11, 2019, https://www.propublica.org/article/trump-inc-podcast-trump
-organization-suing-towns-property-tax-breaks.

220 *Trump National Golf Course in Jupiter, Florida:* Christine Stapleton, "Did
Trump Falsify Value of Jupiter Golf Club?" *Palm Beach Daily News*,
March 12, 2019, https://www.palmbeachdailynews.com/news/20190301/did
-trump-falsify-value-of-jupiter-golf-club.

220 "Trump tells voters his properties": Greg Price, "Trump Is Suing Palm Beach
Course for Fifth Time over Valuing His Golf Course Too High," *Newsweek*,
January 29, 2018, https://www.newsweek.com/trump-suing-golf-course-palm
-beach-794275.

220 "They play around with valuations": David Barstow, Susanne Craig, and Russ Buettner, "Trump Engaged in Suspect Tax Schemes as He Reaped Riches from His Father," *New York Times*, October 2, 2018, https://www.nytimes.com/interactive/2018/10/02/us/politics/donald-trump-tax-schemes-fred-trump.html.

220 *being president had cost him a fortune:* Steve Benen, "Trump Complains the Presidency Is Costing Him a 'Fortune' (It Isn't)," MSNBC, November 21, 2018, http://www.msnbc.com/rachel-maddow-show/trump-complains-the-presidency-costing-him-fortune-it-isnt.

221 *Barbara Underwood filed:* Danny Hakim, "New York Attorney General Sues Trump Foundation After 2-Year Investigation," *New York Times*, June 14, 2018, https://www.nytimes.com/2018/06/14/nyregion/trump-foundation-lawsuit-attorney-general.html. Text of complaint available at https://int.nyt.com/data/documenthelper/38-lawsuit-against-the-trump-foundation/5e54a6bfd23e7b94fbad/optimized/full.pdf#page=1.

222 *Michael Cohen also told Congress:* Sarah Cascone, "Michael Cohen Just Told Congress That President Trump Directed His Charity to Buy Yet Another Portrait of Himself," *Artnet*, February 27, 2019, https://news.artnet.com/art-world/trump-painting-1475962.

223 "sleazy New York Democrats": Donald J. Trump (@realdonaldtrump), Twitter post, June 14, 2018, 11:09 a.m.

224 "did not fully capture": Devlin Barrett and Matt Zapotosky, "Mueller Complained That Barr's Letter Did Not Capture 'Context' of Trump Probe," *Washington Post*, April 30, 2019, https://www.washingtonpost.com/world/national-security/mueller-complained-that-barrs-letter-did-not-capture-context-of-trump-probe/2019/04/30/d3c8fdb6-6b7b-11e9-a66d-a82d3f3d96d5_story.html?utm_term=.e29f88c2b1d2.

224 "If we had confidence": Mueller Report, II:2, Special Counsel Robert S. Mueller III, "Report on the Investigation into Russian Interference in the 2016 Presidential Election," March 2019, searchable document and index available at https://www.nytimes.com/interactive/2019/04/18/us/politics/mueller-report-document.html.

226 *No crime not to remember:* "Witness Says Cohn Told Him 'It's No Crime Not to Remember,'" *New York Times*, April 4, 1964, https://www.nytimes.com/1964/04/04/archives/witness-says-cohn-told-him-its-no-crime-not-to-remember.html.

226 "As described in Volume I": Mueller Report, II:76, Special Counsel Robert S. Mueller III, "Report on the Investigation into Russian Interference in the 2016 Presidential Election," March 2019, searchable document and index available at https://www.nytimes.com/interactive/2019/04/18/us/politics/mueller-report-document.html.

227 "Each of us believes": "Statement by Former Federal Prosecutors," Medium, May 6, 2019, https://medium.com/@dojalumni/statement-by-former-federal-prosecutors-8ab7691c2aa1.

229 "on impeachment and conviction for malpractice": Jill Lepore, "How Impeachment Ended Up in the Constitution," *New Yorker*, May 18, 2017, https://www.newyorker.com/news/news-desk/how-impeachment-ended-up-in-the-constitution.

229 *impeachment is of a "political character"*: Excerpt from 1833 commentaries on impeachment by Joseph Story available at https://www.washingtonpost.com/wp-srv/politics/special/clinton/stories/watergatedoc_3.htm.

230 "a consensus developing": Ezra Klein, "The Case for Normalizing Impeachment," *Vox*, January 13, 2018, https://www.vox.com/2017/11/30/16517022/impeachment-donald-trump.

230 *according to Quinnipiac polls*: Mark Swanson, "Quinnipiac Poll: 56% Say Trump Is Unfit to Be President," *Newsmax*, September 27, 2017, https://www.newsmax.com/newsfront/quinnipiac-poll-donald-trump-approval-fit-to-be-president/2017/09/27/id/816161/.

230 *which he bragged in 2016*: Philip Bump, "If Trump Shot Someone Dead on Fifth Avenue, Many Supporters Would Call His Murder Trial Biased," *Washington Post*, March 14, 2019, https://www.washingtonpost.com/politics/2019/03/14/if-trump-shot-someone-dead-fifth-avenue-many-supporters-would-call-his-murder-trial-biased/?utm_term=.43792cb300f2.

231 *Allan Lichtman*: Allan J. Lichtman, "Here Are Five Ways a Democratic US House Might Try to Impeach Donald Trump," *LSE USCentre*, November 7, 2018.

232 *Most Americans, polls show*: Tal Axelrod, "Majority of Americans Don't Support Impeachment: Poll," *The Hill*, April 26, 2019, https://thehill.com/homenews/house/440883-majority-of-americans-dont-support-impeachment-poll.

233 *suing Congress to block access*: Maggie Haberman, William K. Rashbaum, and David Enrich, "Trump Sues Deutsche Bank and Capital One to Block Compliance with Subpoenas," *New York Times*, April 20, 2019, https://www.nytimes.com/2019/04/29/us/politics/trump-lawsuit-deutsche-bank.html.

234 "busy giddy minds with foreign quarrels": William Shakespeare, *King Henry IV Part II*, Act 4, Scene 3.

234 "antic disposition": William Shakespeare, *Hamlet*, Act 1, Scene 5.

235 "No public man": from Sidney Zion, *The Autobiography of Roy Cohn* (Secaucus, NJ: Lyle Stuart, 1988), 150.

INDEX